Reciprocal Mobilities

MARK DIZON

Reciprocal Mobilities

Indigeneity and Imperialism
in an Eighteenth-Century
Philippine Borderland

The University of North Carolina Press *Chapel Hill*

© 2023 The University of North Carolina Press
All rights reserved
Set in Arno Pro by Westchester Publishing Services
Manufactured in the United States of America

Library of Congress Cataloging-in-Publication Data
Names: Dizon, Mark, author.
Title: Reciprocal mobilities : indigeneity and imperialism in an eighteenth-century
    Philippine borderland / Mark Dizon.
Other titles: Indigeneity and imperialism in an eighteenth-century Philippine
    borderland | David J. Weber series in the new borderlands history.
Description: Chapel Hill : The University of North Carolina Press, [2023] |
    Series: The David J. Weber series in the new borderlands history |
    Includes bibliographical references and index.
Identifiers: LCCN 2023025313 | ISBN 9781469676432 (cloth ; alk. paper) |
    ISBN 9781469676449 (pbk. ; alk. paper) | ISBN 9781469676456 (ebook)
Subjects: LCSH: Indigenous peoples—Travel—Philippines. | Anti-imperialist movements—
    Philippines—History—18th century. | Indigenous peoples—Philippines—Luzon—Social
    conditions—18th century. | Indigenous peoples—Philippines—Luzon—Government
    relations. | Borderlands—Philippines—Luzon—History. | Philippines—Race relations—
    History—18th century. | Philippines—History—18th century. | BISAC: HISTORY /
    World | POLITICAL SCIENCE / Colonialism & Post-Colonialism
Classification: LCC DS674 .D596 2023 | DDC 305.800959909/033—dc23/eng/20230602
LC record available at https://lccn.loc.gov/2023025313

Cover illustration: José Honorato Lozano, *Indio a Caballo* (1847).
Courtesy of Wikimedia Commons.

Contents

Illustrations

MAP 0.1 Map of the towns of central and northern Luzon in the eighteenth century. The borderlands of Ituy and Paniqui were located between the provinces of Cagayan and Pampanga.

Reciprocal Mobilities

Manila; the Spanish national library for its digital collections; the library of the Augustinian convent in Valladolid; the library of the Diocese of Vitoria; Ana Hernández of Archivo General de Indias in Seville; Regalado Trota Jose, Jane Flores, Elsie Musni, Joyce San Gabriel, and Arwin Palileo of the University of Santo Tomas archives in Manila; Fr. Carlos Alonso and the late Fr. Isacio Rodríguez of the Augustinian archives in Valladolid; Fr. Cayetano Sánchez Fuertes and Fr. Reynaldo Landazabal Legayada of the Franciscan archives in Madrid; and Fr. Emiliano Pérez of the Dominican archives in Ávila. Perhaps the only thing better than finding the archival documents you needed (including the ones you never thought you needed) was having conversations with the friar-archivists about the most varied topics while taking photos of documents.

Both preliminary and more developed ideas from this book have seen the light of day in various workshops, conferences, and a publication. I am especially grateful to the feedback from the formal workshops and casual conversations over coffee at the EUI. A shortened, modified version of chapter 1 has appeared in *Itinerario* 46, no. 3 (2022).

The last leg of this journey was in the company of the University of North Carolina Press. This book has found a perfect home in the David J. Weber Series in the New Borderlands History. I would like to thank the series editors, Ben Johnson and Andy Graybill, for seeing the potential in my manuscript; Debbie Gershenowitz, JessieAnne D'Amico, Valerie Burton, and Iris Levesque for guiding me through the publication process; the two anonymous readers for their helpful feedback; Lindsay Starr and the art department for creating the book cover; Erin Davis and the copyeditors at Westchester Publishing Services; Bill Nelson for making the maps; Dino A. Battista, Liz Orange Lane, and the marketing department for spreading the word about the book; and all of the people who worked in the background, helping to craft the final shape of this book and bringing it out to the world.

Writing this acknowledgment feels like the end of the journey, but it is also the beginning of a new one. I welcome the readers of this book aboard.

Acknowledgments

The journey of writing this book has been a long one. It probably started with conversations with Ana de Zaballa about doing research on ecclesiastical visitations. Although I never managed to write anything about that topic, I did eventually end up writing this book on visits and mobilities years later. A major milestone of this journey was my encounter with various accounts that detailed the eighteenth-century travels of independent Indigenous people to ostensibly unlikely places, such as colonial Manila, far away from their borderland habitat. Based on the standard historiography, unconquered indigenes should have been cooped up, unmoving in the borderlands, so I wanted to tell an alternative story of Indigenous mobilities that unfortunately get buried in the onslaught of colonial narratives about the Spanish conquest and penetration of the hinterland.

Two locations were crucial in writing this book. One was the European University Institute (EUI), where I conducted the bulk of the research and writing for this project. I received funding from the Italian Ministry of Foreign Affairs and the EUI. Jorge Flores helped me a lot in fleshing out my ideas by suggesting readings, giving critical comments on draft chapters, and handing out sage advice. Stéphane Van Damme, Ann Thomson, Pieter Judson, Regina Grafe, Lucy Riall, María Dolores Elizalde, David Henley, Jon Greenwood, Camille Sallé, Aina Palarea, and colleagues who are too many to name read various portions of the book and gave helpful comments and writing advice. The EUI is a unique place where scholars from different academic backgrounds can meet and exchange ideas. This international setting was conducive to experimentation and looking at things from different perspectives. The other key location was Ateneo de Manila University. Ateneo is, in many ways, home. Even though I occasionally go away, I always come back somehow. The university gave me time off teaching to prepare this book for publication.

Historians live and die by their sources, and their journeys are not complete without visits to libraries and archives. I am indebted to the librarians, archivists, and their institutions who have helped me throughout the years: the European University Institute library in Florence; the Ateneo de Manila University library in Quezon City; the University of Santo Tomas library in

FIGURE 0.1 Pedro Murillo Velarde, *Map of the Philippine Islands*, 1744. This section from Murillo Velarde's famous map shows the most important, Spanish-recognized towns in central and northern Luzon. Besides the colonial towns along the coasts, it also includes independent and mission towns located in the center of the island. https://collections .leventhalmap.org/search/commonwealth:9s161d40f. Map reproduction courtesy of the Norman B. Leventhal Map and Education Center at the Boston Public Library.

Introduction

History is usually associated with the flow of time, with chronology in the abstract. But among late twentieth-century Ilongots, one of the Indigenous communities living in the borderlands on the island of Luzon in the Philippines, history was "mapped onto the landscape, not onto a calendar."[1] Events were rooted in precise memorable places; the temporal was spatialized.[2] As swidden agriculturalists who regularly moved their residence and gardens, what Ilongots remembered were "the places where they had 'erected their houseposts' and 'cleared the forest.'"[3] Walking and movement activated their history. As they walked along paths, they saw and recalled the places they had inhabited and cultivated. History was a stroll through a landscape full of sites of memory. Houseposts, trees, secondary forest growth, and the location of a hunt were their historical sources. For Ilongots, their social life and history were "unpredictable and improvised"; sometimes they walked "single file along paths that shift in direction," but at other times they ran "like wild pigs."[4] Although Ilongot society and history were tied to the landscape, they were very malleable and could go in many different directions, concentrating in particular places or dispersing over a wide area. The anthropologist Renato Rosaldo summarized the Ilongot sense of history in the following manner: "The perspectival sense of the past held by Ilongots is consistent with their view that social life is determined by what people make up as they go along; societal processes, in other words, are seen more as improvised than given, more meandering than linear, more mobile than stationary."[5] If the Ilongot themselves viewed history in such a fashion, perhaps we could benefit from adopting a similarly improvised, meandering, and mobile history of borderlands.

Ilongot communities were dispersed across the landscape. The state of their relationships manifested itself in terms of distance.[6] Geographical distance signified social distance. The farther apart people were, the colder the relationship; the closer together, the warmer. Since Ilongots relocated their residence every several years, they had periodic opportunities to loosen or tighten their bonds by either living closer together or moving away from each other depending on the prevailing circumstances. Mobility allowed people to not only move farther apart but also build and maintain relations with others polities occupied different ecological niches, it induced reciprocal exchanges between them, so even remote interior borderlands maintained threadlike connections with the wider outside world. Southeast Asian borderlands, although geographically local, were thus tied to regional and even global networks through various forms of mobilities.

Mobility in the early modern period tends to conjure up images of long-distance voyages and globe-trotting travelers.[19] Europeans associated travel with a sense of modernity and intellectual and economic expansion.[20] Explorations of and encounters in the New World represent the quintessential cross-cultural contacts of the time. In the case of the Philippines, Spanish Manila was a transshipment port for Chinese silk and Mexican silver, and a site of the intercontinental movements and cosmopolitan encounters of various Asian and European actors.[21] Even though European overseas expansion typically dominates discussions of mobility in the early modern period, Indigenous people from Africa, Asia, Oceania, and the Americas also traveled globally, visiting and settling in European cities like Seville and London in diverse capacities.[22] However, despite the existence of these global travels, mobilities have a counterpoint in friction.

Expanding into a global empire from the fifteenth century, the Spanish monarchy with its vast overseas realm struggled to overcome the friction of distance.[23] Five thousand leagues and two oceans separated Spain from the Philippines and made connections between the two places tenuous and cumbersome. Accustomed to the instantaneous speed of the twenty-first century, we sometimes neglect the sense of moving slowly by land or by sea. Prior to the transportation revolution of the nineteenth century, traveling was generally slow, and distances thus loomed large.[24] In traditional spatial terms, the Philippines was a remote frontier of the Spanish empire.[25] If coastal Manila was already a colonial frontier, then the interior borderlands of the various islands were even a step further beyond that frontier.[26] Besides the two transoceanic crossings, Spanish travelers to borderland settlements, say, at the center of Luzon, had to walk considerable distances and climb mountains to reach their destination. The Spanish empire, a sprawling composite or polycentric monarchy, was stretched thin across the globe.[27]

However, the portrayal of empires as networks with multiple centers and nodes sometimes leads to a simplistic, abstract, and uniform conception of space. Geographical obstacles and frictions complicated connections and mobilities on the ground and across oceans. Taking into account topographical features such as islands and mountains brings back the lumpiness missing in spatial constructions of empire.[28] The rough contours of land and seascapes led to patchy imperial networks of enclaves and corridors. How certain imperial policies developed was intimately linked to specific geographies and landscapes.

Mobility can sometimes conjure up romantic notions of free-flowing, unhindered movement; hence friction brings back the lumpiness and stickiness inherent in mobility. After all, "mobility is always located and materialised."[29] Resistance can take the form of friction of distance or terrain, where spatial separation or rugged landscapes inhibited movements and exchanges.[30] However, friction does not only stand in opposition to mobility. It also refers to the materiality of traveling, such as the moorings and infrastructures that make mobility possible.[31] Friction provides real-world traction for people on the move. Political powers in control of infrastructures can prevent, promote, and channel the flow of mobility.[32] They simultaneously enable and confine movements through particular routes. At a more conceptual level, friction is "the grip of worldly encounter."[33] Even grand universals only enact themselves in the sticky materiality of localities. Moorings and places of dwelling are integral elements of mobility. Traveling borderland actors were not moving for moving's sake. They had a destination at the end of their trip, meeting friends or pouncing on strangers. Traveling to multiple places created social interactions or frictions that enabled relations to be built and consolidated, or broken and destroyed. Since borderlands are diffuse spaces of interaction rather than clearly delineated boundaries, they serve as a conceptual tool for thinking with the feet, no different from how Ilongots constructed their history by walking.

While the early modern period is usually associated with long-distance sea voyages, this book has more modest aims in studying the micro-mobilities in the borderlands of an island.[34] The advantage of focusing on micro-mobilities is that it puts everyone on a more or less equal footing. Transpacific mobilities were limited to a select few, mostly Spaniards. Although "unusually cosmopolitan individuals" who lived global lives existed in the borderlands of Luzon in the form of missionaries, officials, and soldiers from Spain and Mexico, this book is more interested in their micro-mobilities on the island rather than their grand voyages.[35] It is more concerned with nondescript everyday mobilities like visits, raids, trading, and flight. By adopting a smaller scale, it allows other historical actors like Indigenous peoples to appear on stage.[36] Especially in the imperial context, the mobility of colonizers tends to garner a disproportionate amount of attention over native mobility. Even Indigenous peoples who largely remained in the borderlands were cosmopolitan and mobile in their own right. Their smaller circuits might not be typically associated with the global, but the grip of worldly encounters took place even in the remotest corners of an island hinterland. As a consequence, the picture that emerges in this book is the multiple mobilities and frictions of various actors from Spanish soldiers and missionaries to Indigenous traders and raiders overlapping and entangling with each other.

Spanish colonial officials and missionaries almost always viewed the island interior as the unconquered frontier of the colonial capital in coastal Manila. Spaniards who ventured inland saw themselves as agents of colonial expansion and religious conversion. They had a very metropole-centric perspective in spite of their travels, visits, and sometimes even long stay in the interior. As a corrective, mobility can be the guiding principle in presenting a decentered history of an island's borderlands. Instead of a unilinear expansion from the center to the periphery, movements were multidimensional and multidirectional. In their travels, visits, and raids, historical actors created a web of back-and-forth interactions that belied a one-way expansionary inland movement. Borderlands were not only geographical but also relational. Travels and mobility broke any perceived boundaries between center and periphery. Clear-cut boundaries on maps did not reflect the dynamic interactions on the ground. After years of residence in and travels to borderland missions, the Dominican missionary Francisco Antolín flipped the traditional paradigm where borderlands were peripheral: "The missions of Ituy and Paniqui are the center and heart of the Christian provinces of this island of Luzon."[37] In his view, the borderland—and not Manila—was the heartland, which was probably how his Indigenous neighbors saw the situation too. Experience and travels in borderlands changed people's perceptions of geographical relations and hierarchy. Borderlands were not the simple by-products of states as the latter expanded and collided with other polities; they can be appreciated in their own right.[38]

Mobility and friction characterized the interactions in the borderlands of eighteenth-century Luzon. Although historical actors portrayed mountainous interiors as a distinct geographical space from coastal regions, the constant movement within and beyond frontiers showed the interconnectedness of different places on the island. Mobility and friction in the form of mutual visits, violent raids, road openings, and disease transmission shaped and were shaped by the unfolding of encounters and relations. Multiple mobilities and encounters in different places provided the necessary backdrop for how various individuals and polities interacted with one another. Besides the physical movement to a different place, the actual experience of trudging across the landscape shaped the traveler's mentality.[39] Thinking with the feet allows us

to pay closer attention to the landscape and environment and brings us closer to how people experienced the world as they moved about in earlier times.[40] It involves a type of history that emphasizes not only a movement in space but also the experience of movement itself because the latter is an integral part of how human beings feel, think, and act.

Instead of seeing mobility as a unidirectional movement from coastal Manila to interior borderlands on the part of Spanish colonizers, this book views this movement as one among multiple entangled mobilities that involved Indigenous actors, among others. Spanish missionary penetration of the countryside had a counterpart in the visits of Indigenous chiefs to Manila and other colonial towns. Reciprocity manifested itself in these mutual visits that crossed apparent geographical and cultural divides and facilitated the conversion of Indigenous communities and the formation of alliances. Movements and exchanges showed themselves not only in instances of positive encounters but also in violent raids and attacks. Opposing sides borrowed and adapted each other's cultural practices in warfare. A pillar of mobility and friction was the negotiation over access and the gaining of permission. Ostensibly colonial roads built by Spanish missionaries were actually founded on the willing participation of Indigenous communities who granted access and, in fact, controlled who could and could not pass. The establishment of mission towns in the intermediate zone between the uplands and the lowlands not only facilitated the transmission of epidemic diseases between the two areas but also halted the mobility between them by potentially aggravating the malaria situation.

The next two sections use a case study from the late sixteenth and early seventeenth centuries to give a brief historical background to the eighteenth-century mobilities and frictions tackled in greater detail in the rest of the book and to offer a quick glimpse of the book's main themes and arguments. The final section of the introduction provides a description of the succeeding chapters.

Historical Background

After Spaniards established their colonial capital in coastal Manila in 1571, the conquest of the rest of the island, especially its interior, beckoned. From the 1590s to the 1610s, a series of expeditions set off from Manila to Ituy, a borderland between the central province of Pampanga and the northeastern province of Cagayan.[41] In 1591, the governor-general of the Philippines, Gómez Pérez Dasmariñas, sent his son Luis to lead an expedition to explore and

possibly conquer the territory. The governor-general had learned from long-time Spanish residents that "the discovery and conquest of the island of Luzon were not finished" and that just beyond the province of Pampanga "there were a lot of people that had yet to be discovered and taken possession of in the name of His Majesty."[42] According to field reports, brave *indio* (Indian) warriors inhabited this borderland. The indios of Cagayan were always at war and took advantage of the upriver hinterland to supply themselves with food and other necessities. When the governor-general inquired "why there had been twenty years of inattention that they had failed to penetrate inland," the reply was that "a number of Spaniards had gone up the Cagayan River and seven of them were killed by indios."[43] Due to the casualties, they had refrained from going upriver ever since.

The governor-general of the Philippines was surprised by the gap in their knowledge of the island. A completely new land in the interior was yet to be discovered and pacified twenty years after the founding of Spanish Manila, which was unacceptable in his mind. While the conversion, tribute collection, and pacification of indios were the main agendas of the Dasmariñas expedition, the immediate cause of Dasmariñas's campaign to Ituy was the peace and order situation in the province of Cagayan. Serving as a place of refuge for rebels, the borderland of Ituy strengthened Indigenous resistance to Spanish presence. If the expedition was successful, Dasmariñas would be able to gain the allegiance of the inhabitants of Ituy as loyal vassals of the Spanish monarch and eventually convert them to Christianity. Vassalage and conversion in Ituy were a means to win the war in Cagayan by cutting off the refuge and source of provisions of hostile indios. In spite of the governor-general's instructions to carry out a gentle pacification of Ituy, threats and violence pervaded the expedition's immediate cause and its conduct in the face of Indigenous resistance.[44]

The Dasmariñas expedition had contrasting fortunes at different points of its journey. When things went well, local chiefs accepted Spanish offers of friendship and promised to pay the tribute.[45] They sealed the alliance with ceremonies and exchanges. In several instances, the oath of alliance involved the breaking of eggs: "The said Don Luis [Dasmariñas] and the [Indigenous] chief each taking eggs in their hand, which is their customary oath, threw them on the ground in front of everyone declaring that whoever did not comply with the agreement would meet the same fate as the broken eggs."[46] On the one hand, after Indigenous chiefs promised to pay the tribute, the Spanish explorers often gave them pieces of silk.[47] On the other hand, when Indigenous communities fled or resisted, Spaniards exerted a corresponding

amount of force to garner native acquiescence and vassalage. They resorted to common tactics such as seizing a few individuals as hostages-cum-emissaries in negotiations with local communities. When several Ituy chiefs had already made the promise of friendship and tribute payment to Dasmariñas, a chief who had been away suddenly arrived and denounced the situation: "In no way should they let [the Spaniards] move forward or be their friends, and if they still persisted, they should know that the rest of this province would consider them enemies."[48] With mounting opposition, the Spanish conquistadors fortified their position and secured the food provisions they had requisitioned.[49] When natives of Ituy burned the Spaniards' makeshift fort, the latter opened fire in response.

Dasmariñas's expedition might look like a classic narrative of the conquest of a frontier, but details in the historical accounts belie such a simple story. On the surface, there is a one-way expansionary movement from the center to the periphery. The Dasmariñas expedition could be seen as the initiative of the colonial center in Manila to expand its possession to a distant frontier. However, particular points in Dasmariñas's own account undermine this classic narrative. There were usually two sides to each action. Both Spanish and Indigenous participants framed vassalage to the Spanish monarch in terms of friendship and alliance. Besides the payment of tribute, which was simultaneously a Spanish and an Indigenous practice, they sealed their friendship through the Indigenous custom of breaking eggs. Native vassals received silk and other gifts in return for the tribute. More than a unidirectional conquest, the Dasmariñas expedition involved several instances of reciprocal exchanges. The dividing line between oaths of vassalage to the Spanish king and Indigenous oath-taking ceremonies was blurred. These overlaps and ambiguities put into question a monolithic portrayal of conquest.[50] Even on occasions of violence, Indigenous agency manifested itself in flight from or resistance to Spanish intrusion.

An important goal of Spanish expeditions was to discover and pacify new lands for the monarchy, but the building of bonds with borderland inhabitants was just as relevant. Throughout his account, Dasmariñas emphasized the friendship Spaniards offered to the inhabitants of Ituy.[51] While the expedition did not have any qualms about using force in the face of hostility, as much as possible it tried to appeal to indios with the promise of being friends and vassals under one king and lord. Conquest or pacification in the Spanish sense was not purely about taking possession of land; it also meant the vassalage and subjection of people. There was some overlap between Spanish and Indigenous notions of political power, since both emphasized the importance

of building a substantial following and patronage network. Discovering the interior of the island entailed not only the physical act of exploration but also the creation of relationships through pacts and gift exchanges. When Spanish officials and soldiers and Indigenous chiefs and their retainers traveled and met in the island's borderlands, what they tried to accomplish was as much relational as territorial. Even violent conquests recognized the value of personal connections in establishing friendship, vassalage, and alliances.[52]

Mobility rested on more than Spanish military movements and intentions, since Spanish explorers like Dasmariñas were dependent on native go-betweens, guides, and translators and had to take into account local interpolity dynamics. Although the father-and-son Dasmariñas tandem might appear to be the driving force behind the exploration of Ituy in the 1590s, the figure of Dionisio Capolo, a chief from the province of Pampanga, loomed large in the background in many of the contacts with the borderland of Ituy.[53] Accounts of the Dasmariñas expedition do not mention Capolo, but he does appear as the main intermediary in previous and succeeding contacts between Manila and Ituy. The previous governor-general of the Philippines, Santiago de Vera, had sent Capolo to discover the reported new lands beyond Pampanga.[54] After reaching a distance sixty leagues from Manila, his acquaintances warned Capolo not to proceed any further because the people there were belligerent and currently at war. Later on, in 1607, two chiefs from Ituy visited Capolo's house apparently wanting to render obedience and pay tribute to the Spanish king.[55] Through Capolo's mediation, Spanish officials in Manila received them although without much fanfare. Capolo and the chiefs went to Ituy to encourage other chiefs to become Spanish vassals too. Capolo returned to Manila with seventeen chiefs from Ituy, who were received in a similar lukewarm fashion by Spanish officialdom.

Besides the prominent role of Capolo as an intermediary between Manila and Ituy, a number of nameless guides and translators made Spanish expeditions to Ituy possible. In the 1570s, one expedition sent out to explore the interior of the island turned back due to the lack of guides.[56] Spanish conquistadors did not always conform to the image of trailblazers who marked out their own path because they often used local guides to facilitate their explorations. The Dasmariñas expedition received the specific instruction to "always have good translators and guides who know the land and who can show the right path."[57] His entourage was composed of Spanish officials, thirty soldiers, two Augustinian priests, and several chiefs with a hundred of their followers.[58] As was usually the case, local allies made up the bulk of a supposedly Spanish expedition. Knowing the local terrain and people, the

guides and translators not only made sure that the group did not get lost but also acted as negotiators who tried to convince the chiefs in Ituy to accept the friendship of the Spaniards.[59]

Indigenous go-betweens from prominent chiefs to anonymous translators and guides facilitated the movements of Spanish exploration. Ordered by the governor-general of the Philippines to carry out a reconnaissance of new territories farther inland, Capolo in effect performed the role of explorer for the Spanish monarchy. If Spaniards saw Ituy as an unexplored frontier between Pampanga and Cagayan, Capolo viewed Ituy as an extension of his Manila-Pampanga network. He acted as a fulcrum between Manila and Ituy, and between Spaniards and borderland chiefs. His intermediate geographical and social position made him an ideal go-between and ally.

Despite the scarcity of written sources, we can glean that Capolo's clout seems to have grown through the years. The more he traveled, the stronger his connections became. In his first recorded journey, he did not travel very far and turned back even before reaching Ituy. As the years passed, his network of alliances and relations appeared to expand and made him a renowned chief over a larger area with more acquaintances and contacts stretching from Manila to Ituy. By the early seventeenth century, he had visited Ituy several times of his own accord. In these trips, the people of Ituy received him well because they already knew him from before, particularly from an instance when he had treated one of their chiefs with the utmost respect.[60] They were simply repaying the favor. Capolo straddled several worlds: a descendant of a ruler of preconquest Manila, a chief of a town in Pampanga, a loyal vassal of Spanish Manila, and a friend and ally of the chiefs of Ituy.[61] Seen side by side with the figure of Capolo, Spanish expeditions to the borderlands seem less like a unidirectional story of imperial expansion and conquest and more like a multidimensional engagement among a wide variety of actors. With the quick turnaround of Spanish officials and soldiers on short tenure in the Philippines, Capolo was a constant in the Ituy expeditions, which enabled him to create and consolidate the relations that bridged Manila, Pampanga, and Ituy. His repeated visits to the borderland of Ituy and his warm reception of Ituy chiefs at his home were key factors in his growing influence.

While Spanish historical accounts generally focus on the movements of Spanish officials, they nevertheless capture a few of the corresponding borderland travels of indios. If the movements were reciprocal as I argue in this book, then Indigenous mobility should leave some trace, no matter how muted, in the historical documentation. In the case of the expeditions to Ituy, Spanish officials and Indigenous chiefs exchanged tributes and gifts, and they performed their oaths twice in both the Spanish and Indigenous manner. Reciprocity was the foundation of attempts at creating ties. In a similar fashion, the bonds between Capolo and Ituy chiefs grew stronger as they visited each other over the years. Although Spanish sources most of the time concentrate on their own actions, Indigenous actors appeared once in a while in shadow movements when reciprocal practices were involved.

Spanish officials and missionaries did not always initiate the contact. Sometimes travels emanated from the borderlands. Interior mountain populations were not immobile and trapped in an enclosed space at the heart of the island perpetually hiding from outsiders and anticipating an invasion. They took the initiative in various ways. The inhabitants of Ituy regularly ventured to lowland colonial towns in Pangasinan to trade there.[62] In some cases, the visits were more deliberate and calculated in nature. Ituy chiefs visited Capolo, who facilitated their official welcome in the capital city of Manila. Some of them even timed their visits to get the maximum result. In 1609, upon hearing that the provincial of the Dominicans was on a pastoral visit in Pangasinan, thirty chiefs from Ituy decided to drop by unannounced to make a personal request to assign priests in their communities.[63] The Dominicans reciprocated the visit by sending two priests to explore the frontier, but they could not accede to the request of permanent priests due to the shortage of ministers in the archipelago. More than two decades later, inhabitants of Ituy once again resorted to the same tactic, but this time they met with more success.[64] When the Dominican provincial passed by Pangasinan on his pastoral visit, twenty-four borderland inhabitants intercepted him and repeated the same request for resident priests. Following the same pattern, two priests were sent out to reciprocate the visit and explore the land, but this time they did establish a mission in Ituy that lasted for a few years only. In the first few months after founding the mission, the new missionaries spent a lot of their time visiting and being visited by surrounding communities.

Mobility and Connections

Reciprocity can take on many forms from oaths to gifts to journeys. Mutual visits in borderlands often entailed some form of gift exchange, one of the quintessential practices of cross-cultural reciprocity in history.[65] Spanish explorers and missionaries to Ituy often brought gifts with them. When in a welcoming spirit, indios reciprocated with gifts of their own. In some cases, native gifts took on the form of tribute in kind to the Spanish monarch. Besides fulfilling an economic transaction in some cases, gifts constructed,

shaped, and embodied social relations.[66] Even the double oaths of tributes and eggs carried out by both Indigenous and Spanish parties mirrored the reciprocity of gift exchanges. If the gift was more than just the material object, explorations of and travels to borderlands were more than just a straightforward act of possession. Like gift exchanges, they were really about building relationships. More than generic or pro forma travels, they were personal visits that invoked—and sometimes coerced—acquiescence and reciprocity.

While the gift is the classic example of reciprocity in scholarship, hardly any attention is paid to the reciprocity in certain types of movement.[67] In some ways mobility, especially in the form of mutual visits, provides a more encompassing framework for understanding borderland relations than gift exchange because it includes a wider array of interactions. Mutual visits between Ituy and other places—from Manila and Pangasinan to neighboring borderland communities—provided the groundwork for gift exchanges to happen in the first place. While exchange and communication can also provide broad frameworks within which to view historical interactions, they tend to focus on the point of contact and relegate the surrounding context to the background. In contrast, an emphasis on mobility and friction incorporates a greater range of activities from the buildup to the encounter to the aftermath. Mobility and friction highlight the distance that had to be overcome in the process of creating and maintaining relations. They add a kinetic and deliberate element to how interactions emerged from, circulated within, and extended beyond borderlands.

Encounters were not isolated events that happened on a single spot. Neither were gifts or oaths merely points in time that marked the beginning of relations. A whole host of processes before and after these events took place and gave meaning to these individual instances. Spanish officials, missionaries, and soldiers and Indigenous chiefs, intermediaries, raiders, and merchants met one another in a series of occasions at different points on the island. Rather than focus on isolated encounters, the notion of mobility brings these geographically scattered encounters together for a more holistic, processual analysis. A network of movements underpinned individual encounters, a multisided reciprocity characterized interactions, and actors conquered social distance through reciprocated movements, even in moments of violence.

At first glance, the idea of mutual visits as the foundation of relations may prove overly benign and saccharine to the detriment of the reality of violence in these interactions. In the published accounts of Spanish officials and missionaries, narratives of conversion and alliance-making often follow a fixed rhetorical template.[68] They usually start with natives requesting Christian

baptism and alliance with Spaniards and end with natives sealing the agreement by traveling to the capital city to sign a treaty. Leaving out important details like the friction involved in the negotiations, these standardized reports oversimplify the complexity of interactions on the ground.[69] Nevertheless, no matter how compromised these reports are, they still offer a glimpse of the existence of cross-cultural, reciprocal visits despite their sometimes one-dimensional portrayal.

Even if historical sources portray mutual visits in a stylized fashion, outright hostilities constantly appear in them. Archival documents contain an abundance of material on military expeditions, wars, and conflicts. When violence and conflicts broke out, they usually left a documentary trail. While mutual visits may seem too benign in their portrayal of borderland interactions, more violent forms of friction are available to balance the picture. Spaniards and lowland indios carried out military expeditions in the frontier; hill people conducted their own raids on lowland communities. Despite their violent nature, military expeditions and raids still performed reciprocal movements in borderlands, a conflictive type of exchange but an exchange nonetheless. The use of force and coercion does not change the fact that targeted movements embodied social relations no matter how negative and antagonistic they were.[70] Friendly visits and vicious raids were two sides of the same coin. They both expressed a desire to manage social distance, whether to shorten or lengthen it, in the same way Ilongots concentrated and dispersed in borderlands. Mobility and friction are open-enough concepts to encapsulate the tension between the two apparent extremes. They also have the ability to capture the physical, spatial element in borderland relations, which involved traveling distances, welcoming outsiders, attacking them, or blocking their access.

If borderland movements can encompass the opposing actions of visits and raids, then borderlands also have the ability to embody the spatial contradiction of being an integral but separate part of a bigger geographical area. In Luzon, interior uplands occupy a distinct ecological niche from valleys and plains, which created difference but also complementarity. On the one hand, the rough topography and the sparse population of borderlands were not conducive to mobility. The center of Luzon has mountain ranges that made travel more cumbersome compared with the surrounding valleys and plains. Spanish observers always noted how rough and difficult the terrain was.[71] Reaching the heart of the island was a challenge, and small villages were scattered across the landscape. At least for Spanish travelers, the lack of roads—or what they considered roads—made journeys twice as long as they

were supposed to. Geographical distance did not always correspond with the duration of travel. A place might be physically close but difficult to reach due to the topography, which created the "friction of terrain."[72] Besides the terrain, constant warfare and headhunting among the diverse borderland polities made travelers fear for their lives.[73] Difficult, dangerous journeys created social distance between coastal and interior communities. In Southeast Asia, inland polities exhibited substantial levels of independence because of the factors mentioned above.[74]

On the other hand, the borderland's ecological difference from the littoral zone also made it an ideal partner for coastal communities. The products of interior and coastal areas were complementary and thus conducive to trading.[75] Interior upland settlements provided forest and agricultural products; lowland coastal ones supplied manufactured and overseas goods. In the case of Ituy, they specialized in wax and deerskin. Trade in these products might have been one of the reasons why Capolo maintained ties with Ituy and Manila. He might have been not only a political ally to Spanish and Ituy chiefs but also an economic middleman between them. Besides the opportunities for commerce, borderlands were sites of refuge for the apostates and fugitives of the colonial lowlands. Hostile indios used the inaccessible interior as a hiding place and supply base for their resistance. The Dasmariñas expedition to Ituy wanted to cut one of the heads of the Hydra-like resistance in Cagayan, which had a network of communities that straddled the downriver lowlands and the upriver uplands. Even in cases of contrasting reactions to colonial rule, indios in borderlands maintained kinship ties that crossed ecological, political, and religious lines. Such ties aided access to and movement in remote parts of the island's interior and opened a realm of possibilities and options.

With the rise of port cities in the early modern period, coastal polities like Spanish Manila exerted greater regional impact, but even then their power over interior upland polities remained tenuous at best. Military force was not sufficient to exact obedience, especially in hard-to-reach frontiers, hence the reliance on less antagonistic means of establishing ties through gift-giving, oath-making, and feasting. A combination of cooperation and independence pervaded upland-lowland, interior-coastal ties. Hinterland and coastal regions were separate but connected spaces.[76] Access to the inland frontier was limited, but that did not prevent movement to and from the interior. In fact, the punishing terrain and limited access made inland travels and visits even more significant, since people exerted more effort in the move. Visiting someone in a far-off place meant that person was important enough to warrant

such time and dedication. A visit manifested the strength of existing bonds, resurrected dormant ties, or consolidated them. Visitors enjoined their hosts to come and see them and repay the visit.[77] Mutual visits created and sustained long-distance relationships.

The time period of this book is the eighteenth century, which seems to have witnessed an increase in borderland mobility. Whether this apparent increase is merely an offshoot of the availability of more documentary sources is a distinct possibility. Historians are mostly reliant on Spanish written sources due to the scarcity of Indigenous writings in early modern Philippines, especially the borderlands. From a historian's perspective, the documentary situation is even worse in the precolonial period, prior to the arrival of Spaniards, because there are even fewer extant written sources in general and none from the borderland communities in Luzon. A strong oral tradition in Philippine polities, which does not always get written down and recorded, leaves us with a lopsided set of largely Spanish source materials, which imposes a clear limitation on the task of fleshing out Indigenous agency and motivations. Nevertheless, Indigenous activities and movements can be gleaned from Spanish accounts.[78] Missionaries out in the field gave very detailed reports on their interactions with Indigenous communities. From these snippets of details, we can partially reconstruct not only the changing relations between Spaniards and indigenes but also the role of borderland actors in shaping the trajectory of colonial history.

If the increased mobility in the eighteenth-century borderlands of Luzon was a reality on the ground rather than a mere fiction of the archives, what motivated Indigenous actors to act in particular ways? Why did borderland chiefs visit and ally with Spaniards in some instances but attack and resist them in other moments? It is much easier to ascertain Spanish intentions—typically formulated in terms of conquest and conversion—because of the abundant documentation they left behind. In Southeast Asian and Philippine studies, the notions of persons of prowess and mandalas provide the standard explanations for the dynamics of Indigenous polities.[79] Leaders of polities or mandalas were persons of spiritual prowess who had strong connections to the spirit world and brought prosperity and good fortune to their followers. The dynamics and hierarchy among leaders and mandalas changed constantly depending on their relative power to one another. Followers aligned themselves to powerful leaders because it was beneficial to be part of a strong mandala. In a similar fashion, weak mandalas would foster ties with stronger ones for, say, protection. At the same time, followers might leave their chief and change their allegiance with the rise of a more powerful upstart. Chiefs

and their polities went to war against weaker opposition and threatening rivals. In light of this background, eighteenth-century borderland inhabitants in Luzon must have visited and aligned themselves with Spaniards when they thought the latter were in a position of spiritual power and would be able to bring prosperity and good fortune to them. Conversely, they must have attacked colonial towns and resisted Spanish overtures when they felt they were in a dominant position to impose their will or felt threatened by the emerging Spanish power. These broad explanations for Spanish and Indigenous motivations, of course, need to be contextualized in the specific conjunctures of each individual case. For example, based on the existing Spanish sources, we do not conclusively know what drove the early seventeenth-century Ituy chiefs to visit Manila and align themselves with Spaniards. But based on what we know of the general contours of Philippine polities, they probably saw the Spaniards as powerful chiefs and thus ideal allies. Each chapter in this book attempts as much as possible to reconstruct the complexity of each situation to highlight the different actors' agency and intentions despite the clear limitations of the documentary sources.

In terms of the conjunctures that led to the borderland mobilities and contacts in the eighteenth century, I posit that the closer proximity among the different historical actors and the dispersed yet connected nature of Southeast Asian polities provided the overarching framework for these movements and interactions. A more extensive Spanish presence in the archipelago by the eighteenth century and deliberate policies on the part of the Spanish monarchy to approach borderland communities opened more opportunities for contact. From the late seventeenth century onward, Spanish royal policy pushed for the conquest of interior provinces and encouraged the dispatch of missionaries to animist communities, some of whom responded in kind.[80] Existing parishes extended out their hand to nearby animists in the frontier by sending out emissaries and intermediaries. Closer physical proximity and increased attempts at contact were sufficient conditions for more interactions and movements to occur.

Although it is more difficult to unearth the contributions of Indigenous dynamics to greater borderland mobilities in the eighteenth century, the dispersed but connected structure of Southeast Asian polities offers a possible rationale for the flexibility of borderland communities in welcoming or rejecting Spanish alliances. While the decisions of individual persons and communities are important in understanding specific historical cases, these decisions were not made in a vacuum. Although counterintuitive, the dispersal of Southeast Asian polities was conducive to maintaining connections because their differences were often complementary. For instance, border-land communities with access to forest products would find it convenient to foster ties with coastal polities with manufactured goods. Perhaps such complementarity was the driving force for the Ituy chiefs' attempts to build ties with Spanish Manila. Indigenous chiefs and their polities were acutely aware of what was happening around them and what others were doing. Individual polities were geographically scattered but connected in more ways than one. This spatial distribution of Southeast Asian polities at the local level gave them room for maneuver.

Distance and dispersal, although often considered as manifestations of loose social ties, were strategic when viewed from a wider interpolity perspective, since they offered people a variety of options. Kin members who lived far away from each and chose different paths could remain spread out, or they could rekindle their dormant relations and decide to live together. The open-endedness of borderland dispersals partly explains the constant reversals, switches, and changes of mind, say, between conversion and apostasy or between alliance with and hostility toward Spaniards throughout the years. It was never a purely binary choice when kin, neighbors, enemies, and allies at the individual and group level made their own coinciding or conflicting decisions. In a networked but dispersed Southeast Asian borderland, there was always a relative, friend, or enemy you could join, whatever decision you took. As borderland actors traveled and moved around, we can see these various choices and mutating ties in action, which is particularly significant given the paucity of historical sources that explicitly spell out their inner motivations.

Borderland is a useful framework to use in thinking of the history of Luzon because of the fluidity and improvisation inherent in the interactions. Although colonial binaries—upland/lowland, Christian/infidel, civilized/barbaric, nomadic/sedentary, and so on—have pervaded the historiography, the mountainous interior was never solely a bastion of resistance. Uplanders went to the lowlands to trade, Christian indios apostatized and fled to the mountains, and colonial subjects and independent islanders lived together in settlements and also moved around in different directions. More importantly, communities and kin groups were spread across a wide area with some members living in the mountains and others in the valleys, some professing Christianity and others animism, several cooperating with Spanish colonizers and a number antagonizing them. Capolo had ties with Manila Spaniards, Ituy chiefs, and his Kapampangan followers. Christian belligerents in lowland Cagayan sought refuge with and assistance from their animist relatives in

upland Ituy. Borderlands capture this fluid, mixed dynamic of polities. They are an antidote to clear-cut, rigid colonial binaries. Connections spanned ostensible geographic, ethnic, religious, and cultural divides whether in precolonial or colonial times. Variety and differences among allies and kin facilitated opportunities: Capolo acting as a go-between between Ituys and Spaniards, an animist uplander trading with his Christian relative living in a colonial town, or an indio apostate rejoining his animist family in the highlands.

In a tentative, halting dance that dragged on for years—reminiscent of Ilongots' slow, measured movements as they traveled—Spanish missionaries and Indigenous chiefs inched closer and closer to one another and negotiated issues of access and conversion.[81] Some Indigenous chiefs returned the favor with their own visits. Perhaps Spanish movements sometimes coincided with Indigenous phases of concentration and dispersal. At the very least, this combination of proximity and controlled dispersal provided the conditions for interactions to occur and relationships to develop, stagnate, or deteriorate.

When the initiative or reception was lacking or not reciprocated, the relationship did not prosper. The frequent visits between Capolo and the Ituy chiefs strengthened their bond, but Spanish Manila's cold reception of the Ituy chiefs did not amount to anything despite the latter's seeming willingness to initiate relations. The contingency of favorable circumstances played a decisive factor on whether reciprocal mobilities worked or not. The unpredictability of the results rested on the actors' improvisations as they went along, sometimes walking in single file, at other times choosing diverging paths, and in special occasions running like wild pigs.

For late twentieth-century Ilongots, their society and history were spread out across the landscape, following an improvised rhythm of concentrations and dispersals. They go against the stereotype of an unconquered Indigenous people cooped up in their mountain abode because mobility—expanding and contracting, maneuvering and meandering—was an integral part of their activities. Scattered settlements and kin were part of their social landscape, the rekindling of old distant ties possible at a moment's notice depending on the circumstances. This condition conforms to the sprawling networks characteristic of borderlands and Southeast Asian polities. More than individual or local, Indigenous agency was relational, closing and opening ties whenever it was opportune. Structures and hierarchies of power existed, but they were always malleable and at best tenuous even during colonial times. Even in the face of enclaves and corridors that limited the extent of mobilities and relations, agency and power were diffused across the borderlands and never concentrated in a single ruler or authority. Perhaps this is the appropriate way to

retell the eighteenth-century history of borderlands in Luzon—through mobilities and frictions, through the unexpected twists and turns of cultivated and abandoned relationships.

Structure

Eighteenth-century encounters in the borderlands of Luzon were processes of mobility and friction where limitations of and negotiations over access shaped and were shaped by the building and breaking of relations. The book's four chapters come in pairs. The first pair covers the initial borderland exchanges and interactions from the late seventeenth to the early eighteenth century. The second pair of chapters explores the deepening borderland relations from the middle to the end of the eighteenth century. The book's conclusion discusses the ever-increasing entanglement of lowlanders and uplanders, Christians and animists, and Spaniards and natives after a century of greater borderland mobility.

Chapter 1, "Mutual Visits," analyzes the initial contacts between Augustinian, Dominican, and Franciscan missionaries, on the one hand, and Indigenous borderland communities, on the other. It highlights how movement was crucial in the consolidation of ties between missionaries and potential converts. While missionaries and their lowland Christian intermediaries visited the frontier, inland chiefs made the corresponding visit to Manila and provincial capitals. Missionary chronicles and government accounts of the various visits are the key sources that track the movement of friars and natives in and beyond the borderlands. Reciprocal visits underpinned the creation of social and political ties between them. Travels, permissions, and access were fundamental to how Spanish administration functioned and how upland communities created kinship ties with others. By taking into account Indigenous borderland movement, the chapter counteracts the inherent tendency of the historical sources to portray mobility as a unilinear, unidirectional Spanish penetration of the interior frontier. Borderland interactions were multidimensional, multidirectional, and multisited.

Chapter 2, "Violent Exchanges," delves into the more antagonistic side of borderland exchange. In a way, it balances the perhaps benign portrayal of borderland relations in the preceding chapter, but it is also a simple recognition of the reality of violence. Military expeditions and raids were an essential part of frontier movements. The Spanish government employed military forts and expeditions to soften upland resistance to Spanish presence, protect colonial subjects from upland attacks, and carry out the law that prohibited

upland-lowland commerce. At the same time, upland communities carried out raids on mission and colonial towns. In some areas, the conversion of several communities to Christianity created a distinct Christian alliance, which altered the power balance in the borderlands and threatened the communities that remained animist. In these cases, mission towns were a prime target for burning and headhunting raids from independent groups. Besides the written accounts of the missionaries, the other main source for the chapter is the government reports on Indigenous raids and the Spanish proposals to build defensive forts. Although the chapter presents the more unseemly side of borderland relations, it also shows how exchange and mobility continued through the use of violence and force. Mobility, exchange, and violence were interrelated phenomena. Soldiers who manned forts usually engaged in upland-lowland trade and tried to use their military power to monopolize it. Forts also facilitated the movement of people through hostile territory. Spanish and Indigenous warriors adapted to each other's fighting style by borrowing and targeting specific cultural elements in order to be as effective as possible in combat.

If the first and second chapters explore the friendly and violent sides of borderland mobility and exchanges, the third and fourth chapters track the increasing borderland connections and their consequences. Like the previous pair, they also reveal the tensions and contradictions inherent in greater mobility and contact.

Chapter 3, titled "Roads and Crossings," discusses how the religious orders and Indigenous communities created a road through a borderland in 1738. In general, the rough terrain hindered Spanish penetration and mobility at the center of the island. Protected by distance and topography, hostile independent polities in the frontier attacked colonial towns at will with largely no repercussions, and apostates and other runaways fled from Spanish-administered towns to the unconquered hinterland. For Spaniards, the construction of a road through the center of the island was a solution to these perennial colonial problems. However, the road was not simply a logistical issue of finding a viable path in uncharted territory because it depended on building the necessary social relations. The religious orders needed the acquiescence of local chiefs; otherwise, the project would not have pushed through. Without the local support of some borderland communities, cleared roads would have simply been overrun by mudslides and undergrowth without proper maintenance. For certain Indigenous communities, cooperating with Spaniards in opening the road furthered their political position in shifting borderland alliances. While a variety of traveler's accounts flesh out the difficulties inherent

in everyday mobility in the mountainous, muddy interior, friar chronicles and correspondences retrace the obstacles encountered in negotiating the opening of the borderland to outsiders. Mobility had a social as much as a physical dimension. The missionaries were acutely aware of this, as they simultaneously explored the logistics of traversing mountains and ridges and negotiated with and tried to convert the communities along the proposed road. Indigenous communities, nevertheless, exercised paramount authority over who could pass and use borderland roads.

Chapter 4, "Deadly Transitions," investigates the epidemiological consequences of greater mobility and resettlement projects in the borderlands. In the face of the preponderance of death in the tropics, European settlers typically blamed it on the hot, humid climate. Although Spanish missionaries noticed the pestilential character of the borderlands of Luzon, they did not attribute it to the scorching heat but rather to the harsh, cold weather of the interior mountains. While the harsh upland climate allegedly debilitated and killed off lowland Spaniards and natives who attempted to reside in the foothills, upland converts who moved in the opposite direction and relocated to missions in foothills and valleys succumbed to epidemic diseases. These population movements had detrimental epidemiological effects on both Spaniards and indigenes as they entered different ecological zones. While historical actors largely attributed health-related deaths in the borderlands to the climate and epidemics, the chapter proposes that mission towns also found themselves in a malaria zone that was more likely to kill newcomers in the area. Mosquitoes that carried and transmitted malaria thrived at a specific altitude, from 800 to 2,000 feet above sea level, precisely in the zone where Spaniards set up their mission towns to attract animist communities from the uplands. The sources for this chapter are the missionary accounts of the relocation of upland converts to foothills and valleys and the chronicles of flight caused by the outbreak of epidemic diseases. Besides exposing their population to epidemic diseases like smallpox through greater outside contact, mission towns in foothills most probably exacerbated the incidence of malaria in the borderlands as they became the perfect breeding ground for malaria-carrying mosquitoes with their combination of the right altitude, slow-moving water, better access to blood meal for mosquitoes, and newly arrived inhabitants without any prior immunity.

Connections in borderlands had previously existed even during precolonial times, but the closer proximity and meandering mobilities of various borderland actors in the eighteenth century led to more encounters. Despite the prominence of the upland-lowland divide in the mental map of Spaniards

and indigenes, increased mobility ensured that the trajectories of the two areas became more entangled than ever. More people converted and apostatized, aligned with and connived against Spanish colonizers, and visited their friends and attacked their enemies. Whatever people did to avoid disease and death—whether quarantining themselves or migrating from the uplands to the lowlands or vice versa—it became more and more difficult for them to escape the same fate. As networks of cooperating and competing polities, borderlands were in a continuous state of flux, like Ilongots walking and crouching along paths and encountering long-lost friends or unsuspecting passersby.

CHAPTER ONE

Mutual Visits

The day after Ash Wednesday of 1785, the governor-general of the Philippines, José Basco, traveled to the town of Santa Cruz in the province of Ilocos, as part of his tour of the northwestern provinces of the island of Luzon.[1] While in Santa Cruz, he had a meal and witnessed a spectacle of dancing Igorots. One of Basco's companions described the scene in the following manner: "A company of Igorots came forward to bid him [Basco] welcome with a dance, which was very curious to us. Ten or twelve placed themselves in a line forming a circle, resting their two arms on the shoulders of those nearest, and, bending their bodies over, they slowly went around some paces; they let go of each other and squatted down on their haunches, chanted some words of good wishes in a very solemn tone, accompanied by the music of a little gong."[2] Although Basco's trip involved performing his serious administrative duties as governor-general, it also had its lighter ludic moments. Feasting and Indigenous dances were an unofficial but arguably integral part of his job. The premier representative of the Spanish monarch in the archipelago was surveying the royal domain. As the king's embodiment, he brought the royal presence to subjects in far-flung provinces during his travels. What could be more personal and intimate than sharing food and admiring a dance up close?

The chance encounter between Basco's entourage and the dancing Igorots was curious in many ways. Besides the strangeness of the dance to unaccustomed Spanish eyes and ears, it defied expectations that the most powerful Spanish official in the archipelago would meet face-to-face with independent Igorots in a most nondescript place. It was curious enough for Basco's companion to write an account of it in his diary and for a religious chronicler to mention it again a few years later. Almost 200 years later, a historian still found the event to be somewhat unexpected.[3] What we find curious and surprising depends on what we find normal and predictable in our daily affairs. In the town of Santa Cruz, the meeting of Basco and the Igorots seemed like a strange encounter of opposing cultures: Spanish and Indigenous, colonial and independent, Christian and animist, lowland and upland, and center and periphery. It was portrayed like a unique occurrence in the history of cross-cultural encounters on the island. However, what is perhaps even more curious and surprising is that such meetings happened more often than expected.

Spanish colonial geography advanced the idea of a frontier.[4] Urban towns in the Indies embodied the outposts of Spanish civilization.[5] In contrast, territories beyond colonial towns represented savagery. Colonial geography rested on a duality between civilized towns and barbaric frontiers. In the case of Luzon, the mountain ranges at the center of the island represented the unconquered frontier. In colonial historiography, Spanish-administered towns in coastal and lowland areas became the showpiece of Spanish rule.[6] In contrast, the independent polities in the interior mountains became a foil to Spanish domination as a site of flight and resistance.[7] The geographical divide between plains and mountains reflected the dichotomy between state rule and independence.[8] Each landscape favored a particular type of polity. The division that steep mountain gradients created between upland and lowland communities was not only topographical but also political and cultural. Spanish-administered cities were the antithesis of the frontier. In this view, only one movement was possible, Spanish penetration and Indigenous flight into the interior. As a frontier, mountains were either a site of conquest or a place of refuge. In any case, interior hill peoples were always in a defensive position. Spanish officials acted, and Indigenous communities simply reacted.

Such a mental map made the encounter between Governor-General Basco and the dancing Igorots somewhat unusual. Both parties were outside their designated space. Basco was hundreds of kilometers away from the seat of Spanish power in Manila, and the Igorots were in a lowland town away from their mountain abode. Both sides met in a liminal space, a borderland. They both stepped outside their perceived habitat. However, more important than the location of their meeting in a frontier town was the fact that they were both mobile.

Rather than look at the process of interactions from the geographical perspective of a frontier space, this chapter highlights the movement involved in such interactions.[9] The meeting between Basco and the Igorots might have happened in a frontier outstation, but these contacts occurred in a wide variety of places from upland settlements in the Cordillera to colonial cities like Manila. While Spanish colonial sources do emphasize the penetration of the inland hinterland by Spanish officials and missionaries, it was not a one-way movement. Interior inhabitants like the dancing Igorots regularly traveled to the lowlands and occasionally to provincial capitals and even Manila. Since these interactions happened everywhere, it becomes superfluous to use the notion of a geographical frontier as an analytical framework. In the end, the borderland was everywhere, and people's movements and interactions created it. An approach that focuses more on movement rather than on space

lends itself to a mobile, multisited ethnography.[10] It requires the historian not only to observe the various actors in their places of dwelling but also to follow and walk with them in their travels. In this chapter, cross-cultural interactions are put in the context of movement, specifically that of mutual visits. Instead of viewing these interactions as taking place in a specific geographical space, they are interpreted in terms of mobility. In several key moments, mutual visits, or the lack thereof, were critical in the strengthening or weakening of ties between Spaniards and indigenes, and between Christians and animists. Taking into account Indigenous travels from the hinterland balances the analysis by putting the various actors on a more or less equal footing.

The portrayal of the mountainous interior frontier of Luzon as a space of colonial conquest or Indigenous refuge plays to the binary distinction between center and periphery. However, recent trends in historiography have questioned this oversimplistic portrayal of frontier interactions.[11] Instead of envisioning the frontier as a contact zone between two distinct geographical and political entities, I propose an outlook where fluidity and flows that transgressed perceived borders and divisions are the norm. States and frontier polities are not static entities but intrinsically mobile.[12] Movement trumps territoriality. Power depends on gaining access to resources and channeling mobility. In this alternative paradigm, interactions, exchanges, and negotiations are of primary importance as people move about, welcome others, and restrict access. Basco's encounter with the dancing Igorots becomes less curious and less surprising in a vast sea of visits carried out by both Spanish officials and missionaries and Indigenous chiefs and followers.

This chapter's emphasis on movement is not simply a matter of a more pleasing theory. It is true that the historical sources lend themselves to a traditional rendering of the narrative because they revolve primarily around the missionary activities of the Augustinians, Dominicans, and Franciscans who ventured to the island's hinterland. They support a linear, unidirectional narrative of the conquest of the imperial frontier. However, these same sources contain details that undermine such a lopsided story. Alongside missionaries who explored and settled in the hinterland, Indigenous actors like the dancing Igorots occasionally appeared in the written records. They traveled too, not only to frontier colonial towns but also to capital cities. These neglected visits pepper the official Spanish documentation and offer a fuller picture of the back-and-forth dialogue transpiring at that time. Movement was not the sole prerogative of Spanish conquistadors and missionaries. Indigenous people moved too.[13] They were not a permanent fixture of the mountains. Escaping from Spanish oppression and seeking refuge in the interior uplands

were not the only journey they made.[14] They also regularly went to the low-lands to carry out a wide variety of activities from trading and raiding to feast-ing and dancing. The more violent, conflict-ridden exchanges appear in chapter 2. The more benign themes of visits, permissions, and access are the subjects of this one.

The increased contact in the eighteenth century between Christians and animists did not come out of nowhere. In the late seventeenth century, the Spanish monarchy revived the neglected practice of administrative inspec-tion tours called *visitas a la tierra* that partly resulted in the plans to conquer the unsubdued hinterland. At roughly the same time, the religious orders en-couraged their parish priests to take on the role of missionaries by scouting the propensity of animists in the surrounding areas to conversion. These small-scale tentative visits and inquiries led to the grand visits to Manila by potential converts. Visits broached and later on consolidated the conversion of hinterland inhabitants to Christianity and their alliance with the Spanish monarchy. Both sides were involved in visiting one another. Although Span-ish sources portray the events as the conquest of the frontier, the process re-volved around reciprocity. In Indigenous communities, visits usually came in pairs. Being invited, accepting the invitation, carrying out the visit, recipro-cating the invitation, and being visited in turn—all these activities under-pinned the creation of social relations. Borderland actors from Spaniards to Ilongots took part in this dynamic process. Spanish inspection tours and the grand reception of Indigenous chiefs in Manila conformed to Indigenous no-tions of reciprocity. However, mobility was contained and channeled. Not everybody was welcome, and friction also took on the form of rejection. Even in cases where Spanish officials and Indigenous chiefs prohibited access to their towns and thus rejected any sort of exchange or alliance, they still stand as counterexamples that prove the importance of mutuality in interactions. Successful relations manifested themselves in mutual visits, while unsuccess-ful ones failed on the first step of being welcomed.

This chapter starts with the grand visits to Manila by Indigenous chiefs prior to conversion. It then situates these visits within the context of the gen-eral movement of people in the hinterland, particularly the initial feelers sent out by parish priests and their parishioners and the official inspection tours conducted by Spanish judges, bishops, and provincials. However, missionary attempts at penetrating inland depended on intermediaries and permissions. On some occasions, access was restricted, and gaining entry required pa-tience, persistence, and affection. When permission was granted, it opened the door to carrying out reciprocal visits and establishing kinship relations.

Simple everyday visits among friends and kin connected people together at an intimate personal level. Visits underpinned the conversion and alliances that spanned the borderland because they made affinity and kinship palpable and real. Instead of generic concepts of conquest and conversion, mobility in the form of visits and meetings transformed strangers into relatives. Only those who had the aptitude and dedication to foster kinship ties were able to span the perceived religious, political, and geographical divide.

Italons and Many More Go to Manila

On August 25, 1702, several Italon chiefs arrived in Manila.[15] They had traveled all the way from the town of Lublub at the foothills of the Caraballo Mountains about 200 kilometers away. They first stopped by the Augustinian convent in Tondo, where friars from the nearby provinces had already congregated in preparation for the feast of Saint Augustine in three days' time. Together with the other members of his religious order, the provincial warmly welcomed the potential new converts and gave them money. Throngs of people from the surrounding neighborhood flocked to see the unusual visitors whom they had only heard about. Part of the attraction was the travelers' clothing, or lack thereof. The visitors were "all naked according to mountain custom, with their indecent loincloth."[16] A few were armed with lance and shield, others with bow and arrow.[17] The chiefs wore a type of hat made of palm leaves. In preparation for their entry to Manila proper, the provincial had clothes made for them, so they would be more presentable.

The next day, the provincial accompanied his guests to the city to meet two of the most important Spanish officials in the land, the governor-general of the Philippines, Domingo Zabálburu, and the archbishop of Manila, Diego Camacho y Ávila.[18] The governor-general embraced them and, following the Spanish monarchy's typical spiel to attract Indigenous allies, promised to defend them from their enemies. The Italon chiefs kissed the hand of the archbishop, who in turn gave them gifts. The meeting with the governor-general and the archbishop was clearly performative. The Augustinians brought independent chiefs from the hinterland to submit to the monarchy and church as vassals and converts. Even though the Italons had not yet converted at this time, the encounter prefigured what lay in store for them in the near future if they submitted, membership and protection in the Spanish Catholic community.

Although being hugged by the governor-general and kissing the hand of the archbishop might seem like the climax of the whole journey, the trip was

far from over. The Italon chiefs stayed for another six days in Manila.[19] The Augustinians housed them in their convent in Tondo, which was a short distance away from the city proper. From there, the Italons could easily visit the city, soak in the atmosphere, marvel at the churches, participate in the celebrations during the feast of Saint Augustine, and buy goods at the market with the money the Augustinians had given them.

On the return journey to Lublub, the Italon chiefs carried a letter from the Augustinian provincial ordering the various convents along the way to welcome them, house them, and lavish them with gifts.[20] When they arrived home, they became the perfect spokespersons of the kindness and generosity of the Spaniards: "They did not know how to explain what they had seen in Manila. They could not stop talking about the warm reception and care that they had received, and the affection and good treatment that they had experienced throughout the whole trip."[21]

The Augustinians' strategy worked, as the Italon chiefs' wonderful journey to Manila predisposed entire communities in the hinterland to convert to Christianity. The Italons' reluctance to convert was, in fact, the primary trigger for the Manila trip in the first place. The old chiefs had requested that they would love to see Manila before getting baptized.[22] So as not to disappoint them in the least, the Augustinian missionaries obliged because so-called bad Christians were spreading rumors in the area that Spaniards only wanted to convert them to exact tribute and take away their liberty.[23] For the missionaries, the Italon chiefs singing the praises of the Spaniards after the trip to Manila was the precise antidote they needed to counteract the previous unfavorable reports and edge the Italons closer to conversion. For the Italons, the trip sweetened the deal before their definitive conversion and confirmed with their own eyes and ears the grandness of the Spaniards. Although the old Italon chiefs had never been to Manila, it was on their mental map. They knew of its existence. To bring themselves out of their doubts, they had to visit the place where the Spaniards lived, a place that they had only heard about. Travels and visits were part of their social repertoire. The Italons of Lublub and the residents of Manila knew of each other's existence, but it was only through the trip that they finally met one another face to face. Inasmuch as Lublub was a Spanish frontier, Manila was an Italon frontier.

The Italons' visit to Manila was a special event, but it was far from unique. A few weeks earlier, the Ituys and the Dominicans had carried out a similar activity.[24] The Ituys lived in the same general vicinity as the Italons and likewise hesitated about converting to Christianity. The Dominican missionaries brought them to their convent in Manila where high-ranking officials of the order gifted them with clothes, plates, bowls, jars, and cattle. The fondness, affection, and gifts the Ituys received dispelled their misgivings and predisposed their kin group to convert. A few months after the journey, the parents of one of the Ituy travelers to Manila eventually agreed to be baptized.[25]

Even though most of the sources for the visits to Manila only existed as unpublished manuscripts for centuries, they nevertheless exhibit a distinct pattern that could raise suspicions on their authenticity.[26] The narrative always starts with apprehensive indios who were open to the idea of conversion and repeatedly ends with their satisfaction with the Spaniards and their receptiveness to be baptized after going to Manila. The native willingness to cooperate with Spaniards throughout the whole process may seem a little too convenient. It fits in too nicely with Spanish aims of trying to justify colonial rule and Christian conversion by incorporating native participation and acquiescence. At the end of the day, did Spanish priests and officials largely manufacture these stories of Indigenous consent to legitimize their colonial rule?[27] Undeniably, the narratives reflect contemporary European political practices. Part of European courtly ritual involved provincial magnates visiting and paying homage to the monarch, and Spanish and other European powers replicated this practice in their colonies by bringing Indigenous chiefs to capital cities to seal and celebrate their alliances.[28] The grandiosity of these festivities was vital to the exercise of political power. The exchange of gifts was also a normal part of early modern diplomacy.[29] When the Italon chiefs kissed the hand of the archbishop, they took part in the Spanish court ceremony known as *besamanos*.[30] The through line of all these royal rituals was the act of submission. It was the Italons and Ituys who visited the ritual center in Manila, and not the other way around. They kissed the hand of the archbishop as a sign of subservience. Initially "naked" in their loincloth, they eventually donned Spanish clothes as a sign of their civilization under Spanish rule.[31] The cornerstone of the whole trip was their conversion, which was the symbol par excellence of submission to the Christian God and the Spanish monarch.

Although these ceremonies were rituals of submission, they were much more than that. The sources most likely hid, or at the very least simplified, the complexity of the situation more than anything else.[32] While historical accounts did co-opt native participation to legitimize colonial rule, they nevertheless offer echoes of the multiple voices of the various participants, including those of the Italons and Ituys, no matter how muted they are.[33] As discussed later in the chapter, travels and visits were an integral part of how islanders built and maintained ties with friends and relatives living far away.

Gifts of prestige goods, gestures of affection, and wearing Spanish clothes embodied social relations and transformed the participants' identities.

The exchange of prestige goods was standard practice among allied Indigenous polities.[34] It was the duty of the paramount power to distribute prestige goods to allies and please them, so it was not a relationship of utter subjugation. When Spanish friars offered gifts that they knew their hinterland visitors valued, they adopted a policy of attraction not that different from how Indigenous chiefs distributed prestige goods to gain and maintain a following. When the Italon chiefs used the money from the Augustinians to buy the goods that they wanted in the markets of Manila, that was a clear manifestation of their agency in the exchange.[35] They had demanded to be brought to Manila and determined the gifts they brought back home to Lublub. If anything, the trip to Manila was only one side of the equation because gift-giving was usually reciprocal and created a web of relations, and the account is most likely merely silent on how the hinterland chiefs materially reciprocated the generosity.[36]

Gestures of affection were not frivolous ceremonial acts but rather matters of utmost importance in sealing ties. The Ituys' visit to Manila provides a case in point. The Dominican missionary Francisco de la Maza mentioned the one blot in their visit to the capital: "They complained a lot about a charlatan, who treated them badly by calling them Ituys, when they were already half-Spanish, having hugged the king."[37] Although Maza's letter is brief and lacks details, it seems that the Ituys, like the Italons, were welcomed by the governor-general, the so-called king. Their journey to Manila was more than the physical movement from one site to another, the eight days of trek, or even the eventual conversion to Christianity. By the simple act of hugging the king, that is, the governor-general, they transformed their identity from Ituy to half-Spanish. Similarly, when the Italon chiefs kissed the hand of the archbishop in *besamanos*, they most likely interpreted it in the context of Indigenous gestures of affection among kin.[38] Visits, hugs, and kisses engendered a distinct form of *mestizaje* (miscegenation).

Instead of interpreting the hinterland chiefs' wearing of Spanish clothes as their transformation from barbarity to civilization, the new attire was a manifestation of their new alliance and consequent identity. In Southeast Asia, wearing garments from prestigious foreign centers was a source of status.[39] This was not the Philippine version of Adam and Eve realizing they were naked. King Narai of Ayutthaya dressed in the Persian fashion appropriate for a mighty ruler; a seventeenth-century Jambi crown prince found Javanese clothes to be most appealing.[40] Spanish missionaries dressed their hinterland

visitors in Spanish clothes to hide the latter's supposedly embarrassing na-
kedness, but the recipients viewed the situation in a completely different way.
They elevated their status by associating with powerful Spaniards and wearing their clothes. Borderland natives in Spanish clothes was not a curious and
surprising phenomenon, but rather a sight to behold because it was an occasion of honor. Even hinterland residents who had never been to Manila
before were receptive of outside influences. They were so modern and cosmopolitan that their identity shifted based on the people they hugged and the
clothes they wore.[41] The wearing of Spanish clothes was not so much a sign
of submission as that of transformation into honored allies or, in other words,
half-Spaniards.

Even though historical accounts have a tendency to present the visits to
Manila as benign affairs, an undercurrent of tension was almost always in the
background. In the case of the Italons and Ituys, the visits were meant to
counter their reticence to convert because of widespread stories of Spanish
abuse. The journey of several Igorot chiefs to Manila provides a more explicit
example of how missionaries and animists resorted to visits to overcome overt
conflicts. In 1753, while visiting the provinces of Ilocos and Pangasinan, the
Augustinian provincial Manuel Carrillo received news that the Igorots no longer went to lowland Christian towns because the Spanish provincial governor
of Pangasinan had prohibited trade with non-Christians and threatened the
Igorots with a military expedition.[42] During Carrillo's second visit in 1754, several Igorot chiefs met with him, declared their desire to become Christian, and
asked him for help in addressing their grievances against the provincial governor.[43] Instead of merely representing the Igorots' case to the governor-general
in Manila, Carrillo thought it would be better to have the Igorot chiefs themselves present their demands to the governor-general in person.

In Manila, the governor-general met with them and granted their demands, which included the suspension of the planned military expedition
and the lifting of the ban on Christian-animist trade.[44] He also wanted the six
Igorots to be baptized before they went home, since they had already expressed the desire to do so.[45] Their godfathers were the most distinguished
citizens of Manila, who dressed them in the Spanish style. Besides the governor-
general and the Augustinian vicar provincial, priests and residents from all
over Manila packed the Augustinian convent in Tondo. The apparent highlight of the occasion was the governor-general rising from his chair, approaching the six baptized chiefs, and kissing their hand.[46]

But arguably even more spectacular was the Igorot chiefs' arrival in the
town of Agoo in Pangasinan on their way home.[47] With coincidentally many

visiting upland animists in town, the Augustinians took advantage of the situation and made the entrance of the six chiefs arriving from Manila as awe-inspiring as possible: "The six [Igorot chiefs] entered on horseback, accompanied by the officials of Agoo, dressed in the Spanish style, with their appropriate cane of office based on their title and rank, with which the governor[-general] had favored and honored them."[48] The Igorot chiefs were treated like royalty upon their entrance. Their mode of transportation, clothing, and accessories all manifested the marvelous treatment they had received in Manila. It was all a well-choreographed spectacle to convince the animists in town of the grandeur and generosity of the Spaniards. Aligning with the Spaniards had its benefits. The performance worked and left its audience astounded: "All those pagans were amazed upon seeing them [the six Igorot chiefs] so well dressed, and even more upon hearing about the greatness of Manila. For people who have not seen anything besides their shacks, it was shocking and incredible."[49] The Augustinian provincial—a personal witness to the events and one of its masterminds—remembered the utter disbelief of somebody in the crowd who could not fathom that Manila was better than their own town.[50] These spectacular trips were "planned and calculated maneuvers" to amaze hinterland communities and gain their trust.[51]

Rituals and ceremonies were vital in the exercise of political power and the formation of alliances.[52] They diffused a tense situation that could easily have turned into war. Like in the previous examples, seemingly artificial trappings like clothes, canes, and embraces manifested social prestige and ties. In the absence of a complex bureaucratic machinery, personal pleas carried their weight in negotiations. The six Igorot chiefs' journey to Manila broke the impasse between Christians and animists. It resumed the commerce between the uplands and the lowlands; upland animists were back in colonial towns like Agoo to visit, trade, and convert. While the original motive behind the trip to Manila was to personally present an urgent plea to the governor-general, the spectacle of it all was just as important. Word spread quickly in the hinterland about the kindness and generosity of the Spaniards to the six Igorot chiefs.

Several elements of the Igorots' trip stand out compared with the previous cases. First, the governor-general kissed the chiefs' hand rather than the other way around. In an ironic twist, the direction of the kiss indicates that the Igorots were of higher status than the governor-general. It was such an unexpected move that Carrillo took a note of it in his chronicle. The gesture contradicts the assumption that Spaniards always treated visiting natives as mere "objects of curiosity" during festive ceremonies.[53] Perhaps the governor-general

understood that indigenes expressed their ties through affective gestures and thus momentarily disregarded Spanish protocol. Second, Carrillo's account describes in detail the entrance of the Igorot chiefs not only in Manila but also in Agoo. It decenters the overly Manila-centric bias of most of the accounts so far. Both entries were spectacular, but the one in Agoo especially so. In the visit to Manila, despite the attention and kisses lavished on the Igorot chiefs, the governor-general still occupied the pride of place as the paramount ruler of the city. In the entry to Agoo, the Igorot chiefs held the most prominent position. The details of their entry mirrored the standard practice in royal and viceregal entries, which established or renewed the intimate link between the monarchy and the city.[54] However, the returning Igorots took the place of the king or viceroy in the procession.

The chiefs went to Manila under a cloud of conflict as the provincial governor banned mountaineers from trading in Pangasinan and threatened them with a military campaign. It was only fitting that their grand entrance evoked royal entries where the king and the city renegotiated their relationship. Per Spanish practice, the officials of Agoo welcomed the Igorot chiefs on the outskirts of town and escorted them into town with as much pomp and circumstance. It indicated that town officials respected the governor-general's final decision that overturned the provincial governor's earlier actions. Besides respecting their ties with the royal government, Agoo officials renewed their strained relationship with the Igorots by welcoming the returning chiefs. As city officials in Spain and the Americas were wont to do when entertaining a visiting king or viceroy, officials in Agoo supplied horses to the Igorot chiefs so that their guests could enter town as if they were royalty.[55] In Spanish tradition, horses have symbolized royalty and chivalry since medieval times.[56] In Pangasinan, they received the same reverence, as an old provincial ordinance decreed that only esteemed vicars could ride them.[57] The Igorots' spectacular entrance was as good an indication as any that past differences had now been put aside.

Besides the restoration of peaceful relations between Pangasinan and Igorot country, the visit to Manila established a thin, tenuous link between the capital and the hinterland. Several Indigenous communities in Southeast Asia projected their history on the landscape.[58] Swidden agriculturists had to relocate from one area to another every few years. As they moved across the landscape, they remembered their old swidden plots and houseposts. They had such an intimate familiarity with their surroundings that they still recognized their old forest clearing even when it was already overrun by secondary forest growth.[59] Traveling jogged their memory as the landscape constituted

their history. Even though hinterland visitors never had as intimate a knowledge of Manila or Agoo as their own forests, their visits nonetheless made
lowland colonial towns part of their landscape and memory. To travel was to
be brave and acquire knowledge of new people and places.[60] Fantastic stories
about Manila spread throughout the borderland. Even those who did not
make the trip vicariously lived the experience as they witnessed their chiefs
arrive in royal regalia and as their chiefs regaled them with stories from an
amazing faraway land. Besides the journey and the tales, kinship bonds united
Igorot chiefs and Spanish Manileños in baptismal godparenthood. In Southeast Asia, traveling to sacred sites reinforced the inner spiritual power of
pilgrims.[61] Since Manila was the ritual center of Spanish power in the
archipelago, hinterland travelers to the capital might have interpreted their
trip as a pilgrimage to a sacred site. Arriving in Agoo on horseback dressed in
Spanish clothes with their canes of office, perhaps the six Igorot chiefs physically exuded the spiritual transformation they had undergone during their
journey for everyone to see. Traveling widened people's landscape, strengthened their spiritual prowess, and created a common history that conquered
vast distances.

The magnificent visits to Manila gained a certain renown among missionaries and animists. They were simultaneously special yet relatively commonplace. On one hand, trips to Manila were a unique enough experience for
hinterland travelers and communities to be astounded by it. On the other
hand, Spaniards and indigenes often resorted to it to resolve outstanding issues and clear any doubts between the different parties. Throughout the
years, visits to Manila eventually became part of a standard operational procedure. It was probably no coincidence that in 1702 the Italons and Ituys accompanied by Augustinians and Dominicans, respectively, went to Manila
within a few weeks of each other. Living and working in close vicinity to one
another, they must have been aware of what their neighbors were doing. The
Italon chiefs must have known that their Ituy neighbors had the privilege of
going to Manila before getting baptized and thus made the same request to
their own missionaries. In 1755, after finishing his pastoral visit, the Augustinian provincial Carrillo returned to Manila with four Tinguian men from the
hinterland hill town of Parras because they had expressed their desire to be
baptized in Manila.[62] From a purely pragmatic and doctrinal perspective, a
baptism in Parras was the same as one in Manila. However, from an experien-
tial and social point of view, it was simply not the same. Even the provincial
recognized that the four Tinguian men's baptism should have the same so-
lemnity as that of the six Igorot chiefs. The two baptisms occurred within

months of each other. With the popular precedent of the Igorot chiefs' journey to Manila, both Augustinian missionaries and hinterland converts understood the value of visiting Manila and putting on a show in building affective ties. Even if only a select few made the trip to Manila, they nevertheless represented the rest of their community and savored it for everyone.[63]

The popularity of these visits to Manila transcended vast distances and made them almost de rigueur. In 1755, the Franciscan missionary José de San Pascual wrote to his father provincial, "We just had news about the new Augustinian missions. Some Igorots were baptized in Manila. The governor [-general] attended and even expressed it would be delightful if some from our missions could come. Even before this news, we had already talked about this point and how it would edify the republic."[64] In contrast to the close proximity between Italons and Ituys or Igorots and Tinguians, the Franciscans operated on the opposite side of the island from the Augustinians, and yet they had the latest news from afar. They knew about the six Igorot chiefs who got baptized in Manila, whose hands were kissed by the governor-general, and who made a grand entrance in Agoo on horseback. They had to keep up with the standard set by the precedent; otherwise, their converts would be disappointed.

In 1757, Ilongots from Baler went to Manila and had a similar experience to the Italons and Igorots who had made the same visit in the past half-century. Franciscan missionaries in the mountains of Baler had a difficult time convincing the Ilongots to convert because the latter believed that Spaniards only wanted to kill and destroy them.[65] To disabuse them of this belief, the Franciscans employed the time-honored method of sending them to Manila to see for themselves the good intentions of the Spaniards. Eleven Ilongots made the journey to Manila and met the governor-general, Pedro Manuel de Arandia, in the royal palace.[66] Besides the usual demonstrations of affection, the governor-general gave the loincloth-garbed Ilongots pants and shirts, which delighted them to no end. About two weeks later, the Ilongots were baptized in one of the suburbs of the city.[67] Their godfathers were the governor-general, various city officials, and other Spanish residents. Before the Ilongots finally went home, their godfathers gave them knives and adzes useful for mountain work, and pans and other tools much appreciated in their remote settlements.[68] The meeting with the governor-general, the Spanish clothes, the lavish attention from distinguished Spanish residents, and the well-thought-out parting gifts—part of a routine by now—all contributed to swaying the Ilongots' mind and affection toward conversion.

The visits to Manila were usually long, drawn-out processes. Prior to the journey, both missionaries and animists had to come to an agreement in the

first place. The journey itself to Manila took several days. Even though the main objective of the trip to Manila was to get baptized, the visitors usually stayed in the city for several weeks. The homecoming was curated as much as the reception in Manila. However, the relative frequency of the visits and the smooth narration of the events in the sources should not eclipse the fact that considerable obstacles and distances had to be overcome. Although the religious orders, hinterland inhabitants, and the Spanish monarchy actively participated in carrying out the visits, they all put in a massive amount of time and effort to get past their differences. Bad prior experience with Spaniards and the spread of this infamy created unfavorable working conditions for missionaries. In one case, San Pascual claimed that Ilongots were so afraid of leaving their mountains that it would be impossible to bring them to Manila to be baptized without the missionaries themselves accompanying them.[69] Ironically, the best way to break the impasse was to increase the depth of contact by taking a giant leap of faith and visiting Manila. As a well-choreographed routine, the visit to Manila usually turned out well, as it narrowed down the existing differences between the parties.

What made the dramatic trips to Manila more manageable and imaginable in the long run was the precedent of other trips. When the Italons went to Manila, the Ituys had already gone before them. In a similar fashion, the Tinguians and Ilongots had the comforting example of the six Igorot chiefs to help dispel any of their indisposition. In the same way that stories of tribute and labor exactions created a bad reputation for Spaniards, the fantastic stories of those baptized in Manila spread like wildfire in the borderland and redeemed Spanish reputation. Through word of mouth and occasional letters, the various trips to Manila were interrelated with and reinforced one another.

However, more than the specific precedent of successful trips to Manila, travels and visits formed part of the general social fabric. A wide variety of visits made the grandiose trips to Manila possible. Missionaries and even provincials visiting the hinterland nudged the channels of communication and encouraged potential converts to make the journey to the capital. Upland animists regularly went to lowland colonial towns and sometimes even danced for visiting Spanish officials. These smaller, less glamorous excursions to remote interior towns generated reciprocal visits and initiated the first steps to conversion. The trips to Manila happened in a web of movements, blockages, jolts, and hesitations. They acquired a pattern and rhythm of their own through the years. Other types of travels and visits were similar in nature and provided the backdrop for borderland mobilities in general. On

the Spanish side, from the late seventeenth century the Spanish monarchy revived the inspection tour of provinces, and the religious orders encouraged parish priests to preach to animists in their vicinity. On the Indigenous side, commerce and kinship constituted the stream of travels and visits. While Indigenous travels and even visits to Manila existed in previous centuries (see the introduction), the more concerted effort on the part of Spaniards to explore the hinterland in the eighteenth century encountered fertile ground in Indigenous notions of reciprocal visits.

Visiting the Land

States are inherently mobile.[70] Rather than fixed static institutions, they are more accurately portrayed as dispersed networks of individual experiences and movements. While still true today, the mobility of states was much more evident in the early modern world. In place of a complex bureaucratic structure, rulers were the embodiment of the state.[71] The political and ritual center moved as the ruler traveled. Apart from performing administrative and inspectorial functions, royal tours and progresses consolidated the monarch's political and symbolic power over his realm. If the ruler himself was the state and his domain reached a certain size, his governance inevitably had to be peripatetic. A multitude of rulers in history employed tours and circuits as a form of statecraft from Elizabeth Tudor of England and Kangxi of China to Hayam Wuruk of Java and Alaungsithu of Pagan.[72] The ruler's very presence was necessary to oversee the current state of faraway provinces and renew political ties through the proper rituals.

The Spanish monarchy was also a mobile state. In the early sixteenth century, monarchs were constantly on the move as royal courts transferred from one city to another.[73] They—and not any fixed capital city—embodied the political and symbolic center of the realm.[74] Their very movement signified possession and demonstrated statecraft. The Catholic monarchs Ferdinand and Isabella untiringly visited their entire domain, and Charles V even claimed that "an emperor needed no other residence than his saddle."[75] The domain of the Spanish monarchy expanded by leaps and bounds in the sixteenth century as it crossed the Atlantic, traversed the Americas, and ventured across the Pacific. With a realm that spanned the globe, it became impossible for Spanish monarchs to reconnoiter their entire possession in person. In standard historiography, a shift occurred in the sixteenth century between the peripatetic Charles V and the sedentary Philip II. While the royal territory was as vast as ever, by the end of the century the monarch be-

came more sedentary than before, especially with the establishment of the capital at Madrid. The outward expansion of boundaries coincided with a mooring of the royal center. Insisting on reading every report that arrived on his desk from his vast realm, Philip II could dismissively say that "traveling about one's kingdom is neither useful nor decent."[76] Palaces like El Escorial (Madrid), court ceremonies, and bureaucratic paperwork took on a more central role in statecraft.[77] The visits of the Italons, Igorots, and Ilongots to Manila a couple of centuries later were potentially a later manifestation of this shift. Philippine subjects and vassals traveled to the royal center in Manila, instead of the other way around. As the representative of the Spanish monarch in the archipelago, governors-general were not obligated to do a tour of the archipelago. In Manila, borderland chiefs were the ones who participated in the by-then well-established court rituals.

However, the supposed shift from traveling to moored monarchs is too simplistic. Despite his protestations on the indecency of traveling, Philip II still carried out a surprising number of royal tours in his life.[78] Although Bourbon monarchs like Philip V and Ferdinand IV never set foot on the borderlands of Luzon, the Spanish monarchy was nevertheless mobile but in a different way. Palaces, paperwork, and dispatches never completely replaced the practice of royal visits and tours; the latter simply took on new forms. The Spanish monarch and his vassals utilized a wide variety of methods to overcome the physical absence of the king in the Indies. One method was the use of the king's simulacra, which stood in the place of the king's body.[79] A popular simulacrum was the king's portrait, which subjects treated with the same reverence as if it were the actual king.[80] The portrait took part in royal entries to cities and presided over palace ceremonies. Even though the monarchy was far away, colonial cities celebrated important events in the life of the royal family: the birth of a royal heir, the ascension to the throne of a new king, royal birthdays and weddings, and the passing away of a king.[81] While the king's portrait and the festivities in his honor had the ability to bind him to his vassals across the world, they still primarily operated on a symbolic level. Even with his eyes peering from the canvas and ceremonies making him seem to be everywhere all the time, the king could still not physically intervene in the daily affairs of his distant realms.[82] For a more direct involvement, he needed another way to make his presence felt.

Another method the monarchy used to overcome the problem of distance was the use of representatives, particularly viceroys and royal judges. High-ranking colonial officials combined the dual role of local administrators and royal embodiments. In a way, the term "representative" does not capture the

spirit of the times back then because it downplays the quasi-mystical status that they held. In the case of the viceroy, for example, he was the king's living image.[83] Much better than a portrait, he was a breathing, walking image of the king. The viceroy exercised the same royal power and authority but in a limited jurisdiction.

However, Spaniards were not the only ones who viewed high colonial officials as incarnations of the king; various Indigenous groups shared a similar perception. The Ituy visitors in Manila thought they hugged the king himself in the governor-general. In various occasions, both missionaries and indigenes referred to the governor-general as the king or *hari* of Manila,[84] so meeting with him was an honor. More than the Spanish king's living image or simulacrum,[85] the governor-general was the de facto king of Spaniards for all intents and purposes in the archipelago. This elevation of colonial officials into royalty was a common phenomenon in the region. As the highest-ranking colonial officials, the Dutch governors-general of Batavia and Taiwan often had to assume the role of Dutch "king" from Java to Japan precisely because the Dutch Republic did not have kings.[86] Rather than a mere imposition or diffusion of a European notion of royal simulacra, colonial officials taking on the role of kings also stemmed from local expectations. They were royalty in their own right who held great power and esteem among the local population. For example, Governor-General Zabálburu effectively usurped the royal title and became the Spanish king to his Ituy visitors.

Paradoxically, the greater the distance between the viceroy and the king, the more the viceroy embodied the king's power and the more necessary and lavish the ceremonies and rituals were supposed to be.[87] Viceregal entries—and even those of governors-general—mimicked royal entries in their ostentation and grandeur.[88] Although the entries of governors-general to Manila were a "pale reflection" of royal entrances to Seville and viceregal ones to Lima due to a severely limited budget, that did not stop local officials from demanding for more royal funding and pooling their own personal resources because the entry "manifests and shows the sovereignty of the monarch whom he [the governor-general] represents, and it is more necessary in the Philippine Islands where so many nations gather together, and they make the ostentation more respectable."[89] Despite its meager means, Spanish Manila nonetheless did its best to make the governor-general's entrance as spectacular as possible. As we have seen earlier in the chapter, it offered similar grand receptions to visiting hinterland chiefs who did show a fondness for festivities and ostentation. Manileño celebrations might have paled in comparison with those of other Spanish cities, but they were enough to exalt the status of the visitors.

In traditional historiography, cosmological and political innovations in the conception of space seemed to have mirrored each other in the early modern period.[90] In Europe, the sun represented the king. With the Copernican revolution, the sun no longer revolved around the earth, but rather remained fixed at the center. With the founding of capital cities and the growing popularity of urban court ceremonies, monarchs no longer had a pressing need to tour their realms because they could simply stay in the capital and receive their guests there. The heliocentric revolution in cosmography supposedly went hand in hand with the political revolution toward sedentarism and absolutism. The almost mystical veneration of royal images and life events in the Indies seems to confirm such an interpretation. The king might have been physically absent, but his presence was nevertheless everywhere through various simulacra. However, the portrayal of early modern royal culture as spatially centralized and politically absolutist does not take into account the complex operations of monarchies.[91] Although portraits, viceroys, and governors-general replicated royal rituals that were very urban and ceremonial, colonial officials dispersed throughout the Indies not only relocated to their assigned post but also conducted inspection tours of their jurisdiction.

Viceroys and governors-general often did not visit the countryside and hinterland, but various subordinate officials and specially designated visitors were sent out to inspect the different parts of the monarchy's vast territories.[92] Besides symbolically reaffirming the ties between the monarch and his subjects, these visits were crucial in shaping royal policies in the Indies.[93] José de Gálvez, one of the chief architects in implementing Bourbon reforms in the Indies under Charles III, spent years as an inspector general touring New Spain before embarking on his illustrious career in the Council of the Indies.[94] Whether performing an extraordinary commission or a routine visit,[95] colonial officials on inspection tours had an incredible opportunity to intervene in and shape the lives of royal subjects—and sometimes even those of unsubjugated inhabitants of remote borderlands. Although high-ranking royal officials were more or less sedentary in capital cities, the Spanish monarchy still operated on the principle of mobility and visits that belie exaggerated claims of absolutism and urbanism. The sun-king might have remained at the center, but he was dependent on a vast army of mobile officials who scoured his realm, exhibited a fair degree of independence, and occasionally arrogated his position and status.

Spanish legislation enshrined the practice of *visitas a la tierra*, or periodic inspection tours of the realm, which was a mechanism of maintaining royal control over officials in distant territories. It forced royal officials to leave the colonial capital, visit the different provinces, and investigate the performance of local officials. For the Philippines, the ordinances of 1596 contained a provision on annual inspection tours of the different towns and provinces of the archipelago.[96] Inspectors had the task of evaluating the state of administration in the provinces and addressing whatever shortcomings and abuses they noticed. For the Spanish Indies, a whole section of laws in the *Recopilación de leyes de los reynos de las Indias* detailed how colonial judges were supposed to carry out the inspection tour of their jurisdiction.[97] Usually the most senior judge of a royal court in the Indies had the task of visiting his particular dominion every three years. Even though Philip II expressed disdain toward the act of visiting his kingdom, legislation compensated for "immobile" monarchs by mandating royal officials to do the ocular inspections instead.

Inspection tours in the Philippines had a patchy history. From 1580 to 1603, the royal court in Manila planned eight tours, but only three were definitively carried out.[98] After the aborted visit of 1596, the next tour took place almost a century later in 1691. It was a far cry from the annual or even triennial visits prescribed by law. In response to a complaint from the viceroy of Peru that officials had been remiss in visiting their jurisdiction, a royal decree in 1690 partly resurrected the moribund practice.[99] In the next couple of years, inspection tours took place in Charcas, Quito, and the Philippines.[100] However, the royal court in Manila already launched its very first visit in years in 1691 even before receiving notice of the royal decree a year later.[101] The Spanish judge Alonso de Abella Fuertes visited the provinces of Cagayan, Ilocos, Pangasinan, and Pampanga from 1691 to 1692; Juan de Sierra Osorio the provinces of Oton, Panay, Cebu, Negros, and Leyte from 1692 to 1695; and Juan de Ozaeta y Oro the provinces of Tondo, Bulacan, Laguna de Bay, Balayan, and Cavite from 1695 to 1697.[102] Not only did these three visits cover a significant portion of the archipelago's territory; they also inaugurated a revival of the inspection tour, with six more being conducted in the first half of the next century. The 1690s thus marked a massive shift from a total lack of visits to a relative abundance for a couple of decades.

On paper and in practice, inspection tours dealt primarily with territories under colonial control. Hence, it is not surprising that their two main concerns were tribute collection and the administration of justice. Visiting judges updated the number of subjects who qualified for tribute payment and usually boasted the resulting revenue increase for the royal treasury.[103] They also upheld the principle of justice, which meant examining the violations and abuses committed by local officials, especially in provinces far from Manila, and prosecuting the perpetrators.[104] The traveling judges served as a form of check and balance to local powerholders. They also passed ordinances that addressed the illegal activities they encountered.[105] It was probably no coincidence that Governor-General Fausto Cruzat y Góngora promulgated a revised set of general ordinances in 1696 right after the first couple of inspection tours in almost a century had been concluded.[106] While the judicial punishments and fines that inspectors meted out might have had an immediate short-term effect, the ordinances had a more long-lasting influence in provincial administration. Whenever there were disputes, a party could always cite the ordinances of a visiting judge from decades ago to bolster their case.[107] With the benefit of hindsight, a Dominican historian could wax lyrical on how the ordinances of good government of a visiting judge were "the true ancient code" of a particular province.[108] Since the Spanish monarchy used visits as a means to maintain control over negligent and abusive officials in distant provinces, inspection tours worked primarily within the royal domain, not outside it.[109] However, provincial visits still managed to affect unsubjugated territories, such as the interior of the island of Luzon.

Before embarking on his visit of the four northern provinces of Luzon in 1691, Alonso de Abella Fuertes received a last-minute assignment from the governor-general of the Philippines.[110] Besides monitoring the colonial administration of the provinces, he also had to investigate the feasibility of conquering the borderland between the provinces of Cagayan and Pampanga. The Dominican order had just proposed to the governor-general the possibility of converting the pagans and apostates there. It was Abella's job as the visiting judge to provide an expert opinion on the matter. After informing himself of the situation while in Cagayan, he declared the borderland was flat, fertile, and well populated and proposed a military approach as the best option.[111] The germ of the sustained missionary presence in the borderland between Cagayan and Pampanga in the next century can be traced to the visits and tentative approaches of the 1690s. Even though the Spanish monarchy would eventually adopt a more peaceful approach, Abella's visit consolidated royal support for the conquest of the borderland. The visiting judge's opinions affected even independent communities technically outside his jurisdiction.

The link between inspection tours and pacification campaigns was not limited to Abella. During his visit of the province of Pangasinan in 1704, José de Torralba tackled the issue of Igorot raids on lowland towns.[112] Like most visiting judges, Torralba preoccupied himself with updating the tribute count and verifying the alleged abuses of Dominican friars against natives. Like Abella, he also addressed the issue of hostilities coming from unsubjugated communities farther inland. Pagan Igorots from the surrounding mountains killed Christians in lowland colonial towns, burned their churches, and committed thefts and other insults.[113] In response to the problem, Torralba named several corporals to act as sentries in defense of lowland towns. He promised accosted colonial subjects that the governor-general would provide the necessary additional assistance. At the same time, he also entertained the idea of nipping the problem in the bud by converting the Igorots to Christianity and relocating them to lowland towns.[114]

Besides defending colonial subjects, visiting judges got involved in affairs beyond the strict jurisdiction of colonial towns because they had the duty to uphold a standard of order. Apostates who fled to mountain settlements outside Spanish control were still subjects—albeit renegade ones—in the eyes of the Spanish monarchy, and they had to be brought back to the fold. Fugitives escaping from Spanish justice had to be held accountable for their crimes. The royal inspector was, after all, a judge. During his tour of the Visayan province of Oton in the early 1690s, Juan de Sierra Osorio had military troops burn down the houses and fields of indios who lived in the uplands.[115] He succeeded in bringing back some apostates to resettle in colonial towns, and it was all part of his duties. While visiting judges concerned themselves mostly with colonial tribute and justice, their responsibilities often entailed dealing with communities outside colonial rule.

Besides the judges of the royal court in Manila, ecclesiastical officials such as the archbishop of Manila and the provincials of the religious orders also ventured outside the capital to conduct official visits of the provinces but with a focus on the administrative running of parishes.[116] In fact, royal inspection tours had their juridical roots in pastoral visitations conducted by bishops in their diocese.[117] Like their secular counterparts who intervened in issues involving unsubjugated communities, ecclesiastical visitors also expanded their scope beyond the narrow confines of parishioners and made tentative approaches to nearby animists. In some cases, unsubjugated hinterland towns even knew when visiting provincials would arrive and used the encounter to further their own interests.[118]

Although episcopal visitations were rare in the Philippines due to jurisdictional conflicts with the well-entrenched religious orders, the archbishop of Manila Diego Camacho y Ávila managed to carry out one from 1698 to 1699 in southern and central Luzon.[119] Despite the severe limitations on the number of parishes he could visit, the archbishop proudly proclaimed that he had performed the sacrament of confirmation on 80,000 Christians. Besides administering to the pastoral needs of his indio parishioners, the archbishop also took advantage of the journey to convert animists who lived in adjacent mountains. If missionary friars were stepping on the jurisdiction of secular priests by holding on to parishes, the archbishop returned the favor by personally getting involved in conversions. Toward the end of 1698, when Camacho visited the southern provinces of Taal and Balayan, he instructed a few Christian indios to go up the mountains to persuade the animists living there to relocate to lowland Christian towns.[120] In the town of Antipolo, he climbed the mountains of Paynaan and San Isidro, where he stayed for eighteen days, which was much longer than originally planned, because Aetas had come down to Paynaan and he could not resist the opportunity to convince them to stay among Christians permanently. He personally gave them rings, necklaces, earrings, clothes, tobacco, and other trinkets in order to attract them.

The next year in 1699, Camacho went north of Manila to the provinces of Bulacan and Pampanga.[121] He reached the area surrounding Mount Arayat, which was near the northern limits of Pampanga. It was a particularly dangerous territory because unsubjugated communities there had a habit of killing passersby. As he tried to visit the parishes of his archdiocese and administer the sacrament of confirmation, Camacho gathered information about the Aeta raiders who menaced the province and wreaked havoc on colonial subjects. He informed the Spanish government that the suspension of military maneuvers and slave raids against hostile communities only emboldened them in their attacks. Besides reporting on the actual situation on the ground, the archbishop even took part in a peace pact with upland Aetas in order to remedy the situation. In the same way visiting judges influenced and intervened in the conduct of unsubjugated communities, visiting prelates had plenty of room to maneuver and coordinated interactions with independent animists.

Timely visits fed Spanish interest in the borderlands and their independent inhabitants. In his episcopal visitation, Archbishop Camacho went out of his way to deal with upland animists and apostates because a royal decree from a few years earlier had ordered the conversion of the countless indios who still lived in the mountains of the archipelago.[122] Even Abella's earlier visit to Cagayan, which endorsed the conquest of a borderland, did nothing more than enact a royal decree and carry out the special commission triggered by an earlier pastoral visit to Cagayan. With the provincials of the religious orders having effectively usurped the power of episcopal visitations from secular bishops, the Dominican provincial Cristóbal Pedroche visited Cagayan in 1690. After his visit, he claimed that four provinces between Pampanga and Cagayan—namely, Ituy, Paniqui, Sifun, and Yoga—were full of pagans and apostates and that they could be conquered cheaply through a variety of methods (figure 1.1). The provincial's report of his visit prompted official interest in the borderland and resulted in Abella being explicitly instructed to vouch for the veracity of the various reports coming from the field.[123] Three visits—Pedroche's in Cagayan in 1690, Abella's in Cagayan in 1691, and Camacho's in Pampanga in 1699—predated the missionary efforts of the next century. Official tours were highly influential in shaping royal policies toward borderlands. Judges, bishops, and friars were the gears and cogs of the Spanish monarchy as they set out and visited the provinces. Located at the interstices of these movements were ever more intricate, smaller-scale visits. This complex web of travels and visits laid the groundwork for the more intimate interactions in the eighteenth century.

Networks and Access

At the base of the dramatic visits to Manila and official inspection tours were more mundane but equally crucial travels and visits that occurred at the local level. At the forefront were the Spanish friars scattered across the island, who left the majority of the written documentation. Their main goal was to convert the animists in the island's interior. While relocation to permanent settlements and doctrinal issues were vital themes in missionary activities, just as important were the tentative approaches and the sounding out between missionaries and animists.[124] The messages and visits exchanged between them formed the basis of the social relations that could potentially lead to conversion. The religious orders honed a strategy of small, calculated movements as they tried to inch closer to their animist neighbors. Visits straddled the tension between waiting for permission to be granted and going ahead without any prompting.

In the late seventeenth century, provincials of the Franciscan order in the Philippines gave an overview of how they carried out missionary work. In 1680, Fernando de la Concepción said that they had been complying with a government decree that mandated that in case of news of the presence of Aetas, Zambals, and other pagans in the vicinity of parishes, their religious order should have four or five ministers always at hand dedicated to the work of conversion.[125] In situations where there were not enough friars, ministers performed the double role of parish priest and missionary. The nearest parish priest was responsible for the conversion of surrounding animists. In 1690, Juan Bautista Martínez confirmed the effectiveness of this strategy of approaching nearby animists.[126] To attract the animists dispersed throughout

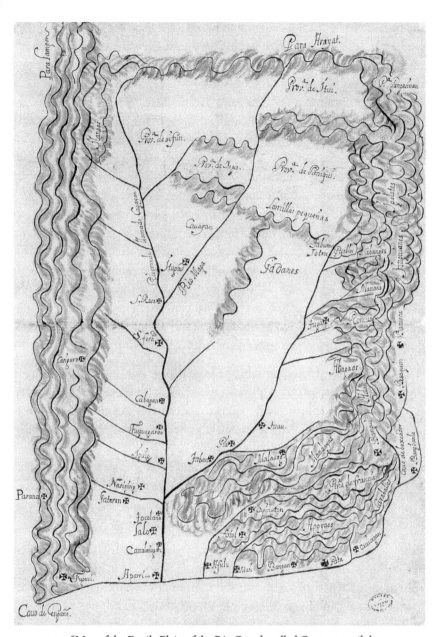

FIGURE 1.1 "Map of the Fertile Plain of the Río Grande called Cagayan until the Provinces of Sifun, Yoga, Paniqui, Ituy, etc.," 1690. The map's orientation has the north at the bottom and the south at the top. With the Pacific Ocean to the left and Cagayan at the bottom, the map lists four interior provinces at the top that are yet to be conquered in the late seventeenth century, namely, Sifun, Yoga, Paniqui, and Ituy. Ministerio de Cultura y Deporte, Archivo General de Indias, MP-FILIPINAS, 140.

the mountains, a parish priest would set up an upland outstation or *visitilla* where catechumens could congregate. These outstations also served as jumping-off points to facilitate missionary movement in the mountains. While visiting the mountains of Lupi and the outstations there, Martínez received news of the presence of many apostates and pagans close by. He sent a messenger bearing gifts of necklaces, medals, and crosses with the proposal of relocating them in a designated spot where the nearest parish priest could easily visit and preach to them. A network of outstations stemming from parishes facilitated mobility in the hinterland. It allowed parish priests to move around more easily and administer to upland catechumens, even enabling the provincial himself to reach remote mountain outstations during his pastoral visits. Converts could also move in stages in the opposite direction from upland outstations to lowland parishes if they chose to do so.

Besides the network of parishes and outstations, mobility in the hinterland relied on people and relationships. Provincials and priests used visits, gifts, and intermediaries to court potential converts. The Franciscan provincial Martínez emphasized the coordination and organization required in conducting successful forays into the interior:

> It is thus essential that ministers do not go haphazardly because that will only mean to depart and return without being able to enter. If they do enter, they will not be able to stay for many days due to the mentioned inconveniences and harshness of the terrain. It is of necessity that they first establish a connection with somebody who is already converted . . . and from there inquire about the entries and exits, and the settlements of the pagans. . . . In this way, the prelate can visit and assist them [the pagans]. . . . However, if parishes are on one side and missions on the other, they will have a difficult time getting the necessary and timely help and assistance.[127]

Parish priests and missionaries had to work hand in hand, if they were not already the same person. Insider information was important, and indio parishioners who had ties with upland communities were the critical informants and intermediaries to mobility in the borderland. Everything was well coordinated before a priest even thought of taking the first step toward the mountains. Missionaries had to rely on parish priests and parishioners because the latter already had existing ties in the area that stretched up the mountain, no matter how tenuous they were. The newly arrived missionary was in most cases a total stranger.

From a certain perspective, the way the Franciscans established lowland-upland ties is highly reminiscent of the settlement pattern prevalent in island

Southeast Asia that connected coastal polities with interior mountain settlements.[128] In this networked system, coastal towns maintained connections and exchanges with upland settlements but only exerted at most a weak authority over them. Departing from lowland parishes, missionaries likewise established loose but functioning connections with upland animists through intermediaries and gift exchange. The Franciscan missionary method did not reinvent the wheel; it simply repurposed existing Indigenous strategies for its own end. Whether consciously or not, Spaniards had the habit of adapting their plans to local conditions and landscapes from Mexican municipalities resembling Nahua *altepetl* (ethnic states) to Peruvian *repartimientos* (distribution of Indian communities to Spaniards) patterned after Incan political organization.[129] The arrangement of colonial polities followed the contours of the terrain and built on existing Indigenous settlement patterns.

When the Augustinians founded the mission in the mountains of Pantabangan and Carranglan in 1702, they followed the same procedure as the other religious orders. They started out from parishes on the plains before progressing to their hill missions. Compared with previous centuries, the eighteenth century marked a shift in missionary activities in the area. The different religious orders were finally able to have a relatively sustained presence in the borderland between Pampanga and Cagayan. Such a foundation can be partly attributed to the much-avowed method of parishes and missions working together. Although missionaries take the lion's share of the acclaim in historical accounts, the Augustinian parish priest of nearby Santor played a key role in setting up the mission.[130] The lowland town of Santor hosted various visitors and explorers of the borderland that facilitated religious conversion.

Previously a *visita* or outlying barrio of the town of Gapan, Santor became a town in its own right in 1689.[131] As a separate town, it now had its own set of *visitas* in Bongabon, Pantabangan, and Carranglan. A couple of advantages of being declared an official town were the assignment of a dedicated parish priest and the election of local officials. More than a simple administrative reclassification, the recognition of Santor as a town marked a deeper colonial presence in upper Pampanga. As a sort of religious way station in a remote borderland, Santor made subsequent missionary endeavors in the mountains of Pantabangan and Carranglan much easier by smoothening travel and communication between the plains and the mountains.

An Augustinian missionary in upper Pampanga from 1705 to 1746, Alejandro Cacho recognized how indio parishioners were the key intermediaries of missionaries trying to gain access to upland animists.[132] When the different religious orders advocated for the cooperation between parishes and missions, they had more than a physical network of towns in mind. They were thinking of a network of people who could facilitate access and contact. While going about their regular tasks, both parish priest and parishioners sent out feelers to the surrounding animists whether they were willing to convert to Christianity. While performing his pastoral duties of visiting Pantabangan and Carranglan, the parish priest of Santor, Tomás de Villanueva, had the perfect opportunity to test the receptivity of the animist communities scattered across the nearby mountains: "Whenever one or another priest visited these towns [of Pantabangan and Carranglan] which had contact with the said pagans, he sounded them out himself or with the aid of one or another Kapampangan he had brought there to see if they could be attracted and converted through messages, gifts, or caresses."[133] If bishops and provincials performed long-range episcopal visitations, parish priests conducted their own pastoral visits at a smaller scale. With townspeople dispersed in far-flung barrios, parish priests like Villanueva had to regularly visit their parishioners out in the hinterland, and the priests took advantage of these occasions to do some missionary work. The principle of blurring the division between pastoral and missionary functions exhibited itself in the very act of the visit. Although the identity of the Kapampangan companion of the priests was not specified, he was almost certainly a Christian parishioner. Parish priests and parishioners together were the ones making the missionary advances in the hinterland.

When Antolín Alzaga, the first officially designated missionary of Pantabangan, arrived in 1702, he had a list of instructions from the parish priest of Santor, who had already done the initial explorations.[134] The missionary's arrival signaled the transformation of Pantabangan and Carranglan into a proper mission. With the parish priest taking a back seat, indio intermediaries took an even more prominent role in guiding the missionary in his new assignment. The instructions to Alzaga explicitly told him to go to Pantabangan in the company of two local chiefs who were the closest friends of the Italons.[135] Once there, he should look for Nicolas de los Santos, a Christian indio from the town of Guagua who would serve as his guide and interpreter.[136] De los Santos had been living in Pantabangan for several years already. Although not explicitly stated, he must have been one of the Kapampangan companions of the parish priest of Santor in previous approaches to upland animists. Having a dedicated missionary stationed in Pantabangan made visits to the surrounding communities much easier. Nevertheless, the basic dynamics of the visits remained largely the same with parishioners working with the friars.

With mountain animists having declared prior interest in converting, Alzaga sent four intermediaries to inform them of his arrival in Pantabangan.[137] Two of these messengers were his main guides, Nicolas de los Santos and Marcos Malalbon.[138] Various chiefs came to visit Alzaga, who received them with as much kindness and affection as possible. Without many gifts to give, Alzaga compensated for the material shortcoming with his apparent natural affability. They all decided to meet again on a later date in Lublub at the foot of the mountains. At the designated date, more than forty Italon families in Lublub welcomed the missionary with a feast, built a church, and planted a cross in a public spot. The eventual establishment of a mission town in Lublub rested on a series of incidental visits that spanned several years: animist communities giving indications to nearby parishes of their willingness to convert, the parish priest of Santor and his Kapampangan companions going to the hinterland barrios, Italon chiefs visiting Alzaga in Pantabangan, and Alzaga in turn visiting them in Lublub. This network of contacts was bound together by exchanges and visits. The foundation of towns and *visitas* in the uplands aided this reciprocal interaction by bringing people into closer proximity.

As Augustinian and Dominican missionaries entered the mountainous borderland, Italons and Ituys made the journey in the opposite direction as they visited Manila. Hinterland intermediaries continued playing a role in these longer-distance travels. Fray Villanueva, the parish priest of Santor, accompanied the Italon chiefs of Lublub to Manila.[139] Malalbon, a chief in the mission town of Carranglan, escorted the Ituys being courted by the Dominicans to Manila.[140] Previous ties smoothened the trip to Manila. While Spanish friars and Kapampangan parishioners penetrated the mountainous interior, hinterland inhabitants like Malalbon traveled just as widely. The parallels in the mediating role of Villanueva and Malalbon are striking. Both prepared the ground for the arrival and movement of missionaries in the borderland. Both participated in the feasting of potential converts in Manila. Intermediaries were not mere accessories and perfunctory conduits for other people's travels. They themselves were veteran participants in borderland mobility and more than likely enjoyed being so. Friars assigned in distant provinces often relished the opportunity to visit Manila once in a while.[141] More than a mere escort, Malalbon was a vital piece in Augustinian and Dominican missionary activities and most likely got feted himself in Manila together with his animist companions. Being a local official in Carranglan and holding the military rank of *maestre de campo* (colonel), he must have been one of the guests gifted with cords and titles, as it was customary during these visits for the governor-general to officially recognize visitors' status and rank.[142] Friars and indios moved in a network that stretched from Manila and Guagua to Santor and Lublub.

Everything, however, was not smooth sailing in borderland mobility. Travelers encountered friction. As Spanish friars had lookouts and messengers to gauge the willingness of animist communities to convert, they patiently waited for a positive response, which sometimes took years. At least in central and northern Luzon in the early eighteenth century, it was unusual for missionaries to simply enter an upland village without any prior permission or invitation. While some communities willingly opened the door to further contacts and visits, others were just as likely to say no and close the door shut. In Cagayan, an independent animist town told a Dominican missionary that until they knew he who was, they would not let him enter.[143] Intermediaries facilitated the getting-to-know-you process. Malalbon as an intermediary embodied the dual nature of mobility and friction in borderlands. Inasmuch as he got praised for helping friars contact, visit, and settle in upland communities, he also received plenty of flak for preventing them from setting foot in certain villages. Whether it was Malalbon or the communities themselves that rejected Spanish presence, mobility and access in a world of permissions were highly fickle. They rested on a knife-edge and could easily go one way or another. The difficulty of gaining permission and access is best exemplified in the attempts of Francisco de la Maza to enter Apayan and those of Alejandro Cacho to enter Buhay.

The Dominican missionary Francisco de la Maza accused Malalbon and the other chiefs of Carranglan of preventing him from exploring the surrounding area of his mission town of Burubur and from visiting independent communities in the valley on the other side of the mountain range. Filled with evangelical zeal, he had attempted to do so three times, only to be forced to turn back by the Carranglan chiefs every single time.[144] In his first attempt, he arrived at Carranglan and went no farther. In his second attempt, he reached the peak of the mountains of Ituy. In his third and last attempt, he was not even able to leave the confines of Burubur. All three attempts were foiled because missionaries, especially new ones, were highly reliant on guides and interpreters to show them the way.

From one perspective, de la Maza did not follow standard missionary procedure. Instead of asking for permission to enter and waiting for the affirmative response, he wanted to barge ahead and make headway on the other side of the mountains despite the protests of his intermediaries. Following standard practice, the Carranglan chiefs approached the animist communities and relayed the latter's apparent refusal to be visited by Spanish missionaries.[145] Based on a seemingly loose federation, the valley towns had an agreement to let outsiders in only if there was unanimous consent from everyone. Even if just one village dissented, permission could not be granted. However, from de la Maza's perspective, the sticking point was the honesty of his Carranglan intermediaries. He felt that they had vested interests in preventing him from visiting the animist towns on the other side.[146] In his mind, when they described "the open sky and sun full of spears and arrows," it was not because they were faithfully transmitting the animist communities' hostility.[147] They were simply looking after their own welfare because they wanted to "sell at a profit to the pagans what they get from us [missionaries] for free."[148] In de la Maza's view, there was absolutely no danger at all. Borderland intermediaries were only protecting their trade interests under the guise of respecting the animists' wishes. Whether the towns on the other side of the mountains were actually hostile or the Carranglan chiefs were deliberately isolating them to maintain the trading status quo, access was not forthcoming for the Dominican friars.

De la Maza felt like a fish trapped in a net set up by precisely the people who were supposed to help him, but he was not someone to stand around and do nothing.[149] Defeat was not in his vocabulary. If he could not rely on his Carranglan intermediaries, he had to try other means and find a gap in the seemingly closed borderland network. He found a new intermediary in a twelve-year-old boy named Andres who assisted him in the mission.[150] He sent Andres to Apayan, one of the main valley towns on the other side, to ask its chief Mangalipto for permission to visit. Mangalipto's approval was important because he was the paramount chief in the area. In Apayan, Mangalipto met with Andres and declared that he needed more time to consult with his Cagayan friends before giving his final answer, so Andres should come back in a few days bearing gifts as a sign of peace. After eighteen days of waiting, Andres finally got the answer. Mangalipto and another chief had decided to let de la Maza enter but only in Marian, the very first town of the area. In addition, they asked him to keep the arrangement a secret from everybody. Of course, the Dominican missionary welcomed the good news; however, it was still not good enough for him. His main goal was to reach Apayan, and he was going there whether Mangalipto liked it or not.

Borderland mobility was not as straightforward as moving from point A to point B. Contacts and intermediaries were more important than roads and maps. Even with the secret go-ahead from Mangalipto, de la Maza could not simply go to Marian because of the overwhelming opposition to any journey from the mission chiefs. He needed somebody who could help him, and circumstances played out in such a way that he encountered an even better liaison than little Andres. On Christmas day, de la Maza baptized a chief named Ligaguen and his wife.[151] Their five children had already been baptized, and one of them was even part of the entourage that had gone to Manila. It so happened that Ligaguen was born in Marian and had many relatives there. He was the perfect companion on the secret trip. After staying with his relatives in Burubur for six days after his baptism, it was now his turn to host de la Maza in his hometown of Marian. During the trip, de la Maza divulged to Ligaguen their true destination—Apayan—and that he had permission from Mangalipto to go there. The ruse shocked his companion, and it quickly spread among the other chiefs in the borderland. De la Maza was too far into the journey, so it seemed too late for anybody to stop him from reaching his avowed destination. In one fell swoop, the steadfast friar completely disregarded the opposition from the mission chiefs, lied to Ligaguen, and broke the secret nature of his arrangement with Mangalipto.

In Canaan, a town on the way to Marian, Mangalipto intercepted de la Maza.[152] He welcomed the missionary, but he also warned him to stop telling people that he gave him permission to enter. De la Maza should admit that it was all his own idea. Mangalipto gave the priest strict orders to stay in Canaan until further notice. While waiting, de la Maza received several chiefs from the Carranglan and Burubur missions who tried to convince him that he was putting not only his own life but everybody's in danger. Apparently, the Ilongots of Apayan were armed and ready to kill him. The mission chiefs also feared for their lives because they were the ones being blamed for letting de la Maza reach the valley, but the missionary was adamant in continuing his journey. He challenged the chiefs on what they had previously boasted about: "You have always said that you only feared the Cagayanes, that the rest of the Igorots and Ilongots are your friends and have always been so, and that when they were your enemies, you just ignored them."[153] While the mission chiefs now cowered in the face of the imminent Ilongot threat, de la Maza was prepared to face martyrdom.

As a last-ditch effort, the mission chiefs faked a dispatch from Mangalipto ordering de la Maza not to come to Apayan.[154] Even then, the missionary was determined to go ahead just to confront Mangalipto and his fickleness. De la Maza only discovered the deceit when Mangalipto returned to Canaan. The chief of Apayan chastised everyone involved in the phony message. In the end, he relented to de la Maza's wishes and allowed the priest to set foot in Apayan. During his eleven-day stay in Mangalipto's town, the novelty of de la

Maza's presence attracted people from all over the valley to visit him. They were curious about the Mass and prayers and enchanted by the music of the harp and violin. They also liked the combs, needles, and animal figurines they received from the Dominican friar.

It is debatable whether the Carranglan chiefs or de la Maza was right all along. The principal source for the events is de la Maza himself in one of his letters, so any analysis needs to contend with the missionary's predominant viewpoint. On one hand, although de la Maza eventually got Mangalipto's second and final permission to enter, there was still an underlying hostility to his presence in Apayan.[155] One of the Carranglan chiefs who had failed to stop de la Maza's entry could not sleep at all because every night Ilongots would menacingly surround his house in Apayan. Even Mangalipto's wavering stance from a secret arrangement to a temporary halt to a final approval seemed to imply that the Spanish priest's presence was not universally welcomed by everyone in the valley. In constant consultation with other communities, Mangalipto seemed to have failed to gain any consensus. The open sky might not have been raining spears and arrows, but the threat was more than real. On the other hand, de la Maza's contention that trade was at the heart of the opposition received partial confirmation when an armed Ilongot chief visited him in Apayan.[156] After talking about religious matters, the Ilongot chief questioned why de la Maza did not bother to ask him for permission to enter Apayan. After all, he was the "terror of the mountains" who had killed ten people.[157] Nonetheless, the chief granted de la Maza permission to go to Apayan once in a while to buy and sell goods. Like de la Maza surmised, trade was at the forefront of people's mind when talking about access. River valleys were traditional sites of upland-lowland trading in the region.[158]

Even after all the waiting de la Maza had to go through as Mangalipto—the apparent paramount chief in the area—consulted with neighboring communities to allow a Spaniard in his very own town, absolute permission was dependent on so many distant chiefs that it all seemed like a futile, impossible endeavor. A chief from the mountains had a stake in it too and, when completely bypassed in the decision-making process, had to voice his concern. A network that crossed mountains and valleys linked towns together and influenced who had the right of access to any one town. But at the same time, despite the oversight, it did not take much effort for the "terror of the mountains" to change his mind and welcome de la Maza to Apayan. In an ideal world, it was better to ask permission first, but under straitened circumstances de la Maza's unconventional, brusque strategy got him to his destination at least temporarily.

In contrast, the Augustinian missionaries led by Alejandro Cacho took nine years to enter the town of Buhay (figure 1.2).[159] When the chief of Buhay refused to let the priests enter, Cacho remained persistent in his overtures, but he took his time and waited calmly for a positive response even if it took years. In the face of threats from animist communities, Cacho thought missionaries should "be patient, trying to gain their trust and asking for permission to move forward."[160] Reciprocating resistance with patience was common wisdom in the mountains. In the early years of the mission, a Carranglan chief gave an Augustinian missionary the following advice: "For our plans to turn out well, it is necessary to proceed slowly until they [the people of Buhay] mellow down."[161] Despite Spaniards' official advocacy of the international law that gave them freedom of movement to preach wherever they wanted, missionaries like Cacho adhered to local customs that called for prudence.

Without forcing the issue, Cacho continued to send out feelers to Buhay.[162] In 1713, without any success at all and fearing that the people of Buhay might simply have not understood their motives, the Augustinians wrote a letter that explained their purpose and had an intermediary go to Buhay to read it in front of everyone. The chief of Buhay was still not receptive to the idea of welcoming Spanish priests and converting to Christianity. The next year, under the leadership of their provincial who was on a pastoral visit, the Augustinian friars in Pampanga decided to renew their efforts at trying to enter Buhay. Cacho sent another petition to the people of Buhay. He used the Isinay converts living in the mission town of Puncan with kinship ties to Buhay as his intermediaries. The strategy bore fruit because in 1715 a group from Buhay went down to Puncan. Although Cacho failed to convince them to convert, it was a step in the right direction. A few weeks later, several chiefs from Buhay returned to Puncan, but this time they were ready to convert. The new converts opened the door for missionaries to finally set foot in Buhay. A protracted process of unending petitions preceded the granting of permission to enter the promised land of Buhay. But if it took years to gain permission, it only took an instant to revoke it. That was the highly fickle nature of mobility in the borderland.

In 1716, Cacho, together with eighty chiefs from several Kapampangan parishes and mission towns, embarked on the long-awaited trip to Buhay.[163] Following mountain custom, they notified Buhay of their impending arrival. They stopped just outside the town as they waited for the messengers to return with the go-ahead signal to enter. A chief from Carranglan insinuated that they should enter anyway even if the people of Buhay said no, but Cacho

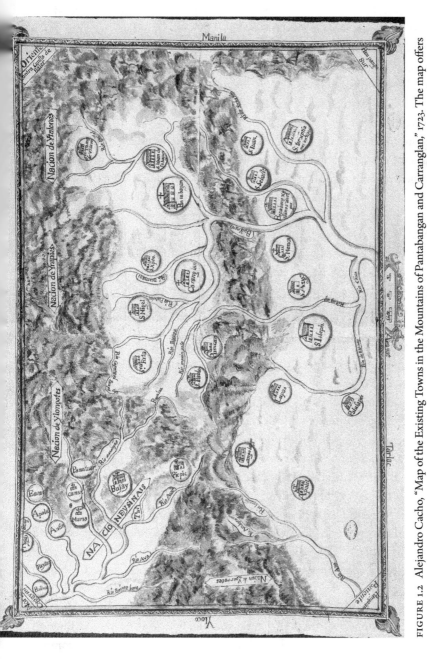

FIGURE 1.2 Alejandro Cacho, "Map of the Existing Towns in the Mountains of Pantabangan and Carranglan," 1723. The map offers a snapshot of the progress of the Augustinian mission of Ituy in upper Pampanga. Mission towns are represented by circles with a church inside (*center and bottom of the map*), while independent towns are simply encircled (*top-left corner*). The mission town of Buhay is at the vanguard of the advancing mission. Ministerio de Cultura y Deporte, Archivo General de Indias, MP-FILIPINAS, 148.

would have none of it and preferred to simply turn back if it was the town's wish. The final reply was a negative. Apparently, the people of Buhay were ready to welcome Cacho and his entourage in Buhay with all the food prepared. However, what caused the sudden change of mind was a traitor in Cacho's camp, one of the messengers sent to notify Buhay of their arrival. The messenger-traitor was an Abaca chief who wanted to exact revenge on Cacho for asking him to leave his wife. To spoil the missionary's plans, he quickly sponsored a feast in Buhay, made the participants swear not to admit priests in their town, and got his way.

The contrast between de la Maza's and Cacho's approach is striking. De la Maza was impatient and forced his way to Apayan. He did not bother to wait for the proper approval from his destination community. Even if Mangalipto had denied his entrance, he would have entered anyway. Cacho, on the other hand, took measured steps and played it on the safe side by respecting mountain customs. He always canvassed the disposition of animist communities toward preaching and conversion. When they refused missionary presence, he respected their wishes even when he was right at their doorstep. De la Maza entered Marian and Apayan almost by himself with no support at all from mission chiefs. Cacho traveled to Buhay with a large contingent of Indigenous chiefs from colonial and mission towns. Both cases demonstrate how intermediaries were important in mobility and how consensus among a plethora of villages and actors determined access to a single town. Although the two missionaries followed opposite methods in gaining access to borderland communities, they both eventually reached their destination.

In the case of Buhay, the town convened the various stakeholders from the Christians of the mission towns to the animists of the neighboring settlements to decide on what they should do.[164] The Augustinian provincial, once again on a timely pastoral visit, made sure that the Christian towns sent the best representatives to the talks. In 1717, Cacho and the other representatives from Carranglan finally set foot in Buhay, where they were received with affection and feasted on pigs, "which among them is the greatest sign of friendship and order."[165] The different parties agreed that priests could come to baptize them, but only if certain postbaptismal conditions were met. No soldiers should enter their town; the new converts should not be obliged to pay tribute; and they should also not be expected to provide for the needs of the priests. Missionaries could also enter the nearby towns as long as they obtained their permission. With Cacho's slower method, borderland communities were well informed of the intentions and movements of the missionaries. They reached a preliminary consensus prior to welcoming their Christian visitors. However, with the snail's pace of getting the necessary permissions, Augustinian missionary progress was slow. On Cacho's 1723 map, mission towns are represented by circles with a red-roofed church inside (figure 1.2). In the top-left corner of the map is converted Buhay with its red-roofed church, but it is still surrounded by nine colorless circled towns, signifying they have not been converted yet. It took years to convert Buhay and its neighbors. In contrast, de la Maza defied his allies' advice and surprised the settlements he visited. He only tried to resolve their differences, if at all, much later when he was already there.

Before going back to Marian, de la Maza received a special request from the Ilongot chief who claimed to be the "terror of the mountains." The chief wanted to have the honor of witnessing the priest dance in the Spanish style.[166] De la Maza was in no mood to do so because his feet were hurting from all the traveling. Overcoming his fatigue, he put on his hat, picked up the skirt of his habit, and held it with both hands at the waist. With Andres playing the harp, de la Maza followed the rhythm of the music and danced for the Ilongot chief, who chanted "hu" whenever the missionary came close to him. At one point during the dance in an amazing exhibition of dexterity, de la Maza kicked his foot half a yard above the chief's head. Dancing seemed to have been a sign of peace and contentment.[167] Later in the day, they had dinner together and slept in the same house sharing the same bed. The Ilongot chief also told de la Maza that if de la Maza were ever to go to Tujay, he should notify the chief.[168] The chief would gladly accompany the priest because the people of Tujay were his relatives and friends. With the Ilongot chief as his companion, de la Maza would not encounter any resistance. Even on his return trip to Marian, de la Maza was not alone. A few of the people he had baptized in Apayan accompanied him along the way.

Seemingly minor, superficial actions were critical in how people interacted with one another. Obliging the other side's ostensibly trivial wishes like dancing for them, calling them half-Spaniards, or giving them trinkets initiated and sustained relationships. Simple acts like sending out tentative approaches and acquiring permission marked how Spanish priests and indio parishioners slowly gained access to borderland communities. De la Maza's precarious predicament showed how dangerous it was to move beyond colonial bounds without the proper permission from locals. Although he did reach his final destination, it was at the cost of substantial commotion, physical threats, and desperate appeals to turn back.

While de la Maza's version of events in his 1703 letter provides the specific details of his tumultuous trip, one of the indios he baptized in Burubur called

Pigu left a historical account that offers a glimpse into how inhabitants of the borderland remembered de la Maza's brazen attempt to reach Apayan.[169] After the Dominicans abandoned the Burubur mission soon after de la Maza's death, Pigu continued in the new faith and became an interpreter of the Augustinians working in the nearby Carranglan and Pantabangan missions. According to Cacho, Pigu "has no equal as an interpreter and preaches more than the Father, when he is among his peers. . . . The mission's faith owes as much to Pigu as to the Fathers, until they had a good grasp of the language."[170] While Pigu's account is not dated, it must have been written sometime between 1711 and 1777. The earliest he could have written it was in 1711 because this was the last year referenced in the narrative, the latest in 1777, the year he passed away. An intermediate alternative would be 1756, the year he finished writing the sequel of the narrative.[171] Whatever the precise date of composition, years of hindsight had blurred the details found in de la Maza's more contemporary account, but at the same time they had distilled the story to its essence for locals like Pigu. Years of working with the Augustinians might have colored Pigu's recollection, but contemporary Dominican chroniclers had no problem preserving and citing it. What stands out in Pigu's version of events is the idea of permission, whose absence became the downfall of de la Maza.

In Pigu's narrative, de la Maza used deception to reach Marian and Apayan.[172] He asked the men of Burubur to accompany him out on the fields, but in reality he tricked them into joining him on a much longer journey. When the men realized what was going on, they questioned de la Maza: "Father, why are we going to Marian without having notified them first? Plus them being pagans, if you had told us, we would have brought lances and shields."[173] De la Maza's answer was a curt "We're going ahead." In Pigu's version, the initial foray of Andres and the secret agreement with Mangalipto never happened, but de la Maza's stubbornness was still there. What remained were the deceit and the lack of respect for social protocols in visiting communities. While de la Maza's letter written at the flush of victory after having just gone to Apayan without getting killed inevitably exuded a strong sense of optimism, Pigu's narrative with the benefit of hindsight was cognizant of the fleeting nature of the achievement. It avoided the hubris oozing in the missionary's glowing account. Instead of seeing de la Maza as a trailblazing priest who bravely overcame insurmountable obstacles, Pigu implicitly condemned the man's arrogance.

In Pigu's version, de la Maza's trip followed the same itinerary from Burubur to Apayan with a short stopover in Marian. However, the events were compressed in a shorter time frame with de la Maza's first arrival in Apayan being conflated with his death about a month later. Instead of dancing for an Ilongot chief and being accompanied by his new converts back to Marian, de la Maza met a different end in Apayan. According to Pigu, an Ibalibon chief sent de la Maza a piece of cloth, which he instinctively smelled.[174] Two days later, the Dominican became sick. He returned to Burubur and even went to Carranglan to receive medical and spiritual attention, but it was all in vain as he died within ten days. Based on the eyewitness account of his fellow Dominican missionary in Burubur, de la Maza died of a sunstroke on a much later date.[175] However, in Pigu's recollection, de la Maza died from a poisoned handkerchief on his first trip to Apayan.[176] For Pigu, two elements bookended de la Maza's journey: his complete disregard for social protocols and his untimely, violent death. Pigu's story presented a cautionary tale for unwelcome visitors. Taken aback, unwilling hosts might just retaliate in the worst possible way. People moved around, but they needed to follow a certain code of conduct.

While de la Maza's and Cacho's contrasting approaches do lend themselves to a black-and-white comparison between a right and a wrong way to access borderland settlements,[177] de la Maza's method was far from being completely alien to mountain customs. It was aggressive, but it still coincided with a few local practices. Even in his less-than-stellar example, de la Maza nevertheless tried to create his own network and wriggle his way through whatever opening he could find. Excluding the use of blatant deception, he still resorted to accepted methods of establishing contact and gaining access. For example, he first sent Andres to scout out Mangalipto's disposition to being visited before embarking on the journey and thus followed the convention of both Spaniards and indigenes in borderlands of asking for permission first. At least in his version of events, he got a conditional permission that he deliberately stretched beyond its limits. He might not have asked the people of Marian first, like Pigu claimed, but he supposedly had a secret agreement with Mangalipto. De la Maza's visit did not faithfully follow protocol, but it had some foundation on mountain customs no matter how flimsy it was.

Without the support of the Carranglan chiefs to act as a bridge to the valley communities, de la Maza created his own connections when he did not just barge his way through. On the way to Marian, he wrangled new converts like Ligaguen to facilitate his visit. Likewise, the Ilongots he recently baptized in Apayan escorted him on his return journey. The missionary astutely used the new bonds created by conversion as conduits to ease his movement in the borderland. De la Maza might not have completely obeyed mountain customs, but a couple of the strategies he used still somewhat adhered to them. Recently baptized and warmly welcomed in Burubur, Ligaguen understood that it was only proper to return the favor by hosting de la Maza in Marian. What de la Maza asked for was nothing out of the ordinary. Even in desperate times, he relied on conventional methods of gaining access and assistance.

Reciprocity

Interconnections and symmetry pervaded the visits of Spanish priests and Indigenous chiefs. Spaniards sponsored the visit of Malalbon and Burubur animists to Manila. In return, missionaries like de la Maza expected their former guests to accompany them in visiting other borderland communities. One of Ligaguen's children participated in the trip to Manila, and Ligaguen felt at home whenever he visited Burubur. It only seemed logical for Ligaguen to host de la Maza in his hometown of Marian. The same principle held even with non-Christians such as the Ilongot chief who visited de la Maza in Apayan. After a short introduction and some feasting and dancing, he felt comfortable enough to offer to accompany de la Maza to Tujay. One visit resulted in another, unleashing a domino effect and creating a web of visits that tied people from distant communities. Even after de la Maza's demise, at least for a time his successor maintained a relationship with Mangalipto and other valley chiefs. He could go visit them in their towns whenever he wanted because he was already their friend.[178]

A reciprocal give-and-take characterized the building of relations in the borderland, and part of the process involved asking permission and visiting one another. Visiting each other's home engendered a certain level of trust. When the Italons of Lublub had second thoughts about converting, they visited Manila, the home of the Spaniards on the island. The parish priest of Santor, a person with whom they had previous interactions, accompanied them and offered an additional layer of assurance. Preliminary visits and exchanges preceded the formal welcome to priests in Buhay. Besides the location and the journey, the reception was a pivotal point in building relationships. Whether in Manila, Agoo, Burubur, or Buhay, massive celebrations, shows of affection, pageantry with costumes and horses, and fantastic feasts punctuated the visits. Manila residents were curious about the visiting Italons and flocked to see them; Ilongot crowds did the same with de la Maza in Apayan and with Cacho in Buhay. Igorots danced for the traveling governor-general; the intruder de la Maza danced for an Ilongot chief. Mutual welcomes in multiple sites conquered considerable physical and social distances.

Visits created and sustained kinship ties among people living in different towns.[179] In the mid-eighteenth century, the Franciscan missionary Bernardo de Santa Rosa described how both Aeta communities and Christian towns used the same strategy to build friendship and kinship with one another. Respect and affection stemmed from fictive kinship and reciprocal greetings: "[Aetas] spend a lot on *maguinoo*, and we have entered by this means. They become relatives of the people of the town, and call them siblings. They tell their friend, 'You have to visit our mother, our father, etc.' The indios tell them the same thing, 'When are you coming to town? How is our mother, sister, etc.?' To those who are still young like the children of their friends, they call them their children, etc. They do all of this because of the conceit they have of becoming relatives of the people of the town."[180] The concept of maguinoo underpinned the building of relationships between animist Aetas and Christian indios. When Aetas visited Christian towns, they invited their indio friends to visit their Aeta relatives. Indios reciprocated the gesture when they saw their Aeta friends and invited them to do the same. Friendship and kinship were one and the same thing. Everyone belonged to one big extended family. Therefore, it only made sense to inquire about the welfare of and regularly visit relatives who lived in different settlements. Familial ties and visits bridged the gap between animist Aetas and Christian indios. Everyday visits might not have the same glamour and panache as the reciprocal trips between Manila and, say, Burubur, but they operated under the same basic principle. Visits blurred the line between Aetas and indios in the same way they turned Ituys into half-Spaniards. Kinship was not given at birth or acquired only through marriage, but constructed through everyday practices, including visits and greetings.[181]

What facilitated—and at the same time obstructed—travels and visits in the borderland was precisely the fluid, on-off character of kinship ties. When ties existed, mobility was much easier; when it did not, communities isolated themselves from each other. The small, dispersed communities in the hinterland were generally kin groups.[182] Their relationship with their neighbors would determine how easy it was to travel across the terrain. If two communities were rival kin groups, then travel between the two sites would be dangerous. Conversely, kinship provided access and security. Expanded kin groups meant more people cooperating with each other. At least in the cases of Apayan and Buhay, they each seemed to have a loose connection with nearby settlements that influenced who could enter the town. Initial inter-community consensus was against allowing priests in their towns because there seemed to be an underlying enmity between mission and valley towns. Eventually, friends and relatives were the channels that enabled missionaries to enter the towns and explore the surrounding areas. In several instances, visits, feasts, and conversion melded into one another to create intercommunity bonds that smoothened borderland mobility.

If Augustinian and Dominican missionaries encountered partial resistance from the network of valley towns in Paniqui, Franciscan missionaries from the Pacific coastal town of Baler had an easier time entering the network of Ilongot mountain settlements. Reciprocal hospitality among Ilongots made traveling across considerable distances feasible. It was most likely practiced by communities with kinship ties—or at the very least not hostile—to one another. In 1757, the Franciscan missionary José de San Pascual described this mountain custom in the following manner: "They are people who do not know how to refuse respite to a pilgrim. They give food to all those who enter their house at meal time. That is why they travel from town to town with little provision and without fear of lacking anything because the owner of the house has to give them their ration. He will not ask them to go away."[183] Each community and house was an effective rest stop for travelers. Hospitality was a requirement. It made the logistics of traveling much easier with no need to worry about where to find the next meal or overburden oneself with heavy supplies over rough terrain.

Even San Pascual had to follow the practice in spite of his reluctance to do so because the mission was still in its infancy and did not have enough provisions.[184] Every day he had guests join his aides at meal time. In one instance, he had two visitors from another town stay with them for two weeks straight, eating and drinking to their heart's content. San Pascual did not particularly like that these people were sponging off of them, but he could not bring himself to tell them to go away. Although a Spaniard, San Pascual acted like a true Ilongot who could not turn away his uninvited guests. He understood that there was a flip side to accommodating travelers. They would treat him with the same hospitality in the future: "When I visit hamlets, I already know that they need to give me what they have, which is rice, sweet potatoes, and vegetables. They are simply returning the favor. They do the same with their countrymen. What a person eats today in my house, he will repay me tomorrow in his house."[185] Feeding visitors might be a daily burden, but when San Pascual was not a host, he became a traveler and guest himself who benefited from the mutual hospitality.

Reciprocity made mutual visits almost inevitable in how people interacted with each other. More than the practical benefits, the custom somewhat forced people to be welcoming of others. It created a domino effect of opening doors to visitors and travelers. In San Pascual's generic description, hosts and guests did not necessarily have any close ties with one another. San Pascual, for one, did not particularly appreciate the two guests who stayed for two weeks. However, such accommodation could be the seed of a deeper future relationship. It nurtured a tendency toward further contact because eating in someone's house created a debt of gratitude that had to be repaid. If extravagant communal feasting marked the big trips to Manila and Buhay, simple shared meals of sweet potatoes and vegetables distinguished everyday mobility in the borderlands.

Although he disregarded certain local practices, de la Maza still understood the importance of food in building relationships. When he doubted the veracity of Malalbon's claims about the hostility of nearby Ituy communities, de la Maza partly used food to gauge the inaccuracy of the claims.[186] When the missionary and his companions found themselves in a place where they did not have anything to eat, the Ituys gave them three bowls of rice in exchange for a bowl of salt. When the Ituys ran out of rice, they offered mung beans instead, so that de la Maza's group did not have to eat lowly sweet potatoes. In de la Maza's mind, the fact that the Ituys were willing to trade with him and not let him starve indicated that they were not as hostile as Malalbon had insisted. They even went out of their way to offer rice, a prestige food. Without any prompting, other Ituy communities volunteered to be de la Maza's middlemen. They got clothes, plates, and salt from the mission and exchanged these goods for rice with the valley settlements. In this way, de la Maza and the mission were well-provisioned with rice. The supply of rice was not only a matter of subsistence but also a manifestation of a willingness to enter into an exchange.

De la Maza primarily interpreted the provision of food as the openness of Ituy communities to Spanish missionary presence, but a distinct possibility exists that even Ituys conceived the exchange more in kinship terms. If kinship was constructed through everyday practices like visits and greetings, it was also "built up through appropriate feeding throughout life."[187] Sharing food and feeding someone are ways of creating kinship ties.[188] A mother's bond with her child is not born at the moment of birth. It is nurtured and developed through the very act of feeding, such as breastfeeding.[189] As nourishment sustains individual bodies, it also fosters interpersonal relations. Feeding visitors in borderlands performed an analogous role. Ilongot kin groups, particularly the women who were in charge of swidden gardens, needed to cultivate more rice than they could consume on their own because they had to take into account feeding their numerous visitors.[190] Ilongots had the habit of visiting each other a lot during the dry season, a special time of the year for people to reconnect. Of course, rekindling ties involved feeding visitors, so there had to be enough food for everyone. If it was rice, then so much the better. Feeding guests nourished kinship bonds. For Ilongots, welcoming visitors during the summer months of abundance was of paramount importance because the onset of the rainy season made traveling and seeing each other much more difficult. Visiting, feeding, and reconnecting were intimately interconnected actions, bringing dispersed communities closer together.

Reciprocal mobilities underpinned the actions and interactions of Spaniards and Indigenous peoples in Luzon. The Spanish monarchy relied on an itinerant court culture that toured its domain and welcomed visiting dignitaries and subjects. Colonial officials replicated this same pattern of circulating the royal realm in the Indies. Indigenous kin groups in Luzon practiced mutual visits to incorporate new kin and renew ties with old ones. Traveling was an integral part of maintaining social relations among dispersed communities. More than a scholarly analytical tool, networks among individuals and polities were a reality on the ground reinforced by continuous travels and movements. Spanish and Indigenous practices of mobility sometimes coincided and reinforced one another in reciprocal visits. The different parties valued ritual and ceremony in the transformation of identities into vassals, converts, kings, mestizos, Ilongots, and siblings. Spatial movements and restricted access mapped out the dynamics of social relations. They were the channels that underpinned the multiple and sometimes conflicting motivations of the various actors. Converting pagans to Christianity, acquiring new vassals for the Spanish monarchy, gaining powerful allies in baptism, becoming kin with strangers, taking advantage of economic opportunities, or reciprocating a debt of gratitude—all these different intentions manifested themselves through the same process of reciprocal mobilities when they aligned with one another.

However, despite the possible benign images that reciprocal mobilities may evoke, the thin filaments of connections they created were tenuous and contingent. In certain instances, they had a clear undercurrent of conflict from the stories of Spanish abuse and violence to the hostile reception of missionaries like de la Maza. The connections engendered by mobility did not necessarily derive from group consensus. Different Spanish officials enacted different policies toward unsubjugated communities. Even missionaries like de la Maza and Cacho used contrasting approaches in their dealings with Indigenous peoples. Independent towns and even individual kin groups had contradictory responses to, say, offers of conversion. Amid the discrepancies within them, the different groups nevertheless tried to influence and coordinate their actions from the governor-general cooperating with missionaries to valley settlements in Paniqui forming a loose confederation among themselves and with nearby polities. Being welcomed and denied access were intimately linked with one another in a milieu of constantly shifting allegiances.

The open-armed hospitality of Aetas, Ilongots, or missionaries like Cacho mentioned in this chapter should not be romanticized and taken out of context because violence was ever-present in the borderlands. Cacho might have exercised extreme patience in courting the people of Buhay, but he also had no qualms about using military force. While Aetas welcomed their indio siblings and Ilongots hosted random travelers in their home, they were also known headhunters. The notion of reciprocal mobilities encompasses not only the benign, friendly exchanges but also the violent, bloody ones. Movement also creates friction, and reciprocity can be antagonistic too. Chapter 2 tackles the more unseemly side of reciprocal mobilities that led to death and destruction. In place of visits, gifts, and hugs, it has raids, weapons, and chopped heads.

CHAPTER TWO

Violent Exchanges

On his way back from his ecclesiastical visit of the province of Cagayan in early 1703, the provincial of the Dominican order, Francisco Jiménez, decided to make an impromptu stop at the mission town of Burubur.[1] He had visited the town a few months earlier and had witnessed how chiefs of the neighboring towns flocked to Burubur to welcome him. He carried out his second visit in more dire circumstances with the viability of the mission in serious doubt, after the resident missionary had died and animist Ilongots had burned down the church and missionary's house. Upon hearing the devastating news, the provincial decided to come to support the distraught Christian community. However, his presence did not make the situation any better. At sunrise, the town of Burubur woke up to the war cries of hostile Ilongots who cut off the head of the provincial's Pangasinense escort.[2] The Christians of Burubur tried to defend themselves from the onslaught, but they were clearly outnumbered. They had to temporarily abandon the nascent mission, the provincial and his entourage seeking refuge in the Augustinian mission town of Carranglan, and the converts and catechumens of Burubur hiding in the nearby mountains.

Visits had the power to bring people together. Congeniality and joy marked the Dominican provincial's first visit to Burubur, which aided the consolidation of the mission. However, visits' ability to connect had their limitations. By his second visit a few months later, the situation had changed dramatically for the worse such that his friendly visit was not enough to stem the tide of Ilongot hostility toward the mission. The stark contrast between the two visits lends itself to a binary reading of borderland interactions, opposing peace and violence, friendship and enmity, and success and failure. Shortly after escaping the Ilongot attack, the provincial immediately requested for the legitimate use of "Catholic arms" to defend the besieged faithful, and the government obliged by dispatching a military campaign against the attackers.[3] The way the events unfolded is conducive to a linear narrative that moves from harmony to chaos. Where peaceful visits failed, war seemed like the next logical step. However, rather than conceiving it as a sharp historical break, it can be construed as the continuation of contact and exchange, albeit of a more antagonistic nature, because violence and cultural interaction are not mutually exclusive.[4] Violence and warfare are also forms of cultural exchange and reciprocity.[5] More than vicious cycles of revenge and back-and-forth sallies, violence had meaning and carried a message to the various contending parties. Although violence might have brought people apart like in the temporary abandonment of Burubur, communication never ceased as the Dominican provincial and governor-general of the Philippines sent out a retaliatory force against the Ilongots. Contrary to a facile association of reciprocal mobilities with benign interactions, I argue that Spanish and Indigenous raids in the borderlands at their core also followed the logic of reciprocal movements.

If violence was not an absolute barrier to further interactions, it also had an ambivalent relationship with mobility. On one hand, threats to and fear over one's life made travelers think twice before setting out from their community and led to immobility. On the other hand, military expeditions and raids were yet another form of mobility. Friction is an indispensable component of mobility not only in terms of resistance and setbacks but also its materiality and lumpiness.[6] Movement does not occur in an idealized, frictionless vacuum but in a real world full of social opposition and natural obstacles. The military forts that take center stage in this chapter embodied this tension between mobility and friction as they simultaneously launched raids against enemies, blocked upland-lowland commerce, and perpetuated existing borderland interactions and movements. This seeming contradiction is inherent in mobility because friction is not the antithesis of movement but rather the conditions on the ground that shape which mobilities take place and which ones are hindered or stalled. Revenge raids were as much a part of reciprocal mobilities as mutual visits. If anything, the violence only highlights the friction involved in all types of mobility.

The mutual visits spanning several decades described in chapter 1 occurred in parallel with violent clashes. Visits and raids did not simply reflect alternating periods of friendship and hostility; they coexisted. Friend and foe were sometimes one and the same person. Mobility and proximity did not always lead to smooth relations; they also produced friction and clashes. Francisco de la Maza (see chapter 1) and the Dominican provincial carried out their visits in the face of severe opposition and threats to their life. De la Maza was not quite sure whether his intermediaries were actually helping or preventing him from achieving his goals. From the 1690s when the Spanish government started to plan an official occupation of the borderlands of Ituy and Paniqui to the establishment of actual missions in the succeeding decades, the age-old debate between pacification and conquest kept rearing its head in the discussions on how to best deal with resistance and hostility. Missionaries had to decide whether they would take up the option of using armed escorts and forts to facilitate their evangelical work. The use of force defended vulnerable converts and catechumens from enemy attacks, but it could also lead to greater antagonism with hostile communities, which sometimes resulted in their flight or destruction rather than their submission and conversion.

Different cultures convey and interpret violence in different ways.[7] In Southeast Asia, warfare usually entailed the capture of slaves and portable wealth rather than the physical seizure of enemy towns because the relatively low population density in the region meant that the control of people was more important than the occupation of territory.[8] With an abundance of land and a scarcity of people, the latter became a more sought-after resource among competing polities. The incorporation of additional labor in the form of captives was a clear sign of victory. The theoretical possession of vast lands meant nothing if there were no hands to cultivate them. At least in the Philippine archipelago, surprise raids and plunder rather than field battles between armies characterized warfare.

The island of Luzon was the stage for multiple types of violence, which had different effects on people's movements and configured borderland space in different ways. Spaniards used soldiers and armed escorts to conquer and navigate the hinterland. Victory meant the establishment of permanent settlements. The dotting of colonial towns and forts across the countryside was also a means of maintaining control over the territory. With Spaniards construing native flight from colonial settlements as tantamount to rebellion, mobility and violence were intimately linked in their worldview. In contrast, Indigenous violence usually involved surreptitious raids rather than set-piece battles. At least in the borderlands of Luzon, one of the main objectives of raids and ambushes was to kill somebody by decapitation, so it made traveling all the more dangerous. Although headhunting could be a part of warfare where the acquisition of heads was a form of victory, it was as much a ritual to mark the passing of a recently deceased relative and bring prosperity to the community.[9] The choice of headhunting victim was mostly random and not based on any animosity or desire for vengeance. Violence on others was not always committed in the context of warfare. Although Spanish-style warfare was more direct and territorial, it nevertheless shared a few characteristics with Indigenous hostilities. They both practiced raiding that included the plunder of goods, the burning of houses and fields, and the seizure of captives.

Different visions and practices of warfare not only clashed with one another but also influenced each other. Opposing sides not only interpreted their opponent's values and behavior in terms of their own beliefs and practices; they also tried to understand their opponent's world and use that knowledge to inflict the most harm. In some cases, natives of the Philippines saw Spanish conquistadors as no different from Indigenous men of prowess who exhibited immense spiritual and military capabilities.[10] Indians in Brazil explicitly targeted slaves, the most valuable property of Portuguese settlers, in order to unleash the worst economic havoc and drive the invaders away from their lands.[11] A certain level of mutual understanding and exchange thus pervaded even the most acute conflicts.

The various actors in the borderlands observed and learned how to best deal with their adversaries. They did not have monolithic, impermeable cultural differences in the conduct of violence. With increasing Spanish presence in the borderlands between Cagayan and Pampanga, belligerent natives adapted to the situation and became more deliberate in their attacks. Rather than ambush random passersby, they started to target mission towns and burn churches, the quintessential symbols of Spanish colonial incursion. Mostly associated with mourning rituals and isolated raids, headhunting became more prominently incorporated as a tool in a sustained warfare against Christian communities. Spaniards also adapted to the particular situation in the borderlands. Fixed settlements in the form of mission towns and military forts made Spaniards and their native converts particularly vulnerable to constant attacks from hostile hinterland communities. In response, they resorted to recruiting native soldiers in their military expeditions who brought their Indigenous skills like knowledge of the terrain and headhunting capabilities in the service of the Spanish monarchy. Throughout the years, the different sides in the conflict borrowed from and adjusted to each other amid the open antagonism.[12] There was as much mutual understanding and exchange in revenge raids as there was in reciprocal visits.

Mirroring the previous chapter, the current chapter starts with the late seventeenth century and lays out contemporaneous Spanish plans of using just war against belligerent Indigenous communities in the borderlands between Cagayan and Pampanga. It tackles two areas where indios and Spaniards adapted to each other during times of conflict: headhunting and forts. Headhunting practices were different depending on the location. On the plains of Pampanga and Pangasinan where Spanish colonial presence was relatively light, Negritos and apostates targeted random individuals in isolated places. In the cramped, mountainous borderland between Cagayan and

Pampanga where the expansion of Spanish missions was much more aggressive, Ilongot headhunters deliberately attacked and burned down mission towns. While headhunting was more ritualistic with the Negritos, it was more militant with the Ilongots as they faced a more menacing Spanish presence at their doorstep. Besides mission towns, forts were a pillar of Spanish attempts to gain some semblance of control of the frontier and contain attacks from hostile communities. They functioned as the launch pad for retaliatory attacks and as a border guard to ensure the separation between Christian and animist communities. However, the economic interests of fort soldiers and provincial governors meant it was to their advantage to maintain contact and commerce with unsubjugated mountain communities.

The chapter then discusses how violent warfare nevertheless led to mutual exchanges from severed heads to Spanish weapons. Some apostates, Christian indios, and animists incorporated guns into their fighting repertoire. Spanish troops, like Indigenous warriors, resorted to headhunting when dealing with hostile upland communities. Agonistic animists destroyed churches and plundered religious images as trophies or prestige goods. The contending sides tried to push each other away, create a buffer zone between them, and minimize their contact, but in the process they became more and more entangled in each other's violent ways. The final section of the chapter argues that despite all of the death and violence, warfare in the borderlands was still primarily about maintaining or gaining control over people. Besides their more well-known goal of acquiring new converts, Spaniards attacked mountain polities in order to forcibly bring apostates and runaways back to colonial towns. With more and more villages converting to Christianity, Ilongots and their allies preyed upon mission towns because the growing number of Christians posed a threat to their paramount political position in the area. The movement of people as they converted and apostatized reconfigured alliances and shifted the balance of power in the borderland. The transfer of people between the different groups was the foundation of the cultural exchanges in the midst of warfare. Although violence and destruction were legitimate responses to conflict, more amicable methods of conflict resolution existed from the exchange of gifts and captives to negotiations and peace pacts.

War Plans

A series of visits by provincial officials and priests in the 1690s set the stage for the relatively peaceful establishment of missions in the borderland between Cagayan and Pampanga in the early 1700s (see chapter 1). Parallel to these developments, several government officials entertained the possibility of resorting to a violent conquest of the hostile communities there. Although the military proposals of the 1690s were not carried out, the deployment of force and soldiers was always in the background in spite of the predominantly benign narratives coming from the religious orders, especially the Augustinians, celebrating the absence of violence in their missionary activities.[13] Spanish officials and priests out in the field constantly debated whether to take the more peaceful or violent route, but the two paths were in reality sometimes complementary.

With a substantial population of animists and apostates living in the borderlands of Ituy and Paniqui, plans were underfoot in the 1690s to finally deal with this effective defiance of Spanish rule. The government consulted various stakeholders from high-ranking officials such as a visiting royal judge and the Dominican provincial to military officers manning the frontier forts on how to conduct the affair. All of them concluded that the use of force was a crucial ingredient to any successful plan to conquer the borderland. The visiting judge Alonso de Abella Fuertes believed that a military campaign was the only viable option.[14] He wanted one set of troops to attack from the north in Cagayan and another from the south in Pampanga to effect a pincer maneuver on the enemies.[15] The Dominican provincial Cristóbal Pedroche suggested a similarly aggressive but more multifaceted strategy.[16] Besides the usual plan of simultaneously attacking the borderland on two military fronts, Pedroche also advocated for the construction of a new fort and the use of converted natives as intermediaries. While there was already a Spanish fort in Itugud, he wanted another one deeper in the hinterland of Paniqui.[17] To offset the considerable costs in provisions, the provincial suggested that the fort soldiers simply steal food from their enemies during the harvest season or hunt the cows, carabaos, and deer in the area. Combining both harsh and gentle methods, Pedroche wanted converted natives to act as bridges, since they had plenty of animist relatives still living in the hinterland whom they could convince to join them.[18]

Unsurprisingly, military officers in the provinces did not hesitate in urging a violent solution to the problem. Diego de Acosta, infantry captain in the provincial capital of Lal-lo, advocated for the dispatch of punitive expeditions against the bellicose animist and apostate communities in the borderlands.[19] From his own experience, he observed that the lack of retaliation from Spanish-administered towns implicitly encouraged hostile communities to continue their attacks despite their fear of firearms. The problem was, as hostile groups retreated to the hinterland after their assault on colonial towns, they were often beyond the reach of garrisoned Spanish soldiers. To resolve the problem, Acosta wanted military expeditions to march into the hinterland and attack hostile mountain settlements in their very backyard. Sebastián de Asensio, a corporal in various frontier forts, offered the same advice as everyone else—retaliation.[20] Gentle methods were not as effective as violent ones. A combination of expeditions and a new fort should root out belligerent natives from their places of refuge. In his assessment, forming an expeditionary force and building a fort did not pose any major difficulties, except for the danger involved in sourcing materials and provisions for the fort in enemy territory.

An eye for an eye, a tooth for a tooth. It was the law of reciprocal justice. The advice mentioned above all coincided on the use of force. Hostile hinterland communities infringed on ostensibly Spanish-controlled spaces without any repercussions. While unsubjugated upriver and upland communities were free to carry out their attacks, Spaniards and their indio allies had a more difficult time penetrating the hinterland and seeking retribution. In some cases, they were just not familiar with the terrain. In one instance, when they brought along guides who did not know for certain where their attackers lived, they simply burned down all the towns they encountered as they roamed around.[21] Retaliation does not quite work when it does not hit its precise target. In other cases, their targets simply went farther inland to avoid direct confrontation, which was a common problem encountered by coastal powers trying to impose their military might over interior polities.[22] To counteract the attacks from the hinterland and the flight of apostates inland, Spanish officials wanted to reciprocate the attacks and forcibly bring back the apostates to the Christian fold. Spanish war plans in their desire to weaken the enemy partially mirrored in reverse the movements conducted by agonistic borderland communities.

The parish priest of Tocolana in the province of Cagayan, Pedro Sánchez, proposed ideas along the same lines as the others, but his military vision was more dynamic. Instead of two fixed forts and military expeditions coming from either side of the borderland, he wanted a combination of settlements and forts to act as a moving colonial frontier as Spaniards and their indio allies moved deeper and deeper into enemy territory.[23] If the forts of Cabagan and Itugud were removed, it would free up the resources to establish a new fort a day's travel farther upriver. The new fort would eliminate hostile groups from its immediate surroundings "by fire and bloodshed" because amicable requests to hand over the apostates always fell on deaf ears.[24] Their harvests should be burned and destroyed, so that they would starve and be forced to surrender. Once this was accomplished, another fort town should be built a day's walk farther inland so that both forts could work together. A string of forts would eventually corner all the hostile groups with no room to escape.

Sánchez's plan shared similarities with the pincer maneuver suggested by the others; however, instead of using expeditionary troops to effect it, he wanted the more permanent structure of forts to carry out the maneuver. It would be a massive resource strain on the province of Cagayan to sustain an ever-increasing number of forts, but it also presented a more enduring solution to the problem by completely eliminating the zones of refuge that hostile animists and apostates took advantage of.[25] Flight was one of the main tactics used by indigenes to escape from Spanish retaliatory expeditions, so the existence of a vast frontier made it almost impossible for Spanish-backed soldiers to decisively catch, punish, and subjugate their enemies.[26] Forts were supposed to eliminate, or at the very least minimize, the role played by the hinterland as an escape hatch. If fixed cities epitomized Spanish order in the Indies, forts acted as the muscle that tried to impose this order on the unconquered borderland.[27] In Sánchez's plan, forts were dynamic structures at the vanguard of an expanding colonial frontier.

Despite the overwhelming number of voices clamoring for violent retribution, the governor-general of the Philippines, Fausto Cruzat y Góngora, decided not to implement any of the war plans. In his view, the conquest of the lowlands was always going to be easier than that of the uplands.[28] Experience had taught old hands in the country that retaliatory military campaigns always stumbled upon the intractable problem of enemies just fleeing to inaccessible mountain ranges. Thus, Cruzat favored the time-tested method of using missionaries, implementing a royal decree of 1677 that required all religious orders to have four or five missionaries dedicated to the conversion of animists and apostates living in the mountains of the archipelago.[29] The governor-general's stance can be construed as cooler heads prevailing on a heated topic, but the reality was that the construction of forts and the payment of soldiers' salaries were a heavy burden on the Manila government's finances.[30] Funding missions and missionaries did not only adhere to the lofty goal of saving souls but also presented itself as a cheaper, more effective option to brute force. Cruzat's decision to favor missions over forts fits in nicely with the Augustinians' official narrative that their subsequent evangelization in the early 1700s hardly had any recourse to violence. Although mission activities in the borderlands between Cagayan and Pampanga were relatively peaceful in the early part of the eighteenth century, the ominous presence of violence was never far away. A few decades later in the 1730s, the same debates on how to best manage hostile attacks from unsubjugated groups would resurface. This time it would be in relation to the Negritos inhabiting the mountains of the archipelago and their practice of headhunting.

Random Murders in Isolated Places

Different types of violence had different effects on borderland mobility. On one hand, Spanish-backed forts tried to implement order in the face of mostly haphazard attacks coming from unsubjugated communities. Besides launching retaliatory campaigns, forts also tried to create a border between colonial subjects and independent communities by prohibiting all types of contact between the two sides. Ironically, however, the intermediate position of garrisoned soldiers made them prone to commit abuses that undermined their avowed goal of acting as a barrier because more often than not they took economic advantage of the porous nature of the borderlands. On the other hand, Indigenous headhunting sowed fear and immobility in colonial towns because everyone was a potential victim and avoiding travels was an obvious, simple preventive measure. For headhunting communities, the taking of a head had its own logic with the head becoming an object of exchange that transferred good and bad fortune from one community to another and elicited anger and reprisals from the victim's community.

In contrast to Spanish-approved military expeditions that were direct and had a precise target in mind, Indigenous headhunting was unpredictable and indiscriminate in its victim. In the Spanish war plans above, retribution acted as a deterrent only when the culprits received their just punishment. Random acts of violence on innocent victims disturbed Spanish notions of honor and justice. In Indigenous headhunting, however, the main goal in general was to cut any stranger's head off. It did not matter who it was as long as he was not a member of the raiders' community. Although it sometimes led to vicious cycles of revenge raids, headhunters did not specifically target the individual perpetrators of previous attacks. At most, they would exact revenge on anyone from the perpetrator's community. Nonetheless, a series of headhunting raids could create a domino effect and become reciprocal.

Many Indigenous communities in the frontier practiced headhunting for a wide variety of reasons. Ilongots and Aetas went on headhunting raids to end the mourning period after the death of a kin and acquire a bride-price for marriage.[31] Besides marking crucial stages of the life cycle, the decapitated head was also a clear physical manifestation of social prestige and spiritual prowess.[32] Balugas were "much inclined to kill people and put the greatest honor and valor in having cut the most heads."[33] For Negritos or Aetas, the skulls of their victims served as cups during their celebrations.[34] Ilongots decorated their houses with skulls and bones: "It is a source of pride to have many animal bones in one's house as a symbol of the owner's bravery. The bones of the many pigs, chickens, and other animals that they kill are hung in their houses that consequently look like slaughterhouses."[35] The Franciscan missionary José de San Pascual lived in precisely such a house. Although his Ilongot hosts had already removed a good portion of the animal bones hanging around the house, there were still twelve skulls from past headhunting raids that kept him company and showed he was being accommodated in an important person's home.[36] Longtime Augustinian missionary Alejandro Cacho described headhunting with the following metaphor: "What all these nations [Italons, Panoypoys, Isinays, and Ibalibons] most agree on is to go headhunting with more pleasure than a Spaniard goes to a bullfight."[37] Headhunting was not only a popular tradition like Spanish bullfighting; it was also a joyous occasion for raiding communities. Murders and feasts were not mutually exclusive phenomena because pleasure and vitality could entail death.

Typical Spanish explanations for Indigenous violence—such as an innate cruelty and barbarity due to a lack of civilization—do not provide much guidance on why certain communities hunted heads.[38] Unable to comprehend the viciousness of headhunting, the Franciscan missionary Bernardo de Santa Rosa preached to animist Aetas the Christian virtues of compassion and respect for human lives: "You like to kill, but you do not want to be killed, so God punishes . . . all killers in the afterlife because they do not love their fellow human beings. Deer, pigs, cows, and chickens do not kill their own kind."[39] In his view, headhunters were worse than animals because they killed their fellow humans, even people from neighboring communities.

However, several Spanish accounts do provide clues to the motivations behind Indigenous headhunting such as when they emphasize the prevalence of fear in kin groups suffering from the loss of a loved one. The death of a kin instilled tremendous apprehension among the living because they believed that the deceased's spirit continued to lurk around and could possibly cause harm and misfortune on them.[40] When an Aeta chief passed away, the mere mention of his name evoked fear because they believed that "when one of them died, he turned into a devil."[41] Ancestor spirits could be either good or evil depending on specific circumstances, such as whether the community had performed the proper propitiation rites. Aetas in the area started hearing melancholic voices, apparently of their recently departed chief, following them throughout the landscape.[42] With the Aeta chief's spirit making its ominous presence felt, Aetas limited their travels and ran away scared whenever they sensed him nearby. While Spanish missionaries' negative portrayal of ancestor spirits made sense in their attempt to demonize animism and present a better alternative in a Christian afterlife, late twentieth-century anthropologists nonetheless observed similar emotions of grief and passion in Ilongot headhunting after someone's death.[43] The emotions might not exactly be the fear missionaries described in the eighteenth century, but they pointed to the same idea of initial devastation and loss in someone's passing.

Headhunting had opposite effects in the perpetrators' and victims' community. It led to fertility and renewal in the former but grief and death in the latter. In effect, headhunting involved not only the physical transfer of a head but also a shift of misfortune from one community to another. For raiders, the taking of a head was a way of appeasing the deceased relative's spirit and bringing good fortune to the community.[44] Negritos followed the mourning taboo of abstaining from food and drink until they had cut a certain number of heads: "They fulfill them [their vows to cut heads] with rare punctuality because it is well known that the devil appears and talks to them, and afflicts them if they do not perform these offerings."[45] Igorots refrained from hunting or traveling in order to avoid bumping into the spirit of the recently dead, which was considered bad luck and even lethal.[46] Although headhunting led to additional deaths, it nevertheless brought prosperity and fertility to the raiders' community. Headhunting raids culminated in feasts, which usually ended the mourning period for the community by placating the deceased relative whose feted spirit should no longer harm the living and should in fact favor them with health and wealth.[47] The initial death of the kin could be transformed into renewal and social reproduction as successful headhunters became eligible for marriage.[48] Through headhunting, a menacing spirit became a spiritual ally, the death of a kin potentially led to marriage and procreation, and the misfortune enveloping a community reconfigured itself into prosperity for the surviving kin.

For the victims, headhunting obviously had more detrimental consequences. News of a death in one community spread fear in surrounding communities because of the clear danger of becoming the unwitting target of a headhunting raid.[49] The dry season was the time for not only traveling and harvesting but also headhunting.[50] The coincidence of rumors of a death and the dry season made inhabitants extra cautious, so they usually traveled armed or in groups.[51] Fear engendered fear, and death more deaths. If the victim of a headhunting raid belonged to a headhunting community, a single death could trigger a chain reaction. Headhunting raids were prevalent enough in the 1730s that the Spanish government in Manila requested reports from priests and officials living across the archipelago on the phenomenon of mountain Negritos attacking colonial subjects.[52]

Although Spanish-backed military expeditions and Indigenous headhunting raids can be seen as two sides of the same coin, headhunting was usually not even a form of warfare, especially when raiders and their victims did not harbor any sort of enmity between them. In complete contrast to set-piece battles, headhunting often entailed random ambushes on unsuspecting victims. The key was to avoid detection, chop the head as quickly as possible, and escape without any casualties on the side of the raiding party.[53] With these objectives in mind, an ambush was the best strategy: "Twelve, twenty or more of them join together, and they come very hidden covered by the dense thicket. They carry out their ambush in a spot where they think some indio would pass by, somebody running away from town, hunting, or going to a far part of town or a lone remote farm."[54] Isolated areas—out-of-the-way fields or uninhabited stretches of road—were headhunters' favorite hunting ground, and lone individuals were their most vulnerable prey.[55] The cautious, circuitous maneuvers of headhunters took advantage of the dispersed nature of frontier settlements on the plains of Pampanga and Pangasinan. Although raiders discreetly targeted isolated individuals, they nevertheless struck fear and wreaked havoc right in the heart of mission and colonial towns, dissuading most forms of travel. Yet technically speaking, it was not warfare. Headhunting raids occurred even when the contending parties never had any ongoing feuds.[56] It was a form of ritual violence where the renewal and prosperity of one community inadvertently depended on another's misfortune.[57] Headhunting rituals were a way to sublimate death in a community.[58] The feast and sacrifice after a successful headhunt not only placated the departed kin's spirit but also transferred the problem of death to another community.

While a strict comparison of Spanish-backed military expeditions and Indigenous headhunting may seem like an exercise in comparing apples and oranges, the actors themselves often viewed one activity through the lens of the other. Spanish sources unfavorably compared the barbarity of headhunting with the gallantry of their own style of warfare. Upholding a sense of moral superiority as they sought to bring hostile animists and apostates to justice, Spaniards viewed their military campaigns as a way of setting the world aright. They were simply meting out the law and its just punishment. In contrast, in their view, headhunting was intrinsically dishonorable. Raiders pounced on the first innocent victim they chanced upon, and worst of all, they did it in a cowardly manner by ambush rather than in a dignified face-to-face combat.[59] Of course, Spanish perceptions situated Indigenous head-hunting in the context of Spanish military warfare rather than the more congenial one of local spiritual sacrifices and rituals. Spaniards could not see the logical causal link between a death in one's community and the need to kill a random person.

Spaniards had a difficult time processing the randomness of headhunting attacks. Unlike Spanish-backed expeditions that targeted the territory of specific hostile communities by burning down houses and fields, headhunters were not interested in territorial acquisition. In fact, they were more likely to avoid direct confrontation with colonial towns and simply turned their attention to isolated farmers and travelers in the countryside. Even though official Spanish reports constantly referred to the "robberies and hostilities" of the mountain Negritos, incidents of robbery were almost nonexistent compared with the prevalence of physical violence because the Negritos' "principal cruel appetite is to kill in order to carry away heads."[60] A lack of interest in acquiring territory or a victim's material possessions pointed to the head-hunter's greater devotion to spiritual matters, at least of the animist kind. In the spiritual realm, the victim's identity was hardly relevant when he turned into either a sacrificial offering or the new focal point of death and misfortune. From the perspective of warfare that valued territorial conquest, head-hunting raids were unconventional, uncoordinated, and weak attempts at violence. If Spanish military maneuvers largely focused on permanent settlements such as towns and forts, headhunters thrived on descending upon unsuspecting individuals in scattered, isolated places. Everything beyond the immediate vicinity of colonial towns was a danger zone where everyone was vulnerable to a surprise decapitation. In the face of random headhunter hostilities, a standard Spanish military response was to defend settlements and gain control of the territory through the construction of forts and the dispatch of expeditions.

Fortifying the Frontier

Missions and forts were the classic institutions of the Spanish colonial frontier.[61] Missionaries and soldiers—cross and sword—usually worked together toward the complementary goals of creating Christian converts and Spanish subjects. They used fixed settlements as the primary means to spread their notion of civilization. As discussed in chapter 1, missions slowly penetrated into the hinterland in the eighteenth century to establish a level of influence and control. As mentioned earlier in this chapter, the war plans of the 1690s envisioned forts as performing a similar function by pushing hostile communities into a corner. In principle, Spaniards in the archipelago conceived of space in terms of fixed settlements such as towns and forts. The unpredictable, mobile nature of headhunting raids ran counter to this conception. Aside from being at the forefront of the Spanish conquest of the frontier, forts had a vital role in separating colonial and independent spaces. Besides attacking hostile polities, soldiers had the task of preventing trade and communication between animist and Christian communities as a means of starving independent communities of supplies and forcing them to join colonial settlements. Ironically, the intermediate position of forts in the borderlands put soldiers in an ideal position to actually facilitate and profit from a lucrative upland-lowland trade. Fort soldiers were put in the awkward predicament of straddling the line between creating and blurring the boundaries of the frontier.

Although the different proposals to build forts in the borderlands in the 1690s were never carried out, garrisons would again become a major talking point in the 1730s. While forts had always been a tool in the Spanish colonial repertoire, they would acquire ever more prominence throughout the eighteenth century with the Spanish monarchy growing less and less fond of missions.[62] In early eighteenth-century Philippines, coastal and land attacks from European rivals and unsubjugated indigenes, respectively, required the placement of defensive forts in strategic but compromised areas.[63] Despite the lack of a cohesive defensive logic behind the organization of its Philippines forts, which would fail miserably during the British invasion of Manila in 1762, the Spanish government nevertheless paid meticulous attention to the defense of its territories and subjects, placing garrisons as a centerpiece of its operations.[64]

In the 1730s, local officials and priests recommended the use of force and forts to contain the headhunting raids from mountain Negritos. Despite the recent relative success of missions at the center of the island of Luzon, in the face of hostilities Spaniards had no qualms about resorting to violence. Like a déjà vu of the debates of the 1690s, they revived old arguments about whether to employ peaceful or violent means in subjugating belligerent independent polities. Sections of the provinces of Zambales and Pampanga that were near mountains were prone to Negrito attacks. The Recollect provincial vicar Benito de San Pablo threatened to pull out his five missionaries in Zambales if the government did not provide adequate military support because their lives were in grave danger.[65] In Pampanga, hostile Negritos inhabited the areas of Lubao, Porac, and Gapan. Particularly prone was the line running from Arayat to Magalang to Tarlac.[66] Travelers going from Manila to the provinces of Pangasinan and Ilocos had to pass by this dangerous stretch of road.

While the various religious and civil officials consulted presented a wide spectrum of proposals to deal with the problem from starving the Negritos out to enslaving them, the different religious orders consistently supported the idea of building forts and sending out military expeditions. The Recollect parish priest of Mabalacat, Pablo de San Agustín, had lost hope on the traditional missionary methods of showing affection and giving gifts to the Negritos because they did not produce the desired effect.[67] In their place, he wanted forts and punitive campaigns to remind Negritos that there were consequences to their actions.[68] He believed that "only the rigors of justice and not love" could contain these worst-case scenarios.[69] Similarly, three Dominicans endorsed a defensive, vindictive war because so far gentle, peaceful means had not succeeded.[70] In response to the dry-season headhunting raids of the Negritos, they wanted colonial soldiers to carry out two retaliatory expeditions each year to the mountains with at least 200 men, with each campaign lasting at least a month.[71] To protect travelers traversing the treacherous twelve leagues from Magalang in Pampanga to Puntalon in Pangasinan, the government should establish two forts along the road that would continuously attack the Negritos in their mountain habitat. The Recollects advocated for the construction of six strategically located forts because the establishment of towns in the Arayat-Magalang-Tarlac area failed to bring about the desired subjugation of Negrito communities.[72] It seemed like the supposed civilizational, calming influence of cities and missions had clear limits. In such cases, resorting to the more violent institutions of forts and expeditions was a standard Spanish response.

While the proposal of building forts in the 1730s might seem like a simple rehash of the old war plans of the 1690s, a crucial difference was the greater emphasis on the prohibition of trade and contact with independent upland communities. In 1691, the provincial governor of Cagayan broached the idea of using animist communities' Christian relatives as interpreters and intermediaries in the conquest of the borderland.[73] Except for the Dominican provincial Alonso Sandín, the other expert witnesses at the time did not entertain or even mention the possibility of economically isolating mountain communities.[74] By the 1730s, however, the idea of completely cutting off trade between upland animist and lowland Christian communities was much more prevalent in official discussions.

Perhaps Governor-General Cruzat's ordinances of 1696 heralded a gradual shift in government policy that only became more prominent in the succeeding decades. Ordinance 37 prohibited "natives of the towns from conducting any trade and commerce with pagans and runaways because this made the latter's pacification and subjugation impossible."[75] In 1705, the succeeding governor-general Domingo de Zalbáburu banned Chinese merchants from selling arms and other goods to animists in the hinterland of Pampanga and ordered them to relocate far away from the frontier.[76] Besides their negative cultural influence on catechumens and new converts, the Chinese allegedly strengthened the military capability of potentially hostile animist communities by selling them weapons.

In the war plans of the 1690s, forts performed an offensive military function in their conquest of a borderland and their elimination of refuge zones. In the 1730s, the proposed forts were more to defend colonial towns from the attacks of Negritos and other hostile groups. While the shift to a more defensive role had much to do with their location on the plains of Zambales and Pampanga rather than deep in the mountainous hinterland of Ituy and Paniqui, forts had a new task in maintaining the boundary between colonial and independent populations. Not only were forts supposed to conduct raids on antagonistic upland communities; they were also supposed to enforce the latter's complete isolation from the lowlands. Performing a sort of siege on the mountains had the intention of eventually forcing all their inhabitants down to join lowland Christian towns. The economic siege performed in Philippine borderlands ran counter to the late eighteenth-century Bourbon reforms in the Americas that placed greater emphasis on mutual trade as a tool in controlling frontier populations and further assimilating them to a colonial lifestyle.[77]

In a few instances, both animist towns and Spanish forts tried to maintain a boundary with outsiders. They both took advantage of the landscape to prevent intrusions onto their lands. Upland communities maintained their relative isolation through distance and rough terrain.[78] Rebels had the habit of occupying inaccessible forests and scrubland.[79] Runaways in Pampanga lived in a place called Marangley composed of "very wide and closed jungles, with several hills overrun by undergrowth and towering trees that sunlight can barely penetrate."[80] If their settlement's isolated location and nature's undergrowth were not enough, independent communities could always resort to more deliberate means to keep outsiders away. One common method was to litter pathways with spikes.[81] In 1787, a combined expeditionary force from Carig and Bayombong "encountered the paths filled with small spikes buried in the ground and other bigger ones positioned in trees."[82] The spikes might not have killed anyone, but they did slow down the progress of the invading troops by forcing them to stop to remove the embedded spikes in their feet.[83] When material obstacles did not do the job, some frontier communities resorted to actual physical attacks on intruders. Negritos in the Marangley were known to kill people for trespassing on the lands where they hunted, fished, and gathered firewood and wax.[84]

The status of the relationship between villagers and outsiders manifested itself in the state of the vegetation surrounding the town. If thick underbrush and spiked roads were a sign to keep out, cleared pathways were a welcoming embrace. Whenever Spanish missionaries were invited by the towns themselves, they were usually greeted by clean roads.[85] When Franciscan missionaries entered the town of Tabueyon in 1754, the town was "clean and spruced up, all the grass plucked out and the shrubs trimmed, so that they could not disturb their [the missionaries'] path and offend their sight."[86] While clean paths were signs of peace, untended grasslands posed a danger to visitors. Besides being a physical obstacle, dense thickets and tall grasses were a major security concern because raiders could potentially hide within them. The Dominican Vicente Salazar described the terrain of Paniqui in the following manner: "The valley, which is in this scrubland and . . . is composed of dense reeds, which can hide a man on horseback and are as thick as a finger. There are no open roads in all this country. They do not burn those reedbeds, but only enough to build their house and work their small fields. . . . With each one in their own hamlet, the expansive thicket prevents anyone from seeing very far. You can see a hamlet only when you are already there."[87] The situation in the valley of Paniqui might not have been representative of the whole frontier, but thick tall grasslands were common on the island. With reeds taller than a person on horseback, it was very easy for raiders to lurk within, shoot their arrows unseen, hit their targets, and escape without being noticed.[88]

Even in the nineteenth century, the same danger of traveling through grasslands persisted (figure 2.1). Igorot warriors took advantage of the tall cogon grass of the Caraballo Mountains to spring their attack: "Those mountains and also uncultivated plains are covered in very thick fields of cogon (a type of reed) that are tall enough to cover a person, and a great number of Igorots hide in them well stocked with cane arrows that they use. When somebody passes by inattentive or the escort happens to notice something, they [the Igorots] rise up with a horrifying cry, unleashing a rain of arrows to see if they can injure someone or get somebody to be left behind."[89] For Igorots, cogon grass was ideal not only for surprise attacks but also for a defensive escape:

FIGURE 2.1 José Honorato Lozano, "Pass at the Caraballo Sur Mountain on the Island of Luzon," 1847. A group traveling in the Caraballo Sur is heavily armed, while headhunting Igorots prepare an ambush hidden in the tall cogon grass. Imagen procedente de los fondos de la Biblioteca Nacional de España (image from the collections of the Biblioteca Nacional de España).

"It is not easy to discover them in advance because of the thickness of the cogon, nor is it easy to pursue them for the same reason."[90]

With the dangers posed by thick vegetation, Spanish forts adopted the opposite strategy of clearing their immediate surroundings of plant life to defend themselves from an attack. When Governor-General Fernando Manuel de Bustillo Bustamante planned to build a fort in the province of Sifun, his first advice was "Before anything else uproot the trees in all areas with the biggest possible circumference because in the surrounding forests and thickets enemy indios manage to ambush and harm us."[91] For Indigenous towns, the unrulier the vegetation, the better it was for defense. For Spanish forts, a clean terrain with a clear view of the surroundings was the best defensive strategy. Ideally, the fort should be in a spot where garrisoned soldiers could see the whole countryside.[92] In borderlands, either abundant vegetation or the lack of it could function as a barrier against intruders. While Indigenous settlements hid in the thickets, Spanish forts with their palisades were structures that stood out in the open.

With their double function as both an attacking front and a boundary line, forts were enmeshed in issues that were not purely military in nature. In order to enforce the separation between the mountains and the plains, garrisons had the tough task of halting all types of contact between these two areas, especially those related to trade. In the eyes of the Recollect Andrés de San Fulgencio, the main culprit for the lack of progress in the evangelization of pagan communities was precisely the "commerce, trade, and contact between Christians and pagans."[93] If soldiers in the proposed forts prevented mountain Negritos and Aetas from going down to the plains to hunt and get their provisions, then the upland communities would eventually be forced to settle permanently in the lowlands because they would not be able to survive otherwise.[94] The Dominican order came to a similar conclusion that trading only strengthened mountain polities because it supplied them with everyday goods that they desperately needed in the highlands, especially iron that they could turn into work implements and weapons.[95] For instance, iron axes were a useful tool for cutting trees in swidden gardens and boat building, but they could also be used as weapons.[96] Years later, the Franciscans were still worried how Ilongot trade with the mission towns of Pantabangan and Carranglan counterproductively armed hostile communities with weapons such as spears, swords, and arrows.[97] Although San Fulgencio's proposal did not exclude the possibility of directly attacking upland towns, it leaned toward a more holistic approach to the problem. Starving uplanders of their subsistence needs was an indirect but effective way of waging war against hostile groups.

Besides making life difficult for uplanders, enforcing a boundary line had an even more practical purpose. Upland traders and raiders were often one and the same people. In fact, trading turned them into better raiders. The Augustinian parish priest of Bacolor, Francisco Sensano, observed, "Experience has shown that when mountain Negritos communicate and trade with these natives [of the plains of Pampanga], it is as if they were never enemies. They enter their towns and go up their houses with a little wax, deer meat, and other mountain products that they sell. They trick them so that they are welcomed in their towns without realizing that with this falsehood they pass by the roads, entries, and exits of the towns. With [the towns'] minimal care and diligence in preventing dangers, they are able to commit their hostilities and end their invasions happily."[98] A distinction did not exist between good traders and evil raiders. The seemingly friendly traders of today were the bloodthirsty raiders of tomorrow. Sensano's description conforms to the standard portrayal of headhunters as dishonorable, duplicitous individuals. Not only did headhunters cowardly attack people in ambushes; they also targeted people from the communities they traded with. Occasional benign trading relations made colonial towns comfortable with the presence of animist hill people and caused them to unadvisedly let their guard down.

The Augustinian Jerónimo Sanz Ortiz arrived at the same conclusion as Sensano in describing the commercial exchange between Igorots and Christians in the provinces of Ilocos and Pangasinan: "Intending to sell their gold, they [Igorots] go down to the towns in pretend peace and measure every inch of the whole land. At little cost, they learn all the designs, movements, and opportunities to wreak destruction and robberies on those who maintain this contact with them. All trade and commerce with those Igorots naturally weaken them [the lowland towns]."[99] Igorots were effectively using their trading sojourns as opportunities to scout the layout of lowland colonial towns and the movement of their inhabitants. They learned where to best spring their surprise attacks when needed. Like the Negritos who discovered the ins and outs of Christian towns as they traded, Igorots also gained intimate knowledge about their potential targets and adversaries. With no apparent distinctions between traders and raiders, the safest option was to simply cut off all types of contact with animist uplanders. Standing guard between mountains and plains, garrisoned soldiers were ideally placed to enforce this separation.

An even worse scenario for fort soldiers trying to maintain a cordon sanitaire was the possibility that animist and Christian trading partners were colluding with one another. Ecological differences between the uplands and the lowlands meant they produced complementary products that were ideal for exchange.[100] While Christian towns on the plains supplied iron, tobacco, salt, clothes, wine, and other goods, upland communities provided wax, gold, and other mountain products.[101] As long as the two sides maintained a mutually beneficial commercial relationship, there was no point for uplanders to convert and leave behind their mountain habitat to relocate to the lowlands. In fact, such a move would be economically detrimental to both parties. Missionaries often suspected that Christian indios in the frontier had a vested interest in preventing the conversion of their animist trading partners (see chapter 1), hence their alleged attempts to spread rumors that Christian life brought with it only hardships in the form of excessive tribute and compulsory labor.[102] The same suspicions followed apostates who escaped to the mountains. Perhaps in some instances, more than a religious choice, apostasy was a strategy to cross the divide, become an intermediary, and make a profit from the lucrative hinterland commerce.

Besides the exchange of wax for iron and arms, information also changed hands between animist uplanders and Christian lowlanders when they traded. Representatives of the Dominican order claimed, "They [the natives] will not stop giving him [the Negrito trader] warnings about the plans and dispatches of military expeditions, so the Negritos will be able to escape to a safe place and nothing will be achieved."[103] Shared economic interests trumped whatever perceived differences existed between Christian indios and animist Negritos. Continued cooperation between the two groups undermined Spanish attempts to force mountain Negritos to relocate to the lowlands. It also blurred the line between allies and enemies that Spaniards tried to impose with much conviction.

In some cases, more intimate relationships than trade existed between mountain Negritos and Christian indios, and yet it still failed to bring about the desired goal of fully converting Negritos to the Christian way of life on the plains. More importantly, it made the imposition of any boundary line even more difficult. Besides his official duties as sergeant major and mayor of the town of Betis in Pampanga, Pablo Santiago was the unofficial "godfather" of a sixteen-year-old Negrito who would occasionally visit him.[104] Trying his best to attract the Negrito to the charms of colonial life, Santiago would give the Negrito everything that he needed. Nevertheless, the Negrito would always go back to the mountain and remained animist. In an ironic twist, Santiago claimed that instead of being grateful, the Negrito "godson" called upon his upland relatives and friends to hunt and kill his ostensible "godfather." Gifts and kinship somewhat brought the Kapampangan "godfather" and Negrito "godson" closer together, yet they were not enough to prevent murderous plans from being hatched. Santiago's version of events clearly perpetuates the image of the duplicitous, backstabbing Negrito. Even if his perceptions did not faithfully reflect the Negrito's motivations and intentions, they did attest to his confusion and uncertainty when dealing with uplanders. What seemed like steps in the right direction were actually leading to his demise. A tighter bond counterintuitively produced the opposite effect. Relationships were highly changeable, and boundary crossings quite normal. Bonds could be broken just as easily as they were formed in the fluid borderlands.

Santiago witnessed an even worse example of treachery, or perhaps just another instance of the lack of clear geographical and cultural borders in the frontier. Of the few Negritos and Aetas who had converted, the most promising ones eventually went back to the mountains.[105] As punishment, they were captured and sent to Manila and Cavite apparently as prisoners, but some managed to escape and return to the uplands. If the apostasy was not bad enough, the once exemplars of Christian conversion became the caudillos and guides of other Negritos in robbing and killing in the vicinity of colonial towns such as Guagua, Bacolor, and Mexico. Moving several times and adopting multiple identities, the Negritos relocated to colonial towns as Christian converts, then escaped to the mountains as apostates, and finally returned to the colonial towns as raiders. Although violent, this was a story of boundaries being constantly crossed. Negritos switched their identities from colonial Christianized subjects to hostile headhunters in an instant. At the crossroads of various societies, borderlands were the ideal setting for these boundary crossings.[106]

The twin goals of civilizing and converting indigenes entailed the transformation of people and the physical and cultural traversing of borders. However, such crossings opened up colonial towns to predations from hostile communities. The Spanish monarchy and the Catholic Church welcomed new subjects and converts with open arms, yet they had to balance this with security and safety concerns. Forts should have closed the door to all types of contact with independent animist communities, but the reality on the ground was far from the ideal espoused in military plans. Converts themselves were sometimes the problem as they traded with and aided their animist friends and as they themselves apostatized and became the enemy.

Porous Borders

If the law decreed a no-contact policy between independent animists and Christian indios, was it even possible to identify who was a colonial subject and who was not? Agustin de Vergara, the captain of two Zambal barrios, was stationed in a garrison at the edge of a forest in Pampanga.[107] A mountain Negrito arrived and introduced himself as a colonial subject from Mabalacat.[108] Given permission to enter by the garrisoned soldiers, he took with him a Christian india and Vergara's bull and brought them to the mountain. The victim of another Negrito treachery, Vergara mused, "There is more danger with those who pass themselves off as colonial subjects than the others because those are homegrown enemies while the others are known enemies."[109] Soldiers had to keep enemies out, but it was incumbent on them to make a quick decision on who was an enemy. Internal enemies were the big problem. Apostates, runaways, and others who had substantial dealings with Christian indios could imperceptibly cross boundary lines. The mountain Negrito pretended to be a Christian convert with no problem at all. The borderland was a gray area of changing allegiances and identities, and fort soldiers had the impossible task of sorting black from white.

In spite of all the difficulties, forts nonetheless tried their best to impose their particular sense of order on the frontier. In response to the blatant disregard of the trading ban with independent animists, proponents called on fort soldiers to punish recalcitrant merchants, including Christian ones.[110] Even Spanish provincial governors were deemed legally liable for not enforcing the law. To counteract the intimate ties between animist and Christian traders, the Franciscans recommended a discriminating selection process for the soldiers in the six forts that they proposed.[111] As much as possible, fort soldiers should have no "familiarity, contact, and dealings" with the mountain Negritos, so those previously stationed in Manila and its environs were thus the ideal candidates.[112] They were the antidote to the entanglements created by commerce and conversion in borderlands. In contrast to the missionary strategy discussed in chapter 1 where social bonds built through mutual visits were important factors in gaining access to the hinterland, forts fostered separation not only by trying to minimize contact but also by selecting soldiers who were aloof and above the daily realities of upland-lowland relations. Forts were both physical and social barriers to movement. They were the material structures that marked divisions in borderlands, but they were also the soldiers who stood in the way of animist-Christian interactions. If intermediaries facilitated movement and exploration in borderlands, garrisoned soldiers performed the opposite role as the antithesis of go-betweens.[113]

After a few years of consultation, in a seeming flashback to the final official position taken on the 1690s war plans, the Spanish monarchy's resolution on how to deal with Negrito raids took on a relatively dovish—yet still definitely violent—stance compared with the more hawkish voices. The Manila government in 1733 and the Spanish monarch in 1735 advocated for cutting off the commerce between animists and Christians and sending out occasional punitive military expeditions.[114] However, they both rejected the most extreme proposals of enslaving antagonistic animists and constructing the six forts. Like in previous situations, both moral and financial considerations tempered an overly aggressive approach to the problem. The Spanish monarchy often went for the cheap, conservative option. The final decision combined a variety of strategies: an offensive one with military campaigns, a defensive one with a cordon sanitaire, and a constructive one with the foundation of towns, farms, and ranches. It was the carrot-and-stick method with punishment and attraction working hand in hand.

Besides being financially expensive and logistically difficult to build and sustain, forts were not the bastions of propriety and order their most ardent supporters usually claimed.[115] Whether as a defensive or boundary line, they struggled to accomplish their stated goals. As defensive measures, forts and their particular way of conducting warfare were out of place in Philippine borderlands. In the midst of quick Indigenous raids, Spanish forts were too slow-footed and cumbersome. Despite the occasional glowing endorsement from missionaries, forts did not always provide a sufficient deterrent to attacks.[116]

Although an advocate of violent methods such as military campaigns, the Dominican Alonso Sandín was highly critical of the forts in the province of Cagayan.[117] He thought they were absolutely useless to the Spanish monarchy and the indios they were supposed to defend. For example, in the town of Tuao, "the enemies go down to cut heads in plain sight of the fort. When I was there in [16]89 they cut off one or two. (I do not remember the exact number.) What the corporal does is gather all the soldiers and lock themselves in the fort, claiming that his only duty is to guard and watch over the fort."[118] European forts in the colonies were not always built around villages, but sometimes only near them as places of refuge.[119] This seemed to have been the spatial arrangement of most forts in Cagayan's frontier based on illustrations and their small size.[120] However, at least in the case of Tuao, only soldiers had the luxury of hiding inside the fort during attacks. Worse than not having any desire to go after the headhunters, the soldiers valued their own safety first and left the townspeople to their own devices open to the risk of being decapitated. Primarily designed to defend and hold onto territory, forts were ill-equipped to handle Indigenous ambushes that had no desire whatsoever to occupy enemy land: "It [The Spanish fort] does not provide any defense to the town, as the enemy does not go after the town, nor steal from it, but rather goes after people to kill and decapitate without putting himself in danger of getting killed or injured."[121] Forts kept their soldiers safely ensconced inside but pretty much left everyone else open to headhunting raids.

Francisco de Olmedo, the Dominican missionary of Pata in Cagayan, had a similar experience: "If the enemy comes to infest the garrisoned towns, they [the corporals] ignore it, or if they go after them, after half a league of pursuit, they become tired and return very happy, saying that the enemy already fled."[122] Fort soldiers had the same attitude whenever a fire broke out in the town they were meant to protect. They would simply hole up inside their garrison instead of helping to put out the fire. Perplexed after having witnessed this inaction several times, Olmedo asked them why they did not do anything, to which they replied, "They guard their fort because they are afraid there might be enemies."[123] In effect, these were not random fires, but possibly deliberate attempts by the enemy to burn down the town, and yet the soldiers did absolutely nothing.

Apparently, the blasé attitude from the garrisoned soldiers emboldened hostile indios to come to fortified towns and commit assaults by setting fire to houses and throwing lances into the fort. In Capinatan and Fotol, raiders successfully killed a Spanish and an indio soldier, respectively, by hurling spears into the forts in broad daylight.[124] The garrisoned soldiers were like sitting ducks cooped inside their fort, and they were just as vulnerable as the people they were called on to defend. Ironically, forts were attracting direct attacks from enemies, which was slightly unusual given the prevalence in Indigenous raids of random attacks on unsuspecting individuals in isolated places. Sandín observed that headhunters found garrisoned towns to be easier targets "because they [the enemies] know that although they are heard, they have plenty of time and space to escape and flee. Forts serve no other purpose than as an impediment and hindrance."[125] Instead of actually protecting Christian converts, forts seemed to have been making the situation worse.

As a barrier enforcing an upland-lowland, animist-Christian divide, forts left much to be desired in spite of the outsider origins of most of their soldiers. In 1672, out of a total of 223 officers and soldiers, only fifty-one soldiers or 23 percent were indigenes in the forts of Cagayan.[126] Being Spaniards and theoretically impervious to local politics, the vast majority of the troops should have been ideally placed to implement a blockade in borderlands. The generic label "Spaniard" masked their diverse origins of Spain, Mexico, and possibly the Philippines. Their exact breakdown based on their country of origin is not known, but Mexico had the obligation to always send soldiers to the Philippines in the galleon ships, and they were mostly Mexican-born Spaniards.[127] Spaniards had a predominant presence in forts for two reasons: one was to balance the mixed composition of the troops and ensure their loyalty, and the other was to help spread Spanish cultural influence across the archipelago.[128]

Despite having a significant number of garrisoned Spaniards, forts in Cagayan's frontier recruited soldiers of various backgrounds. The fort soldiers in Burubur were composed of eight Spaniards, ten Merdicas, twelve harquebusiers from Manila, ten Kapampangans, and twelve Pangasinenses.[129] For a proposed fort in Sifun, the recommended composition was twenty-five Spaniards, twelve Merdicas, and twenty Kapampangans.[130] At least in these two forts, the ethnicity of the soldiers was spread out almost equally among different groups, and no local warriors from Burubur or Sifun seemed to have participated. As outsiders, soldiers supposedly embodied an impartiality in implementing order and division in the borderlands.

Proposals to hire nonpartisan soldiers who were not embedded in hinterland trade and relations most likely reflected the stark reality on the ground where the provincial governor and garrisoned soldiers had vested economic interests in breaching the divide. Contrary to their official image as impregnable neutral barriers, forts were very much enmeshed in local wheelings and dealings. In some cases, Christian indio merchants traded on behalf of Spanish officials, but in other cases, Spaniards did the trading themselves.[131] While performing their duties as encomenderos, some indios maintained economic ties with uplanders. Responsible for collecting the tribute and providing religious instruction, they took advantage of their position and engaged in trade. The Dominican provincial prior Bartolomé Marrón noticed how some prioritized tribute and trade over proper religious instruction and the relocation of mountain Negritos to mission towns.[132] They seemed more interested in keeping their Negrito proselytes up in the mountains living like pagans and apostates because it gave them access to valuable mountain products. In Pangasinan, an indio encomendero reneged on his official Christian duties when he showed no inclination to bring his Negrito tribute payers to town whether to live there permanently or to drop by for a quick confession.[133] In fact, the Negritos carried out their yearly headhunting raids in the lowlands without any protest from the encomendero as long as he received their tribute payment and kept part of it for himself. If indio encomenderos were deeply enmeshed in hinterland commerce, Spanish officers from provincial governors to fort soldiers were no different. In many ways, they merely copied the Indigenous middlemen who sustained the lucrative trade between the mountains and the plains.

More than any Spanish official, provincial governors exerted the most imposing presence in the countryside as the highest-ranking Spanish authority there.[134] Hence, they also had the greatest opportunity to abuse their position and flout the law that prohibited trade with independent upland communities. Like other garrisons in the Indies, forts in Cagayan effectively operated as if they were trading posts or customs houses.[135] The provincial governor usually arrived at his post loaded with merchandise such as clothes and iron to sell.[136] He consigned his goods to trusted soldiers who traded them throughout the province. Through these soldiers and Christian indios, the wares eventually reached the animists and apostates of the mountains.[137] Under the pretext of going to the provincial capital in Lal-lo to pick up supplies, indios would bring down the mountain products they had amassed for the provincial governor. In Tuao, twenty to forty indios went to the mountain every month to sell the provincial governor's goods.[138] During the week they were there, they also hunted carabao meat, which they unfortunately could not bring back with them because the corporals of the fort requisitioned it, making a healthy profit from selling it themselves. Wild game meat from the hinterland had a ready market in Manila, so vessels regularly traveled from Lal-lo to Manila carrying the product.[139]

The Dominican Sandín partly blamed provincial governors for the poverty of Cagayan.[140] In Sandín's mind, Spaniards taking money from the province and spending it somewhere else like Manila made Cagayan poorer. Like other Spaniards assigned in the province, provincial governors bought goods cheaply in Manila only to sell them at a marked-up price in Cagayan. Effectively, the money they generated from upland trading ended up in Manila with hardly any of it remaining in the remote province for its own development. Like indio encomenderos who turned a blind eye to animist atrocities, provincial governors adopted the same attitude in the name of personal profit. When the Spanish judge Ignacio de Arzadun visited Cagayan in 1743, he noticed how the provincial governor used prisoners and other natives to trade with animists and apostates.[141] With his priorities focused on making money, the provincial governor made no effort to relocate uplanders to mission towns or bring to justice the murderers of the Christian merchants who had gone to the mountains to trade. If the profits went to the provincial governor, the burden and labor primarily rested on the shoulders of indios. When he needed vessels to transport his merchandise to Ilocos or Manila, Christian indios had to source the wood and construct the boats themselves.[142] Without any saws and with only axes at their disposal, they expended an inordinate amount of labor and resources, hacking away at humongous tree trunks.

Although provincial governors wielded a significant amount of power, they mostly stayed in the provincial capital away from the daily grind in the hinterland. In contrast, soldiers stationed in frontier forts not only had greater contact with local inhabitants but also exercised a substantial degree of autonomy in the absence of direct supervision from higher authorities. Left to their own devices in the hinterland, corporals of the forts acted like "absolute lords."[143] They were "treated with great ostentation as if they were provincial governors not only in the town where the fort is located, but throughout the whole province."[144] Like provincial governors ordering their subordinates around, garrisoned corporals demanded whatever they wanted from the townspeople. Indios had to hunt meat, pound rice, and fetch water and firewood for them. If fort soldiers were like provincial governors of the frontier, indios were "nothing more than the slaves of the corporal and the fort."[145]

Spaniards assigned in remote forts were not necessarily the best speci-
mens of the upright soldier.[146] Although officially composed of voluntary re-
cruits and convicts, almost all of the soldiers from Mexico were really forced
migrants to the archipelago and belonged to the Spanish urban underclass
of Mexico City and Puebla.[147] These convicts exiled to the Philippines were
mostly thieves and social pariahs.[148] They were predominantly career pick-
pockets, rustlers, and highway robbers, or indolent sons involved in shady
activities disowned by their parents. While the majority of soldiers from
Mexico joined the king's fixed regiment in Manila, the rest were assigned to
various garrisons across the archipelago.[149] The worst criminals were often
sent to the most unpleasant assignments outside Manila, rowing galleys and
manning remote forts. In fact, the most troublesome soldiers in Lal-lo were
reassigned to even more isolated frontier forts where out of sight they
were ostensibly less of a problem.[150] If Spanish soldiers in the Philippines were
mostly social miscreants from New Spain, the worst of the worst ended up in
the hinterland forts of Cagayan.

Whether in Mexican cities or Philippine garrisons, convict-soldiers maintained their reputation as troublemakers. Instead of ensuring peace and order
in the colonies or reforming their life of vice and crime, some of them took
advantage of the situation and tried to profit from it. Several did not even
serve a single day in the military and just became the servants of Spanish residents and friars in the Philippines.[151] At least in the case of Cagayan forts, the
soldiers simultaneously performed their military duties and became the retainers of the provincial governor. They became part of the provincial governor's patronage network as they bought and sold goods on his behalf. With so
much freedom of action, garrisoned soldiers could easily abuse their position; hence, fort-towns often found themselves overburdened by excessive
demands. Some fort soldiers were even worse than provincial governors as
they drove indios working for them as unpaid servants and porters into the
ground.[152] Not known for their moral integrity, they resorted to beating up
indios who complained.[153]

With so much trading being carried out by Spanish officers themselves,
forts failed to erect an economic barrier between the mountains and the
plains. While garrisoned soldiers were militarily conservative as they hid inside their fort during attacks from upland raiders, they were economically aggressive as they sustained a thriving upland-lowland trade. However, while
forts put provincial governors and soldiers in an advantageous position to
trade with mountain polities, they also marginalized others from taking part
in the same trade. One person's trading outpost was another person's trading

barrier. Forts erected a semiporous, selective barrier. When Spanish judge Abella conducted his inspection tour of Pampanga in 1692, the towns of Candaba, San Miguel, Gapan, Aunas, Pasinan, Santor, and Bongabon all complained to him about the demeanor of the corporals stationed at the nearby fort in Arayat.[154] Apparently, the fort prevented them from freely trading the goods that they raised on their fields and collected from the mountains. Whenever they would travel by Arayat, fort soldiers would block their passage, closing off both land and river routes. Even worse, the soldiers would sometimes sequester their merchandise at a bargain price. Abella agreed with their complaint and issued an ordinance confirming locals' right to freedom of trade. Fort soldiers selectively enforced trade prohibitions for their own benefit.

From indio intermediaries and encomenderos to Spanish provincial governors and soldiers, everybody had a stake in trading with upland communities. Each group tried to gain an advantage over the others. The banning of Chinese merchants in the missions might not have been solely for their bad influence on new converts and their provision of arms to borderland communities. It might have also been a ploy to eliminate one more competitor in the upland-lowland trade. Even the missionary method of giving gifts of clothes and cows to new converts and mountain animists must be seen in the context of the exchange economy, as native intermediaries sometimes felt threatened by the flow of free goods coming from the missions. With sometimes competing and at other times coinciding interests, the various borderland actors jostled for position favoring trade and contact at some points and pushing for violence and isolation at others.

Although a lot of the criticism of forts came from the religious orders, it was not a simple, straightforward manifestation of the perennial power struggle between church and state. The secular powers were not consistent in their support of forts and trade prohibitions. In the 1690s, while Judge Abella issued several provincial ordinances enshrining people's right to trade with whomever they wanted, Governor-General Cruzat published a general ordinance prohibiting commerce with upland animists and at the same time rejected the plans to construct more forts in the borderland. The Dominicans Sandín and Marrón were highly critical of forts and their detrimental effect on towns, but a few years later Dominicans would establish a fort in Burubur to protect their incipient mission. In the consultations on how to deal with Negrito attacks in the early 1730s, an overwhelming majority of local officials and parish priests were keen on using force and violence, particularly the Recollects who advocated for a six-fort defensive line.

At least during the consultations on the 1690s war plans and the 1730s Negrito raids, the Spanish monarchy opted not to build forts but rather supported the establishment of missions and the prohibition of trade with independent communities. Despite its occasional misgivings, the government was not against the principle of forts and constructed several of them throughout the eighteenth century. By 1753, there were forts in Lal-lo, Capinatan, Cabicungan, and Playa Honda in the provinces of Cagayan and Pangasinan.[155] In the borderland between Cagayan and Pampanga, forts appeared in Ajanas in 1746, Bagabag in 1752, and Carig in 1773.[156]

With the debatable military value of forts, Spaniards noticed that there were more effective ways of dealing with headhunting raids such as constant vigilance and instantaneous reciprocal attacks. In 1686, Bishop Ginés Barrientos noticed that the town of Malaueg, deeply nestled in the interior surrounded by enemies, never experienced any attacks despite the absence of a Spanish fort and soldiers to defend it.[157] The residents had a system of lookout posts and sentinels that dissuaded any type of encroachment, including the rain of lances that befell forts. Compared with expensive, imposing forts and palisades, vigilance seemed to have done a better job in preventing unwanted movements like sneak attacks. Even without the organized system of Malaueg, standard Indigenous reactions to raids also drew praises from Barrientos and Sandín. Instead of cowering in fear, residents of fort-less towns simply went after their attackers.[158] Once invading headhunters achieved their goal of cutting a head, they ran in retreat to avoid getting caught by town residents, who were always armed and poised to retaliate immediately.[159] While in pursuit, the first responders shouted along the way so that others farther behind would know where they were, follow their path, and provide the necessary backup. Since local residents knew the terrain better than the raiders, they often caught up with the attackers and succeeded in chopping a few heads themselves in a clear case of violent reciprocal mobilities. Perhaps small victories like these provided inspiration for Spaniards to rely more on military expeditions than forts and recruit indio soldiers experienced in this style of warfare.

Indio and Spanish combatants used whatever military strategy was available as long as it worked. As forts failed to keep headhunters out and halt upland-lowland commerce, Spaniards and Christian indios aligned under the banner of the Spanish monarch got entangled in vicious cycles of violent exchange with mountain communities. Their styles of warfare adapted to the circumstances and to each other. The encroachment of missions farther into the hinterland in the eighteenth century induced more targeted attacks from threatened Indigenous communities. Instead of relying completely on Spanish soldiers and forts, local Spanish officials coordinated with their Indigenous allies who carried out the bulk of the military operations. The mixing of fighting styles partly stemmed from the intermingling of people as apostates joined hostile uplanders and as Christian indios and Spanish soldiers fought together in military expeditions. Locked in a vicious cycle of mutual attacks, each side borrowed and adapted tactics from one another from Christian troops beheading their enemies to mountain communities using Spanish muskets and targeting sacred Christian images. Besides the adoption and subversion of military techniques, emotions played a deliberate part in arousing retaliatory headhunting raids and inflicting suffering among the victims of attacks and plunder.

Cycles of Violence

Headhunting in Southeast Asia has generated a couple of debates regarding the nature of warfare in the region. First, the abundance of land and the scarcity of people meant that warfare in the region generally avoided the act of killing because gaining captives was more important than occupying land.[160] However, the existence of headhunting practices in certain societies, among other factors, belies this point.[161] If people were such a scarce resource, then why did some communities still practice headhunting? A possible solution to this puzzle leads to the second point of contention, whether headhunting was actually a way of conducting warfare. Unlike historians, anthropologists are more likely to view headhunting as a form of ritual than of warfare; hence, they are able to sidestep the issue altogether, since headhunting operated on a completely different symbolic plane from ordinary combat.[162] However, even taking into account its ritual and sacred aspects, headhunting was nevertheless sometimes an integral part of Indigenous warfare. While sporadic Negritos raids could easily fit in the anthropologist's interpretation of headhunting as ritual, more overt cases existed where warring communities attacked each other's village, fought face-to-face, and beheaded their opponents. Less reliance on generalizations and an acknowledgment of local varieties of warring and headhunting practices are possible solutions to both conundrums.[163] Having a close look at specific cases and comparing them opens the window to spotting variations across time and in different circumstances.

Headhunting seemed to have adapted to immediate spatial and political contexts. In the reports on early eighteenth-century Negrito and apostate raids on the plains of Zambales and Pampanga, headhunting was composed of isolated ambushes on individuals as they traveled or worked in remote areas. The various reports consistently stated that the settlements themselves were not the target. Headhunters wanted to avoid detection and confrontation, so they veered away from towns. The situation was different in the borderland between Cagayan and Pampanga, where hostile groups directly targeted mission towns and their inhabitants. They were bold enough to attack fort-towns despite the presence of armed soldiers. Although the elements of stealth and surprise were still present, headhunting raids in this borderland were more direct and aggressive than on the plains of central Luzon.

Rather than attributing the difference to the ethnicity of the headhunters, say, Negritos being less violent than Ilongots, it seems more appropriate to see the difference as a result of varying circumstances.[164] On one hand, the Negritos' mountain settlements were never under sustained direct attack from colonial towns on the plains. Vast stretches of road that led to Pangasinan and Ilocos were uninhabited and thus unprotected, making travelers vulnerable to predation. At the same time, nearby colonial settlements offered an opportunity to Negritos to execute their annual headhunt. On the other hand, the borderland between Cagayan and Pampanga was a relatively tight, confined space. Mountain and upriver settlements were under threat from the constant encroachment of mission towns since the start of the eighteenth century. Even though the pincer maneuver of the 1690s war plans was not approved, the Augustinians and the Dominicans effectively carried out its ecclesiastical version in the succeeding decades by moving in on the borderland from either side. Although their evangelization was often peaceful, they nevertheless presented a political threat to animist communities. In the words of the missionary Antolín Alzaga, a subjugated Ituy was a "fort against the pagans."[165] Missions had the same effect as forts as they edged out animist communities on their home turf. Threatened by the unwelcome incursion, the remaining independent animists retaliated by going after mission towns. While no reports mention the burning of houses and fields in Negrito raids, these assaults were the norm in the borderlands of Ituy and Paniqui. A more imminent threat required more drastic measures.

With the Ituy and Paniqui frontier's independence from Spanish rule being eroded by expanding missions, alliances among the different polities shifted and buckled with the emergence of colonial Christian communities, a topic discussed in greater detail in chapter 3. Christianity altered the political relations in the area. The new religion created a new, or at least an additional, identity and solidarity among converts. Previously subservient to Ilongots, Isinays became more assertive after their conversion because "with the fraternity that they gained in baptism, many of them will soon join together in defense and offense."[166] In a place where kinship was the foundation of group identity and allegiances, converts became part of a wider alliance of Christian indios and Spaniards. Membership in the new religion was potentially the equivalent of belonging to a new kin group or "ethnicity" that threatened the status quo in the borderland.[167] Ilongots declared war against Christian Isinays "because the conquest had arrived at their doorstep."[168] A paramount power in the area, Ilongots now felt besieged by the apparent alliance among Christians.

The situation was completely different earlier in 1703 when Ilongots and Isinays had concluded a pact that "they would not become Christians nor permit priests in their towns, and that they should burn all the churches . . . built on the lands of Ituy."[169] The crux of the matter had been the recent intrusion of Christians in the borderland, particularly the foundation of a new mission town in Burubur. Besides putting a stop to further encroachment from the missions, the old Ilongot-Isinay alliance had threatened to "burn down even the towns of Carranglan and Pantabangan, which are old towns of the province of Pampanga . . . because the chiefs of those two towns helped the Father missionaries enter the mission of Ituy."[170] If the Christian chiefs of Kampampangan towns had previously been the target of Ilongot ire for aiding missionaries, the newly converted Isinays of Ituy were now in the crosshairs of Ilongot hostility for their apparent betrayal.

In previous centuries, Ilongot settlements had had a sufficient buffer zone with the Christian towns of Pampanga, so the Ilongots had not attacked the towns directly. However, the eighteenth century saw the expansion of mission towns, and their closer presence became an unbearable menace to Ilongots, who felt compelled to retaliate by hunting heads and burning towns. When their previous Isinay allies eventually converted to Christianity, their situation became more dire. A line had been crossed. Random headhunting raids in isolated places would not have had the same effect. Ritual and warfare were not mutually exclusive, but in some instances like the overt Ilongot-Isinay, animist-Christian conflicts, the combative aspects of headhunting were much more prominent.

Certain characteristics of headhunting were conducive to warfare. Although it usually had an air of randomness in its choice of victims, headhunting could also be very deliberate and vindictive. When a community that suffered a beheading retaliated against the perpetrators' community, it could unleash a potentially never-ending run of mutual killings.[171] Headhunters were not too particular on cutting the head off the actual perpetrators; getting the head of somebody from the perpetrators' community was often enough. With a specific community in their sights, raiders could be very measured on how they launched their assault. One method they used was to sneak into the target community before sunrise.[172] Before entering the village, they would throw a few roots and herbs in a pool by a river and perform their spells and rituals. Apparently, the concoction would produce a strong wind and agitate the water, so that the ensuing noise would cover their entrance. Another method was to simply pretend friendship with the enemy and ask to stay over in his house for the night.[173] When the host was fast asleep, it was the perfect time to cut off his head. When headhunting took place inside the victim's own house, the act became more calculated and pinpoint accurate, precisely the characteristics one would expect in warfare.

The taking of heads was a form of violent exchange that elicited rage and ensured further attacks. Besides the skulls that decorated the headhunter's house, the victim's teeth also adorned the handle of the headhunter's cutlass.[174] When the victim's kin saw their relative's teeth displayed on the enemy's weapon, it only enraged them more and pushed them to seek vengeance like "rabid dogs."[175] A group of Aeta chiefs whom a Franciscan missionary was trying to convert gave the following justification after listening to a sermon on the evils of headhunting: "The thing is, we did not want to kill anyone. However, when we see our enemy, we cannot control our emotions, so it is best if we don't ever see him."[176] An uncontrollable visceral reaction prompted the urge to hunt heads. On the reverse side, not being able to avenge the death of a kin was a grave source of embarrassment.[177]

While the portrayal of emotional headhunters might lend itself to the stereotypical trope of the savage native with an uncontrollable urge to kill in complete opposition to the rational, self-composed European colonizer, a couple of late twentieth-century anthropologists observed the vital role feelings played in headhunting.[178] While strong emotions accompanied the whole headhunting process from the desire to kill to the celebration afterward, an emphasis on the historical and cultural context of the emotions involved prevents the reduction of headhunting to an innate barbarity or intertribal animosity of Indigenous peoples. For instance, the Recollects suggested sending Italons in military raids against the Zambals because of their "special aversion" toward the latter.[179] However, rather than attributing the aversion to the Italons' savagery or tribalism, it may be better to view it as a possible retaliation to previous headhunting raids or as a showcase of the growing alliance between Italons and Spaniards as a result of the former's recent conversion. Headhunters felt deep emotions, but the urge to take a head was rooted in the specific situation that they found themselves in.

As one community raided another community, they were effectively performing an exchange.[180] Instead of voluntarily trading goods for each other's mutual benefit, they forcibly took heads from one another to the other's detriment.[181] The head held a special meaning for communities, so much so that burying a headless cadaver was an omen of misfortune.[182] At the news of someone's death, the first thing they worried about was the head: "What does it say that they quickly ask about the head by chance? They do not mention the tragedy, say, that an alligator ate someone, that Negritos killed a traveler. Later the person who heard the news asks without much care, 'And the head?' It appeared!"[183] The head was so important that whole communities searched for it whenever it was missing. Even Christian indios were not interested in a headless corpse, which they deemed unworthy of Masses or a proper funeral, so they would simply wrap it in a mat and disposed of it in front of the church for the priest to take care of.[184] In the case of very important persons, communities seemed to exert an extra effort to regain the head. Zambals cut off the head of the Dominican Antonio Pérez when he served as the chaplain of a woodcutting expedition in the forests of Mexico, Pampanga.[185] Christian communities decided to retrieve his head, launching a military expedition to the mountains of Playa Honda, where they successfully recovered it.

In field battles, combatants tried their best to keep the bodies of their deceased comrades away from enemy hands. As an Ipituy warrior fell from the musket fire of Christian indios and Spanish soldiers, another Ipituy took his place in the vanguard and swiftly moved the dead body to the back, so the enemy could not take its head.[186] Although part of a violent exchange, decapitated heads were nevertheless highly esteemed objects that traveled reciprocally from one community to another.

Both indigenes and Spaniards practiced styles of warfare typically associated with the other side. While in some cases it was down to coincidence, in others there was clear evidence of exchange. Historical studies used to emphasize the crucial role of guns in the Spanish conquest of the New World.[187] Whatever the validity of these claims, it did not take long for indios to learn how to use Spanish weapons. Runaways and apostates were some of the main conduits that brought guns to borderlands.[188] Of course, the possession of guns was useless without access to gunpowder. With porous economic borders despite trading prohibitions, apostates in borderlands managed to source gunpowder in Pampanga and Pangasinan, and they used Spanish weapons against Spanish-backed expeditions.[189] To fight fire with fire, provincial governors and missionaries supplied Christian indios with guns. In the spirit of self-defense, the Augustinian José González requested firearms from his provincial because his mission was surrounded by hostile settlements.[190] He wanted to arm his converts because firearms were supposedly the only thing that pagans feared. He even cited the precedent of the Dominicans who supplied weapons to their Cagayan missions. Besides self-defense, indio soldiers also needed Spanish weapons when they launched their military campaigns.[191]

When dealing with particularly bellicose animist communities, missionaries and converts alike recognized the efficacy of armed expeditions.[192] Whenever hostile groups succeeded in their raids, they became more defiant and less amenable to conversion.[193] In the 1740s, when the Isinay converts of Dupax asked for reinforcements from the visiting judge Arzadun against the intensifying assaults from animist Panoypoys, the government sent out a ragtag group of Pangasinenses who did not know how to use firearms and had no battle experience against hostile uplanders.[194] Incompetent and unprepared, the Pangasinense troops lost and only emboldened the recalcitrant Panoypoys even more.

In 1745, the Spanish government organized another military expedition against the Panoypoys, but this time composed of experienced warriors from Cagayan and the missions.[195] Christian indios and Spaniards believed that only a crushing victory could strike fear and terror in the heart of the enemy. More astute than the previous troops, they deployed various tricks from stealth to blanks to catch the enemy off guard. The expeditionary force tried to sneak upon the main town of the Panoypoys by avoiding conventional paths and trudging through thickets; however, several Panoypoys happened to notice the recent tracks left by the Christian troops.[196] Prepared for the incoming assault, the Panoypoys held their ground in their walled town at the top of a mountain, where they had a distinct tactical advantage. They had piles of big boulders, spears, and pines that they could throw down at anybody who attempted the narrow ascent.

Guns, however, were novel items for some Indigenous peoples and could thus create fear and confusion. Igorots, for instance, showed "horror and fear of bullets and gunpowder."[197] When Spaniards and Christian indios attacked the Panoypoys, they creatively used guns to overcome their compromised position and unleash the most havoc possible. Experienced in fighting against uplanders, Lorenzo Dipagang, the sergeant major of the mission of Paniqui, had the brilliant idea of shooting at the Panoypoys without bullets first because he wanted to lull them into a false sense of security by letting them believe that guns were nothing to be afraid of.[198] As the Panoypoys grew bolder and left their commanding position, it gave the Christian troops the perfect opportunity to surprise their opponents and finally shoot them with loaded rifles. Dipagang, an indio, had not only learned how to use Spanish weapons but also developed an innovative use for them in the specific context of borderland warfare.

But non-Christian indios were just as innovative and learned how to deal with the Christians' novel weapons. In 1703, when the Dominican provincial Francisco Jiménez arrived in Burubur with armed guards, two Isinays from nearby hostile towns put up a friendly façade and welcomed the provincial.[199] However, they secretly put water in the provincial's guns to immobilize them for the planned attack the next morning. Even in cases where indios rejected Christianity and did not use Spanish guns, they were wily enough to counteract the advantages of new foreign weapons.

While indios had no problems adapting to elements of Spanish warfare, they also stuck with Indigenous methods of fighting. For Spaniards, nothing stood out more as the antithesis of their style of warfare than headhunting. They consistently condemned the headhunting raids carried out by mountain polities as utterly barbaric and lamented its continued practice among new converts.[200] Despite the blanket denunciation of headhunting, they seemed to allow it when performed by Christian troops against enemies in battle. While the vast majority of Spanish sources do not mention their side resorting to headhunting, a few surprisingly do.[201]

In 1750, the Dominican Vicente Salazar narrated how a military expedition against the Panoypoys involved headhunting.[202] "Experienced in such undertakings," Agustín de la Puerta, a Spanish corporal major at the fort in Lal-lo, was named the commander of the expedition.[203] During their march, the regiment under Puerta encountered ten Panoypoys by a river making salt. Waiting for the right moment, later that night they tried to sneak on the unsuspecting Panoypoys, whose dogs, however, started to bark loudly, which woke up their masters.[204] Startled, the Panoypoys tried to escape, but Puerta's men were able to spear six or seven of them, while the rest escaped unscathed. Out of the people that they hit, they were able to behead two of them. Without knowing his ancestry, we could have easily mistaken Puerta for a native based solely on the way that he conducted warfare. The stealth, the lances, and the headhunting were all ingredients of Indigenous warfare. Salazar described the headhunting carried out by the missions in a very matter-of-fact way with no hint of condemnation. He even praised Puerta for conducting a previous campaign against the Ipituys "with such brilliance."[205] Spanish sources often talked about a particular style of fighting in the border-lands: "the savages' system of war demands a special discipline and tactic."[206] Soldiers who did not know how to deal with it were bound to lose, and it seemed like headhunting was a normal—though often unacknowledged— part of borderland warfare whether one was an animist uplander, a Christian indio, or a Spanish corporal major. All was fair in love and war, even a few chopped heads.

With animists, apostates, and Christians all headhunting and using guns to varying degrees, contacts and exchanges led to a certain level of commonality and understanding.[207] When hostile uplanders wanted to manifest their dis-dain for Spanish, particularly missionary, presence in the borderlands, they deliberately targeted mission churches because they understood the struc-tures' value for Christians. A better understanding of the opponent made them better warriors.

The images of saints played a similarly coveted role in warfare, as they were equally beloved by Christian converts and scorned by hostile animists. For converts, saints were like ancestor spirits, their images like animist wood carvings.[208] Missionaries gave and confiscated images from catechumens and converts to sway them to do their bidding. In 1755, before agreeing to becom-ing Christians, Tinguians asked the Augustinian provincial Manuel Carrillo who would be their town's designated patron saint.[209] Carrillo promised to send them an image of the Santo Niño especially made in Manila. When the converts refused to follow the missionaries' orders, the latter threatened to take away this prized image. In 1741, the converts of Limanab did not want to relocate to Duliao as requested, so the missionary seized their saints until they acquiesced.[210] They were so forlorn that they went to the mission-ary to retrieve their images, but to no avail. In 1743, the missionary Juan Ormaza used the same strategy to convince the town of Diangan to resettle in Mayon.[211] Seeing the reluctance of the people of Diangan to move, he said, "What are the [images of the] saints doing here? These do not enter the town, neither do they want to. If the pagans burn them, it will be a loss. It would be better to bring them to Mayon."[212] Despite their very real concern of being exposed to Ibalibon attacks in Mayon, the people of Diangan finally relented and followed their saints to the new town.

Since the images of saints were so important to Christian priests and in-dios, an effective way for belligerent animists to express their hatred toward Christians was to attack these very same images. For instance, the Ipituys stole sacred images from mission towns and broke them into pieces, which they sent to their allies.[213] This affront was not only sacrilegious for the priests but also devastating for the converts who treasured these statues. Even worse, the chief of the Ipituys hung the broken pieces of Christian images on the door of his house, dangling like trophies from a headhunting raid.[214] Unlike the burning of houses, churches, and fields, which led to the vital material loss of shelter and subsistence, the destruction of images was predominantly symbolic, but it thrust a dagger right in the heart of what Christians held dear. Despite all the violence and hate, mutual brutality still demonstrated at the very least a modicum of cross-cultural exchange, emotional understanding, and reciprocity. In the face of their seeming proclivity toward escalating warfare, the various borderland actors still had alternatives like gift-giving and peace pacts to negotiate their way out of a spiraling violence.

Breaking the Cycle

The vicious cycle of violence in some ways entangled the various actors closer together. Headhunting encapsulated the almost inescapable vortex of nonstop killings. Among headhunters, a death in a community had to be repaid by a death in another. The practice had a self-reinforcing momentum as the victim's kin became enraged as they saw their loved one's skull and teeth displayed in the headhunter's house and weapons. While recovering the victim's head was sometimes a possibility, simply taking somebody else's head seemed like the easier option. The mutual violence forced warring communities apart as they avoided each other, but also brought them closer together as they brutally exchanged heads. Even in the case of hostile animists who wanted to push Christians priests and indios away from their lands, commerce—both economic and cultural—still continued. Decapitated heads traveled from one community to another with Spanish soldiers even taking part in the exchange. Animists plundered the images of saints not only to insult the enemy but also to acquire trophies to proudly display their prowess. The different borderland actors adopted different styles of warfare as they interacted with one another.

A narrow focus on headhunting in warfare heightens the paradox of murder in a people-scarce area, but adopting a wider perspective on why different polities attacked each other brings back the prime importance of gaining people rather than killing them in warfare. At its core, what drove both Spaniards and indios to raid whoever their opponent was, was the loss of people. The flight of people from the lowlands to the uplands or vice versa was a greater loss of population and power for colonial and independent polities, respectively, than the occasional deaths from wars. Although casualties were somewhat inevitable in warfare, the main priority of Spaniards and indios was to regain control and influence over people. In the early 1690s, when the Dominicans sent their petitions requesting the conquest and conversion of the borderland communities between Cagayan and Pampanga, one of their primary concerns was recovering the vast number of apostates who had fled there rather than gaining fresh new converts.[215] The mass migration of apostates had desolated the colonial towns of Cagayan: "Apostatized Christian indios are plenty in the mountains. From the province of Cagayan, so many have fled that Christian towns seem deserted."[216] While royal decrees restricted the use of force on non-Christians who could not be attacked unless in self-defense, bringing apostates back to the Christian fold was one of the conditions of just war, so apostates were subject to the use of violence.[217]

Apostasy and flight by themselves were acts of rebellion. In the colonial church's eyes, there was no room for a renunciation of the faith—once a Christian, always a Christian. The movement away from colonial towns had clear religious and political implications. Like Indigenous chiefs who valued people over land, Spanish missionaries and officials who clamored for the conquest of the frontier wanted to regain control of their former converts and subjects. They wanted to stem the tide and reverse its direction. They envisioned apostates as hostages of the devil or ancestral spirits in the mountains, and in taking the apostates back to the Christian lowlands they were simply restoring the rightful order of things.

Even in instances of actual warfare, Christian troops nevertheless prioritized capturing or converting their enemies rather than actually killing them. During the debates on how to contend with Negrito headhunting raids, most of the suggestions were violent but not necessarily lethal. The trading prohibition was a benign method to bring hostile communities to their knees and surrender. Rather than promoting the execution of Negritos, various officials proposed the idea of enslaving them instead.[218] Not only would it stop the violent raids, but enslaved Negritos would be beneficial to colonial society. Even the popular strategy of conducting punitive campaigns on the mountains was primarily designed to instill fear in the enemy. Most of the time Christian troops only burned settlements and fields, another way of weakening enemies without necessarily killing them. Of course, field battles resulted in deaths, but capturing the opposition was still a common practice. During the military campaigns in Ituy and Paniqui in 1748, the battle at the town of Banazi left twenty-seven animist fighters dead, but fifty-one surrendered to the Christian victors.[219] Christian indios and Spaniards brought almost one hundred captives in total back to Bayombong.

Unlike Spanish missionaries who deplored the flight of converts to the mountains, uplanders did not necessarily see the conversion of their kin as detrimental to their status. Having relatives in colonial towns meant they had intermediaries to facilitate trading relations. In one instance, Ilongot traders beheaded a new convert not because he became Christian, but because he failed to pay them for the tobacco and wax delivered.[220] Belonging to the new religion by itself was not abominable to indigenes because animism was not monotheistic and could seamlessly accommodate a wide variety of gods and spirits, including the Christian God and saints.

However, there was a tipping point where being closely surrounded by Christian communities became a threat to the remaining animists' power and influence. At least in the case of the Ilongots, when nearby subservient polities converted and aligned with Christian indios and Spaniards, they sensed the loss of their paramount status in the area. The increasing presence of Spanish missions and the gradual conversion to Christianity started to wrench a religious divide in the borderlands. When hostile animists deliberately hunted heads and destroyed structures in mission towns, it was a strategy to restore their previously prominent position and maintain a buffer zone between the two parties. Successful raids were a manifestation of their superiority over Christians and hopefully a signal to the new converts to realign with them once more.

If Christian troops used punitive campaigns to intimidate hostile upland communities, the latter employed analogous escalating intimidation tactics. Ilongots harassed the mission towns of Carranglan and Pantabangan in the following manner: "Squadrons of armed Ilongots shot arrows and spears at them, but they never saw any dead bodies, although they did find weapons and blood all over the ground. . . . The same thing had happened in the missions of Baler before the entry of the religious."[221] The spilled blood and the discarded weapons were most likely part of Ilongot scare tactics to dissuade the further arrival of missionaries, hence the lack of actual casualties. Nevertheless, the Christians of the mission towns felt real terror and danger, despite the apparent theatricality of the violence. When the intimidation did not work, hostile groups ratcheted up the attacks by beheading mission residents and burning their houses and fields, so there was a logic to the progression of violence.

Even in headhunting, alternatives existed besides the taking of more heads, which shows that transfers and reciprocity could take on many forms. In 1743, despite the physical proximity of animists and Christians to one another and the greater potential for friction, amicable exchanges continued to occur. Two Panoypoy traders, for example, went down to the mission town of Meuba to sell a few slaves.[222] For no apparent reason, however, the Isinays of Meuba decided to behead one of the Panoypoy traders. After hearing the news, the Panoypoys were understandably fuming mad, but they did not want to kill anyone. The aggrieved Panoypoys only wished to receive clothes in compensation and scare the Isinays of Meuba a little to teach them a lesson. Negotiation was often a possibility, and violence was not always the immediate response.

But things got out of hand when the converts of Dupax and the *maestre de campo* of Buhay got involved, sided with the Panoypoys, and took things to another level.[223] Instead of a little intimidation, Dupax demanded that Meuba abandon their town altogether for the offense. To mollify the Panoypoys, Dupax gave them gifts, and the *maestre de campo* of Buhay even volunteered to give them an old man to sacrifice. The death of the Panoypoy trader could have been handled in multiple ways, from intimidation and headhunting to the gift of clothes and a sacrificial victim. There was plenty of room to maneuver in settling the score. Crossing the religious divide, the Christian converts of Dupax and Buhay did their best to appease the animist Panoypoys, to the detriment of their fellow Christians in Meuba.

The function of frontier forts was to regulate the movement of people: prevent attacks from mountain settlements, carry out punitive expeditions on them, and halt the upland-lowland trade. Although various actors questioned the efficacy of forts, these military-commercial structures nevertheless had an impact on borderland mobility. After a successful expedition against the Ilongots of Apalan in 1703, about fifty soldiers—a mixed group of Spaniards, Merdicas, and indios—decided to stay behind, build a fort in Burubur, and protect their gains.[224] The fort soldiers imprisoned an Ilongot on the request of the Isinay chiefs of Burubur, who wanted him detained because he was married to someone in town and they suspected him of returning permanently to Ilongot lands and abandoning his wife.[225] Garrisoned soldiers might have often failed to catch headhunters, illegal traders, and apostates, but in this instance they did manage to capture someone trying to escape his wife. In response to the detainment of their fellow Ilongot, the Ilongots of Apalan threatened to burn the mission town of San Agustin and kill its inhabitants unless the fort released the hostage.[226]

Like what happened with the aggrieved Panoypoys, the missionary of Bu-rubur, Joaquin de la Torre, and the rest of the mission entered into negotiations with the angry Ilongots rather than go to war.[227] After close to two hours of discussion, they all came to a resolution: the Ilongots would no longer harm Christians or give Isinays refuge in their towns, among other conditions. Both parties solemnized the peace pact twice.[228] First, they attended Mass the next day and proclaimed their vows inside the church. De la Torre promised that if the Christians harmed the Ilongots in any way, they would die in violation of the pact. An Ilongot representative made the equivalent vow that Ilongots would meet the same fate of death if they inflicted violence on the Christians. Second, outside the church, they sealed the pact once again with feasting, music, and dancing. After the meal, somebody fired an arquebus and shouted, "Anyone who would harm Ilongot Christians would have his stomach blown up in a similar fashion."[229] There was a certain symmetry between war and peace: an eye for an eye, a tooth for a tooth, a death for a death.[230] While independent polities could enter into war pacts against Christian missions, they could just as well make peace pacts with them. Ironically, however, it was the threat of mutual death that buttressed the state of peace. Reciprocity and its concomitant mobilities and exchanges reflected the current state of relations, whether peaceful or warlike.

Headhunting and forts epitomized the vicious cycle of borderland violence. However, there was always a way out, whether in the form of oaths and pacts or the exchange of gifts and hostages. Forts were known for maintaining a barrier between the animist uplands and the Christian lowlands, but in reality they also facilitated exchanges. The *maestre de campo* of Buhay offered a sacrificial victim to the Panoypoys; the fort soldiers of Burubur released their Ilongot prisoner. Without the proper exchange, burned villages and severed heads would have been the end result. While forts did escalate the cycle of violence, they also had the ability to diffuse it through alternative forms of reciprocity.

Forts facilitated movements that furthered their cause. In Spanish plans, forts and roads were inseparable infrastructures in borderlands. Besides sending out military expeditions, forts were meant to provide safe passage to travelers in potentially hostile territory. The ad hoc fort of Burubur had the auxiliary role of opening a road in the frontier.[231] Mobility relies on moorings, whether in the form of hubs or channels.[232] It is rooted in the ground and pathways that produce friction and allow encounters to happen. Fort-towns and roads had to take into account Indigenous agency and movements. They were not purely violent colonial impositions. In their day-to-day activities, soldiers and missionaries had to negotiate with and gain the trust of frontier polities because Indigenous cooperation was crucial in channeling mobilities.

Chapter 3 on the construction of a road in the borderland between Cagayan and Pampanga shows how Spanish missionaries and officials had to constantly resort to nonviolent means to achieve their goal. Since the road connected multiple polities with each other, arriving at a consensus and forming alliances were of vital importance. Going to war was not always the best option. Behind their grandiose designation as "Spanish royal roads," colonial roads in the borderlands merely concealed their Indigenous moorings and mobilities.

CHAPTER THREE

Roads and Crossings

Pedro Murrillo Velarde's *Hydrographic and Chorographic Map of the Philippine Islands* published in 1734 is arguably the most famous historical map of the archipelago.[1] It has been praised for being the "mother of all Philippine maps" or "the first accurate map of the archipelago."[2] Due to its unprecedented cartographic precision, other mapmakers used it as the template for their own maps of the Philippines. The map's popularity is understandable given the time and effort Murillo Velarde spent crafting it. He tried to get the distances, directions, latitudes, and longitudes as accurately as possible.[3] However, his map merely reflected the state of geographical knowledge at that time. The coastlines were pinpoint precise, but the interior spaces of islands only had vague and generic topographical features. Spanish colonizers had largely conquered the seas and coasts but not the inland frontier. Charting and traveling across the landscape were more difficult endeavors than voyaging out to sea.

Despite all the praise heaped on Murillo Velarde from the eighteenth century to the present, he was not immune from criticism even back then. In 1789, Francisco Antolín criticized certain inaccuracies on the map, especially those relating to inland spaces: "Still, there have been no exact measurements made of the interior and center of this wide island [of Luzon]."[4] In his 1734 chart, Murillo Velarde placed evenly spread-out legends of tiny plants and hills throughout the interior of the island of Luzon as if in an attempt to fill up the blank, uncharted space (figure 3.1). Anyone familiar with topographical maps of Luzon today can easily identify the glaring discrepancies on Murillo Velarde's map. Central and northern Luzon are not uniformly hilly but punctuated by several mountain ranges: the Cordillera, the Caraballo, and the Sierra Madre. Rather than the mountains, the topographical features that stand out on Murillo Velarde's map are the rivers and, to a lesser extent, the roads. Instead of the Cordillera mountain range occupying the spine of the island, the Jesuit mapmaker gives pride of place to the Cagayan River. Besides the rivers, roads are a distinct feature on Murillo Velarde's cartography of Luzon. Faint dotted lines indicate the roads that crisscross the island, but what jumps off the map is the road to Cagayan. A unique feature of his 1734 map is the text that runs vertically alongside the Cagayan River and reads, "Aquí se halló un camino que en tres días se pasa a la parte de Cagayan" (A road was found here

FIGURE 3.1 Pedro Murillo Velarde, *Hydrographic and Chorographic Map of the Philippine Islands*, 1734. On his map, Murillo Velarde wrote a text that runs vertically at the center of the island of Luzon and reads "Aquí se halló un camino que en tres días se pasa a la parte de Cagayan" to indicate the discovery of a road to Cagayan. Courtesy of the Library of Congress Geography and Map Division (www.loc.gov/item/2013585226/).

that reaches Cagayan in three days). In an unusual move, instead of resorting to the standard dotted line for roads, Murillo Velarde visually recorded this one in bold textual form. It seems like what interested him were the passages of mobility rather than the obstacles on the island.

It was not as if Murillo Velarde was not aware of the mountainous topography of the area. In his ten-volume series on world geography, he described the province of Cagayan in the following manner: "The land is mountainous, and the mountains so enclosed by forests, thickets, and outcrops that this province could hardly maintain overland contact with others."[5] And yet the landscape of cartographic Cagayan is devoid of mountain ranges and forests. Nevertheless, viewers of the map still get a hint of the province's topography from the absence of roads. While the province of Ilocos to the left of the Cagayan River has two dotted-line roads that run from north to south, the province of Cagayan has none. Three dotted-line roads approach Cagayan from the south but never actually venture into the province, except for the recently discovered textual road that reaches Cagayan in just three days. It was likely a deliberate choice on Murillo Velarde's part to emphasize rivers and roads because they epitomized the channels used and the progress achieved by missionaries in reaching the borderlands of Luzon.

If Murillo Velarde's cartographic masterpiece would eventually acquire the symbolic status of "the first map of the Philippines," the road to Cagayan would become a legendary icon of its own in accounts of the Christianization of the province's frontier.[6] Antolín's unpublished magnum opus on Dominican missionary work in Cagayan throughout the centuries has the grand title of "Chronological Compendium of the Road to Cagayan through the Province and Mission of Ituy."[7] Even if Antolín's manuscript details everything and everyone involved in the entire history of the Cagayan missions and not just the road itself, the road to Cagayan nevertheless has a central place of honor in the title.

The image of roads held a powerful sway over how Spanish missionaries and officials envisioned their project in borderlands. Besides the religious missions and military expeditions discussed in the previous chapters, roads were another symbol and tool of Spanish conquest and control.[8] The Spanish realm was an empire not only of towns and forts but also of roads. Road networks connected the distant territories of a far-flung empire. For the Spanish monarchy, distances and routes were crucial concepts in understanding the layout of the land, hence its preoccupation with gathering spatial coordinates from local officials.[9] In the fifty-item questionnaire of the "Relaciones Geográficas," several questions try to ascertain the distance of a town to its neighbors, the nearest capital, and its diocesan headquarters.[10] The following question on distance and terrain appears repeatedly: "Are these leagues long or short, through flat or hilly land, over straight or winding roads, easy or difficult to travel?"[11] Friction was calculated in terms of not only distance but also terrain.[12] Traveling a long distance on a smooth, flat road was preferable to covering a short distance on a rough, mountainous path. Travelers conceived of distance more as the time they spent traveling rather than the space they actually covered, so the perception of how long a league was changed depending on the nature of the route.[13] Roads had the job of filing away at the friction of terrain and bringing faraway towns closer. The road to Cagayan not only slashed the province's distance but also stood for the progress in penetrating a borderland.

For the early modern period, plenty of attention is paid on long-distance sea navigation in the context of the "age of discovery," but few studies focus on more common forms of overland travel and everyday mobility.[14] Although towns and forts might seem like static structures in the landscape, they manifested and facilitated borderland movement, as chapters 1 and 2 have shown. Roads were even more explicit expressions of mobility in the island's interior. The movements of people imparted a sense of coherence to a geographical space.[15] Like towns and forts, roads were not mere infrastructure that channeled movement. Each element played a part in constructing each other; all three provided moorings that enabled friction and mobility. The construction of and access to roads were inseparable from the exercise and shaping of political power.[16]

Distant observers like Murillo Velarde might have viewed the road to Cagayan as the triumph of Spanish imperial power over the frontier, but missionaries out in the field were acutely aware of the social dimensions of the undertaking. On the ground, long-distance travel on roads meant going on an adventure full of uncertainties, improvisations, and negotiations.[17] A whole host of factors were involved in the construction, maintenance, and traversing of roads. Building the road was not solely the task of clearing a pathway through forests and thickets. It also involved negotiations with local communities whose permission and compliance had to be gained or teased out. Roads as points of access were manifestations of the current state of alliances, or lack thereof, among neighboring polities. Rather than mere imperial impositions, even colonial roads were borderlands in themselves where Indigenous inhabitants took an active part in forwarding their own interests.[18]

A common refrain among Spanish observers, along with a few indios, was how difficult overland travel was. Rough terrain, thick vegetation, steep inclines, overflowing rivers, torrential downpours, and other environmental factors inhibited mobility. While it is true that geographical distance and terrain had a strong influence on how communities developed and became relatively isolated, absolute detachment almost never occurred.[19] In European overland travel, for example, "so-called regions of difficulty or hardship are defined not by inhabitants but by outsiders."[20] Although traveling over rough terrain entailed a lot of time and effort, local inhabitants had little choice in the matter, especially in earlier time periods.[21] They exerted the effort anyway since it was the only way to stay connected. It is usually the "myth of blanket impassibility" that laments the lack of roads and the impossibility of travel.[22]

In the colonial setting, English, Spanish, and Portuguese settlers often despaired in their inability to travel quickly and safely, but that was as much a reflection of their lack of knowledge of Indigenous routes and communication networks as a problem of the terrain itself. In early New England, English settlers for the longest time had to rely on Indian messengers and pathways for their very survival.[23] In peripheral Guatemala, Spanish settlers and their documents were highly dependent on Indian informants and messengers who had a vastly superior knowledge of the local terrain.[24] In the Brazilian frontier of the eastern Sertão, the Portuguese monarchy attempted to prohibit settler incursion and road building in the so-called forbidden lands, and yet there were Indian trails everywhere that Portuguese smugglers even used for their own benefit.[25] In the remotest colonial outposts, road and communication networks—however rudimentary—already existed even before colonizers co-opted or attempted to ban them. Many colonial roads simply followed the tracks of existing pre-Hispanic roads in New Spain, Peru, and even Cagayan.[26]

When Murillo Velarde and Antolín used the term "road," they implicitly perpetuated the myth of impassibility. It was as if nobody had passed from Pampanga to Cagayan or vice versa ever before. Indigenous chiefs from Ituy had traveled to Manila throughout the years, and Spanish conquistadors had already ventured to Ituy in the sixteenth century (see the introduction). At a more general level, commercial exchange had been a permanent fixture between uplanders and lowlanders, and runaways from Pangasinan and Cagayan had been seeking refuge in the interprovincial borderland for years. They all must have used a variety of roads not recognized in Murillo Velarde's map. What was new to the missionaries was likely common knowledge among the locals.

The importance Murillo Velarde and Antolín gave to the road to Cagayan most likely had more to do with their particular context and definition of what a road was than the road's actual novelty. Europeans usually distinguished between a road—the physical infrastructure on the ground—and a route—the imaginary line linking two sites.[27] With their strong emphasis on materiality, European observers like Antolín were wont to dismiss Indigenous roads for not conforming to their particular conception of how a road should look like. For Spanish settlers in the Indies, a road was a road because it connected two colonial settlements. It was part of the civilizational infrastructure of cities and forts.[28] Thus, in the same way that Indigenous settlements that did not conform to Spanish notions of civilization were not really cities in a strict sense of the term, roads that did not link Spanish-administered towns were not really roads. In this hierarchy, roads in the unconquered borderlands were mere trails and pathways. Physically speaking, the great Dominican road to Cagayan was barely different from the rest of the roads or trails in the countryside, but existing roads remained imagined routes until they were traversed by colonial subjects on the way from one colonial town to another.

The analysis in this chapter combines the materiality and experience of everyday mobility with the changing social configuration of borderland communities. Unlike other studies where infrastructure and social relations are analytically kept apart, this chapter explores how the two co-constructed each other.[29] The chapter continues with the mechanics and technicalities of everyday mobility in the borderlands. It tackles how people traveled, what means of transportation they used, and what obstacles they encountered on their way. With almost all the sources coming from outsiders, they often depict traveling as difficult and pathways as impassible. Although they accurately portray the relative inaccessibility of the hinterland, mobility still occurred in a wide variety of situations. The chapter then discusses Spanish plans to construct a road running directly from Manila to Cagayan to solve the problem of mobility in the island's interior. In the first couple of instances, the planned road served a military purpose in attempts to finally conquer the frontier and suppress revolts. In 1738, with the help of their Augustinian counterparts, Dominican missionaries successfully crossed the borderland, traveling from Cagayan to Pangasinan and opening the famed road.

The rest of the chapter shows how the process of opening the road was not a purely infrastructural or topographical issue. Negotiations with and the acquiescence of key communities along the route were crucial in the success of the project. The increasing penetration of Christian towns in the hinterland caused tensions with resistant animist settlements that had to be resolved before passage could be granted. The road was symptomatic of the shifting interpolity relations in the borderland. Although the road signaled the integration of several borderland communities to the Spanish monarchy and the Catholic Church, it also exacerbated the dividing line between Augustinian- and Dominican-administered towns. Now working in adjacent missions without a buffer zone, the Augustinians had to cede several of their northernmost mission towns to the Dominicans, and some converts affected by the transfer decided to pack up and migrate to the Augustinian missions. Even though missionaries claimed ownership over the opening of the road, in the final analysis local communities generally determined who had access to the roads. With a corridor through the borderland, a stronger Christian presence in the river valley provoked violent reactions from upland polities that resented the new intrusion.

Friction of Terrain

After traveling thousands of kilometers and enduring months on galleons sailing the Atlantic and then the Pacific, for the vast majority of Spaniards who landed in Manila, they had finally reached their destination. For a selected few assigned to the provinces, the journey was not yet over. If the tyranny of distance characterized the remoteness of Manila from Madrid, the friction of terrain made two points on the same island of Luzon seem farther than they actually were.[30] Prior to the transportation revolution of the nineteenth century, travel whether by land or sea had always been relatively slow and drawn-out for centuries.[31] While bad roads led to sluggish pace, sea journeys seemed never-ending. If "Napoleon moved no faster than Julius Caesar," then globetrotting Spanish conquistadors and missionaries were no better than Philippine islanders once they were off their galleon ships.[32] Like in the rest of the early modern world, traveling by water in the Philippines was generally easier and quicker than doing so by land, so the arduous overland journey to an island's hinterland was as much an adventure as a long ocean voyage.[33] To avoid traversing the mountain ranges in the center of Luzon, Spaniards preferred to travel by sea or river whenever possible. When overland travel was the only feasible option, they tried to use various modes of transportation like animals and porters to make their life easier. However, whether they walked, were carried, or rode horses, they still encountered difficulties along the way. In the end, they would attempt a more permanent solution to the problem by clearing the landscape and constructing roads.

From very early on, observers noted how the rough terrain in the interior of Luzon made everyday mobility a struggle. The Dominican chronicler

Diego Aduarte described the borderland of Ituy as a "land that is so rugged and difficult to visit."[34] The Augustinian Manuel Carrillo said that new missions in the interior were in a very precarious situation because their very newness meant that missionaries did not know the land and had not yet discovered the necessary roads.[35] In the Dominican Francisco Antolín's view, where Spaniards settled in the Philippines was largely determined by basic geography and logistics rather than any elaborate plan: "The few secular and religious Spaniards who arrived in Manila spread out along coastlines, navigable rivers, and various islands without being able to go to the mountains due to rough roads and the lack of riding animals."[36] They were reliant on horses and rivers for quick travel across an island. Unfortunately, horses were initially not readily available. River travel was also limited because navigable rivers often did not reach deep into the hinterland. The rivers of the province of Pampanga were far away south from the mission of Ituy. The Cagayan River up north provided access only to the northernmost mission towns of Paniqui. Without horses and rivers, access to the mountainous hinterland remained difficult.[37]

The relative ease of water over land travel pushed Spaniards to use coastal towns as their primary nodes of mobility. Following sea routes that hugged the coast was the rule in the early modern period.[38] It was more practical to go the long route by sailing from one coastal town to another rather than run a more direct route overland. Manila on the southwest of Luzon and Cagayan on the northeast were on opposite ends of the island. No direct road connected the two areas until the eighteenth century. As a result, Spanish officials and indio merchants in Cagayan had to send everything by boat to Manila from official dispatches and animal meat to tobacco and wheat.[39] Vessels would even stop by the coast of Ilocos along the way to complete a tripartite trade. After the goods were collected from the interior, they were brought to the nearest river dock and loaded on sampans, the primary means of long-distance transportation on the island. The objective was to make the overland journey as short as possible. Even the transpacific galleons avoided landing at any other port in Luzon than Manila unless it was an emergency because it meant commandeering natives to haul all of the ship's silver and merchandise overland to Manila without the aid of mules through densely forested mountains.[40]

In 1700, the galleon *San Francisco Xavier* arriving from Acapulco unexpectedly found itself docking off the coast of Cagayan after being ordered to follow an unconventional route back to Manila and being blown off course by strong winds.[41] Instead of opting to transport the bulk of the ship's cargo overland as was the common practice in cases of shipwrecks and pirate attacks, the crew decided to finish the voyage aboard their battered ship.[42] They barely reached Manila on an almost submerged ship, but the alternative trip overland was hardly more promising. Apparently, Augustinians onboard the galleon decided to abandon ship and finish the journey from Cagayan to Manila on foot, which took them two months.[43] The ship's crew, however, waited it out a few weeks before resuming their sea journey and arrived in Manila almost two months later on a sinking ship.[44] Neither option was entirely appealing, and both ended up lasting almost the same time, but barring unforeseen circumstances sea voyages were the preferred way of traveling significant distances. Overland travel was a last resort. Incidents like this show that mountainous island interiors were difficult to access but not impenetrable. Even before the eventual opening of the Dominicans' famed road to Cagayan, Augustinians had already made this north–south land crossing, and surely others had made similar but undocumented journeys.

Besides the sea, another body of water that facilitated movement were rivers, which evaded the problem of dealing with the rugged terrain. Even though several rivers connected the coast with the island's interior, most of them were no longer navigable farther inland. But up to the point that they were, officials, travelers, and merchants took advantage of them as a primary means of transportation. In Cagayan, towns in the interior had to build bamboo rafts to bring tobacco leaves to the provincial capital downriver.[45] The Dominican missionaries Manuel Moliner and José Marín used the Itugud River to travel from their mission town of Cauayan: "Although the journey is shorter by land, we prefer to go upriver by boat to avoid any incidents because the pagans hunt the animals and people in those uplands, and while the riverbanks are also infested with Negritos, the latter are not as fierce as the former."[46] In Tayabas, missionaries took note whenever sites were accessible by river because it made traveling back and forth much easier.[47] A Franciscan missionary in Baler told his visitors to travel overland from Manila, but to finish the final leg of the journey from Santor to Dingalan by river so that they could "arrive like kings without much work."[48] Journeys on water, whether by sea or river, were the preferred means of mobility in the archipelago, but they also had their limitations.

Although sea travel had the advantage of avoiding the vagaries of topography, it was nevertheless subject to the whims of the wind. Remote coastal towns were isolated in times of rough seas and adverse winds.[49] In the case of Baler on the east coast of Luzon, both Spaniards and indios used vessels to travel from one coastal town to another; however, it was far from ideal because even short journeys were dangerous.[50] Monsoon winds made the seas very rough and prevented ships from sailing to Baler during particular times of the year.[51] Vessels venturing out in open water were also prone to pirate attacks.[52]

While rivers did facilitate movement in the island's interior, they also posed as obstacles to overland travelers. As streams and rivers meandered across the landscape, travelers on foot encountered the problem of crossing them several times.[53] With more than a hint of hyperbole, the Franciscan Juan de Ocaña claimed that overland travelers would have to cross the same river "more than seven hundred times" to get to Baler.[54] The Augustinian Pedro Vivar had to cross a river by jumping from rock to rock, but he slipped, fell into the water, and arrived at his destination unscathed but soaking wet.[55] Rock hopping was a fairly common way to cross rivers, but some travelers were not as lucky as Vivar when they lost their footing and injured themselves.[56] Most towns had very basic bridges: "two canes laid across, which is the same as crossing a razor because, as we [priests] have not learned how to walk a tight rope, it is not easy for us to cross that obstacle."[57] When there were no bridges, determined travelers had to be creative: "The Igorot tied a piece of rattan to a tree on the bank of the river, swam through the current to the other side with the rattan, and tied it to another tree there; then, hanging from this rattan by their hand, they crossed the river with the tips of their toes just touching the water."[58] The danger of drowning in rivers was very real. On a few occasions, strong currents swept away and drowned missionaries trying to cross rivers on horseback.[59]

If the rainy season made the seas too choppy for sailing, it also caused rivers to flood and flow too fast to be crossed. In various frontier missions, missionaries and converts recognized the difficulties and dangers presented by rushing rivers during the rainy season.[60] For the fortunate few, the raging waters only slowed down the missionaries, as they were still able to conduct their pastoral visits.[61] For the unlucky others, heavy downpours suddenly made rivers impassable and trapped travelers wherever they were caught unaware, waiting for days for the water to subside.[62] Ilocano godparents, for example, could not come and attend baptisms in inland missions during the rainy season.[63] In extreme cases, the solution was to go with the flow. During heavy downpours that flooded the lands, the missionary Antonio del Campo frequently swam about two leagues downriver from Bayombong to Apiat.[64] It was not the most sophisticated way of traveling, but it got the job done.

The realm of polities and villages shrank with the onset of the monsoon rains.[65] Their livable world did not go far beyond the immediate confines of their land. Even Spaniards who had traveled halfway around the globe had to conform themselves to such a basic constraint in the Philippines. Traveling by sea and river was a popular way to get around the archipelago, but it was a seasonal and restricted mode of traveling. During the months of strong winds and rains, travelers had better chances relying on land routes. Seas and rivers also gave limited access to the hinterland. With gale-force winds and incessant rains beyond human control, the landscape was a more malleable medium for human mastery, and Spaniards spent more time and effort trying to tame it. With most coastal settlements already charted and monitored by the Spanish monarchy, island interiors and their roadways posed a greater challenge for Spaniards in the eighteenth century.

Nature made traveling in the hinterland difficult. In the mission of Ituy, a succession of mountains, crags, and rivers made certain areas inaccessible.[66] Hamlets near the main mission town were sometimes unreachable because trails were quickly overrun by undergrowth. Steep inclines and thick mud also made some roads impassable.[67] A meandering route up a mountain offered a safer, more comfortable—but longer—journey.[68] In contrast, a direct assault up a mountain took less time and covered less ground but was infinitely more dangerous. In the mountains of Tabueyon, climbing and descending slopes was an arduous but normal part of mobility: "Just the climb up the mountain took half a day, but it was so hard because it was vertical without the usual roundabout way of going up that usually made it less daunting. So as not to fall off, it is necessary to grab trees, shrubs, and several vines that they [the locals] themselves have put there for when they descend and ascend."[69] Travelers had to crawl over the terrain and grapple whatever was at hand if they wanted to cross mountains as quickly and securely as possible. Only the physically fit could climb the craggy slopes of these mountains.[70] Even walking on flat lands battered the bodies of travelers as their feet became bloated and sore from the rocky terrain and wet ground.[71]

To avoid the slow, tedious activity of walking, Spanish missionaries and locals resorted to various means of transportation from boats and rafts to horses and hammocks. Technology partly solved the drudgery of overland travels; however, it often rested on the hard, unpaid labor of ordinary indios. Vessels had to be rowed, and hammocks needed to be carried. The ease and comfort of passengers depended on the grueling exertions of oarsmen and porters. Among Ilongot communities near the Pacific coast, men built the boats and helped priests cross rivers, while women carried the cargo on land.[72] When the Spanish judge José Ignacio de Arzadun conducted his inspection tour of the province of Cagayan from 1738 to 1741, he unraveled the abuses in

FIGURE 3.2 José Honorato Lozano, "Indios Carrying Hammocks," 1847. The elite in the Philippines traveled by hammock or palanquin carried by porters. Imagen procedente de los fondos de la Biblioteca Nacional de España (image from the collections of the Biblioteca Nacional de España).

transportation committed not only by Spanish priests but also by the Indigenous elite.[73] Based on Spanish law, hiring rowers and porters was legal as long as they were paid. Gabriel Balagan, a resident of Piat, testified that they were not. Priests and chiefs boarded vessels in Piat to go to Tuao, Malaueg, and distant places without paying their rowers.[74] The porters of hammocks endured the same treatment (figure 3.2).[75] With no cows or horses in Piat, the elite relied on being carried around when traveling. Chiefs, their wives, and priests all rode hammocks when moving from one town to another to spare themselves the burden of walking the rough terrain. The priest had eight men carry his hammock without giving them a centavo or even a morsel of food. Testimonies from other witnesses confirmed the prevalence of these practices in the region, even where horses and cows were available as riding animals.[76]

While Arzadun's resolutions expressed his vision of how overland travel in the archipelago should be conducted, the objections from parish priests revealed the harsh reality of mobility on the ground. In Arzadun's view, the exploitation of porters could easily be avoided with the clearing of roads and the provision of horses, cows, and oxen in each town.[77] He condemned traveling by hammock because of the unnecessary burden it placed on unpaid porters. Animals should be the beasts of burden, not indios even if they willingly did it for free.[78] Four laws of the *Recopilación de leyes de los reynos de las Indias* had very specific guidelines on how Spanish officials and priests should travel in the colonies: one encouraged the use of horses, another forbade traveling by hammock, and two prohibited indios from working as porters.[79] Arzadun wanted an infrastructure of roads and bridges to facilitate movement between the different towns. To this end, he expected wide roads to be constructed and maintained on a yearly basis.[80]

Arzadun's ordinances caused an uproar among the Dominican priests in Cagayan who staunchly defended their right to travel by hammock. Their objections rested on two issues: the advantages of hammocks over horses and the impracticality of Arzadun's orders based on local conditions. Francisco Roxano complained that the ordinance banning hammocks did not make any sense because the province did not have any passable roads, which were very rough at best and traversed steep hills and mountains.[81] During the rainy season, the ground turned into a marshland. With a lack of horses, no bridle roads, and a pressing need to administer the sacraments in dispersed settlements, priests in the province claimed that they had no other option but to ride on hammocks to fulfill their duties and obligations.[82]

Diego Saenz, another Dominican priest in Cagayan, echoed Roxano's arguments that traveling by hammock was a common and acceptable way of moving about in Cagayan.[83] With Arzadun's grand mobility plan still all a pipe dream, he justified the continued use of hammocks in the meantime: "Even if they are able to supply fully-equipped horses and oxen, build bridges across estuaries, construct streets, straighten roads, and flatten mountains, until this impossibility becomes possible . . . there should be no prohibition on hammocks that would leave the province incommunicable."[84] Saenz doubted the feasibility of implementing the ordinances because of the seemingly untamable nature of the terrain, which was "swampy, flooded, and uncultivated, full of dense reedbeds and grasslands, and most of it hilly, and during the rainy season it seems more like a sea or large river rather than land."[85] Laws had to succumb to more mundane, immutable realities on the ground because at the end of the day "it is not for the law to demand that people travel on a river on horseback."[86] In the eyes of the Dominican order, until the infrastructure of roads (including elevated pathways that passed over marshlands), bridges, and river boats was fully set in place, the current practice of hiring indios to carry hammocks should be respected.[87]

The clash partly stemmed from different traveling practices in different parts of the world. While in Spain and the Americas travelers commonly used horses and mules, on the island of Luzon and the rest of the region the use of human carriers and porters was quite normal.[88] Arzadun's ordinances and the Spanish laws of the Indies tried to implement a particular vision of transportation that relied heavily on mules in an area where this pack animal was not prevalent and the use of human porters was an acceptable practice. While Spanish officialdom followed Spanish and American precedents, Spanish missionaries on the ground decided to adapt and travel on hammocks just like the native elite.

At least in the eyes of several Spanish observers, indios were more adept at traversing the difficult terrain in the island's interior and covered the same distance in a shorter span of time.[89] In the same way that perceptions of distance changed according to the ruggedness of the route, travel times changed according to who did the traveling.[90] The trailblazing missionary José Marín in one instance reckoned the journey time in terms of "indio days," implying that Spaniards would need to expend more time doing the same trip.[91] Fray Antolín compared indios to agile forest animals when they moved: "Like deer, the pagans don't bother to make any trails."[92] When escaping their enemies, they fled through areas where only wild boars and deer managed to pass.[93] Descriptions comparing indio and animal agility could be either a recognition of Indigenous nimbleness and expertise in tackling the terrain or an attempt to demean indigenes by comparing them with animals and implicitly contrasting them to Spaniards who were supposedly more civilized in their use of paved roads. These stereotypes derived from the idea that indios were more acclimatized to the weather and terrain and thus predisposed to work as porters for Spaniards without any problems.[94]

An indirect way to track borderland mobilities is to trace the circulation of messages and documents.[95] Unlike travelers and visitors, messengers are less prominent and almost invisible in the sources; however, they were the foundation of a whole informal system of postal service. Without them, long-distance communication between Manila and the hinterland or among mission towns would not have been possible. Dispatches from the Franciscan provincial in Manila to his missionary brothers in Baler might have followed a long, circuitous path reliant on a series of Indigenous messengers, but they eventually reached their recipients. The Franciscan missionary in Binangonan gave the official letters from Manila to a messenger from Umirey, who gave them to the Augustinian missionary Alejandro Cacho in Pampanga, who in turn sent an Ilongot to deliver the dispatch to the Franciscan Santiago de Jesús María in Casiguran.[96] From Binangonan to Casiguran, it took more than two months for the letters to arrive. Ilongot messengers were clearly not the express runners of Persia who covered twenty leagues a day, but two months was not bad when a coastal mailboat would have made seasonal deliveries at best.[97]

While Indigenous messengers were the conduits of written communication on the island, they also held the senders and recipients at their mercy. Fray Jesús María blamed the shamelessness of the messengers for taking their time in making the deliveries.[98] The informal postal service had to rely on whoever was available and willing to do the task. In the case of the Franciscan dispatch from Manila to Casiguran, the letters passed through several hands from priests of different religious orders to indigenes of different ethnic groups. When mission residents in Santa Cruz fled during an epidemic outbreak in 1741, the stationed missionary could not send correspondences and updates to his provincial because nobody was left to deliver the messages.[99]

While the circulation of letters and messages proves the existence of an underlying borderland mobility, both Spanish and Indigenous residents were unenthusiastic in carrying out the task. When Franciscan missionaries had to go and pick up their dispatches in Baler, it was a complicated undertaking that involved eighty Indigenous escorts to take care of them from pounding their rice to carrying their cargo.[100] It was a strain on everyone from the porters who barely had any time to rest to the missionaries who sometimes succumbed to injuries like Manuel Olivencia, who injured his foot and could no longer move. Four messengers in Baler wanted to quit their job delivering mail and even requested a visiting commissioner for a tribute exemption in compensation for their service.[101] From the very beginning, the Franciscan missionary in Baler, Juan de Ocaña, had misgivings on whether he could trust them to reliably bring the dispatches coming from Manila. When he heard about the exchange between the messengers and the commissioner, he reprimanded them for complaining and prohibited them from presenting an official written request as ordered by the commissioner. If they did not want to pick up the letters from Santor, he wanted lay brothers to do the job instead.[102] The Baler messengers' demand probably reflected the difficult nature of the job and their desire to be compensated for it. Despite their renown for slicing through thickets and moving up mountains like deer, even indios found traveling in the countryside a thankless task.

Delivering letters during the rainy season complicated matters. A bad storm usually delayed the delivery of the post.[103] When the missionary of Tabueyong, Manuel Fermoselle, sent a dispatch in early August during the height of a downpour, the messenger had to swim across several overflowing rivers and got the letters so drenching wet that they were no longer salvageable.[104] During the rainy season, mobility in the countryside was still possible, but it was a challenge. While the myth of blanket impassability might not be true, neither was overland travel frictionless. A patchy network of short-distance travels created a tenuous but functioning mobility that required a lot of coordination and effort.

Many roads on the island of Luzon received the designation of "royal road."[105] While Spanish royal roads did refer to both public routes of the first order and roads traveled by the royal court, secondary local roads also shared in the regal title.[106] More than an aberrant lofty label—even in the case of rough frontier trails—royal roads were a manifestation of the power and reach of the Spanish monarchy.[107] With its vast realm, the Spanish empire paid attention to basic matters of logistics and mobility. If Philip II tried to run a road through France to connect his European possessions and facilitate troop movements, a couple of centuries later Bourbon monarchs and their Philippine officials would do something analogous in constructing a royal road through the borderland of Cagayan.[108]

Constructing a Road

Although an unofficial network of well-traversed roads and unmarked routes dotted the landscape, Spanish officials and priests in the borderland still wanted a direct overland link between Cagayan and Manila. While the patchwork of trails made mobility possible, they did not conform to what Spanish travelers expected of a road, a pathway cleared of obstacles and composed of compacted earth. A missionary account describes how the Spanish government instructed indios to build roads as part of their required labor services: "The first task at hand was to cut down the big trees that blocked the path, burn the undergrowth, tall grass, and scrubland . . . dig the ditches, and throw the excavated soil in the center of the path, road, or street, flattening it later with heavy wooden planks."[109] This way of building roads was probably more the ideal rather than the reality because the topography of certain areas—rough and hilly terrain in the island's interior—simply did not allow for wide, flat roads.

Ease of travel was at the forefront of most travelers' mind. When Fray Marín had to trudge through a league of reedbed, he imagined a bridle road in its place where travelers could breeze by on horseback.[110] Alonso de Abella Fuertes and José Ignacio de Arzadun, two Spanish judges on an inspection tour of Cagayan in the 1690s and 1730s, respectively, opted to take a ship to reach their destination, which took them about a month, because they did not have much choice.[111] Another Spanish judge, who did not want to do the inspection tour, made the excuse that Cagayan "being too remote and with the rainy season having already started . . . it is well-known that the passage [from Pangasinan to Cagayan] closes."[112] Even if on the off chance he reached Cagayan, he was afraid he was going to get stuck there for months until the rains stopped. Of course, the sea route was the most feasible way to travel between Manila and Cagayan, but he emphasized the hard overland slog to strengthen his case for not going.

The absence of a direct link between Manila and Cagayan caused many other concerns besides the mobility of Spanish officials and the governance of a remote province. In the mind of a few observers, mobility and prosperity were intimately linked to each other. In 1690, the Dominican Pedro Jiménez thought that the conquest of Paniqui would allow a Manila–Cagayan road to be opened, which would bring about several benefits.[113] In terms of mobility, Dominican priests assigned in Cagayan would be able to attend the meetings held in Manila, and the provincial carry out his pastoral visits moving from one town to another from Pangasinan. Economically, Cagayan residents could go to Manila, sell their merchandise there, and become rich. In 1740, during his visit of Cagayan, Arzadun concluded that the province's poverty was partly due to its lack of commerce and isolation whether "by sea or land, without any assistance except for the few vessels that return from Manila every year."[114] The land was rich and fertile, but the limited number of laborers and commercial opportunities hampered any chance of economic development. Militarily, Manila and Cagayan could assist one another during times of conflict. While Manila could supply gunpowder, bullets, and ammunition, Indigenous communities from Cagayan could provide backup to a Manila under attack. In 1691, after visiting the province of Cagayan, Abella believed that a road defended by forts would make it easier for the Manila government to maintain its control over hostile frontier groups.[115] The road would effectively bring the hinterland closer to Manila. A road to Cagayan stood for a whole body of improvements that would primarily benefit Spanish interests but nonetheless ameliorate the living conditions of Indigenous communities isolated from the rest of the island.

For the Dominicans, who continuously made a big deal of it, the road was a key to unlocking the potential and salvation of the whole island. It was all about geography because the road would pass right through the center of the island. It was not a simple matter of linking peripheral Cagayan with metropolitan Manila, but of resolving a central puzzle piece that would affect a much wider area. After conquering and staying primarily on the coast, Spanish presence would finally penetrate the ostensibly untouched heartland of Luzon. In the 1740s, the Dominican provincial Manuel del Río lauded his order's successful attempt to clear borderland paths. They linked Cagayan not only to Pampanga and Pangasinan but also to Ilocos.[116] Río thought that opening roads had a civilizing effect on the surrounding pagan communities because by "making that place passable those barbaric people will be domesticated by contact and commerce with the provinces, and the impenetrability of their territory would no longer make them so intractable."[117] Slashing their way through dense thickets, roads would open up the inaccessible interior to these so-called positive outside influences. Ideally located at the center, the mission of Ituy could facilitate communication and commerce for the betterment of all nearby provinces.[118]

At the end of the eighteenth century, the chronicler Antolín harked back to the same key ideas of centrality and mobility. He considered the missions of Ituy and Paniqui to be "the center and heart of all the Christian provinces on this island of Luzon."[119] He envisioned the formation of a strong Christian front in the face of a largely animist hinterland: "It was perfectly ordinary and normal that these Christian provinces should have communication and commerce among themselves, and for this reason it was always intended from the very beginning to have some roads for mutual communication."[120] Unlike Río, who saw roads primarily as inroads into enemy territory, Antolín envisaged them as a unifying factor among Christians first and foremost and as an offensive tactic against pagans secondarily: "The motto of those old [missionaries] was this: let a land route be opened through the interior of this island and there will then be more communication among the Christians, and the Igorots and other pagans will be exposed."[121] Plunging right to the heart of the island, the road to Cagayan would eventually drive out animist communities from their hiding places. Despite the slight differences, both Río and Antolín shared the view that mobility, contact, and location all worked together to bring about civilization and progress in borderlands.

Specific incidents in the 1690s and 1710s made the project of constructing a Manila–Cagayan road an immediate and pressing concern. Rebels and apostates seeking refuge and consolidating their position in the unconquered hinterland were a constant threat to Spanish authority in the provinces. Along with missions (see chapter 1) and forts (see chapter 2), roads were another socio-infrastructural institution deployed to gain control of those spaces. When Abella carried out his inspection tour of northern and central Luzon in the early 1690s, he gathered important information for the planned opening of a road through the center of the island.[122] He described his trip as going to "the most remote provinces of these islands" and passing through "mostly deserted mountains and hostile rebel territory."[123] Besides being the home of runaways, elopers, malcontents, and layabouts, upriver Cagayan was now the refuge of the perpetrators of the recent uprisings in Cabagan, who had threatened their neighbors against receiving any priests from Cagayan.[124] To counteract the menace and attacks coming from borderland rebels and outlaws, Abella wanted the two provinces of Cagayan and Pampanga to work together and hack a road right through the heart of enemy territory.[125] The road would be the "open door" that would expose this nesting ground of rebels and their relatives who succored them, and make greater control from Manila possible.[126] Based on Abella's calculations, the shortest and easiest route to Manila would pass by Itugud, Paniqui, and Arayat.[127] From the town of Itugud to the province of Pampanga, it would take a mere twelve days of travel.[128] By opening up the borderland, the road would reconfigure the spatial dynamics of the island by bringing remote, inaccessible places closer to Manila.

Like the contemporaneous war plans to invade the borderland of Ituy that came to nothing (see chapter 2), Abella's road stayed on the drawing board. However, another uprising in Cagayan would revive the old project of building an interprovincial road. In 1718, a revolt started in four Cagayan towns and immediately spread upriver.[129] Local histories blame the long-standing abuses committed by Spanish provincial governors and garrisoned soldiers for the armed uprising, which specific events and offenses in 1718 simply triggered.[130] A locust infestation that decimated the rice harvest in Luzon that year initiated the maelstrom.[131] Taking advantage of the dire situation and their political position, provincial governors requisitioned rice at a cheap fixed price in the provinces and sold it at an exorbitant rate in Manila. The forced requisition of rice would explain why there was unrest not only in Cagayan but also in Pangasinan and Pampanga.[132] Rebels in Tuguegarao destroyed the Spanish-owned boats loaded with rice, maize, and other provisions.[133]

While a general unrest pervaded several provinces of the island, it was Cagayan that garnered the special attention of the Manila government. The superintendent of royal works and fortifications, José Francisco de Torres, claimed that the agitation in Cagayan was due to its distance of more than one hundred leagues away from the colonial capital.[134] Whether by sea or land, the northeastern province's inaccessibility made it a breeding ground for unrest. In the superintendent's eyes, the immediate dispatch of troops to quell incipient rebellions was the optimal solution, so a road network had to be built to better connect the province with the rest of the island.[135] Eight to ten days was an acceptable travel time to reach the other provinces by land instead of the usual thirty-day sea voyage. Other provinces like Pampanga and Pangasinan were within easy reach of colonial troops in case of an uprising; consequently, the unrest there garnered less attention from the government. In contrast, Cagayan's relative isolation surrounded by mountain ranges engendered greater colonial anxiety and thus required a special solution, the construction of an interprovincial road a year after the outbreak of the uprising.

The 1719 road project shared several characteristics with the plans from the 1690s. Disturbances and rebellion were the main causes of both. Although separated by several decades, Abella and Torres proposed similar solutions to the logistical problem of constructing a road in hostile enemy territory. Like Inspector Abella in 1691, Superintendent Torres recommended the cooperation between the provinces of Pampanga and Cagayan.[136] He also wanted forts to accompany the road construction, one each for the two provinces. About ten to twelve leagues apart, the two forts could open the lines of communication across the frontier. Torres's plan was the pincer maneuver of the 1690s all over again.[137]

Governor-General Fernando Manuel de Bustillo Bustamante followed Torres's proposal to the letter.[138] To quell the rebellion, General Juan Pablo de Orduña, along with his Spanish-Kapampangan infantry and Ilocano-Pangasinense troops, descended upon the problematic towns in Cagayan.[139] To construct the road, Sergeant Major Luís Estacio Venegas approached from Cagayan and built a fort in Sifun (figure 3.3), while Sergeant Major Miguel Navarro replicated the maneuver in Pampanga.[140] The goal was to eventually meet up with the other in the middle, which would effectively open the road. From the use of forts to the two-pronged approach from either side, Abella's plans, Torres's proposal, and Bustamante's road all mirrored each other.

However, a few differences distinguished Bustamante's 1719 road from Abella's 1690s plans. Although both road projects had the aim of finally subjugating the animist and apostate communities in the borderland, the 1719 road had a wider remit in attempting to gain greater control not only of unconquered natives but also of recalcitrant colonial officials.[141] The vast majority of contemporary observers, especially ecclesiastical authorities, blamed the

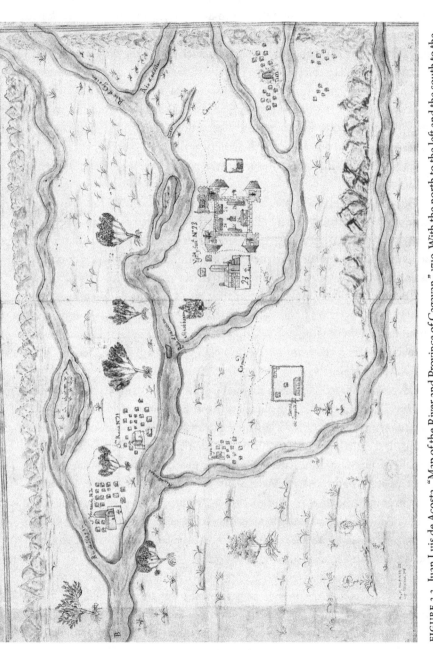

FIGURE 3.3 Juan Luis de Acosta, "Map of the River and Province of Cagayan," 1719. With the north to the left and the south to the right, this section of Acosta's map depicts the fort of Itugud, the farthest Spanish military outpost in upriver Cagayan near Sifun. Ministerio de Cultura y Deporte, Archivo General de Indias.

uprising not so much on the rice shortage, but on the blatant opportunism of Spanish officials during the crisis. Beyond the reach of Spanish Manila, provincial governors and garrisoned soldiers abused their power and caused the uprising in the first place. Unlike the abandoned proposals of the 1690s, the 1719 road partly became a reality or, at the very least, left a few traces on the ground. Paradoxically, the road quickly turned from a tool of administrative control to an open target for critics, especially after citizens of Manila murdered Bustamante soon after. Succeeding Spanish officials accused the now defenseless, deceased governor-general of making the situation worse. He was held accountable not only for the extortions in Cagayan but also for exacerbating the situation with his road project.[142]

With a new interim governor-general in Francisco de la Cuesta, archbishop of Manila and archnemesis of Bustamante, it was inevitable that the tide would turn against the planned projects of the previous governor-general.[143] Instead of being a solution to the problem of exploitation and unrest in Cagayan and its hinterland, the road quickly became a symbol of everything that was wrong with the previous administration. De la Cuesta dug up the complaints against the road filed by the Augustinians—specifically the missionary Alejandro Cacho and the provincial Tomás Ortiz—and used them as justification to stop the project.[144] Missionaries working on either side of the borderland despaired at the disruption caused by the soldiers and the road construction. In his chronicle, Cacho observed the changed atmosphere in his mission after the arrival of Sergeant Major Navarro and his troops to open the road from the side of Pampanga.[145] A sense of unease reigned among the potential converts who now wanted to go back to their mountains. Through Cacho's imploration, most were convinced to remain, but they still decided to disperse a little just in case something happened. The Dominicans witnessed a similar situation on the side of Cagayan. Their provincial reported that borderland animist communities fled to the mountains due to their fear of the soldiers, among other reasons.[146] With no one to preach to, the Dominicans pulled out from the site. From the missionaries' perspective, the road had a counterproductive effect because instead of aiding the conversion of animists and apostates and bringing them into the Spanish-Christian fold, it was repulsing and dispersing them deeper into the hinterland.

Unlike their support for the violent war plans of the 1690s, the religious orders disapproved the fort and road constructions of 1719 and preferred a method of conquest that was more missionary than military. The reversal in policy was partly due to the past antagonism with Bustamante and partly due to the slow but steady progress of the missionaries themselves. The road was a hindrance to missionary activities. It was not an innocent infrastructural project of clearing a path through forests and across mountains because it involved forts and coercive force that affected mission and Indigenous settlements in unexpected ways. The dispute between Cacho and the Augustinians, on one hand, and Bustamante and the Manila government, on the other hand, conformed to the classic conflict between religious and secular authorities. The Manila government accused Cacho of blocking eighty indigenes who had come down the mountains to meet with Sergeant Major Navarro and denying the latter's request for guides to open the proposed road.[147] In his defense, Cacho protested that not a single person had gone down from the mountains and that he had not refused a request for guides. Whatever the veracity of each side's claims, the tension manifested a power struggle around who was in charge in the borderland and whose method would prevail.

The conflict resolved itself with the death of Bustamante and the accession of the archbishop to the vacated post. The Augustinians would still open a road, but they would do it their own way through the slow process of conversion, even if it took years.[148] Bustamante and his military officers would probably not have been happy with such a slow pace of road building, but the missionaries at this time wanted mission towns—and not forts—to be the nodes of the road in the making. Instead of two military sergeants meeting in the middle and creating the road as soon as possible, missionaries, converts, and catechumens would crisscross sections of the borderland for years before a deliberate attempt would be made to finally link Cagayan with its neighboring provinces to the south.

In the Augustinian method, missionaries like Cacho focused on establishing colonial towns and converting natives, and roads were simply the offshoot of their evangelical activities.[149] This was the anti-Bustamante, missionary style of constructing a road, which was built on conversion and mutual reception rather than military campaigns and force. As much as possible, it only relied on armed force as a last resort. It laid the groundwork for the so-called Dominican road that would open a couple of decades later, but it was a long, seemingly aimless way of going about it. While Bustamante's sergeant majors made immediate progress on the ground despite the disruptions, Cacho and his flock made slow, halting movements, coming upon one pathway or another that connected mission towns but never bringing the project of an interprovincial road to its completion.[150] The Dominicans had to step in years later to accomplish that. The missionary method was always at the mercy of the acquiescence of a wide variety of animist groups in the borderland, hence the glacial pace of its progress. Although the missionaries of the different religious orders were the primary sponsors of road construction, they had to rely on local actors and adapt to the social dynamics of the borderlands by getting the cooperation of allies and gaining the confidence of opponents.

Negotiating a Passage

A road connected not only sites but also communities. It opened interactions and communication among different towns and villages. Constructing roads in borderlands was as much taming the rough, overgrown landscape as hashing out the differences of the communities along the way. Besides clearing a trail through the vegetation and flattening the rugged terrain, roads connected communities that had varying relationships with each other. Allied communities would appreciate the opportunity for greater contact, but antagonistic ones would reject the unwanted proximity. While Spanish officials and friars envisioned a *pax hispanica* of commerce and contact built on the foundation of roads, connecting previously detached polities sometimes resulted in greater conflicts.[151] When the Augustinians and Dominicans started working on the road to Cagayan in earnest in the second half of the 1730s, they still remembered how the lack of roads had made the suppression of the revolt in Cagayan two decades earlier very difficult.[152] The road became a cornerstone of the project to conquer the borderland and establish Spanish control there (map 3.1).

When the Augustinian and Dominican orders opened the road to Cagayan in the late 1730s, they had to resort to persuasive as well as violent methods. They ironically revived certain elements of Bustamante's earlier plan such as the use of forts and force. The conversion of several borderland communities to Christianity both minimized and exacerbated existing antagonisms in the area. The Isinays of the mission town of Buhay were crucial in creating the road to Cagayan as they provided all kinds of support to the missionaries. Converted to the new religion and backed by the Spanish government, their growing influence in the hinterland, however, also antagonized several Indigenous groups who became more resistant to letting outsiders pass by, much less enter, their territory. Resolving this social puzzle was all part of road construction.

The establishment of a mission in Buhay in 1717 was a central piece of the puzzle to the opening of the road to Cagayan in 1738. If it took the Augustinians almost a decade to enter Buhay (see chapter 1), it took them more than twice as long to penetrate the towns of the Magat River Valley, such as

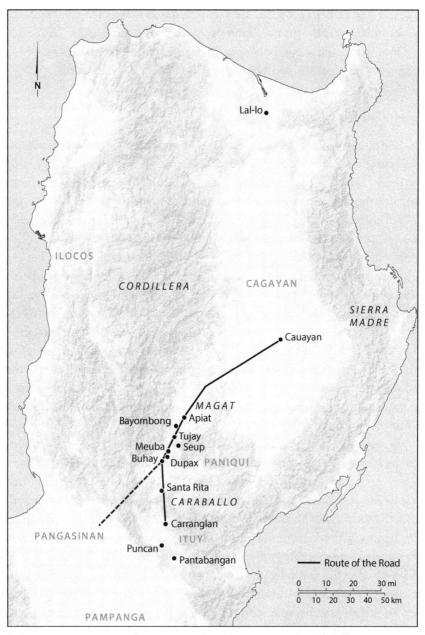

MAP 3.1 Map of the towns along the road between the Cagayan Valley and the central Luzon plains from the late 1730s. José Marín traversed the road connecting Cagayan and Ituy *(solid line)*, and succeeding Dominicans used an alternative route between Buhay and Pangasinan *(dashed line)*. The opposition of key towns and the mountainous topography of the borderlands restricted the number of viable routes.

Bayombong, farther north that led to Cagayan. Despite the seeming lack of progress, Buhay became a crucial staging point for missionary explorations. Diego Noguerol, a veteran missionary in the area, claimed that Buhay "has always been the column and castle built on rock that maintained the whole mission."[153] After finally welcoming the missionaries, the people of Buhay offered invaluable support in fostering ties with receptive animist communities and offering protection against hostile ones. For example, they sponsored councils, ceremonies, and gift-bearing embassies to surrounding animist communities.[154] They also built the churches and houses of the new converts to encourage them to relocate to mission towns. In times of war, the Isinays of Buhay defended their Christian brethren. Noguerol's Buhay companions, particularly Domingo Lumayon and Antonio Ilayat, saved him from certain death at the hands of the hostile Ibalibons of Seup.[155] Besides its central geographical position in Ituy, Buhay was the backbone of missionary activities in the area.

Although most histories of the opening of the road to Cagayan emphasize the role of Augustinian and Dominican friars as the trailblazers, the basic building blocks of the road were the shifting alliances and antagonisms among the different borderland communities.[156] The Spanish ability to enforce road building in the area was partly dependent on the relative power of their Isinay allies, who started out weak but gained some strength through the years. The conversion of Buhay was both a boon and a bane. On one hand, the Isinays of Buhay had the propitious opportunity to be at the forefront of the Christian wave sweeping northward from the 1720s. Alongside Dominican friars, they converted a long list of towns in the region: Bayait, Bantang, Anting, Apean, Duliao, Erran, Guinayompongan, and others.[157] More importantly, the new religion gave them access to a growing Christian alliance and progressively emboldened them in their status and authority. On the other hand, in the social milieu of the hinterland, the Isinays were not the dominant group. Other Indigenous groups such as Igorots, Ilongots, and Ibalibons held sway in the area and were not receptive to Spanish presence.[158] The Spaniards had effectively aligned themselves with one of the weaker borderland groups; missionaries even had to pay tribute to the stronger Ilongots and Ibalibons. It was the complete opposite of their avowed goal of gaining vassals and tribute payers for the Spanish king. In their alliance with the Isinays, they were vulnerable and open to attacks from stronger groups, which forced them to adopt an appeasing and cautious strategy.[159]

Although the Isinays of Buhay eventually gained greater social power as other borderland towns also converted, they suffered a lot of setbacks and opposition in the process.[160] Belligerent animist communities, primarily the

Ibalibons of Seup, burned their granaries and church.[161] The Christian towns of Buhay and Carranglan wanted to retaliate against Seup, but they were dissuaded by the missionaries who did not want the violence to escalate and lead to the mission's total ruin. Seup attacked again, but this time they burned down the whole town of Buhay. Incensed, Buhay finally retaliated and burned the animist towns of Seup and Tujay, who in turn burned the mission town of Meuba.

The back-and-forth attacks between the different borderland communities were part of the normal churn of shifting alliances and antagonisms, but the conversion of towns like Buhay added another layer to the interpolity dynamics. In the region, polities constantly jostled for supremacy among one another: powerful ones subjecting weak ones, subordinate ones aligning themselves with paramount ones, polities splitting into competing factions, or upstarts taking control of regional leadership.[162] Individuals and communities looked for the best opportunity for themselves, which sometimes meant subordinating oneself to more powerful polities for protection and at other times meant defeating a rival polity for supremacy. The conflict between Buhay and Seup certainly cannot be blamed solely on the presence of Spanish missionaries.[163] However, that animist and Christian towns were often on opposite sides of the conflict was no coincidence. The reductionist perspective of the Spanish religious sources, which viewed the world in terms of an eternal war between good and evil, definitely colored the way they portrayed the conflict. Nevertheless, borderland inhabitants—both Christian converts and animist practitioners—quickly learned that baptism involved membership in a Christian family and the Spanish monarchy.[164] In other words, conversion meant entering into an alliance with Spaniards and other Christians.

The battle lines between animists and Christians in the competition over strategic towns like Tujay prove the point. On one side were the main opponents of further Christianization in the area: the Ilongot Beiran of Seup and the Ibalibons Danao of Apiat and Talimazon of Bayombong.[165] The three chiefs and their towns were against the recent conversion of the towns of Duliao, Erran, and Guinayompongan under the stewardship of Buhay. On the other side were Buhay and the other Christian towns. In their attacks on Seup, Buhay had the backing of lowland Kapampangan troops and the new converts in Dupax.[166] A conflict between opposing animist and Christian sides is a too-simplistic portrayal of the situation. Of course, factors other than converting to the new religion and aligning with Spaniards were at play;

however, the threat of a looming, growing Christian alliance was a concern to the paramount Ilongot and Ibalibon chiefs. Tujay was a major Isinay town, and its potential conversion to Christianity posed a threat to the animist triumvirate of Beiran, Danao, and Talimazon because too many towns were then joining the Spanish-Christian alliance. When the Isinays of Tujay showed a willingness to receive Spanish missionaries, the Ilongots of Seup burned Tujay to demonstrate their displeasure and dissuade more Isinays from joining the other side.[167] The animist chiefs vowed to destroy the mission and kill any missionary who made any further advances into their territory.[168] When Noguerol visited Duliao, that was exactly what they tried to do to him.

This predicament was the roadblock that inhibited any significant progress in building a road to Cagayan. Converts and missionaries could not even set foot on enemy territory without the distinct possibility of being killed, much less construct a permanent route through it. Wars and head-hunting raids commonly hindered movement in the countryside.[169] Sections of Cagayan dominated by animist communities were intransitable for the longest time until the establishment of missions because attacks from hostile groups made traveling very dangerous, at least for those on the receiving end.[170] In the mission of Baler, Franciscan missionaries had never set foot in Dinarayauan for twenty years because of the notoriously violent Aetas living there.[171] In one area, an Aeta chief gave passage only to those who offered him tribute.[172] The missionary Bernardo de Santa Rosa gave him rice and tobacco so that he would leave the mission alone. Even if roads and pathways existed, ambushes and enmities rendered them practically unusable. Manuel Olivencia, a missionary in Ilongot country, could not find anyone to accompany him to the next village because "the succeeding towns were their enemies, and the roads were closed."[173] One of his companions had the candor to ask him, "Father, if they kill me, will you resurrect me?"[174]

However, roadblocks were not insurmountable. On the positive side, the existence of a federation among towns made roads safe for travelers.[175] If alliances were so malleable that the emergence of a new Christian identity had a ripple effect in the borderlands, they could also be shaped to incorporate one's enemies. After all, before it all came to a head and they were thrown out, Augustinian missionaries had already been in Seup, Apiat, and Bayombong and converted a few people there.[176] In the midst of all the burned churches and towns, Beiran, Danao, and Talimazon continued to visit mission towns where the priests usually warmly received them with gifts in an attempt to convince them to convert.[177] In fact, these chiefs were major players in the trade between Ibalibons and Isinays.[178] These malleable, even if sometimes tenuous, relationships allowed borderland mobilities to occur in the midst of opposition and violence.

Ibalibons like the three generations of Danao, Dayay, and Ganaban who wavered in their allegiances opened the door to conversion and led to a reconfiguration of borderland interpolity dynamics. Among the three Ilongot and Ibalibon chiefs, Danao seemed to be the most willing to work with the missionaries.[179] Whenever he visited Pantabangan, Cacho would try to woo him and give him gifts. In return, Danao made promises of wanting to be baptized and welcoming priests in his town, but he always reneged on them, alleging that the other two chiefs prevented him from doing so. Danao's son, Dayay, was even more receptive of priests as he tried to convince his father to welcome them with open arms. At one point, he even sent his two sons, Piran and Ganaban, to be raised by Noguerol in Buhay.[180] This was the classic missionary strategy of using a chief's children as the entry point for conversion.[181] Like his grandfather Danao, Ganaban found an excuse not to get baptized: "Father, if God willed that those elders passed away soon, I would then get baptized."[182] If Danao used the other chiefs as an excuse, Ganaban used the town elders as his.

Whether these were valid justifications or merely a "big dissimulation and shamelessness" on the part of so-called deceitful natives, they were evidently plausible explanations given that in the Indigenous world individuals were bound to communities and communities to their neighbors.[183] Individual choice was constrained by what other chiefs, elders, and a host of other people thought. In the face of a seeming wall of opposition, missionaries looked for every opening they could find whether in interpolity or generational differences. They constantly searched for the weak link that would break the resistant chain.

Gaps in the battle lines permitted communication between the opposing parties, and a certain leeway existed for alliances to buckle and shift. In an Isinay's account of events, it was the missionary of Buhay, José González, who initiated the peace talks with Seup in 1736 and calmed down the combative spirit of his parishioners.[184] When the contingent from Buhay arrived nearby for a conference, elders from Seup told them that they could not enter because the town was burned down and had nothing to offer them to eat. The Isinays of Buhay knew this was a good sign, since the Ibalibons of Seup were, at least in principle, willing to receive them, if not for the dire circumstances. Sure enough, the following month the people of Seup visited Buhay, where they feasted and danced their way to peace.

In hindsight, the pact with Seup was the turning point that led to the opening of a road to Cagayan and the conquest of the Ibalibons.[185] Even though most Ibalibons were still against the idea of conversion, the missionaries now had a more stable foothold in the borderlands. Afterward, González frequently went to Bayombong without major issues.[186] Reciprocal visits (see chapter 1) were the conduits that brought people together even in times of violent conflict. The missionaries themselves emphasized the crucial role their Christian converts played in sponsoring these peace ceremonies in mission towns.[187] With the mutual devastation of Isinay and Ibalibon towns, no clear superior power emerged in the battle. The once clearly weaker Isinays of Buhay had already proved their mettle, and an alliance with the enemy—or at least maintaining peaceful relations with them—was a way out of the impasse. Visits and feasts were the standard procedure to achieving peace and forming alliances, but a novel, additional method was conversion to Christianity.

Peace pacts did not necessarily lead to conversion or completely open the door to the frontier. Beiran of Seup eventually died without converting, but he did advise his daughter to do so.[188] While Beiran and his town adopted a more receptive stance toward the Spanish-Christian presence in the area, Danao and Talimazon remained steadfast in their opposition.

At this stage, the Augustinians approaching from the south, particularly the Buhay-based González, had been coordinating with the Dominicans coming from the north. As early as 1735, the Augustinians had observed "signs of softness" on the part of nearby animist communities, so in 1736 González wrote a letter to the Dominican in charge of the province of Pangasinan, Manuel del Río.[189] Reminiscent of the idea proposed by Abella in the 1690s and Bustamante in the 1710s, he wanted Augustinians and Dominicans to work together in a pincer maneuver on the animist communities in between Pampanga and Cagayan. A local chief backed González's proposal, since flanking the enemies on two fronts would box them in with no other option but to surrender.[190] When González's letter arrived in Pangasinan, it so happened that both the Dominican provincial and a missionary from Cagayan, Diego de la Torre, were also there for a meeting.[191] The provincial immediately ordered de la Torre to explore the frontier between the two provinces and assess the disposition of the Indigenous people there to conversion.

What greeted de la Torre during his investigation was not promising. He found the hut for priests in the Dominican mission's farthest outpost burned down by unfriendly animists.[192] Two of the most powerful chiefs in the area, Danao and Ansimo, were not exactly receptive to Spanish presence. Apparently, Danao had already had conversations about opening a road with some

Christians years ago, but Ansimo had threatened to kill him if he proceeded with the plan. With Danao somewhat receptive, convincing Ansimo was the key to unraveling the deadlock. De la Torre spoke with Ansimo about building a road through the borderland, and Ansimo found the whole idea repugnant, making several excuses including how rough the terrain was.[193] Due to the Spaniards' insistence, he vowed to reconsider the issue, but it was not a matter that could be resolved in a single day, since he had to consult the other chiefs first. Ansimo eventually informed de la Torre of the council's decision to allow priests to move about but with certain limits.[194]

The next year, in 1737, Governor-General Fernando Valdés Tamón approved the assignment of four Dominican missionaries to the mission of Diffun in Cagayan.[195] In the short span of a year, the Dominican side of the two-pronged approach to the frontier was taking shape. However, the new missionaries encountered the perennial problem of resistance from the Ibalibon chiefs who refused to let them in their towns.

Even after a shower of gifts and demonstrations of affection, the best concession the priests could achieve was that they be shown the way to Manila under six strict conditions: no residence in their towns, no preaching, a guarantee of the natives' safety in case soldiers arrived, no passage to any Spaniards, the provision of food during the trip, and gifts of jewelry.[196] While the last two conditions were fleeting transactional dealings, the first four conditions were more permanent in character. They barred Spanish presence in Ibalibon towns, which clearly highlights the one-off nature of the negotiated trip to Manila. The Dominican missionaries accepted the far-from-ideal proposal because it might be the first step toward closer relations. However, the animist towns held another round of consultations and added five more conditions to their initial proposal: fifty cows, fifty horses, a basket of gold, and a man from the town of Tuao and one of the priests to kill as sacrificial offerings.[197] The last two requests, especially the last one, made the deal untenable. Setting their sights lower, the Dominicans simply asked for permission to visit the animist towns once in a while. The hard-bargaining animists agreed but only under the condition that they traveled alone without any escorts.

The Augustinian and Dominican missionaries were stuck between a rock and a hard place. On one hand, they could not make any significant progress in their road building without the acquiescence of the Indigenous communities along the way. Joint resistance from a federation of borderland towns made the simple act of gaining access almost impossible. Neighboring chiefs and communities put pressure on individuals who showed any willingness to welcome the Spaniards. When the alliance of towns made a concession, it was under strict conditions that severely limited the movement of priests and other Spaniards in the hinterland. On the other hand, in the eyes of the religious orders, the road was the solution to the staunch resistance exhibited by the animist communities: "Opening the road from Cagayan to Pangasinan would fix the difficulty of their subjugation because the most resistant... based their confidence in the impenetrability of the route, which being intransitable made their lands very distant from both provinces."[198] Even animist communities knew that this lack of outside access improved their chances of maintaining their independence.[199] In a catch-22, the Spanish road project stumbled on the resistance from animist communities, but at the same time the best way to break this resistance was to construct a road. This circular logic was conducive to a stalemate and would explain the slow process of negotiations and road building.

The situation did not look promising, but the missionaries persisted. In a short span of time, four Dominican missionaries suddenly died in the mission of Paniqui.[200] Two of them died violently in quick succession as if they were poisoned.[201] The fact that a dog died at the same time raised the concern that hostile animists had given them poisoned food, which was a known method of surreptitiously murdering somebody in the area.[202] The other missionaries were not quite sure if foul play was involved or if it was just a simple case of overfatigue from all the hard work and traveling.[203] If their suspicions were right, then this was yet another sign of Ibalibon resistance. The message was indirect but clear: priests were not welcome in their towns. However, the Dominicans also saw glimmers of hope. In 1738, a well-respected chieftess sheltered and defended them from their attackers, which led others to follow her lead.[204] Several chiefs went down to the provincial capital of Cagayan to ratify peace pacts with the Spaniards. Even Danao was once again willing to help the missionaries open the road. Before passing away, his son Dayay shared the following vision with him: "My father, some men dressed in white will come here, and they will come for your good, not your harm, and so I ask you, my father, to receive them kindly and to help, protect, and favor them."[205] Although this story might be casually dismissed as apocryphal, dreams and visions involving relatives and ancestral spirits were common elements of Indigenous decision-making.[206] Danao also noticed a softening in the stance of the once hardliner Ansimo. However, as some borderland animists became more accommodating of missionaries, others became more defiant like Talimazon and the people of Bayombong.[207]

With the situation in a state of flux, González, the Augustinian missionary of Buhay, thought that on balance the recent trends were working in their favor. In a letter to the Dominican missionaries in Diffun, he informed them of his latest dealings with Danao and Talimazon, who had contrasting responses.[208] Danao said all the animists would be happy to receive the Dominicans the following year. González had given gifts to Danao, and he encouraged the Dominicans to do the same with any Ibalibons who visited them. In contrast, Talimazon did not want priests to even pass through his land. Nonetheless, González was still optimistic that the road could still be opened because he believed Talimazon was not that important of a figure to impede the priests' passage in the area.[209] Out of the fifty households in Bayombong, in González's estimation, half were more loyal to Danao than Talimazon. Neither did Talimazon have the general backing of Isinays, Ilongots, or Igorots.

Even though other Dominican missionaries from Cagayan had previously reached the Isinay missions of the Augustinians, history would attribute the opening of the road to the daring feat of the trailblazing José Marín in 1738 (map 3.1).[210] Marín's other expeditions cutting out of Cagayan to adjacent provinces on the most daunting routes would only add to this renown.[211] It was as if the opening of the road to Cagayan were a watershed moment, but in reality multiple, shorter, segmented trips and visits had preceded Marín's crowning achievement. A certain amount of boldness, nonetheless, pervaded Marín's trip because he proceeded despite the threats coming from the chiefs of Bayombong like Talimazon. González had advised the Dominicans to travel with plenty of armed escorts, since pagans could never be trusted completely.[212] Along with the show of affection, intimidation through the show of force was part of dealing with enemies. This approach entailed the use of the carrot and the stick or, to be more precise using González's very own words, the bread and the stick.[213]

Disregarding González's advice, Marín crossed the borderland in secrecy with only a few animist guides.[214] Attempting to blend in the background and raise the least amount of suspicion, he traveled barefoot and dressed like an Ibalibon with a hat and cape made of leaves. Besides going incognito for his safety, Marín had other practical reasons for his choice of attire. It was common for missionary explorers to go barefoot just like the natives when climbing very steep slopes.[215] Marín most probably wore a loincloth made of tree bark because it was much lighter than his usual priestly habit, which would have weighed him down over the rough terrain, especially during river crossings, and exhausted him under the heat of the sun.[216] He also traveled under the cover of darkness to avoid detection from hostile towns such as Bayombong and Daruyag.[217] With stealth, he eventually reached Buhay and put on his habit before meeting with González. In the words of the Dominican pro-vincial, "ya se avia rompido la valla,"[218] the barrier had been broken; some-thing difficult and unprecedented had been achieved in their eyes. The road was finally open.

But Marín was far from alone in his adventure and success because he had the support of Danao and Ansimo and, more importantly, he had native guides showing him the way and protecting him. Danao even assigned him a special guide—his very own grandson Piran, whose recently deceased father Dayay had the vision of cooperating with the men dressed in white.[219] Throughout the journey, they stayed with people who were on their side. They spent a night in Buaya, a village of slaves who farmed and fished for Danao, specifically in the house of one of Piran's slaves. This assistance contributed more to Marín's success than his apparent ingenuity and physical attributes.[220] The opposition from Talimazon and company made traveling treacherous, but having the right allies also made it feasible.

The crossing of the borderland did not end with the arrival in Buhay or the meeting between Marín and González. The road connected much more than the Dominican and Augustinian missions in the provinces of Cagayan and Pampanga, respectively. Piran, along with Marín, continued traveling all the way to Pangasinan, where the Dominicans, together with their visiting pro-vincial, feasted him, dressed him in Spanish clothes, and honored him as best they could.[221] A few months later, after personally supervising the creation of a shorter, more direct route between Cagayan and Pangasinan (map 3.1), the provincial vicar of Pangasinan Río went to Manila with twenty-five animist chiefs from Paniqui, including Danao, Ansimo, and the grandchildren Piran and Ganaban.[222] In Manila, the Dominican order housed them and lavished them with gifts. The residents of Manila, including the governor-general, did not spare any expenses to give them the money, clothes, and other things that they asked for. The road to Cagayan was supposed to connect this distant province and its hinterland to the colonial capital in Manila. It did that and more.

While the road facilitated the movement of Spanish priests and Spanish-backed soldiers, it also served the purposes of borderland chiefs. Highlight-ing the immediate benefits of roads, religious chronicles always mention how missionaries used them straightaway to travel and preach to borderland animists. After Marín reached Buhay, two other Dominican missionaries, Pedro Sierra and Juan Flores, followed suit and joined him all the way to Pangasinan.[223] A Dominican priest from Cagayan used the same road a few months later to reach Manila.[224] The newly appointed missionary, Antonio del Campo, used the road to reach his assignment in Cagayan.[225] On his journey, he had the company of Danao and the other Ibalibon chiefs who had just come from Manila and were on their way back home, and four Isinays sent by Sierra and Flores to escort them. Later on, government officials and soldiers would use the same road to exert a semblance of colonial rule. In 1741, the provincial governor of Pangasinan would personally travel to the missions of Ituy and Paniqui to conduct an inspection tour.[226] In 1745, a government official sent troops from Pangasinan on a punitive campaign to the Cagayan frontier to contain the hostile Panoypoys there.[227] Successive descriptions of colonial movement demonstrate how the road made the hinterland much more accessible and open to outsiders. The road became a symbol and conduit of Spanish penetration of pagan territory.

However, even Indigenous communities utilized the road for their own ends. By allowing passage through their towns, they were able to widen their ties beyond their immediate neighborhood. They settled peace pacts in upland Buhay and lowland Lal-lo, and went to provincial Agoo and metropolitan Manila to be feasted and honored by the Spaniards. The road multiplied the sites of encounters and rituals, which escalated the competitive feasting to ever-grander scales.[228] After all, Isinays and Spaniards were dealing with Danao, "the main sponsor of sacrifices in the region and the person those in need consulted and turned to."[229] All of them had a reputation to maintain by hosting the most lavish feasts and ceremonies. As much as missionaries and soldiers used the road to penetrate and cross the borderland, Indigenous chiefs also used it to expand their alliances by traveling to different points across the island. Interpolity networks had existed before, but the opening of the road readjusted these alliances and was itself a product of new alliances. When Ibalibons like Danao and Ansimo permitted passage through their towns, it was a manifestation of their desire to align themselves with Isinays, Spaniards, and other Christians. Even the Ibalibon holdouts of Bayombong who eventually decided to convert claimed that they had dreams of a man telling them to get baptized soon because those who did it too late might suffer plenty of misfortune.[230] With Danao and Ansimo switching sides, the balance had already shifted in the Ibalibon alliance.[231] More than an apocryphal story or a vision of the future, the dream was a reaction to the stark reality of an ever-changing present.

More than the peace pacts per se that allowed safe passage, reiterative rituals in different places created a network of aligned polities that enabled mobility.[232] Traveling itself was important, as it was a transformative, reciprocal process. At its most banal, Marín went native on the way to Buhay in Ibalibon attire, and Danao and Piran returned from Manila dressed like Spaniards. Fellow travelers and visitors became closer and more alike. Exchanges through clothes and visits deepened the bonds among potential allies, which explains why opening roads, undertaking journeys, and celebrating them were such a big deal for both Spaniards and indigenes. Not everybody was welcome, as the almost murdered Noguerol and the dead dog could attest to. Offerings of food could also be poisoned. Traveling to and feasting in different places was definitely a privilege.

New Fault Lines

In spite of all the praises heaped on them, roads—whether Marín's or the Isinays'—were far from perfect. When Marín and Piran came back from their trailblazing adventure, Talimazon felt betrayed by Danao and Ansimo for breaking their pact and offended by Piran for not visiting him on the way.[233] Outraged, he strictly forbade Marín from coming anywhere near Bayombong, so Marín and the other Dominicans had to relocate to Danao's hometown in Apiat. As one door opened, another closed.

Friction in borderlands manifested itself in jurisdictional conflicts among religious orders and Indigenous communities, and the struggle to control the movement of people on the roads. The opening of roads brought the Dominican and Augustinian missions uncomfortably close to each other. When the Dominicans tried to look for alternative routes, it was not so much to save time and avoid a long, circuitous route, but to bypass the missions administered by the Augustinians.[234] It was not an accident that the opening of roads to Cagayan coincided with the territorial rift between Dominicans and Augustinians. Alongside their cooperation in road building and the smooth transfer of nine Augustinian mission towns to the Dominicans in 1740, the two orders had vehement disputes over boundary and jurisdictional lines. Even with roads physically open for transit, certain groups tried to control who could pass. Dominican missionaries in Cagayan had to confront new opponents in antagonistic Panoypoys despite the new road to Cagayan and the gradual alignment of Ibalibons—including Talimazon—with Christians and Spaniards. With a plethora of polities and communities in the borderland, for each one that welcomed Spanish presence and opened its town to outsiders, there was another that rejected the intrusion and refused to cooperate.

The road to Cagayan created a rift between Dominicans and Augustinians and their respective missions. While the road to Cagayan was a cooperation between the two religious orders, the very same road that brought them into closer proximity also created tensions between them. The Augustinian González was always in touch with the Dominicans in Pangasinan and Cagayan, coordinating the road-building efforts, giving advice, and even dispatching escorts. When the Augustinian order ceded their nine mission towns in Ituy and Paniqui, including Buhay and Bayombong, to the Dominicans in 1740, it had all the hallmarks of a selfless, generous gesture. After almost four decades of painstaking progress expanding the mission, they were giving it all up, except for Carranglan, Pantabangan, Puncan, Santa Rita, and a few other towns. The Dominicans wanted the northern section of the Augustinian mission because of the road. They thought that Buhay was key to maintaining the new road and thus keeping the lines of communication open between Pangasinan and Cagayan, two Dominican-administered provinces.[235] The Dominicans even argued that mission towns like Bayombong were better handled by them from Cagayan rather than by the Augustinians from Pampanga due to the relative distances and topography.[236]

Official documents relating to the transfer show no signs of rancor or dismay. The royal decree described the Augustinian order as acting "so freely and selflessly" to "facilitate the spiritual conquest of the rest of heathendom" and cooperating in "true brotherhood" with the Dominicans.[237] Yet despite the seemingly smooth transfer of mission towns, there were underlying tensions and open disagreements.

Proximity and mobility necessitated that the Dominicans and Augustinians clearly delineated the borderline between them. The handover was effectively part of the redrawing of the boundary between the provinces of Pangasinan and Pampanga. Five Augustinian-administered towns—including the main mission towns of Pantabangan and Carranglan—felt aggrieved by the new division and robbed of valuable lands and resources.[238] The Dominicans, in contrast, argued that the new division between Pangasinan and Pampanga was a purely jurisdictional issue and should not have any major repercussions because it did not involve moving any towns or parishes.[239] In their view, nothing had changed except the provincial assignment of certain places for administrative purposes. The five Augustinian towns might have used the filing of a complaint as a defensive strategy to protect their remaining territory in light of the recent cession of the nine mission towns farther north to the Dominicans.

The road to Cagayan provided a wider range of movements, including unwanted ones. After the handover of certain towns to the Dominicans, some converts decided to relocate and follow their old Augustinian missionaries to the mission towns in the south. This migration went against one of the pillars of the transfer of the mission towns, which was to clearly separate and delineate the jurisdiction of the two religious orders. In 1739 in the run-up to the cession, the Dominican provincial Jerónimo Sanz Ortiz made the following case: "But finding that the diversity of opinions and ministers could become an obstacle and hindrance in continuing what has already been started, so Our Lord the King . . . always held as the best policy to divide the provinces and assign them to the religious orders with each one responsible for the conversion of the pagans that are found in their assigned district."[240] In principle, clear pastoral jurisdictions brought order and avoided potential conflicts. The provincial pointed out that by "mixing ministers from different religious orders, even though they all have the best zeal and intention, you often tend to have impediments to major progress not so much because of the ministers, but because of the natives' natural temperament of being jealous and harboring grudges to any perceived demonstration of distinction whether in a change of town or minister."[241] Natives were acutely aware of distinctions by constantly comparing themselves with others. If the Augustinians did one thing and the Dominicans another, converts automatically compared the two and resented any perceived disadvantage. A simple town relocation or the arrival of a new missionary could engender enmity if certain communities thought it heightened the social status of another to their comparative detriment. If the natives were already socially competitive to begin with, having missionaries from different orders working side by side only made matters worse.

By bringing the Dominican and Augustinian missions into closer proximity, the road exacerbated the problem Sanz Ortiz had feared despite the seemingly orderly transfer of mission towns and the delineation of a new boundary line. In the self-fulfillment of a prophecy, new Dominican ministers took over the nine Augustinian mission towns as a result of the handover in 1740, and it unleashed the comparisons and resentments that Sanz Ortiz had predicted but hoped to avoid. For instance, the Dominican Ormaza took over the mission town of Buhay, but the Isinay converts of the town did not take kindly to such an ostensibly innocuous change. As early as 1741, Ormaza noticed a worrying flow of migrants from Buhay to Santa Rita, a mission town under the Augustinians: "Regarding some people of Buhay who went to Santa Rita, and they will continue to go if a remedy is not found, Father Cacho wrote to me saying that he had already given them permission. I wrote to him that I did not."[242] While Alejandro Cacho, a then veteran minister of thirty-six years in the Augustinian mission of Ituy, warmly welcomed the Isinay migrants from Buhay, Ormaza who was relatively new in his post felt abandoned and unloved by his parishioners. In 1744, the situation did not improve for the Dominicans with Isinay converts from Buhay, Dupax, and Meuba migrating to Santa Rita and Puncan.[243] Sensitive to changes in personnel, the Isinay converts wanted to stay with their Augustinian missionaries of old even if it meant relocating their abode.

At the core of the conflict between Dominicans, Augustinians, and Isinays was the question of mobility, specifically who controlled it.[244] There was no frictionless circulation of people, as the reality on the ground demanded that mobility be allowed, diverted, or prevented depending on conflicting interests and differing situations. Although roads did provide better communication and contact between communities, they did not completely eliminate the issue of access and permission. Even if the opening of the road helped to convert the defiant Talimazon, new Talimazons would emerge who would attempt to control who could pass and where they could go.

On one hand, the religious orders and their Indigenous allies advocated for freedom of movement. Dominicans encroached on and eventually took over Augustinian mission towns. Their Ibalibon allies in Apiat promised to facilitate movement on the road recently opened by Marín: "We should not harm but in fact help in their transportation the many Christians and the very reverend Fathers who pass by the said road."[245] In a way, Spanish penetration of the borderland lowered the barriers to mobility. On the other hand, the road to Cagayan partly led to the acute awareness of a borderline between Dominican and Augustinian missions, and the standoff between Ormaza and Cacho. Witnessing the depopulation of Buhay, Ormaza mocked Cacho as "the king of those roads" for letting Isinays relocate to Santa Rita without his permission.[246] He wanted to stop the emigration from the Dominican missions and establish a clear residential boundary between the missions of the two orders. In a letter to his provincial Río, Ormaza complained about Cacho's lack of initiative in stopping the flow of converts: "If only Father Cacho sent me the people who went to Santa Rita the way I do with his [parishioners] who come here, and stopped giving those from here permission to move there."[247] More important than the roads themselves were the persons who controlled them. Cacho effectively owned the roads as Isinay converts flocked to him and disregarded Ormaza's prohibitions.

Besides Cacho, Indigenous communities were the kings of the roads. Just like Ansimo and Talimazon before, they regulated who could pass on the newly opened routes. The converts of Augustinian mission towns such as Santa Rita, Puncan, and Carranglan closed borderland roads at their will.[248] To the north, Santa Rita did not want Cagayanes to use the road because this was not what had been agreed upon. To resolve the issue, Ormaza gathered all the Ibilaos of Santa Rita, including those in Buhay: "They came to the convent, I gifted them salted meat and gave them a heart-to-heart talk, and we agreed that those who had my permission would be allowed to pass, and those who did not would be made to return."[249] Ormaza wanted to wrestle control and authority over road usage from the Indigenous communities. To the south, the towns of Puncan and Carranglan did not want Pangasinenses to pass. Ormaza thought it was unfair and made it clear to them "that they were not the kings of the land and that it was a sin to block those who have the permission to pass by their land and earn a living."[250] The two towns reasoned that they were simply following orders, but Ormaza was skeptical: "I have never believed that the religious are involved in this, especially since it all goes against what Father Cacho and I have agreed upon." Even though Ormaza and the Dominicans occupied a central position in the mission of Buhay, they were outflanked by the converts of the Augustinian mission towns on either side who made the decision on who could traverse the Cagayan–Pangasinan road. The Augustinians might have given away nine pivotal mission towns to the Dominicans, but their remaining towns still exercised a significant amount of control in the borderlands.

While history books and chronicles remember the royal road as the Dominican trail inaugurated by the intrepid Marín, the situation on the ground showed who really was in charge of the road on a day-to-day basis. Despite the designation of some borderland routes as royal roads, regular tasks like road construction and maintenance were commonly delegated to local communities, hence the lack of direct intervention on the part of Spanish officials.[251] Royal control was more jurisdictional than anything else. In Spanish tradition, the king's road was the responsibility of local inhabitants—not the king himself or his officials. More than imperial royal structures, roads were Indigenous pathways where locals played a preponderant role.[252] Since roads were not top-down affairs in the first place, Indigenous borderland actors were naturally the protagonists in their construction. While the road to Cagayan might have served imperial and missionary ends, it would not have opened without the local communities who cooperated in the pursuit of their own ends.

Apart from implementing a quarantine against epidemic diseases (see chapter 4), two plausible reasons for blocking travelers were commerce and warfare. Linking Cagayan with the rest of the island created economic opportunities for the entrepreneurial. In his letter quoted earlier, Ormaza said that Pangasinenses were simply trying to earn a living as they traversed the road. Río noticed a new trade taking place along the new Cagayan–Pangasinan road since its opening three years earlier: "Natives of Cagayan . . . come with great ease to traffic and trade their merchandise on beasts of burden, and they also bring their livestock to sell in this city [Manila] which until now had not been done."[253] In his eyes, the road was a success because it brought Christianity and commerce to a previously isolated frontier. Although still a long trek, Cagayanes now reached Manila on a regular basis by land, an alternative to the circuitous and seasonal coastal sea route. It made a remote province ever closer to the colonial capital.

However, the new road and merchants might have disrupted existing trade networks, hence the desire of certain towns to block the passage of Cagayanes and Pangasinenses. Among upland Igorots, trade networks were segmented between numerous polities but at the same time dominated by certain frontier communities acting as nodes: "Contact and commerce among hamlets is huge, and, they say, they trade from hamlet to hamlet until the most interior one, but frontier hamlets generally do not let others go down to the provinces to buy and sell; they want everything to pass through them. . . . And they also resell them the merchandise or animals that they bought in the province."[254] An analogous situation might have existed in the Augustinian-administered mission towns that acted like monopolistic nodes of a frontier network. In a borderland landscape composed of hills, valleys, and mountain passes, it is especially important to think in terms of channels and corridors rather than boundaries and territories because certain sites were geographically well-positioned to control movement and exchange in the area (map 3.1).[255] The emergence, or at the very least the increase, of provincial traders from Cagayan and Pangasinan traversing the borderland perhaps threatened the Ibilaos' once dominant economic position.

Interpolity warfare was another reason for blocking travelers from using certain roads. Santa Rita and other towns did not want Cagayanes and Ibalibons to use their roads because of outstanding enmities that were yet to be avenged: "A long time ago, they have said, they should have killed a long time ago, so the feud does not end."[256] The Ibilaos of Santa Rita were prepared to kill Pangasinenses and officials from Cagayan who passed by, and warned their enemies to avoid the Augustinians' road and take an alternative route instead.[257] Ormaza entertained the idea of constructing an alternative road for the benefit of the Dominican mission, but he also detested the thought of succumbing to the whims of a bunch of "mangy scoundrels."[258]

The antagonism between different ethnic groups was not necessarily based on primordial cultural differences.[259] It could easily have had its roots on more contemporary events. When the Dominicans explored alternative routes to

Cagayan, they had to negotiate their passage with various Igorot communities. After accepting several gifts, the Igorot town of Pava agreed to let the Dominicans pass but reminded them, "Whoever does harm even once on the roads would no longer be allowed to pass a second time."[260] Conflicts more often than not had recent roots even though they were portrayed as primordial. If ethnic or cultural differences were not a sufficient basis for internecine warfare, neither was religious difference. Even though they were all converts, the Ibilaos of Santa Rita hated the Ibalibons and Pangasinenses enough to block their path. In other cases, animists and Christians willingly worked together to provide safe passage like in the case of the Dominicans of Pangasinan and the Igorots of Pava.[261] Warfare—and enmities in general—did not run along any strict ethnic, cultural, or religious line. It seemed like specific offenses were the root cause of enmities and the desire to deny access to certain groups.

Despite a sharpening division between Christians and animists, there was no hard-and-fast rule based on ethnicity or religion on where different communities and individuals stood. Fellow Ibalibons Danao and Talimazon argued for the longest time on whether to open the road to Cagayan, and the Christian Ibilaos of Santa Rita prevented other Christians from using the Pangasinan–Cagayan road. The patchwork of competing and aligned borderland polities continued on as before but with a new twist in the appearance of mission towns and the opening of roads.

The Dominican missionaries wanted to conquer the frontier by opening roads and populating them with mission towns. In theory, an expanding road network and increasing contact with Christians should facilitate the conversion of animist communities. However, this ideal of roads teeming with co-operative Christians was far from the reality because some roads were actually run by hostile animists. Ilongots were all over the road between Buhay and Bayombong and prevented Cagayanes from going to Manila and the people of Bayombong from reaching Dupax to get some rice.[262] Mission towns ran out of provisions because Isinay converts did not dare to travel and get supplies, since they were too afraid of being attacked by hostile animists.[263] Even though roads existed, using them was a completely different matter.

In 1741, when the people of Bato wanted to convert, the missionaries asked them to relocate to Meuba by the royal road as a sign of their faith.[264] The mission towns of Buhay, Dupax, and Meuba helped them move all their belongings and rice to their new home. The three mission towns recently had an oath of alliance, which was a big deal, since just a few months previously Ilongots had burned Buhay, Dupax had switched to the Ilongots' side, and Meuba had entertained the same move as Dupax.[265] Partly abandoned by other converts,

Buhay had persisted in defending the mission and its priests, and had even convinced Dupax and Meuba to return to the Christian fold. As part of their oath, the newly formed Christian coalition vowed to help and defend the converts of Bato and Paytan "as our siblings."[266] In the meantime, Ilongots continued to ambush the Christians traversing the road on the way to Meuba.[267]

A dividing line between Christians and animists made borderland mobility difficult, but the division was fluid and malleable. Meuba wavered in its loyalty between Christian Isinays and animist Ilongots. A few years later in 1745, Christians and Ilongots would unite in their fight against a common enemy, the Panoypoys.[268] Converts had an expectation that baptism made them members of a Christian alliance that would protect and defend them from enemies, but sometimes that was not the case. The Ibilaos of Santa Rita killed someone from Bayombong in the context of a long-standing feud, and the converts of Bayombong despaired that "the Fathers baptized them only to be killed" because as Christians they were prohibited from going to Santa Rita to avenge the death.[269] Not only were the Christians of Santa Rita blocking roads; they were also killing their defenseless fellow Christians. Nevertheless, just several months after the murder, Ormaza was happy to report that a new road had been built to Santa Rita, a significant achievement in light of the recent history of tension and killings.[270] In a short span of time, things could change very quickly as communities and individuals switched sides, and roads opened and closed.

Rather than permanent structures on the ground, roads were transitory. Rains washed away the soil and stones that travelers walked on. Vegetation eventually covered once clear pathways. Attacks and warfare closed off roads. A whole set of circumstances from the weather and topography to interpolity alliances and rivalries had to be aligned to make roads viable. Although Spanish documents sometimes refer to them as royal roads, the Spanish monarch only had a titular role because local borderland actors and communities were the real owners and kings of the roads. Different polities had to deliberately cooperate with each other to open, maintain, and secure them. However, when such cooperation was as fickle as the weather, roads had to be constantly renegotiated and fought for because otherwise they would be here one moment and gone the next.

A Changing Landscape

In 1741, José Zacarías Villareal, the provincial governor of Pangasinan, personally visited the missions of Ituy and Paniqui.[271] During his inspection tour, he traveled on the famous royal road to Cagayan: "All the road is almost flat with a vast countryside. There are only a few slopes between Paniqui and Ituy, but they are not very harsh. Some pagan hamlets occupy the plains and depressions. Looking out to the provinces of Pangasinan and Pampanga, only the mountain of Buhay is somewhat steep but not for long. The people are so domesticated that they do not run away from travelers as they used to, but warmly receive them and generously offer them what the land produces, which already has horses, cows, carabaos, and other animals."[272] Zacarías Villareal might have idealized the missions and the road too much. Isinays and Ibalibons might have welcomed Spanish visitors, but plenty of hostile animist groups still abounded in the area. The road section along the Magat River might have been relatively flat and easy, but the section from Pangasinan to Buhay was the opposite.

Despite the provincial governor's overly optimistic portrayal, advances had been made in terms of accessing and traversing the borderland. A few decades made a massive difference in Spanish mobility there. Before, the most common way of traveling to Cagayan had been a month-long sea route. By midcentury, an overland journey of about a dozen days was now a viable alternative. In 1718, Spanish Manila had a difficult time quelling the uprising in Cagayan because it could not dispatch military troops there immediately. By 1745, Spanish and indio troops were able to directly attack the upland base of the Panoypoys.

Besides people, animals were also mobile and took to the roads. People from Cagayan took advantage of the road and started selling their merchandise in Manila. They transported their goods on pack animals. Even livestock was a commodity that they sold. Instead of merely shipping the meat by boat, they were now able to bring the live animals to the markets in Manila. In the borderlands, cows were also a currency of mobility. Ansimo demanded fifty cows and fifty horses in exchange for showing the way to Manila. When the Dominican provincial Río entered their territory without permission, the Panoypoys demanded cows among other things as compensation.[273] In 1740, borderland roads were closed off due to the ongoing feud between the Ibalibons and Panoypoys and the outbreak of a smallpox epidemic on the island.[274] Travelers might meet an untimely death in the crossfire or simply under the suspicion of being infected. Ormaza, however, broke the cordon sanitaire with a simple trick—giving cows to the mission inhabitants who were blocking the pathways—so Pangasinenses continued to use the supposedly forbidden roads.[275]

Spaniards partly achieved their goal of using contact and commerce as a tactic to soften the resistance of animist communities and bring them under colonial control. Missionaries, officials, soldiers, merchants, and even cows were now crisscrossing the center of the island thanks to the widening road network. However, it also seemed like mobility brought in more deaths. Besides the casualties from raids and battles, newly arrived missionaries in the borderland died inexplicably. Religious chroniclers could not quite decide whether it was due to overfatigue, environmental factors, or poisoning. When Zacarías Villareal made his trip to the missions, he witnessed settlements moving back to the mountains as they fled from a smallpox epidemic.[276] The Isinays of Buhay blocked the roads and forbade anybody from smallpox-infested Pangasinan from approaching, including the Dominican provincial.[277] Perhaps the increased mobility and deaths were related to each other. Perhaps mobile cows and other animals were somehow involved in these deaths. Perhaps they all came in an interconnected package. These "perhapses" are the subject of the next chapter.

CHAPTER FOUR

Deadly Transitions

Toward the end of the eighteenth century, the Dominican Francisco Antolín wondered about a number of issues that largely revolved around the question of population decline.[1] Although the religious orders were more successful than ever in setting up missions in the mountainous borderlands of Luzon, he observed that the mission population was actually decreasing. In principle, missions should experience consistent population growth because they ostensibly brought the benefits of civilization to once barbaric communities. However, by the late eighteenth century, in Antolín's view the opposite trend seemed to be happening instead. Antolín had the unique perspective of someone who combined practical experience in the missions and scholarly insight culled from libraries and archives.[2] From 1776 to 1789, he served as vicar in the mission towns of Aritao and Dupax. From 1790, he became an official chronicler of the Dominicans in the Philippines. In 1788, he wrote two tracts on the population situation in the missions of Ituy and Paniqui.[3] Antolín's demographic pessimism most likely stemmed from the just recently concluded smallpox outbreaks of 1786 and 1787, which had devastated the missions. There is nothing like death and destruction to force people to pause, reflect, and question their achievements.

Missionary progress in Ituy and Paniqui partly depended on two complementary movements: the resettlement of upland communities to the lowlands and the Spanish penetration of the hinterland. In both cases, Antolín noted that the relocated populations did not fare too well. In fact, he placed the blame for the population decline squarely on increased mobility and contact.[4] Having just lived through the havoc wrought by smallpox, Antolín had epidemic diseases front of mind in his musings. He surmised that mountain populations were previously much larger because they had been "shut off and isolated in the corners and refuges of the mountains. Plagues like smallpox had not hit them so easily as they did now. Ancient Ilongots, Panipuys, and other secluded pagans had no experience of smallpox."[5] The construction of a road (see chapter 3) introduced new diseases in the borderlands and facilitated their transmission. As Antolín succinctly observed, "The fewer the contacts they [mountain inhabitants] had before, the bigger the population."[6]

One side of the greater borderland mobility was the resettlement of up-land communities to missions in foothills and valleys. Antolín noticed that new converts and catechumens who relocated to mission towns were more prone to get sick and die.[7] He compared their predicament to that of wild animals corralled and locked in cages. Where previously they had been free, dispersed, and unsociable, they were now reduced and subjugated. Where previously they had thrived in nature, they now found themselves tamed but rendered useless and more susceptible to death. Antolín's portrayal of life in the mission was surprisingly forthright and despondent. His words seemed to be out of character for a missionary out in the field trying to save souls. He implicitly questioned the whole logic of uprooting people from their natural habitat. Reminiscent of previous debates on the demographic collapse in the Americas, his analogy boiled down to the following question: Was it worth it to attempt to convert and civilize mountain people when they were more likely to succumb to death in the missions?[8] The standard religious answer would have been a yes. Of course, the eternal salvation of the soul in the afterlife was more important than physical survival in the earthly realm, but Antolín entertained alternatives that avoided transplanting converts from their mountain homes.

Another side of borderland mobility was the Spanish penetration of the island's interior. In tackling the question of why it took Spaniards so long to carry out their conquest of borderlands, Antolín named two primary factors at work: distance and nature.[9] For the first factor, the island's distance from Spain made it difficult to bring in a sufficient number of priests to undertake missionary work. The few priests who successfully made the journey tended to cater to the more populated coastal settlements. For the second factor, distance was also an issue, but at a much shorter range and in the context of the terrain. Once Spaniards were on the island, they had a tough time traversing the thick vegetation of the interior. The climatic combination of abundant sunshine and rain fostered the growth of dense forests that hindered movement.[10] In Antolín's words, "In these lands, the sun beats down really hard, it rains a lot, and forests and thickets grow that are difficult to penetrate. Nature has defended these people with a thousand walls."[11] Climate and geography seemed to have conspired against the missionaries and protected borderland communities from outside contact. Even when missionaries reached and settled in the hinterland, they were susceptible to become sick and die from "the bad food and shelter and the many responsibilities and work."[12] When they did pass away, there was no one to replace them in the mission due to the scarcity of priests. The twin problems of distance and impenetrability formed a vicious circle of friction that tested the hardiness of missionaries, but mobility between mountains and plains also caused its own set of problems.

Contradictions abounded in the borderlands. The establishment of mission towns brought elements of Spanish-style living but also epidemic devastation. Instead of creating thriving Christian populations in the frontier, missionaries were unintentionally bringing their new flock to the slaughter. At the same time, missionaries were dying in a land of apparent natural abundance. Taking inspiration from Antolín's recognition of the paradoxes inherent in borderland mobility, this chapter explores the tension between mobility and the environment, especially in relation to diseases. I argue that borderland missions largely occupied an ecological transitional zone between mountains and plains. Although Antolín never explicitly mentioned tropicality in any of his tracts, the concept not only pervades his discourse but also explains many of the contradictions that he noticed, such as the simultaneous existence of natural abundance and widespread death in the same place. He, however, placed a unique emphasis on a harsh, cold climate and incorporated upland-lowland and inland-coastal binaries popular among historical actors in the region. In this chapter, I focus on how reciprocal mobilities in borderlands were grounded in the surrounding environment.

Located along foothills, piedmonts, and river valleys, the missions of Ituy and Paniqui occupied a crossroad that uplanders and lowlanders traversed as they conducted their various activities. Throughout the eighteenth century, growing contact between uplanders and lowlanders at the foothills increased the prevalence of disease in this transitional space. On one hand, missions located in foothills were a breeding ground for malaria that most probably earned this area its reputation for being pestilential. The foundation of mission settlements and the concomitant promotion of cattle and horses potentially made the situation worse by diversifying the blood meal options of mosquitoes and thus multiplying the mosquito population and possibly the incidence of malaria. On the other hand, lowlanders brought with them contagious diseases such as smallpox that decimated the upland population. As Spanish missionaries and indio lowlanders occasionally spread epidemic diseases in the hinterland, uplanders sometimes shut themselves in and prevented lowlanders from entering their highland realm. With foothills harboring malaria and uplanders closing themselves off, the intermediate zone of the missions effectively became a disease barrier that halted attempts at increased mobility. Mission life and domesticated animals brought the colonial lowlands and independent uplands closer together but also kept them apart.

The chapter ends by exploring the epidemics of 1786 and 1787 and showing how movement gave indios the opportunity to reevaluate their situation and escape illnesses. The shared devastation of both uplands and lowlands made the decision perhaps superfluous, but visits and journeys allowed upland animists and lowland converts to better assess their current predicament, compare it with alternatives, and make their move. Greater borderland mobility helped spread epidemic diseases and resulted in more infections and deaths, and yet people continued to move and cross the upland-lowland divide despite everything.

A Tropical Paradox

Without mentioning the term, Francisco Antolín resorted to the general idea of tropicality to explain what he experienced and knew about the island of Luzon. However, he also formulated his own distinct ideas on how tropicality operated on the island. Like other Europeans who ventured to the tropics, Antolín encountered the paradox of the coexistence of tropical abundance and death.[13] Nature blessed the tropics with excessive natural fertility, but tropical lands were also the scene of deadly fevers. Antolín constructed a more nuanced notion of tropicality that incorporated the local geographical distinction between mountains and plains to resolve the contradiction.

Descriptions of the hinterland in Luzon echoed the tropical trope of a vibrant nature that required little human intervention to reap bountiful harvests. In one of his works, Antolín cited the report of a 1633 missionary expedition to Ituy to prove how fertile the area was: "It [Ituy] is very fertile. In sowing their rice, indios do not do anything but burn a piece of the forest and poke holes with a stick on the ground where they throw in the rice grains and cover them with soil. In this way, they enjoy bountiful harvests."[14] Besides being fertile, the land was abundant in natural resources from root crops and fruits to game meat and salt.[15] Their rudimentary lifestyle meant that people had everything they needed at hand. One of the most common goods traded between coastal and inland polities was salt.[16] However, several frontier towns like Aritao and Bambang produced it on their own; hence, they were not dependent on coastal sources.[17] They abandoned their salt production only with the opening of a borderland road. Producing a wide variety of products, the land's richness contributed to making Ituy a self-sufficient and independent place.

Other historical accounts supported Antolín's claim of natural abundance. In 1591, one of the very first Spanish expeditions to Ituy characterized it as "very abundant, temperate, fertile, and with plenty of cattle."[18] In 1737, the Dominican order claimed the island's interior was "partly mountainous and partly level, and all of it happy, fertile, and enriched by two great rivers."[19] In 1755, a Franciscan friar described his Ilongot mission as "abounding with rich waters."[20] He even praised the greater productivity of swidden farming over the irrigated agriculture Spaniards encouraged: "An Ilongot woman does more work with a knife than a Tagalog with two carabaos. The proof is clear. A Tagalog with two carabaos . . . hardly has enough rice for the year, and the Ilongot woman . . . with a bad knife sows and harvests enough rice for the year, not only for herself but also for guests."[21] Sun, soil, and water all conspired to create an excessively fertile land that produced bountiful harvests with the most rudimentary of tools.

The glowing accounts above had an immediate practical purpose and an underlying tropical slant. On the practical side, wanting to convince the Spanish monarchy to support the conquest and conversion of the frontier, Spanish officials and missionaries had a propensity to always describe the lands they explored in glowing terms. The government was more likely to approve the foundation of colonial towns in places with fertile soil and access to water, which it thought would provide a solid base for the prosperity of settlements. On the rhetorical side, the descriptions of the landscape harked back to the tropical trope of natural abundance. Fresh water nourishing a vibrant land and people reaping bountiful harvests with little labor all evoked images of a tropical island Eden.[22] From ancient times to the early modern period, Europeans imagined tropical regions in two complementary ways, one as a torrid zone and another as a terrestrial curiosity or paradise. Ptolemy claimed that just beyond the torrid zone of north Africa was a region called Ethiopia, fed by the Nile River and teeming with exotic flora and fauna.[23] The medieval legend of Prester John and other chronicles imagined an earthly paradise somewhere in Africa that had thick forests, revivifying waters, and wondrous creatures.[24] As early modern European voyagers traveled to the tropics, they searched for this terrestrial paradise of warmth, fertility, and health near the equator. Antolín and other travelers to Ituy might not have been looking for a long-lost garden of Eden in the Philippines, but their descriptions repeated precisely the same elements found in tropical discourse.[25]

In the same way that European voyagers had to grapple with the reality of deadly fevers in the tropics, Antolín and other Spaniards on the island also had to contend with the tropical paradox. Throughout the years, various expeditions to Ituy met with a number of illness-related deaths.[26] In the 1650s, the attempted mission in Ituy lasted only for two years. Among many other factors, epidemics drove missionaries and their military escorts back down to the Cagayan Valley.[27] Based on their assessment, the inclement weather and insufficient sustenance caused the untimely deaths. A military expedition sent to conquer Ituy in 1654 suffered from an epidemic outbreak that decimated its rank.[28] The apparent cause of the epidemic was the intemperate location of Ituy.

The renewed missionary campaign in the eighteenth century encountered the same problem of Spaniards dropping like flies once they set foot in the island's mountainous interior. In 1703, Antolín de Alzaga, one of the first Augustinian missionaries to arrive in the mountains of Pantabangan, fell gravely ill while visiting an upland community.[29] After receiving the last rites, Alzaga had to be evacuated to Manila where the change of airs helped him recover. Based on Spanish medical views at the time, the upland air of Pantabangan was toxic, while the coastal breeze of Manila was healthy. Four years later, back in his upland mission, Alzaga became sick once again, but this time apparently from the fatigue of being exposed to the rain and sun. He eventually succumbed to his illness and passed away.[30] In 1710, his fellow pioneer missionary in Ituy, Balthasar de Isasigana, also fell ill from the strenuous missionary work in the mountains. He left the mission and got better but never fully recovered and never returned to the frontier.

The Dominicans faced similar casualties while working in the borderland of Ituy in the early eighteenth century. While on a pastoral visit in 1702, the provincial of the Dominican order brought along with him two additional missionaries for the upland missions.[31] However, both missionaries became sick upon their arrival in the uplands. One immediately died there, but the other one was lucky enough to make it back to Manila, where he recovered. To make matters worse, an existing resident missionary died at the same time. In the same year, five Dominican missionaries were sent to the valley of Diffun.[32] From their base in the valley, they carried out explorations of the surrounding mountains and hills. Three of the priests became sick and had to return to the provincial capital of Cagayan, where all three of them would die in the span of twenty days. Considering there was an insufficient number of priests in the archipelago, it was devastating for the incipient missionary campaign to suffer so many casualties in such a short period of time.

The death of missionaries by illness was a recurring event throughout the centuries. It is difficult to definitively say whether these deaths were normal for the place and time. However, Spaniards usually offered a variety of explanations from the climate and landscape to the substandard living conditions in the missions. In some cases, they even accused indios for deliberately poisoning them. Doing a retrospective diagnosis of illnesses based on historical accounts is largely a game of guesswork with severe limitations. A large majority of the documents merely state that people got sick or had a fever. Such generic descriptions do not provide enough details to identify the type of illness. For epidemics, sources sometimes mention specific diseases such as smallpox and measles, but in most cases they simply say that there was an epidemic outbreak and not much else.

Although commonalities existed in how Europeans experienced and portrayed the tropics in the early modern period, differences always emerged as they took into account local situations and conditions. The tropical region as a distinct homogeneous part of the world had yet to be invented, which left plenty of room for individual European travelers and settlers to formulate their own distinctive variations.[33] For instance, the standard Hippocratic-Galenic explanation to the tropical paradox argued that both natural abundance and deadly diseases could be attributed to local environmental factors like heat and humidity, which accentuated processes of growth and decay at the same time.[34] Europeans in large part used this basic principle to explain the paradox, but they also added their own unique twists to it. In the case of Antolín, two factors set his argument apart from the classic Hippocratic-Galenic approach to the tropics. First, he emphasized the importance of the intemperate climate—instead of simply heat and humidity—to explain illnesses in the borderlands of Luzon. Constant heat was not the problem; it was the severe weather that caused havoc on people's well-being. Second, Antolín incorporated an upland-lowland divide in his perception of the tropical island of Luzon. Instead of emphasizing the differences between temperate and tropical regions, he made a clear distinction between interior uplands and coastal lowlands. Distance from the sea became a more important criterion than distance from the equator. Antolín combined ancient theories on climate and landscape with his own personal experience and investigations. His perspective was thus highly localized by paying close attention to climate conditions on the ground and by mirroring Indigenous distinctions between mountains and plains.

For many Spanish travelers to the borderland, what made the climate unpleasant was not the heat in itself, but the harsh cold and rain. In his various writings, Antolín argued that torrential rains and chilling northerlies in Ituy made its climate colder and worse than that of the coastal regions.[35] José González gave the following advice to his fellow missionaries: "Do not take a bath because the water is very cold and raw, and drink boiled water. We have also suffered a lot here because of the harshness of the land and the coldness of the wind."[36] Even books decomposed in the excessive humidity of the area.[37] Various observers pointed out how cold winds blowing from the north were detrimental to their health.[38] The cold rather than the heat was the culprit for the physical unease of Spanish visitors and settlers. While the depiction of humidity conformed to the standard Hippocratic-Galenic medical framework, water usually depicted as a curative and revitalizing element in conventional tropical discourse became a harmful and debilitating force in the local context of Luzon. Torrential rains and typhoons during the rainy season most probably created such a negative view of water.

Other Spaniards who had traveled to the interior shared Antolín's sentiments. A common explanation for the illness and death of the missionaries and soldiers who entered the hinterland was the inclement climate. What made the situation worse was that each town had its own distinct microclimate that settlers had to get used to.[39] At the start of the eighteenth century, the main mission town of the Dominicans in Ituy was Burubur. Both missionaries and soldiers were not happy with the town's location. The missionary Francisco de la Maza unfavorably compared the conditions in Burubur up on a foothill with nearby Apean down in a valley.[40] He found the weather in Apean sheltered by the surrounding mountains to be much better with no rain at all during certain months and no strong winds. In contrast, Burubur at the foot of a mountain was exposed to the biting cold, strong winds, and torrential rains. Later missionaries found the site "uncomfortable, humid, and surrounded by wooded mountains."[41] When the rains arrived, Spanish settlers claimed the weather was detrimental to their health.[42] Soldiers at the fort of Burubur escaped from their assignment alleging either discontent or illness. Facing the elements in their day-to-day life, borderland settlers saw multiple microclimates rather than a generic tropical abstraction.

The harsh, schizophrenic weather did not only affect missionaries and soldiers who settled in seemingly unhealthy locations, but also weakened and killed Spanish travelers who were merely passing by. Apparently, a number of missionaries died by traveling on horseback because it exposed them to rain showers and sunshine in quick succession.[43] The climatic contrast made them sick and sometimes killed them off. Covering long distances, missionaries on horseback had to adjust quickly to the diverse climates of the different towns they visited. In this view, such rapid changes had fatal consequences; moving from one ecological niche to another exacerbated the disturbing effects of the inclement weather.

In the European imaginary, the tropics were supposed to be a foil to the temperate zone.[44] The heat of the tropics led to an abundance in nature, which stunted their inhabitants' industry and fostered a culture of indolence. In contrast, the temperate zone represented the golden mean between the climatic extremes of the tropics and the poles. However, Spaniards in the Philippines found the inland mountains and their cold winds to be more problematic than coastal zones and their more stereotypically tropical weather. Spaniards did not embrace the idea of colonial hill stations, which became popular among other European colonizers trying to escape the oppressive, debilitating heat of the tropical lowlands.[45] For other Europeans, hills and mountains in the tropics simulated temperate conditions that were supposed to be conducive to good health. Hence, they became a refuge for convalescing soldiers. Bucking this European trend in tropical colonies, Spaniards found the mountains of Luzon to be unhealthy. The cold upland winds and temperatures were detrimental to the constitution of Spaniards who would visit, much less live there. The difference in perception might have been due to contrasting experiences of the uplands in different colonies.

Contradicting his statements on the fecundity of the land in Ituy, Antolín thought that coasts and plains in general were better in every way than mountains.[46] The uplands suffered from a lack of food and wine because their steep, jagged terrain made farming difficult. In contrast, food and wine were more abundant and varied in the lowlands. Different animals from birds to fish also thrived at lower altitudes. Antolín found that the soil and air on the plains produced healthier livestock and inhabitants. Regarding the quality of the food, "cow meat, which in these mountains is . . . indigestible, is tastier and healthier on the coasts because of the salty pasture."[47] If shadows, mists, and the cold enclosed harsh mountains, coastal areas stretched out under an open sky and imbibed fresh air blowing in from the sea. Hence, people living on the plains were healthier and worked more. On the contrary, the cold, inclement weather made uplanders susceptible to idleness and inaction.

The aversion to cold upland interiors was not a general characteristic of all Spanish colonizers, but a specific response to the circumstances in the archipelago. For instance, Spaniards had no problems establishing colonial towns at much higher and colder altitudes like Potosí in the Andes. It simply shows that in spite of the general rhetoric prevalent in tropical discourse, different historical actors imagined the tropics in their own way based on their actual experience on the ground. Spanish attitudes to Luzon's mountainous interior were partly conventional and partly evolving. They were conventional in the sense that they simply portrayed the Other in a negative light. The uplands, a region that resisted submission to Spaniards, had to be denigrated as being inferior precisely because of their resistance to Spanish presence. The insalubrious conditions in the uplands also justified Spaniards' lack of progress in the conquest and conversion of mountain communities. Spanish attitudes were also evolving because they changed in rhythm with Spanish penetration into the interior. Through the years, constant contact and communication between lowland Christians and upland animists facilitated the transmission of diseases and created the stereotypical portrayal of certain areas as pestilential and unhealthy. As mentioned at the beginning of this chapter, by the late eighteenth century Antolín placed a large part of the blame on the better communication with the interior for the deteriorating epidemiological situation in the borderland. People's perception of the environment changed according to evolving epidemiological circumstances on the ground. Spaniards like Antolín might have even incorporated local geographical distinctions such as the one between mountains and plains.

The Spanish distinction between uplands and lowlands was nothing special. Many Indigenous communities in the archipelago used the same classification. Igorots, inhabitants of the Cordillera mountain range that runs along the spine of the island, made the same distinction between the uplands and the lowlands. They valued their mountain homes and looked down on the lowly plains under Spanish rule. According to their origin myth, Igorots were people of the mountains whose ancient ancestors fled to higher ground to escape a flood that inundated the whole world.[48] A more recent version of the tale from the early twentieth century provided a more detailed version of the story of the great flood.[49] A long time ago, the earth was flat except for a few mountains, and people lived happily. However, one dry season followed another, so people decided to dig up the dry riverbed and look for the spirit of the dead river. After days of digging, water finally gushed out of the riverbed, and torrential rains soon followed. Apparently, they had angered the river god for unearthing his grave. The whole world drowned in a massive flood, except for a couple that managed to escape up a mountain. When the flood waters receded, they saw that the world was no longer flat. New mountains had cropped up. Based on this legend, mountains were not permanent fixtures of the landscape, for the vast majority of them appeared only after the great flood. Upland dwellers attached their identity to the mountains that had saved their original ancestors from drowning.

While Spanish settlers in the lowlands viewed mountains with disdain, upland Igorots reciprocated the feeling by conceiving the plains as being geographically harsher and politically more oppressive than their mountain home.[50] For Igorots, their land was soft and porous. There was no need for plow animals to work the soil when a simple wooden shovel would do. On the other hand, they found "the hardness and solidness of the land in the Christian lowlands strange, for the land in the lowlands is packed down with the pressure of the rains, the tread of the population and the vibration of carts. It is a land, as the saying goes, worn out and baked by the lowland sun."[51] Igorots avoided Christian towns on the plains because they were very hot and the scene of many epidemics and crimes.[52] In their view, the Spanish government also extracted greater amounts of labor and tribute from its subjects than Igorot leaders.

Overall, Spanish and Igorot perceptions of the differences between the lowlands and the uplands mirrored each other but in a reverse fashion. Each side saw the other as plagued by a horrendous climate, infertile soil, and tyrannical government. While Spaniards associated mountains with disease and death, Igorots considered the plains to be the hotbed of epidemic diseases. Antolín straddled the divide and assumed various—and sometimes contradicting—positions: at one point praising the fertile land of Ituy, at another proclaiming the agricultural and health advantages of the lowlands over the uplands, and at yet another blaming lowlanders for spreading epidemic diseases to mountain communities.

Although European notions of tropicality maintained the idea of tropical island Edens, they eventually acquired a more sinister outlook that portrayed the tropics as pestilential places.[53] In an ironic twist, increasing European activities in the tropical world probably caused this shift in representation. Tropical islands were not innately more disease-ridden than temperate countries. They became increasingly plagued with epidemics partly due to European presence and intervention. For instance, newly introduced sugar plantations in the Caribbean created the perfect breeding ground for yellow fever and malaria.[54] While European observers were not completely wrong in portraying the tropics as pestilential, they played a large part in making them so.

An analogous argument can be made for the borderlands of Luzon. For the longest time, scholars have assumed that the Philippines did not suffer the same demographic collapse as the Americas because it had always been part of the Eurasian disease pool.[55] Centuries-long trade with mainland Asia ensured that inhabitants of the archipelago were constantly exposed to crowd diseases like smallpox; hence, Spaniards bringing smallpox from the sixteenth century onward would not have made any significant impact on the local population. However, Linda Newson's study has called this into question because the islands were so sparsely populated that they did not reach the population threshold for crowd diseases to become endemic and thus for inhabitants to develop immunity.[56] Although the demographic decline in the

Philippines was not as dramatic as that in the Americas, the archipelago still experienced a decline with the arrival of Spanish conquistadors and settlers. If Spanish authors described the landscape and climate in the Philippines as lethal, it might have been because there was a historical basis for it. However, they attributed it mostly to the local climate when it was most likely their actions that set the epidemic outbreaks in motion. A few observers like Antolín exhibited great self-awareness in recognizing their own role.

However, missionaries like Antolín put the blame not only on the local climate and landscape but also on the Indigenous inhabitants themselves and their apparently primitive practices. The tropics were as much a cultural construct as a geographical space.[57] Culturally, tropicality rested on the idea of primitiveness and the sensation of traveling back to the origins of time.[58] The tropics were vestiges of nature's unbounded fertility prior to the intervention of human civilizations. In the eyes of the friars, conditions in mission towns would not have been so bad if only they had access to the trappings of "civilization," such as the food and shelter that they were used to. However, in spite of their disdain for upland culture, missionaries were largely dependent on local communities to supply their food and build their churches and houses. Especially in the beginning, they had to make do with what locals ate and where locals sheltered. In their view, the local cultural practices of uplanders exposed them to malnutrition and hunger due to the lack of food, and to the harsh climate due to the lack of proper housing. For instance, Spanish officials did not quite agree with the missionaries' assessment that traveling on horseback was detrimental to one's health.[59] If anything was killing them, it was not horseback riding, but the absence of a proper, balanced diet.

Despite believing that the excessive sun and rain were conducive to the growth of plants and trees, Spaniards did not find the food they wanted amid this apparent abundance and fertility. In Burubur, for instance, when people brought them rice or *mongo* beans with salt for their meal, missionaries were unsatisfied with this limited and—in their eyes—poor selection.[60] Sweet potatoes were readily available, but they supposedly made the missionary's servant sick several times. Without any "palatable" food, it was normal for soldiers to suffer from hunger.[61] The situation was worse in a town near Pantabangan.[62] A visiting missionary could not find any food there. Even if he was willing to pay, there were simply no chickens or eggs to buy. All that was available was some dismal rice. If a priest were to reside there, he would have to arrange for the nearest mission town eleven leagues away to supply him with food acceptable to his palate.

Interestingly, contrary to the missionary's claim, the proposed new mission site near Pantabangan had more than dismal rice at hand. The missionary himself hinted that the inhabitants were more than content with their available resources.[63] The problem was not the food itself, but missionaries' specific dietary demands. They wanted to eat certain foods like eggs and chickens. Bringing in provisions from the lowlands was a common solution to this specific problem.[64] Spaniards' exacting demands on what they ate meant they were dependent on the presence of nearby food supplies. Hence, they could not establish mission towns too deep in the hinterland, far away from colonial food sources on the plains. Mission towns had to be located within a reasonable distance from colonial centers and outposts. With the lack of viable roads and the logistical problem of transporting food over rough terrain, expansion into the interior of the island was partly held back by Spanish eating habits. The eighteenth-century missionary strategy of slowly spreading out from established parishes unwittingly accommodated the dietary demands of Spanish settlers by not overstretching the logistics of their provisions too much.

Besides cold winds, pouring rain, and debilitating hunger, Spanish priests also attributed their illness in borderlands to shoddy houses.[65] If the high humidity and torrential typhoons of the tropics were not bad enough, missionaries did not always have proper houses to shelter themselves from the rain. They found upland houses to be even worse than lowland ones. Spaniards did not even deem these structures to be worthy of being called houses, since they were more like "huts and ostrich nests" that were too flimsy and prone to collapsing.[66] They were mere shanties and huts made of leaves. Houses were meant to shelter their occupants from the harsh outside elements, but from the Spanish settlers' assessment the mountain huts built by locals did not even perform this basic function. Besides building them, locals also maintained these shelters for the missionaries. One missionary's hut was in such a state of disrepair that it was like a sieve that simply let the rainwater in.[67] Without a proper roof over his head and without locals able to make the necessary repairs, the missionary was forced to abstain from taking his post. In the Philippines, however, most houses were made of straw and palm fronds, and no royal decree mandated that indios should construct their houses out of bricks and stones.[68] Although more permanent houses did exist, they were the exception. Missionaries in the archipelago longed for the better housing situation in the Americas, where indios constructed sturdier houses made out of lumber and adobe.

Missionaries on the ground adopted a holistic view of the landscape and climate. The illness that was killing them off was not simply down to the unpleasant weather. Indigenous uplanders' diet and shelter had as much to do with their untimely deaths as the cold winds and rains. Nature and culture together were conspiring against them. Without their usual civilizational apparatus at hand, Spaniards in the borderlands were relatively exposed to the dangers of nature. Accustomed to a subsistence lifestyle, indigenes were unintentionally killing Spanish settlers with their basic food and housing. Since missionaries believed that it would take quite some time to raise the level of civilization of mountain dwellers, in the meantime they had to rely on a network of settlements that maintained links with the so-called civilized world of the plains. With lightly populated Indigenous settlements dispersed throughout the island's hinterland, maintaining such a network for Spanish ends was a difficult task. Although the climate was ostensibly the root cause of the deaths of Spaniards who ventured to the interior of Luzon, everything else also conspired to make them defenseless from the onslaught of the elements. Everything on the island was different from what they had "in our Europe and even in many parts of Asia with manageable peoples and lands where there are towns and shelters, entry and exit points, trade and communication—all of which are very far removed from these mountains and hills that pagans and runaways [in the Philippines] inhabit."[69] The so-called civilization Spaniards were looking for did not exist in the Philippines. In their mind, its absence was killing them one sick person at a time.

Disease Barriers

From their coastal bases, Spaniards viewed the uplands as unhealthy sites. From their upland perch, hill people disdained the lowlands as hot, pestilential places. Their perceptions of each other did not come out of thin air. They had anecdotal experience to support their beliefs. In their reports and chronicles, Spanish missionaries constantly became sick as soon as they stepped on higher ground. With a small number of ministers in the archipelago and an eye to commemorating the martyrdom of their members, the religious orders closely tracked each missionary who got sick and died. Upland converts relocated to mission towns at lower altitudes and got infected by epidemic diseases in their new homes. Both sides suffered casualties as they moved up or down the mountains. Rather than accepting the climatic dichotomy between the uplands and the lowlands in explaining the deaths of people who crossed from one area to another, I argue that the transitional zone between the two areas was a crucial staging ground for the spread of diseases and death. Foothills, piedmonts, intermontane valleys, and other intermediate zones played a more critical factor than they had previously been given credit for. Foothills were the breeding ground of malaria-carrying mosquitoes and the entry point for epidemic diseases like smallpox. That mission towns were situated in these transitional spaces made missionaries and new converts especially prone to illness and death.

While different historical actors mentioned a wide variety of causes to explain health-related deaths in the hinterland, one factor they never mentioned was malaria, which was a vague medical term until the nineteenth century.[70] It was only in 1897 that the transmission of malaria was definitely attributed to mosquitoes. Instead of the cold weather and a subsistence lifestyle making Spaniards sick and killing them off, mosquitoes might have been the unsuspected culprit. In the eighteenth century, the systematic expansion of colonial towns from lowland parishes to upland missions passed through foothills before traversing mountain ranges. Plenty of missions remained at the foothills to maintain contact with existing parishes, avoid the steeper gradients farther up, and be close enough to upland animists to convince them to relocate to the halfway house of the mission.[71] Upland converts made a corresponding downward movement "to first relocate their hamlets at the foot of mountains, and from here they were slowly brought to the towns of the Christians."[72] While missionaries paid attention to winds and rains, they were unaware that they set up their missions in a malaria zone. *Anopheles minimus falvirostris*, the principal malaria vector in the Philippines, thrived from 800 to 2,000 feet above sea level, so missions concentrated at foothills were likely to be endemic to malaria.[73] Unlike some parts of Southeast Asia where coastlands were the ideal breeding ground for malaria-carrying mosquitoes, in the Philippines the uplands were the home of malaria.[74] This might explain why the Dutch in the Netherlands East Indies thought certain highlands were healthy and the Spaniards in the Philippines avoided the seemingly noxious mountains. The absence or presence of malaria might explain their respective perception.

If epidemic diseases like smallpox were a primary culprit in the death of indigenes in the borderlands of Luzon, what could possibly have caused the death of Spaniards moving into the interior? If it was not the climate, the food, the shelter, or Old World crowd diseases, it might have been the malaria-carrying mosquitoes. Malaria was the most destructive disease in the region.[75] Living primarily on the coasts and plains, Spanish settlers were never exposed to *Anopheles minimus* bites and malaria parasites until they set foot in the frontier. Unlike upland dwellers who most likely developed immunity to the disease throughout their whole life, Spanish newcomers were completely vulnerable on the mosquito-infested foothills.[76] It would also explain why some Spanish missionaries were able to stay and live in such places for decades. If they survived the initial bite and infection, they would have stronger immunity from then on. Malaria and migration were intimately tied to one another.[77] Perhaps when Spanish missionaries started blaming traveling on horseback as the culprit for illnesses and deaths, they were inadvertently referring to malaria as they entered endemic areas. It was not the drastic change in weather or their diet that was killing them, but the mosquitoes.

Although malaria might have provided an additional disease barrier between the lowlands and the uplands, it was not a static obstacle. Malaria-carrying mosquitoes were not a permanent feature of the tropical landscape. The incidence of malaria changed depending on a combination of environmental factors that constantly changed.[78] Throughout the eighteenth century, malaria transmission most likely evolved and adapted to the surrounding environment. Since mosquitoes are the vectors of malaria, factors that shape their propagation and biting behavior would necessarily affect malaria transmission. Circumstantial evidence points to the fact that the mosquito population in foothills probably grew throughout the century in step with increasing Spanish presence in the island's interior. Human agency is crucial in facilitating malaria transmission. Malaria retreats and expands in response to the presence of water, humans, and other animals in the surroundings. Borderland settlements, including mission towns, were often located near rivers and streams, which were the ideal breeding ground for mosquitoes in the Philippines.[79] Besides their geographical position, mission towns also attracted upland converts and lowland migrants and introduced cattle and horses, all of which contributed to creating a bigger pool of blood meal for malaria-carrying mosquitoes. Permanent populations at foothills and the rearing of livestock—the hallmarks of the purportedly civilized living that Spanish missionaries wanted to transplant to the borderlands—ironically halted Spanish progress by breeding more mosquitoes that would take their lives.

Civilization in the form of compact mission towns made borderlands more pestilential. An assemblage of actors and processes from the arrival of missionaries and converts to the breeding of livestock and mosquitoes shaped the disease environment in the hinterland.[80] Even nonhumans had a vital role in the creation of a disease barrier that restricted borderland mobility. A network of interactions between slow-moving waters, mosquitoes, and animal blood constituted a dynamic landscape. Mosquitoes took advantage of the breeding ground and blood meal provided by missions in foothills. Invisible in the documentary sources and existing outside the popular medical theories of the time, they surreptitiously infiltrated borderland towns, injected their victims with malaria parasites, and thrived in the favorable conditions of eighteenth-century missions.

Several factors determine malaria morbidity and mortality.[81] One factor is immunity. Previous exposure to malaria makes the survivor develop an immunity to the disease; thus, people who live in malaria-infested areas are more likely to become immune. Absolute newcomers to mission towns in foothills, such as Spanish missionaries and lowland Christian indios, would consequently become the main victims of malaria. Highland converts from the surrounding foothills should have a higher immunity to the disease. Another factor is the mosquito itself, which is an efficient vector in propagating malaria because a single mosquito can bite multiple persons in quick succession. It can easily transfer malaria parasites from one infected person to a mass of uninfected ones. A third factor is the density of the human and mosquito populations. A bigger, denser population makes it more likely for the disease to become endemic. The more people and mosquitoes there are, the easier it is for the disease to spread. Female mosquitoes bite animals because they need blood to develop fertile eggs and reproduce, thus inadvertently spreading malaria. The objective of mission towns in foothills was precisely to concentrate borderland converts around a few settlements. With foothills already endemic to malaria, missions aggravated the situation by offering mosquitoes a bigger, more accessible population to bite.

A fourth and final factor is what animals mosquitoes bite. Mosquitoes can feed on a wide variety of animal blood, ranging from dogs and humans to cattle and pigs.[82] If a mosquito species bites other animals besides humans, a bigger mosquito population can sustain itself and transmit malaria parasites to humans more easily. Missionaries famously brought in livestock like cattle and horses to mission towns. If female mosquitoes in the foothills of Luzon were not selective in their blood meal, they could have indiscriminately bitten humans, cattle, and horses. They would then be better nourished, live longer, and spread malaria parasites over a longer period of time. More livestock, in combination with a bigger human population, could result in a bigger disease pool for malaria to spread.

Whether the additional livestock in mission towns actually exacerbated the malaria problem in foothills is up for debate. Female mosquitoes do not bite animals indiscriminately.[83] Different species of the *Anopheles minimus* have different biting behaviors. Some have a preference for cattle blood, others none at all. When desperate for blood, some mosquito species become less fastidious and feed on whatever animal blood is available. Based on historical documents, it is impossible to make a retrospective identification of the specific mosquito species that inhabited the borderlands of Ituy and Paniqui in the eighteenth century and extrapolate their biting behavior. It seems that mosquitoes in the Philippines are zoophilic, meaning they prefer to bite cattle and carabaos over humans.[84] If this were the case 300 years ago, then the introduction of big herds of livestock in the missions should have made it easier for mosquitoes to reproduce. Being the main biting target of mosquitoes, cattle and carabaos would have spared mission residents from being bitten. However, changes in the status quo like a drop in livestock population could have had detrimental effects on mission inhabitants who would now be the primary target of mosquitoes.

Spanish notions of civilization required fixed, densely populated settlements. Consequently, Spaniards were critical of nomadic activities such as shifting cultivation and hunting. To encourage indios to adopt sedentary irrigated farming, missionaries brought in cattle and water buffaloes to plow paddies. To facilitate contacts between different towns, they promoted the use of horses. Farming with cattle and buffaloes and traveling on horseback not only conformed to Spanish notions of civilized living but also assisted in their attempts to control the native population. However, the increasing popularity of cattle, water buffaloes, and horses in the borderlands of Luzon was not a mere imposition on the part of Spaniards. Indigenous communities also found these animals useful in ways that Spaniards had not entirely expected. This confluence of overlapping motivations made these animals more popular and the area potentially more prone to diseases. Animal mobility in the borderlands shaped not only the landscape but also human communities.

Feasting on Flesh and Blood

Cows and Carabaos

Water buffaloes, or carabaos, already occupied the original site of Ituy that the first Spanish explorers visited in the late sixteenth century.[85] Across the archipelago, they were not commonly used as plow animals.[86] The most common type of farming involved shifting cultivation where farmers cleared and burned the land before planting and where rainfall nourished the crops. The use of water buffaloes for farming only made sense in irrigated paddy fields whose soil needed to be turned before planting. Without a need for plow animals, islanders like the Zambals in central Luzon hunted buffaloes instead (figure 4.1) and sacrificed and ate them in their feasts.[87] Rice and meat

FIGURE 4.1 Zambal hunters, ca. 1590. Two Zambals from central Luzon use a bow and arrow and a knife to hunt a carabao, or water buffalo. Courtesy Lilly Library, Indiana University, Bloomington.

were prestige foods that were not readily available throughout the year, so their consumption during feasts was socially and ritually important for participants.[88]

Pigs, cattle, carabaos, and deer lived and roamed in the intermediate zone of the missions.[89] The grasslands of upper Pampanga—away from colonial towns and adjacent to the mountains of Pantabangan and Carranglan—teemed with deer.[90] This transitional space between colonial plains and unsubjugated mountains proved to be an ideal hunting ground for wild animals. In the eighteenth century, as missions spread out from parishes on the plains toward the nearby mountains, Spanish missionaries decided to set up base in this intermediate zone. Repulsed by the local practice of hunting, they decided to bring in domesticated animals like cattle and carabaos to encourage sedentary farming, increase agricultural yields, and promote fixed settlements.

If the Spanish conquest of the Americas was a form of ecological imperialism, Spanish missionaries in the borderlands of Luzon attempted a similar project to manipulate the local biosphere.[91] Ideally, colonial settlements should be situated in areas with sufficient natural resources; otherwise, they would not flourish. Royal instructions mandated that colonial towns be located on sites that had ample supplies of water, meat, fish, and other subsistence needs.[92] Lands that did not meet these criteria were better left alone or abandoned because they were impractical in the long run. Spanish colonial cities had to have a solid foundation of readily available natural resources. In 1751, in the Magat Valley, a Dominican missionary found the town of Bagabag to be lacking in basic necessities such as rice, cows, pigs, and chickens.[93] There was no wild game, except for a few fish. Without supplies being shipped from the nearby town of Bayombong or from the coastal provinces of Cagayan or Pangasinan, Bagabag would not have survived as a mission.

What missionaries could achieve was limited by the materials they had at hand. However, they did not always surrender to the obstacles of inauspicious places and sometimes disregarded royal instructions on where to establish settlements. If the land was not ideal, they could transform and improve it. Missionaries could encourage converts to cultivate paddy fields and increase agricultural production. They could also introduce cattle ranching to supplement local subsistence needs.[94] For Spanish missionaries, the work of civilization involved performing such ecological transformations, which partly depended on a combination of sedentary farming and domesticated animals.

Food was an important by-product of these changes in the landscape. Like the Indigenous elite, Spanish missionaries had developed a taste for rice and meat, two prestige dishes in the archipelago. Wanting to turn rice into a staple food, they encouraged irrigated farming. To make meat more widely available, religious orders in the Philippines, especially the Augustinians, established cattle ranches.[95] Even the Spanish government in Manila encouraged indigenes to raise their own cows. In the province of Cagayan, a visiting Spanish judge from Manila granted exemptions from tribute payment and personal services to a native official in exchange for taking care of a cattle ranch in 1739.[96] By the end of the century, the ranch had grown so much that it had 1,040 cows. The Manila government even passed laws to protect livestock owners from theft and robbery.[97] Paddy rice and cattle meat were meant to sustain the Spanish population in the archipelago and improve the Indigenous diet of mainly root crops, but it did not hurt that they also tasted good. Recently arrived in his mission in 1702, the Augustinian Isasigana only had praise for cows: "We will try to maintain them as they will help a lot—whether for transportation, milk, or sustenance—because cows sometimes taste like chicken."[98]

Besides their meat and milk, cows were indispensable to missionaries as a form of transportation.[99] They served as pack animals. With missionaries' subsistence needs not always met in the immediate vicinity, cows performed the valuable task of transporting goods to and from the missions. They allowed the missionaries to avoid the problem of using indio porters, who were often subjected to abusive and harsh working conditions (see chapter 3).

With cows forming one of the pillars of mission life, a healthy donation of cows put several borderland missions on the right footing. From its very foundation, Carranglan received 220 cows from the government in 1702.[100] A few years after becoming a mission town, Buhay had more than a hundred water buffaloes and several cows and horses by 1723.[101] Bayombong raised hundreds of cattle and supplied them to Bagabag.[102] In 1745, Ibilaos went down from the mountains to convert to Christianity and establish a new town with a corral of 200 cows.[103] However, Spaniards did not simply impose livestock on Indigenous communities. Mountain dwellers also showed an interest in acquiring cattle and regularly bought some from lowland communities. Missionaries, converts, and animists all had their own vested interests in making livestock readily available in the borderlands. Their mutual love of carabaos brought independent mountain communities closer to mission towns.

With livestock more common on the plains, highlanders regularly bought water buffaloes and cows, among other things, from lowlanders. Ibalibons from the Cordillera traded their wax for cows in the Cagayan Valley.[104] Igorots went down to several lowland provinces, including the missions of Ituy and Paniqui, to buy whole herds of water buffaloes, cattle, and other animals.[105]

In the mission of Paniqui, they would go to the towns of Aritao, Dupax, and Bambang to sell their gold and metal tools and buy a total of 600 cows, carabaos, and pigs a year. Due to the difficulty of transporting animals up steep mountain slopes, upland traders followed the widest, flattest paths they could find.[106] With a regular upland-lowland trade in livestock, the passing carabaos and cows eventually created well-trodden trails. Besides taking routes with the mildest gradients, traders also moved slowly up the mountains to avoid stressing their livestock and killing them in the process. The trip might take longer, but it protected their precious purchases. Although not particularly prevalent, a few upland towns in the Cordillera pastured their own livestock: twenty to thirty carabaos and cows in Kabayan, ten carabaos and two cows in Acupan, and 150 carabaos in Ambuklao.[107] Ambuklao had an unusually large number of livestock because the town performed the special task of tending to the carabaos of nonresident owners, who paid the people of Ambuklao to maintain their carabaos in the meantime prior to their feasts.

While Spanish settlers found cattle meat to be necessary to their subsistence, islanders attributed ritual and social meaning to meat consumption. Like rice, meat was a prestige food because it was not available throughout the year. Local chiefs demonstrated their economic wealth and, more importantly, spiritual prowess by sponsoring extravagant feasts. The more food there was, the more powerful the chief.[108] Without any rice, wine, or meat, it was not a proper feast. In general, feasts lasted for a few days and followed certain taboos. Nobody worked, and no one traveled to avoid bumping into ancestral spirits on their way to the feast. Animal sacrifices played a crucial role in propitiating spirits and bringing good fortune. As one missionary observed, "All these foolish superstitions and omens boil down to eating and drinking well and having many animals to kill . . . their belly is their God . . . everything is fixed with feasts."[109]

Besides their spiritual relevance, feasts performed an explicit social function.[110] A chief distributed prestige food like rice and meat among his guests. In some cases, he simply sent the food to the other towns and chiefs.[111] Feasts and the sharing of food were occasions to cement alliances between a chief and his followers, and among different polities. A popular belief went that "the one who has the biggest pile of rice or food is the most important because it shows that he has more followers and slaves to make him better fields."[112] Allies and followers were more likely to attach themselves to already powerful chiefs, and what better way to assess a chief's strength and prowess than through his generosity in lavish feasts?

Not all meats were created equal. Lowland cattle were more savory than upland ones.[113] While pigs were the most consumed meat, cows and carabaos were reserved for more prestigious gatherings and feasts.[114] Upland chiefs who bought the most cows and carabaos from lowland towns were in the best position to consolidate their political influence in their area. Based on archaeological findings in the highland town of Old Kiangan, Ifugaos consumed more pig and water buffalo meat from 1600 to 1800.[115] Two factors can explain the increase in ritual meat eating. First, the population simply increased, and a bigger population inevitably consumed more meat. Second, upland elites sacrificed more carabao meat in an effort to elevate their status through feasting. More ritual feasting could be an indication of greater political consolidation on the part of mountain polities.

The population growth and political intensification of upland communities like Old Kiangan from 1600 to 1800 coincided with increasing Spanish presence in the interior of Luzon. Perhaps the two trends were not a surprising coincidence. From one perspective, abusive Spanish rule in the lowlands forced some islanders to flee to mountain refuges, consolidate themselves into more centralized polities, and stay in a strategic place to defend themselves from Spanish intrusion.[116] From another perspective, the relationship between the independent uplands and the colonial lowlands might not have been as antagonistic as it is usually portrayed. If the seventeenth and eighteenth centuries saw the steady rise of both upland settlements and mission towns, perhaps the growth of both went hand in hand at certain points. New mission towns with a healthy herd of livestock encouraged reciprocal trade with mountain communities. Upland Igorots, for instance, bought cattle from mission towns in Ituy and Paniqui. With more cows and carabaos readily available from nearby piedmonts and valleys, mountain elites had better access to meat for their ritual feasting and more opportunities at hand to form alliances and consolidate their status.

Relations were built on exchange. Throughout the eighteenth century, Spanish missionaries tried to create rapport with potential converts through reciprocal visits and gift exchange. Besides giving knickknacks and clothes to islanders, they also gifted them cows and carabaos. Cattle served missionaries not only as pack animals and a food source but also as an enticement for indigenes to cooperate and align with Spaniards. Giving pigs, cows, and carabaos to native allies, or potential ones, was a common practice among missionaries throughout the years.[117] When a group of Ituys went to Manila in 1702, they were feted by five provincials of the Dominican order: the provincial superior;

the provincial prior; the provincial of clothes, plates, bowls, and jars; the provincial of cows; and the provincial of carabaos.[118] Two of the five provincials were in charge of giving away livestock! Given the importance of meat eating in rituals and feasts in Indigenous communities, that the religious orders had sizable cattle holdings and gave them away as enticements was not lost on islanders, who viewed these acts in terms of the generosity of Indigenous chiefs.

Rather than always resorting to the inconvenient practice of bringing borderland chiefs to faraway Manila to receive their gifts from the provincials of cows and carabaos, missionaries brought the livestock to the hinterland. The mission frontier promoted cattle ranches. With more livestock close by, mountain chiefs had the opportunity to sponsor more lavish feasts and possibly expand their alliances further afield, which would support the theory of political intensification among independent borderland communities in conjunction with increasing Spanish penetration into the interior.[119] Such a scenario would explain why several upland polities as a group had to reach a consensus on whether to allow any outsider to enter any of their villages (see chapter 1). When missionaries tried to pass by or enter certain upland settlements, they usually had to get the unanimous approval of everyone. It was an all-or-nothing deal. If one settlement declined, then passage or entry to all settlements would be denied too. This coordinated action implied the existence of an alliance among neighboring settlements, which would have been regularly reaffirmed with animal sacrifices in feasts.[120] The greater availability of meat in borderlands would thus make this situation more likely in the eighteenth century. When dealing with aligned upland polities, Spanish missionaries encountered occasional roadblocks that completely halted them in their tracks, but at the same time once they got an alliance to acquiesce, upland conversion proceeded much more quickly in that particular area.

If the greater availability of livestock contributed to more extensive alliances among polities and indirectly affected Spanish mobility in the frontier, livestock also provided an alternative solution to borderland settlements denying entry or passage to Spanish preachers, visitors, and travelers. In the northern part of Paniqui, Dominican priests attempted to pass southward and reconnoiter a road to Manila (see chapter 3).[121] They were denied passage and assistance unless they met a few conditions, one of which was the payment of fifty cows and fifty horses. Although averse to the intrusion of Spaniards in their territory, local chiefs would have tolerated it if they got the livestock that they demanded, which would enable them to sponsor animal sacrifices and consolidate their status as generous powerful leaders. They had to find a delicate balance between rejecting Spanish penetration into the hinterland to maintain their political autonomy and taking advantage of this same presence to bolster their own political position. As a result, they entered into negotiations to find an appropriate settlement.

Feasting kept upland communities open to not only the possibility of forming alliances and federations with other borderland polities but also maintaining contacts with lowland towns. Feasts were rituals that created and renewed ties within the community and with the spirit world. The bigger the feasts, the greater the number of guests, the wider the scope of the alliances. However, mountain communities like the Igorots abstained from rearing their own livestock. Contrary to the Spanish perception that saw the borderland as self-enclosed, self-sufficient, fertile environments, upland polities were dependent on settlements in piedmonts and grasslands for their meat. Missionaries explained Igorots' refusal to raise their own cows, carabaos, and other animals in several ways. Benito Herosa dismissed the unusual practice as simple superstition and left it at that.[122] Antolín noticed that whenever feasts were held in honor of the recently deceased, the community sacrificed and ate all of the deceased's cows, pigs, and carabaos.[123] In effect, all animals joined their owner in the afterlife. With mountain herds constantly being decimated with each elite death, highlanders opted not to raise their own livestock and simply bought them on a regular basis from lowland settlements. This necessity kept mountain communities open to lowland contacts and intervention. With Spaniards encouraging cattle raising in colonial settlements, highlanders bought cows and carabaos mostly from Christian towns and missions. The cattle trade created an opportunity for Spanish priests to build relationships with visiting upland merchants and use cattle as a bargaining tool to achieve their ends. While the supply of lowland cattle impacted even highland communities, the introduction of horses had a more noticeable effect on grassland and piedmont settlements.

Horses

Besides cattle, the other livestock that both aided and hindered mobility in the countryside were horses. Unlike cows and carabaos, horses did not form part of the meat-eating ritual in Indigenous feasts. They were not endemic to the archipelago and did not become incorporated in local animal sacrifices. Spaniards valued horses as a more efficient means of transportation than cattle. Despite not being used for subsistence and ritual purposes, horses still changed the social dynamics in borderlands. Besides facilitating faster overland communication, they transformed how Indigenous hunters caught deer and possibly increased the blood meal options of malaria-carrying mosquitoes.

Unlike cattle and carabaos, which were Indigenous to the region, Spaniards introduced horses on the island of Luzon.[124] When they were unable to
take advantage of quicker, easier river travel to the island's interior, Spanish
missionaries, officials, and soldiers often had to trudge through rough, muddy
terrain. The availability of horses alleviated some of their difficulties. Missionaries always asked for horses to facilitate their movement in the countryside.[125]
With an insufficient number of missionaries to cater to a vast hinterland, anything that aided their mobility was a godsend. Faster communication would
help maintain links between upland missions and lowland parishes. In founding new towns, missionaries considered whether the location was reachable
by horse.[126] If it was not, then the site was unsuitable for a colonial town.
What a horse could travel and reach in some cases determined the realistic
extent of Spanish dominion on the island.

With the limited viability of rivers, missionaries moving inland were in
dire need of horses. The initial lack of horses placed an extra burden on islanders who had to serve as porters (see chapter 3).[127] Whenever cattle and
horses were not available, indios effectively became Spaniards' beasts of burden. They also carried priests, who did not want to walk, on hammocks. The
Spanish government disapproved of this manner of transporting goods and
people because it usually led to the abuse of native labor. Although traveling
by hammock had become a custom among Spanish officials and the local
elite, a visiting judge from Manila reiterated the necessity of horses for the
smooth functioning of Spanish administration in the provinces without an
excessive reliance on local labor.[128] He required all towns in the province of
Cagayan to have at least a horse and an ox to transport people around.

The horse supply in northern Luzon eventually improved. At various
points in the eighteenth century, missionaries and locals testified that they
had a sufficient number of horses in their area.[129] They recognized, however,
that this was a recent phenomenon that partially displaced travel by river
boat, by hammock, and on foot. Missionaries arriving on horseback were a
novelty that inland indios supposedly witnessed only in their lifetime. Although horses were only usable in the dry season, they made administering
whole provinces more manageable.[130] The increasing prevalence of horses in
missions brought the hinterland closer to the rest of the island.

Even if some horses developed the uncanny ability to go up and down
steep gradients, horses were mostly animals of the plains and valleys.[131]
While travelers and visitors saw a few cattle up in the mountains, they did not
see any horses. For Spaniards in the archipelago, horses were meant to transport people and goods.[132] For hunters on the grasslands, they offered a new

way of hunting deer.[133] The traditional method for hunting game was with a bow and arrow. Skilled Italon hunters also caught deer by chasing them on foot and spearing them.[134] With the introduction of horses, Indigenous hunters started hunting deer on horseback.[135] It was an unintended consequence of the Spaniards' reliance on horses to make their control of borderlands more efficient.

Indigenous communities outside the pale of Spanish rule incorporated the new animals in ways that undermined Spaniards' original intention for horses.[136] Spanish missionaries looked down on hunting because it was the antithesis of their vision of civilized life that revolved around a sedentary lifestyle of domesticated animals and irrigated agriculture. Despite the nobility associated with horses in Spanish culture, when mission indios adopted horses to their deer hunting, Spanish condescension toward hunting did not change. Missionaries like Antolín associated hunting with primitive societies and argued that civilizations had arisen without any recourse to hunting at all.[137] "Hunters," according to Antolín, "do not think of or pay attention to anything other than their dogs, horses, lances, and nets. . . . They do not talk about anything else. They neglect everything from their homes and wives to their children and even their Christian obligations."[138] Instead of drawing mission converts away from hunting and making them more noble, horses ironically inspired them to adopt new ways of hunting, become more mobile, and even forget their domestic Christian responsibilities.

Spanish views of horses were contradictory. Domesticated horses were a symbol of speed and grandeur, but they also had detrimental physical effects on their riders. On one hand, horses were a sign of class and nobility.[139] Spanish celebrations in Manila featured citizens astride their horses in magnificent parades through the city.[140] The ceremonial use of horses reflected the splendor of the city as the Philippines experienced economic growth in the late eighteenth century. An old ordinance in the province of Pangasinan showcased a clear hierarchy of animals.[141] Only esteemed vicars had the exclusive privilege to ride horses, while lowly servants had to make do with cattle and carabaos. A local official from Cagayan believed that traveling on horseback was much healthier than doing so on hammock, which was a prevalent practice among Spanish priests and the local elite.[142] Horses offered privileged, healthy mobility.

On the other hand, in spite of their recognized benefits and allure, horses were also associated with pain and illness for their riders. If the weather was not consistently pleasant, Spanish missionaries who traveled on horseback and traversed contrasting climates of heat and rain were liable to become sick and die. The negative effects of an intemperate land of contrasting weather were exacerbated by high-speed travel on horseback. Some mission converts hunted deer on horseback, "which is an irregular, violent exercise, which is why they find themselves suffering from chest pains, asthma, and pneumonia, vomiting blood and ending up destroyed."[143] Although horses symbolized the comfortable, civilized life, they also wreaked havoc on lowland Christians' well-being. Perhaps more than the drastic change of climate or the horses themselves, travelers on horseback became sick because they entered areas endemic to malaria more quickly than ever before. An ambiguity pervaded the usefulness of horses in the frontier. They brought not only pomp and speed to proceedings but also injuries, illnesses, and perhaps greater contact with mosquitoes too.

Mosquitoes

The cattle and horses that started to populate the borderlands more and more throughout the eighteenth century did not only affect the mobility, celebrations, and subsistence of the inhabitants. They also transformed the ecology of the landscape. Bringing their entourage of animals with them, Spanish conquistadors enacted a biological imperialism.[144] Conquest involved not only political and cultural control but also ecological manipulation. In the eighteenth century, as missionaries penetrated deeper inland, they multiplied the number of livestock on the plains and foothills, which in turn possibly increased the number of malaria-carrying mosquito vectors there.

Circumstantial evidence points to the greater preponderance of mosquitoes in the missions of Ituy and Paniqui. Regular rainfall, the concentration of human settlements, and the encouragement of irrigated farming were factors that contributed to the propagation of mosquitoes. Located in foothills, missions shared the same habitat as *Anopheles minimus*. Pools of water, the breeding grounds for mosquitoes, generally accompanied human settlements. With the introduction of more cattle, carabaos, and horses in borderlands, female mosquitoes had a greater opportunity to feed on animal blood, reproduce their kind, and spread malaria to humans.

In spite of all the ecological conditions indicating a greater incidence of malaria in frontier missions, historical sources are understandably silent on the issue. It is almost impossible to find any mention of mosquitoes in missionary writings and official reports because Spanish conceptions of health and disease at the time revolved around ideas of bad air and miasma. As a result, their explanations for illness focused on the sun, the rain, the wind, and the temperature rather than on mosquitoes. However, if only newcomers to the foothills—whether Spanish priests or lowland indios—were becoming sick and dying, their lack of immunity to malaria might have been the cause of their illness and death. It was either malaria or poisoning from hostile highlanders.

Mosquitoes did make an appearance in a description of the town of Santor, which was the starting point of the Augustinians' mission in upper Pampanga. Originally a barrio of another town, it became a separate town in 1689.[145] Fanning out from Santor in the early eighteenth century, Augustinian missionaries established several mission towns in the surrounding mountains and foothills. Indios described Santor as being infested with mosquitoes: "There were so many mosquitoes that a chicken left outside at night would be found in the morning reduced to bones."[146] Even though this account has a touch of hyperbole to it, it nevertheless offers a glimpse into a realistic scenario of massive mosquito infestation in borderlands. Extrapolating the mosquito situation in Santor to the nearby mission towns does not seem to be too far-fetched considering their relatively short distance from each other.

Borderland mobility not only involved people but also entailed bringing in and breeding various animals, ranging from cattle and carabaos to horses, and mosquitoes. More missions and greater mobility brought about a few unintended consequences to borderlands' political and epidemiological situation. Politically, more readily available livestock from lowland missions led to more feasts in upland settlements and strengthened highland chiefs' status. At the same time, it also made these powerful chiefs more dependent on lowland towns for their animal sacrifices. Ecologically, the greater concentration of human, bovine, and equine populations in the borderland made it the ideal breeding ground for mosquitoes and malaria. Several paradoxical trends developed in the eighteenth century. With their more extravagant meat eating and feasting, upland chiefs became more powerful in their own right, but they also became more vulnerable with their reliance on lowland settlements for meat. Missionaries and hunters on horseback traveled more and covered greater distances. However, an increasingly malarial environment also restricted movement between uplands and lowlands.

The transitional space occupied by missions in borderlands made them more exposed to diseases because they were at the crossroads of maladies coming from both the uplands and the lowlands. Malaria was a disease of the foothills of mountains. In addition, crowd diseases from densely populated colonial towns made their way to the mountainous interior. If the higher incidence of malaria required a complex ecology of slow-moving water, mosquitoes, and animal blood, epidemic diseases like smallpox and measles spread through the simpler transmission mechanism of close human interaction. Unlike malaria, these diseases were not endemic to the hinterland. Like malaria, however, they flourished in an atmosphere of greater mobility and contact.

Communicable Diseases

Focusing on bad vapors and inclement weather, Spanish missionaries and officials completely missed the role of animals and mosquitoes in the transmission of disease, especially in the borderlands. However, they were aware that communication and contact were crucial elements in the spread of epidemics in the island's interior. A long history of epidemic outbreaks in both Europe and the Americas taught Spanish settlers in the Philippines that contact transmitted certain diseases. Antolín noticed parallels between the population decline in Europe, the Indies, and his mountain missions.[147] He had no doubt that populations before were bigger, and he blamed better communication among provinces as the main reason for the decline. Aware of the demographic collapse in the Americas, Antolín saw a similar phenomenon when Spaniards arrived in the Philippines. The improved mobility and communication that brought the missionaries' message of peace and salvation were also the factors that brought about death and decimation to borderland communities.

Although no specific figures for epidemic mortality are available, anecdotal evidence shows that more missions resulted in more outside contacts, which in turn produced more epidemic diseases and deaths.[148] Missions introduced previously unknown diseases such as smallpox and measles in the hinterland.[149] Although it could be purely coincidental, the 1738 opening of a road to Cagayan unleashed a wave of smallpox outbreaks in the borderlands of Ituy and Paniqui from 1740 to 1741.[150] The epidemic affected precisely the region where the road passed. Apparently, syphilis also spread into the hinterland for the first time after the construction of the road.[151] The road seemed to have made epidemics more common with additional outbreaks in 1758 and 1786. In 1758, a smallpox epidemic hit the town of Dupax and devastated its population.[152] Missionaries could barely keep up with administering sacraments to the sick, and they ran out of provisions for the burials. They used carabaos to drag the bodies of the deceased. They also had to resort to hiring undertakers from Cagayan and burying the dead in household gardens. Successive waves of smallpox outbreaks struck Dupax in the following years, but with diminishing intensity and affecting mostly the youth. The various outbreaks claimed the lives of 700 persons, which was a significant blow since the combined population of Dupax and another mission town was only 1,290 a few years earlier.[153] More than half of Dupax's population succumbed to the pestilence.

Smallpox struck not only in particular years but also during particular months. The period from March to June was the season for smallpox.[154] The rainy season during the second half of the year prevented people from traveling too much. With no monsoonal downpours, muddy pathways, and impassable rivers, traveling in the dry season was easier and more common. Unsurprisingly, smallpox season coincided with the driest months of the year when people traveled the most. However, whether roads per se were that important in the transmission of epidemics is open to debate because they were temporary trails more than anything else. They were wont to disappear in the undergrowth or be covered by mudslides. Nevertheless, missionaries' promotion of borderland mobility more than likely contributed to the increasing prevalence of epidemic diseases that would continue until the nineteenth century.

The highly changeable nature of borderland mobility manifested itself in the opposite movements of enclosure and flight. While missions and roads increased lowland penetration of the hinterland and introduced epidemics there, uplanders also responded and put a halt to this increasing inward and upward movement. If the rough terrain, steep gradients, and thick vegetation were not enough to form a natural barrier to deter intruders, highlanders deliberately blocked the paths that led up the mountains. One of the biggest fears of mountain settlements was smallpox, and they developed a quarantine strategy to keep epidemics out. When news of a smallpox outbreak spread, "they blocked the entrances to the mountain with trees and shrubs. If somebody had the audacity to enter, they shouted threats that they would kill him on the spot."[155] Upland settlements also blocked access to mountain passes to prevent lowland Christians from reaching the very interior of mountain ranges and contaminating them with deadly diseases.[156] In 1741, after a smallpox outbreak in the province of Pangasinan, the converts of the mission town of Puncan prohibited travelers from using the new road that passed through their territory.[157]

Besides enclosing themselves from the pestilence of the lowlands, borderland communities also migrated to higher, remote ground. Fearful of being infected, new converts in the missions of Ituy and Paniqui fled to and hid in the thickets of nearby mountains because they believed it was a way to escape smallpox.[158] Perhaps such experiences of being infected by lowlanders led mountain dwellers to perceive the coasts and plains as pestilential places.[159] It was one of the main reasons they did not want to relocate to foothills and lowlands because they could not bear to see their relatives suffering and dying in misery: "All our Christian relatives are dying at great speed, and it could finish our generation."[160] While animists in the uplands remained relatively safe, their Christian relatives in the lowlands were getting decimated by diseases; thus, a return to the mountains was always a distinct possibility.

While islanders evaded epidemics by blocking roads and isolating their communities, Spanish priests and officials also suspended their travels and visits during times of epidemics. News of an outbreak made them avoid infected towns. Although priests acted as healers in the archipelago and could gain plenty of adherents during epidemic outbreaks, Spaniards also systematically steered clear of direct contact with contagious diseases.[161] In 1723, a Spanish judge from Manila was conducting an inspection tour of the Augustinian missions of Pantabangan and Carranglan, but he had to cut short his official visit because of news that the rest of the missions were experiencing an epidemic of fevers and throat inflammation.[162] Trying to keep himself safe and healthy, the judge simply turned around after setting foot in the first upland town. In 1756, the bishop of Nueva Segovia was on a pastoral visit of his diocese, while the provinces of Pangasinan and Ilocos suffered from an epidemic of fevers, headaches, and cold.[163] In light of the dire situation, he had to postpone his visit to the following year. Even the provincial of the Dominican order advised him not to continue on his journey to the two provinces because the priests there were too busy administering sacraments and burying the dead to accommodate him. In fact, the provincial governor of Pangasinan had already suspended his own annual inspection tour until the succeeding year.

Since the greater prevalence of epidemic outbreaks was an offshoot of mobility, it only made sense for both islanders and Spaniards to adopt measures that restricted movement to contain the further spread of the disease. However, quarantine measures did not always work. Viruses and their human hosts found ways of circumventing blocked mountain trails and penetrating seemingly closed-off settlements. In times of an epidemic, mobility died down, but it did not disappear completely. Epidemic outbreaks encouraged another type of movement—flight. The pestilence of 1786 and 1787 shows how far crowd diseases could penetrate inland and how retreating back to the interior mountains still remained a viable, if sometimes futile, recourse for new Christians.

During the Lenten season of 1786, an epidemic arrived in Manila and quickly spread to all the islands of the archipelago.[164] Even relatively isolated interior settlements were not spared, with mission towns being a conduit for the disease's propagation. One hundred sixty persons died in the mission town of Bagabag out of a population of 834, and another 1,000 in the rest of the mission out of a total population of about 7,000 souls.[165] The plague not only steamrolled its way right to the heart of the island but also set off a domino effect of calamities. The epidemic lowered the fertility rate of women and depleted the agricultural labor force, which resulted in a famine. Besides directly killing people, the disease initiated a vicious cycle of population decline with fewer children being born and hardly any food to feed the survivors. With a plethora of misfortunes piling one on top of another, the following year of 1787 turned into a devastating "year of pestilence, diseases, and famines" all rolled into one.[166] If that was not enough, the year also witnessed an uprising in the mission of Paniqui precisely in response to these catastrophes. Fleeing to mountain settlements might have been a way to escape the epidemiological catastrophe, but even upland communities were not spared by the disease.

In 1788, four Christians from the mission town of Dupax, together with a few Igorots from Tinok, decided to embark on a journey up the Cordillera mountains to sell carabaos there.[167] They inevitably turned into undercover informants for the Dominicans hungry for any knowledge they could gain about their upland neighbors. The carabao-merchants-cum-undercover-agents came back with a somber report on life in the highlands: that it did not have the conveniences of life in the valley. On the way up, they noticed people "hunting roots and little fruits for their food and they were suffering so from the hunger they asked the Christians for rice, having come round at the scent of food."[168] If the merchants wanted to buy any provisions like betel chew or rice from mountain dwellers, they had to pay an exorbitant amount of gold or silver for it. Even though their statements might have been colored by a condescending Christian tone toward animists, their observations could still have reflected the dire situation among upland communities, which perhaps had suffered more from the previous year's pestilence than lowland ones. That would explain the high price for basic provisions and why lowland Christians were going up the mountains to sell carabaos in the first place when it was common for upland animists to go down to buy their livestock. In Antolín's view, "all these pagans were suffering from hunger because of a general pestilence last year which killed so many there were none to take care of the fields."[169] Hungry, miserable, and emaciated, mountain dwellers had to scour the slopes for shoots, roots, and grasses for their daily survival. Witnessing carabaos ambling their way across the landscape was more like a divine vision, and feasting on them nothing short of a miracle.

After the full brunt of the smallpox epidemic had passed, borderland inhabitants were back to their old ways of moving back and forth between upland and lowland sites. Igorots from Tinok went down and visited Dupax, and Christians from Dupax hiked up and sold their carabaos in the highlands. After only a short pause at best, mobility was back and running. The fact that the epidemic spread in the first place in spite all of the precautions shows how interconnected the various settlements were. Throughout the centuries, Spanish officials promulgated various ordinances that prohibited uplanders from trading with lowlanders in order to cut off their supplies and force them to convert and relocate to the lowlands. These measures inevitably failed to stop upland-lowland commerce. In a similar fashion, uplanders and their quarantine strategy failed too. Contact between mountains and plains continued despite the dangers of infectious diseases. The epidemics of 1786 and 1787 did not spare anyone on the island. They indiscriminately attacked everyone from independent polities on remote mountain ridges to mission towns in river valleys. Connections across political, religious, and ecological boundaries underpinned the broad reach of lethal diseases and the consequent migrations.

Although the carabao merchants from Dupax created a perhaps overly stark contrast between upland deprivation and lowland prosperity, other contemporaneous events showed the opposite case. During Holy Week of 1787, Ibalibons of the mission towns of Camarag and Angadanan in desperation abandoned their new, pestilential settlements in their desire to return to a better life in their old mountain abode. Like the carabao merchants, the runaways from Camarag and Angadanan left the valley behind them as they marched up the mountains. But instead of trying to make a quick profit, they envisioned the mountains as their final destination and home.

Unlike upland settlements, mission towns near plains and coasts had fewer defenses against epidemic outbreaks. In times of pestilence, catechumens and new converts often resorted to retreating up the mountains.[170] With only incipient ties to the new religion, new Christians had no problem abandoning it and fleeing to the highlands. Besides being far away from the epicenter of epidemic outbreaks, the uplands in some perspectives offered a healthier environment.[171] In contrast to the hot, pestilential plains, mountains had fresh rivers, forests, and winds that sheltered inhabitants from the ill effects of diseases.

Like most places affected by the epidemic, Camarag and Angadanan experienced the triple devastation of disease, death, and famine.[172] Catechumens and converts of the two towns endured the hardships until Lagutao's arrival one day during the dry season of 1787. Lagutao was an Ibalibon chief who had decided not to convert to Christianity and continued to live in the highlands. Maintaining ties with his kin who had converted and relocated to the mission towns in the valley, he visited and tried to convince them to abandon the wretched situation they found themselves in. His right-hand man Baladdon told a story from his mother, an Ibalibon animist priestess, that convinced the majority to follow them back to the mountains: "What moved the ordinary people the most was the resurrection of their ancestors who were already waiting for them on the mountain . . . and that they had food there without any labor."[173] The animist priestess had proclaimed through Baladdon the good news of the resurrection of the victims of the pestilence and of a feast of rice and maize awaiting them in the mountains. In the highlands, all illnesses would be cured and everybody would live long, healthy lives.[174] A return home would solve the triple problem of disease, death, and famine. The mountain was a terrestrial paradise.

Most of the Ibalibons of Camarag and Angadanan heeded the call of the mountains and left the two valley towns desolated. About 1,200 people joined the march to the highlands, which included women, children, and dozens of sick people carried on hammocks. They also brought along their carabaos, horses, food, and other possessions.[175] In total contrast to the quarantine measure of isolating upland communities, they brought in sick people, risking contaminating their mountain sanctuary. Unlike ill Spanish missionaries who usually sought refuge and convalesced in Manila, disease-stricken Ibalibons went in the opposite direction. In a time of despair, the animist mountains beckoned with the promise of perpetual immunity to disease and hunger. Pragmatic animists followed the ritual specialist—whether it was an animist priestess or a Christian priest—who offered them the best chance of survival. With the devastation of the valley missions, the Ibalibon converts decided to try their luck with the old belief.

Historical actors from Spanish missionaries to ad hoc carabao merchants to Ibalibon runaways shared a binary view of the landscape: upland versus lowland, mountain versus plain, or hinterland versus coast. Depending on who they were, they always viewed one as better than the other. The carabao merchants from lowland Dupax looked down on upland Igorot communities for their lack of basic commodities. Lagutao and Baladdon despaired at the deplorable condition of their fellow Ibalibons perishing in the pestilential lowlands. Whoever made the observation, they always saw the other side as worse off.

Located in foothills, piedmonts, and valleys, missions occupied a transitional space between the two opposing sides. They gave both uplanders and lowlanders the opportunity to easily switch from one side to another. Changing circumstances could make one location more appealing than the other. A bout of smallpox epidemic made the Igorot mountains unappealing to the carabao merchants in the same way it made the valley mission detestable to Ibalibon converts. Settlements in foothills and valleys provided the ideal location to compare the two sides and join whoever was in a better position. Mission converts had one foot in the valley and another in the mountains, since they never broke their ties with their animist kin who remained in the highlands. One moment they were converts, the next moment apostates. As staging points for migration up and down the mountains, missions gave them options to move about.

Despite various attempts to portray either mountain settlements or mission towns as healthier than the other, the crowd diseases of the eighteenth century flattened the differences between uplands and lowlands. While malaria thrived on transitional spaces like foothills and created an epidemiological barrier between uplands and lowlands, crowd diseases like smallpox infected everyone equally. In contrast to inhabitants of malarial zones who built up immunity to malaria parasites, no one was safe from crowd diseases in eighteenth-century Philippines. Although Antolín and the carabao merchants portrayed the Igorot uplands as worse off than the mission town of Dupax, that was most likely not the whole truth. While Dupax most probably escaped the full brunt of the epidemics of 1786 and 1787, it had not been spared during the earlier smallpox outbreak of 1758, which had hit it hard.[176] Similarly, Lagutao and Baladdon exaggerated the terrestrial paradise of the Ibalibon uplands, unscathed by diseases, deaths, and famines that ravaged the valley mission. If Igorot communities in remote mountains suffered from pestilence and famine, it would not be a stretch to imagine an analogous situation in Ibalibon settlements.

When the refugees from Camarag and Angadanan reached Ibalibon territory, instead of being welcomed by their resurrected dearly departed and a feast of rice and maize, what greeted them was disappointment.[177] The account of what happened next is filtered through Antolín's retrospective narrative that reads like a Christian parable. In the highlands, the refugees did not find the promised rice and maize, only a little sweet potato and taro that they gobbled up rather quickly. Still hungry, they waited anxiously as Baladdon's mother and other priestesses started to cook rice in five pots. Whether intentional or not on the part of Antolín, echoes of Jesus's miracle of the multiplication of the loaves and fish on a mountain in Galilee pervade the story of the Ibalibon runaways waiting for their food in the uplands, but instead of a Christian miracle of abundance, all they witnessed was animist chicanery. In missionary discourse, cooking pots were a symbol of animism because they were used to prepare food in animist feasts.[178] It was not uncommon for missionaries to break them as a religious challenge to animist practitioners. After three hours of impatiently waiting, the hungry refugees saw the priestesses open the pots only to reveal that they were all empty. There was no rice or water. Whatever was inside had been consumed by the fire. Unlike Jesus, the animist priestesses had no power to feed and sustain the hungry crowd. Antolín created an eighteenth-century Ibalibon version of the biblical multiplication of the loaves and fish, but it was an upside-down version where the miracle never took place. Starving and with no multiplication of rice in an animist twist of the Christian miracle, the Ibalibon runaways decided to march back down the mountain and return to the mission. The promised paradise on the mountain fell way short of the reality. They had been betrayed.

The message in Antolín's Ibalibon parable was loud and clear. Animist shamans were phonies and had no power over nature. The story's ending with the apostates returning to the mission telegraphed without a doubt where Antolín's loyalties lay. Real salvation was in Christianity in the lowlands. Framed as a parable, how historically accurate was Antolín's version of events? Did most of the Ibalibon apostates really return to the mission as claimed by Antolín? Population statistics offer a tentative, but far from definitive, answer. The population of the mission of Camarag in 1785 before the outbreak of epidemics was 1,617; in 1787, the year of the flight to the mountains, it was 1,708; three years later, in 1790, it was 1,326.[179] Although the population of Camarag would continue to go down until the turn of the century, it would remain above the 1,000 mark. The disappearance of 382 souls in Camarag, or 22 percent of the population from its peak, can be attributed to the smallpox epidemics of 1786 and 1787. However, the statistics do not reveal what percentage of the population decline was due to death or to flight. Comparable statistics for unconquered Ibalibon communities in the uplands would clarify the issue on how many people joined and stayed with Lagutao, but they do not exist. Nevertheless, a mission population of more than 1,000 was still a considerable number of people who decided to stay put or return to the Christian fold. The fluctuations in numbers also indicate how indigenes entered and left the mission throughout the years before, during, and after epidemics. In spite of the arrival of smallpox in 1786, the population of Cama-rag in 1787 was still higher than it had been two years prior. Despite not dis-tinguishing between the people who fled and those who died, the declining population afterward partly confirms the reality of mobility and migration in the face of a crisis, and yet the substantial mission population that plateaued after the epidemic outbreak seems to partly support Antolín's claim that a sig-nificant number of Ibalibons chose to return to Camarag.

When Lagutao initially tried to convince his fellow Ibalibons to join him in the highlands, he was more somber than Baladdon. He did not promise heaven and earth to them. In fact, he told them that his hometown lacked food.[180] There was not enough food to feed everyone even for a month. When the Ibalibon refugees confronted Baladdon's mother about the mirac-ulous stories of resurrected ancestors and an abundance of rice and maize, she replied that the stories had not come from her but from Baladdon's step-father, who had died from the pestilence.[181] Even Baladdon's hometown up on a mountain was not spared by the epidemic. The improbable miracles that people—whether animist or Christian—clung to stemmed from the same desperation wrought by the common experience of disease, death, and fam-ine. Smallpox was the great leveler. Wherever people went, upland or low-land, they were met by the same destruction and destitution. There was no tropical paradise either in the mountains or in the plains. Mobility did not offer any respite. In fact, it was partly the problem.

Conclusion

Mobilities and connections characterized borderlands. In Southeast Asia, where early modern upland and lowland polities were scattered but nevertheless interconnected, this interpretation is relatively commonplace. Borderlands, or even polities in general, were not isolated entities, hence the need to analyze them in a wider context. Mobilities and frictions made the connections within and beyond borderlands possible. Despite maintaining a mental binary between independent upland animists and colonial lowland Christians, the historical actors nonetheless thought and acted in relational terms. Highland communities went down to and relied on lowland towns for various needs, and vice versa. Straddling the intermediate zone between the uplands and the lowlands, mission towns revealed an understanding of borderlands as an integrated space. The different parts of borderlands constantly adjusted to and affected one another. Traveling Spanish missionaries thought of the conquest of borderlands with a global, comparative perspective, viewing eighteenth-century internal Spanish colonizations in Europe and Asia in the same light. Population movements at mass and individual scales manifested the connected structure of borderlands. Mission towns in Luzon had mixed and growing populations due to migrations, an indication of the dispersed but integrated nature of borderlands. Spanish missionaries and Indigenous chiefs visited one another in Manila and Lublub; borderland polities raided one another in a form of violent exchange; communities at key nodes of borderland networks tried to control access to towns and roads; and greater regional integration facilitated the spread of epidemic diseases across borderlands and led to shared experiences of prosperity and misfortune. These mobilities undermine any strict binary interpretation of borderlands. In fact, timely movements of concentrations and dispersals gave inhabitants the flexibility to choose and chart their malleable, meandering histories.

For Spanish missionaries, borderlands to conquer were located not just in the remote interior of the island of Luzon but all around the globe, including Spain itself. When the Spanish monarchy started consolidating its overseas territories in the eighteenth century, missionaries saw the internal colonizations in Europe, the Americas, and the Philippines as part of the same project.[1] The othering of people in the Indies happened not just across the

Atlantic or the Pacific but also closer to home. European missionaries found
the Indies in Europe, wherever they encountered illiterate, rustic people who
needed evangelization.[2] These people were no different from the indios of
the Americas and the Philippines. The European countryside was the site
of the interior Indies in their own lands. The comparison is understandable
given that missionaries traveled around the world and brought the idea of
the Indies back with them to Europe. For these missionaries, borderlands
throughout the globe followed the same pattern of conquest and had the
same ingredients of success.

Faced with the daunting task of converting the Indigenous communities
of Luzon that had eluded them for two centuries, Francisco Antolín and an
anonymous Franciscan noticed striking similarities between two borderlands on opposite sides of the globe: Sierra Morena in Spain, and Ituy and
Paniqui in the Philippines.[3] The conquest of one was no different from the
other, both being internal frontiers of the Spanish empire. While on a visit to
Spain in 1787, Antolín witnessed the triumph of Charles III's policy of repop-
ulating the mountains of Sierra Morena in southern Spain. Cold, uncultivated, and infested with bandits, Sierra Morena became a success story of
how to turn a harsh, barren highland into the site of flourishing towns. Starting out with a small settlement of Swiss colonists and a new road, Sierra
Morena eventually became populated and developed farms, ranches, and in-
dustries.[4] It was the quintessential example of the "interior colonization of
Spain."[5] Having seen how the Spanish monarchy conquered Sierra Morena,
Antolín thought he could carry out the interior colonization of Luzon if only
he had the same governmental support Sierra Morena had received. For Antolín, Spain's Sierra Morena and the Philippines' Ituy and Paniqui were mirror images of each other. Sierra Morena had humble beginnings in a small
town and a recently opened road. Augustinians, Dominicans, and Franciscans already had several mission towns in the Ituy and Paniqui borderlands,
and they had met with some success in opening roads. If the Sierra Morena
colonization project could prosper with the right amount of assistance, then
so could theirs. Spanish and Philippine borderlands were the targets of a late
eighteenth-century Enlightenment project to colonize and populate the frontier regions of the Spanish monarchy.[6]

Although inspired by the exemplary model of Sierra Morena, Antolín was
circumspect about the prospects of his mission because of the recent epidemic outbreaks and uprising. Like many other Spaniards, he thought the
island's population was in rapid decline. In fact, he recognized how the increased mobility and communication brought about by missions and Spanish

presence in the borderlands were a primary cause of death there. In his view, traveling to and from the mountains and the plains was lethal. When adult uplanders converted and resettled in the lowlands, they became sick and soon died.[7] In Antolín's mind, they were like plants uprooted from their native soil and transplanted to an unsuitable alien ground. It felt unnatural and counterproductive, like domesticating wild animals in cages. The supposedly essential link between people and their homeland was an obstacle to borderland mobility and missionary attempts at resettlement.

Despite Antolín's dire statements about converts inevitably perishing in missions and the mounting number of deaths from sporadic but severe epidemic outbreaks, borderland populations continued to grow in the eighteenth century. The statistics belie a sheer drop in population numbers. The population of the mission of Ituy grew from 2,719 in 1747 to 5,621 in 1800, the mission of Paniqui from 1,812 to 9,021 within the same time period.[8] The population data for the years 1785, 1787, and 1790 can help trace the impact of the smallpox epidemics of 1786 and 1787. For the mission of Ituy, which included Dupax, none of its individual towns experienced any net population loss in that five-year span. In fact, the total population increased from 3,455 to 4,361. For the mission of Paniqui, which included Camarag and Angadanan, there was a slight decline between the years 1787 and 1790 from 9,917 to 9,024. Despite the opening of a road, the greater mobility, and the higher incidence of epidemics, the overall population trend for the second half of the century was still growth, except for a plateauing in Paniqui during the last dozen years of the century.

Antolín was fully aware of these statistics.[9] He knew that the total population for both missions jumped from 5,938 at midcentury to 13,866 just prior to the 1787 Holy Week uprising, an increase of almost 8,000 souls. Antolín attributed the promising population growth to two factors: uplanders joining the missions in fear of military expeditions and the absence of any major epidemic outbreak for about twenty years. Despite more deaths due to epidemic diseases, migration from the uplands at the very least contributed to the mission population and prevented a drastic population decline. Overall, military threats and the attractions of colonial life were more than enough to lure some mountain dwellers to resettle in the missions. Occasionally they tipped the balance in favor of conversion and resettlement despite possible colonial exactions and the greater exposure to deadly diseases, so Antolín's portrayal of colonial and mission towns as death traps for uplanders was not completely true.

Migration, an important part of borderland dynamics, heavily influenced population numbers. On his pastoral visit to the province of Pampanga in

1718, the provincial of the Augustinian order noted how the province was de-populated with most of its inhabitants dispersed throughout the archipelago, especially in the Manila area.[10] In spite of this bleak general picture, the prospects of the upper Pampanga mission was promising because its population was actually increasing.[11] New Christian converts resettled on the mission's grasslands and gladly availed themselves of the abundant deer there. Besides the migration of upland converts, longtime Christians from Pampanga proper flocked to borderland missions to avoid forced labor exactions.[12] Missions received exemptions from tribute payment and corvée for a period of time to entice new converts and shield them from burdensome state exactions. These incentives attracted even longtime Christians who attempted to blend in with the mission population and renege on their tribute and labor obligations. Pangasinenses, Kapampangans, and Cagayanes joined upland converts in the missions of Ituy and Paniqui. Flight did not always equate to apostasy and an escape to the mountains; sometimes it was simply to the intermediate zones occupied by missions. The networked nature of borderlands offered indios nuanced options beyond supposed colonial binaries. The migration of both uplanders and lowlanders partially explains the missions' growing population despite more people dying from epidemic diseases in the eighteenth century. Amid the wars, diseases, and famines, borderland missions were a viable option for some islanders.

In this book, I have tried to capture the multiple micro-mobilities and frictions in the borderlands of Luzon. Despite the popular image of mountains as barriers, these borderlands demonstrated the porousness of the geographical divide between the lowlands and the uplands. Indigenous actors moved in the island's interior and created their histories in the process. The composition of mission towns was a mix of uplanders and lowlanders, so they were not purely grim, isolated outposts, but rather cosmopolitan sites in their own way. Although migration to the transitional spaces of missions exposed both uplanders and lowlanders to greater risks of contracting deadly infections, mission populations still grew in the eighteenth century precisely because of the influx of more people. Its mixed Indigenous composition highlights how mobility was the domain not solely of Spanish colonizers but also of lowland indios and upland converts. Topography was not an impregnable barrier, as people constantly moved from one place to another and adapted to changing circumstances.

Movement in borderlands was not limited to Spanish inland penetration or islanders' relocation from one nearby spot to another. Islanders also traveled considerable distances and reached colonial Manila. A significant enough number of them migrated to Manila and its vicinity that it worried authorities about the possible depopulation of provinces like Pampanga and Cagayan.[13] Antolín heard that there were plenty of single women in Cagayan because the bachelors had left for Manila and other regions to find work. Like Manila, mission towns also attracted their fair share of migrants. Contrary to their popular portrayal as isolated, immobile mountain dwellers, uplanders regularly went down to distant plains and coasts to buy goods like cattle from lowlanders. A wide range of mobilities encompassed the borderlands and presented plenty of opportunities for interaction and exchange.

In response to the arrival of Spanish missionaries, various borderland communities requested that they be brought to Manila or the provincial capital before they would convert. These trips happened so many times in the eighteenth century that they were effectively part of a modus operandi on how to negotiate with borderland inhabitants. The missions were founded on the reciprocal visits of missionaries going to the highlands and animists visiting colonial towns. Even the military threats and expeditions that, according to Antolín, forced many uplanders to relocate to lowland missions had their mirror image in hill people raiding lowland Christian settlements. The whole background story to Lagutao's uprising is an example of these movements to and from the mountains and plains. For every action, there was an equal and opposite—and sometimes complementary—reaction.

Spanish and Indigenous mobilities were intimately intertwined with one another. Religious chronicles present the construction of a borderland road as the achievement of daring, trailblazing missionaries. However, the road would never have been opened without the support of Danao and Ansimo, local chiefs in Paniqui. Despite their insistence, Spanish missionaries and lowland indios would have faced serious obstacles in moving deeper into the borderland without the approval of local chiefs and communities. Incorporating themselves into existing Indigenous borderland networks, missions in foothills, piedmonts, and valleys occupied intermediate nodes in the network and offered residents flexibility in accessing the different ecological niches of the mountains and the plains. Lagutao's Ibalibon relatives had no problem relocating to the valley, fleeing to the mountains, and returning to the valley in quick succession. Mobility was a conscious but often fluctuating choice.

Although the distinction between the uplands and the lowlands was prominent in the minds of historical actors from Spanish missionaries to Igorot mountain dwellers, the situation on the ground revealed a more nuanced reality. The prominence of missions in foothills and piedmonts highlights the appeal of these intermediate zones not only to Spanish officials but also to upland converts and lowland migrants. Instead of always viewing colonial upland-lowland relations in the antagonistic terms of conquest and flight, timely occasional alliances were part of successful borderland mobilities, and in-between places gave more room for flexibility.[14] Even though resistance and opposition existed, they are better seen in the context of violent exchange—but exchange nonetheless. Revenge raids, just like mutual visits, were reciprocal mobilities. The existence of missions in transitional spaces provided borderland inhabitants the opportunity to witness at close hand the viability of a colonial Christian life, try it out firsthand, and leave when it did not suit them anymore. During episodes of epidemic outbreak, mission converts did flee and return to their mountain homes, but it was just one movement in a complex web of other movements. Flexibility and adaptability to the prevailing conditions were key factors in mobilities.

The blurred boundaries between uplands and lowlands manifested themselves not only in people crossing from one side to another but also in how the two geographical areas increasingly shared the same destiny.[15] Improved mobility and the settlement of intermediate zones in the eighteenth century facilitated the growth of links between the highlands and the lowlands. Even when they stood on opposite sides, uplanders and lowlanders prospered and faltered more and more in sync with one another. Although the threat of violence and the actual use of force were never far away, upland converts like Lagutao's relatives found certain aspects of mission life appealing enough to decide to resettle there. The cultivation of cacao, for instance, made mission towns relatively prosperous.[16] Previously, an animal sacrifice had sufficed in a chief's burial. However, with the profits from cacao, prominent chiefs now used silver in their burial.

Instead of looking at the growth of missions throughout the century as inimical to highland settlements, it might have actually contributed to their prosperity. As missions multiplied and expanded, they partly supplied upland communities with goods such as livestock. Archaeological findings point to the greater prevalence of meat-eating in some Igorot communities, which would suggest a pattern of political intensification through ritual feasting.[17] The consolidation of upland communities, however, did not necessarily represent an antagonism to Spanish presence, whether in terms of flight from lowland oppression or defense in the face of colonial aggression. The relationship could also have been complementary, especially between settlements that occupied different ecological niches. Lowlanders effectively supplied the livestock that uplanders needed for their sacrifices, feasts, and political consolidation. Highland prosperity as measured in meat-eating would not have been possible without mission cattle. In general, lowland mission towns and upland settlements increasingly shared contemporaneous moments of fortune and misfortune. The failure of quarantine measures to shield mountain communities from epidemic outbreaks confirms the tighter bonds between the highlands and the plains.

The renown of borderland chiefs also surpassed the traditional division between uplands and lowlands. The Ibalibon chief Lagutao claimed to be "the king and lord of the mountains."[18] Even Ilongots recognized him as a chief. More importantly, with some of his Ibalibon siblings and kin relocating to mission towns in the valley, his field of influence potentially encompassed a wider area. Staying put in his mountain abode and remaining true to his animist beliefs, Lagutao might seem to have lost a large part of his followers when they converted and resettled in mission towns. However, in spite of the popular binary opposition between mountains and plains or between animists and Christians, the bonds between him and his kin were never truly severed. Despite the divergence and dispersal, animist Lagutao's kinship relations with his converted relatives were always there ready to be summoned whenever necessary. The devastation wrought by the epidemics of 1786 and 1787 presented such an occasion to call up past ties and bring distant relatives back home. In Southeast Asia, borderland dispersals were not necessarily a sign of disunity or weakness; they were also possibly a strategic maneuver, a potentiality waiting to be tapped, or a temporary meandering in a long series of movements.

If Igorot chiefs consolidated their political position with grander ritual feasting and Lagutao regained followers with promises of a better life, borderland chiefs like Danao and Ansimo gained greater prominence thanks to their dealings and alliances with Spanish missionaries.[19] In the half-century after they had allowed Spaniards to pass and construct roads through their lands, their families acquired even greater renown and prestige as lords of the region. Borderlands were not solely sites of resistance and opposition to colonial rule; they were also places for negotiations and alliances. Aligning with Spaniards could, in fact, bolster a chief and his community's social standing.

Borderland mobility showcased the porousness of geographical and group categories. While historical actors did view the world in terms of the opposing pairs of mountains and plains or animism and Christianity, their movement from one settlement to another also attested to how different landscapes and peoples were intimately interconnected to one another. The irony here is, the greater mobility of the eighteenth century tied the destiny of uplands and lowlands ever closer to each other, yet in the minds of borderland actors these binary distinctions were somewhat reified as we witnessed in Antolín's essentialist portrayal of uplanders.

What happened in the eighteenth-century borderlands of Luzon was not new nor surprising. Coastal and mountain polities in Southeast Asia had always maintained relations and exchanges with one another, and borderland movements flowed through these networks. If anything, Christian Spaniards and indios simply played a greater role in certain nodes and exchanges in the eighteenth century. Shifting networks encompassed both cordial and combative relations and allowed for improvisations and constant changes. Dispersals and blockages as much as conversions and alliances were part of the rhythm of borderland strategies and mobilities.

Notes

Abbreviations

AFIO   Archivo Franciscano Ibero-Oriental
AGI   Archivo General de Indias
APAF   Archivo Padres Agustinos Filipinos
APSR   Archivo de la Provincia del Santísimo Rosario
AUST   Archives of the University of Santo Tomas
BNE   Biblioteca Nacional de España
n   *número* (number)
r   *ramo* (section)

Introduction

1. Rosaldo, *Ilongot Headhunting*, 48.
2. Rosaldo, 31–60.
3. Rosaldo, 42.
4. Rosaldo, 56–57.
5. Rosaldo, 57–58.
6. Rosaldo, 73, 105, 161, 174; Rosaldo, *Knowledge and Passion*, 182–86.
7. Warf and Arias, "Introduction"; White, "What Is Spatial History?"; Markovits, Pouchepadass, and Subrahmanyam, "Introduction"; Ethington, "Placing the Past"; Acabado and Barretto-Tesoro, "Places, Landscapes, and Identity."
8. Certeau, *Practice of Everyday Life*, 91–110.
9. Grandjean, *American Passage*; Ballantyne, "Mobility, Empire, Colonisation"; Sivasundaram, *Islanded*, 135–72; Markovits, Pouchepadass, and Subrahmanyam, "Introduction"; Pouchepadass, "Itinerant Kings"; Perdue, *China Marches West*, 409–61; Quirk and Vigneswaran, "Mobility Makes States"; Rossi, "Kinetocracy"; Tuck-Po, "Before a Step"; Edwards, "Tyranny of Proximity"; Roche, *Les circulations*.
10. Lester, "Place and Space"; Vivo, "Walking"; Guldi, "Landscape and Place"; Withers and Livingstone, "Introduction," 1–5.
11. White, *Middle Ground*, xi–xxiv; White, "Creative Misunderstandings"; Deloria, "What Is."
12. Herzog, *Frontiers of Possession*; Tagliacozzo, "Jagged Landscapes"; Hämäläinen and Truett, "On Borderlands"; Levin Rojo and Radding, "Introduction"; Barnard, "We Are Comfortable"; Ellis and Esser, "Introduction"; Berdah, "Pyrenees without Frontiers"; Adelman and Aron, "From Borderlands to Borders"; Maier, "Transformations of Territoriality."
13. Levin Rojo and Radding, "Introduction," 1.
14. Hämäläinen, "What's in a Concept?"

15. Curless et al., "Editors' Introduction"; Subrahmanyam, "Connected Histories"; Subrahmanyam, "Holding the World"; Wenzlhuemer, *Doing Global History*, 19–45.

16. Cardim et al., "Polycentric Monarchies."

17. Carey and Lydon, "Introduction."

18. Junker, *Raiding, Trading, and Feasting*, 221–60; Tappe, "Introduction."

19. Kennedy, "Introduction"; Carter, *Road to Botany Bay*, 1–33.

20. Elsner and Rubiés, "Introduction"; Rubiés, "Instructions for Travellers."

21. Flynn and Giráldez, "Born"; Bertrand, "Where the Devil Stands"; Crewe, "Transpacific Mestizo"; Seijas, *Asian Slaves*.

22. van Deusen, *Global Indios*, 1–33; Thrush, *Indigenous London*, 1–27; Thrush, "Walking the Indigenous City"; Fullagar, "Voyagers."

23. Brendecke, *Empirical Empire*; Gaudin et al., "Vencer la distancia"; Braudel, *Mediterranean*, 1:371–74.

24. Braudel, *Civilization and Capitalism*, 1:415–16, 422–30.

25. García de los Arcos, "¿Avanzada o periferia?"; García-Abásolo, "Filipinas"; Crailsheim, "Las Filipinas, zona fronteriza."

26. García-Abásolo, "Filipinas," 84.

27. Cardim et al., "Polycentric Monarchies"; Elliott, "Europe of Composite Monarchies."

28. Benton, *Search for Sovereignty*, xi–xiv, 1–23, 162–66, 222–36.

29. Sheller and Urry, "New Mobilities Paradigm," 210.

30. Cresswell, "Friction," 109–10; Scott, *Art*, 40–48; White, "What Is Spatial History?," 5–6.

31. Cresswell, "Friction," 108–12; Revill, "Histories," 507–8; Sheller and Urry, "New Mobilities Paradigm," 210.

32. Scholz, *Borders*; Quirk and Vigneswaran, "Mobility Makes States," 8–24; Sheller and Urry, "New Mobilities Paradigm," 211.

33. Tsing, *Friction*, 1–6; Cresswell, "Friction," 112–14.

34. Ballantyne, "Mobility, Empire, Colonisation," 37.

35. de Vries, "Playing with Scales," 28–29.

36. Carey and Lydon, "Introduction," 1–7; Standfield, "Moving Across"; Standfield, "Mobility."

37. Francisco Antolín, "Compendio cronologico sobre el camino para Cagayan por la provincia y mision de Ituy" (1790), AUST, APSR, Cagayan, tomo 30, n. 1, 168v.

38. Hämäläinen, *Comanche Empire*.

39. Carter, *Road to Botany Bay*, xiii–33.

40. Ingold, "Culture on the Ground," 323, 330–31; Guldi, "Landscape and Place."

41. Crossley, *Dasmariñases*, 60–110; Fernandez and Juan, "Social and Economic Development," 70–87; Salgado, *Cagayan Valley*, 2:682–97; Keesing, *Ethnohistory of Northern Luzon*, 271–77.

42. Luis Pérez Dasmariñas, "Relación del descubrimiento de Tuy por Luis Pérez das Mariñas" (July 7, 1591), AGI, Filipinas, 6, r. 7, n. 86, 1r, 2r.

43. Dasmariñas, "Relación," AGI, Filipinas, 6, r. 7, n. 86, 1r.

44. Dasmariñas, "Relación," AGI, Filipinas, 6, r. 7, n. 86, 2v.

45. Dasmariñas, "Relación," AGI, Filipinas, 6, r. 7, n. 86, 5v–6r.

46. Dasmariñas, "Relación," AGI, Filipinas, 6, r. 7, n. 86, 6r.

47. Crossley, *Dasmariñases*, 96.

48. Dasmariñas, "Relación," AGI, Filipinas, 6, r. 7, n. 86, 7v.

49. Dasmariñas, "Relación," AGI, Filipinas, 6, r. 7, n. 86, 8r–10v.

50. Lockhart, *Nahuas after the Conquest.*

51. Dasmariñas, "Relación," AGI, Filipinas, 6, r. 7, n. 86.

52. Warf and Arias, "Introduction," 4, 7; Stock, "History," 10, 12–13; White, "What Is Spatial History?," 3; Dizon, "Social and Spiritual Kinship."

53. Crossley, "Dionisio Capulong"; Scott, *Discovery of the Igorots,* 11–12; Fernandez and Juan, "Social and Economic Development," 71, 87–88.

54. Juan Manuel de la Vega, "Relaciones sobre descubrimiento de Tuy y mina de Igorrotes" (Passi, July 3, 1609), AGI, Filipinas, 7, r. 3, n. 45, 1r.

55. de la Vega, "Relaciones," AGI, Filipinas, 7, r. 3, n. 45, 6v–7r.

56. de la Vega, "Relaciones," AGI, Filipinas, 7, r. 3, n. 45, 1r.

57. Dasmariñas, "Relación," AGI, Filipinas, 6, r. 7, n. 86, 2r.

58. Dasmariñas, "Relación," AGI, Filipinas, 6, r. 7, n. 86, 4r.

59. Dasmariñas, "Relación," AGI, Filipinas, 6, r. 7, n. 86, 5r–5v.

60. de la Vega, "Relaciones," AGI, Filipinas, 7, r. 3, n. 45, 6v.

61. Crossley, "Dionisio Capulong"; Scott, *Discovery of the Igorots,* 11.

62. Aduarte, *Historia de la provincia,* 636.

63. Aduarte, 636–37.

64. Aduarte, 637–39.

65. Biedermann, Gerritsen, and Riello, "Introduction"; Algazi, "Introduction"; Liebersohn, *Return of the Gift*; White, *Middle Ground,* 94–141.

66. Thomas, *Entangled Objects,* 7–34.

67. Mauss, *Gift*; Tremml-Werner, Hellman, and van Meersbergen, "Introduction"; Liebersohn, *Return of the Gift.*

68. Herzog, *Frontiers of Possession,* 98–104.

69. Herzog, 99, 102.

70. Langfur, "Moved by Terror."

71. Aduarte, *Historia de la provincia,* 636–37.

72. Scott, *Art,* 40–48; White, "What Is Spatial History?," 5–6.

73. Aduarte, *Historia de la provincia,* 638.

74. Scott, *Art*; Andaya, *To Live as Brothers*; Andaya and Andaya, *History,* 289.

75. Andaya and Andaya, *History,* 51–53; Junker, *Raiding, Trading, and Feasting,* 57–84, 221–46.

76. Tappe, "Introduction," 320; Flores, *Unwanted Neighbours.*

77. Dizon, "Social and Spiritual Kinship," 372–79.

78. Stoler, "Colonial Archives."

79. Wolters, *History,* 16–33; Andaya and Andaya, *History,* 42–61; Scott, *Art,* 40–63; Junker, *Raiding, Trading, and Feasting,* 57–84; Aguilar, *Clash of Spirits,* 32–62.

80. Rodriguez, "La centuria desconocida," 221.

81. Rosaldo, *Knowledge and Passion,* 198.

Chapter One

1. Antolín, "Notices," 245–47; Antolín, "Notices: Part 2," 80–81.

2. Antolín, "Notices: Part 2," 80–81.

3. Scott, *History on the Cordillera*, 4–5.

4. Weber, *Spanish Frontier*; Weber, *Bárbaros*, 1–51; Daniels and Kennedy, *Negotiated Empires*; Crailsheim, "Las Filipinas, zona fronteriza"; García de los Arcos, "¿Avanzada o periferia?," 57–58.

5. Kagan, "Projecting Order"; Kagan and Marías, *Urban Images*, 9–39.

6. Sánchez Gómez, "Estructura de los pueblos"; Abinales and Amoroso, *State and Society*, 53–55; Phelan, *Hispanization of the Philippines*, 44–49; Rafael, *Contracting Colonialism*, 87–91.

7. Scott, *Discovery of the Igorots*; Salgado, *Cagayan Valley*; Salgado, *Ilongots*.

8. Scott, *Art*, 1–39, 58–63, 134–37, 178–219; Lieberman, "Zone of Refuge."

9. Deloria, "What Is"; White, *Middle Ground*, xi–xxiv; White, "Creative Misunderstandings"; Barnard, "'We Are Comfortable.'"

10. Marcus, "Ethnography"; Sheller and Urry, "New Mobilities Paradigm," 217.

11. Stoler and Cooper, "Between Metropole and Colony"; Altenbernd and Young, "Introduction"; Readman, Radding, and Bryant, "Introduction"; Wilde, "Political Dimension"; Norton, "Liminal Space."

12. Hämäläinen, *Comanche Empire*; Hämäläinen, "What's in a Concept?"; Rossi, "Kinetocracy"; Quirk and Vigneswaran, "Mobility Makes States"; Pouchepadass, "Itinerant Kings."

13. Carey and Lydon, "Introduction"; Paredes, *Mountain of Difference*, 32–35, 168–70; Herzog, *Frontiers of Possession*, 104.

14. Scott, *Art*, 25, 135–37; Acabado, "Archaeology of Pericolonialism"; Acabado, *Antiquity*, 123–24; Lieberman, "Zone," 343.

15. Cacho, "Conquistas espirituales," 1904, 33–34; Cacho, "Manifiesto compendioso," 63–64; Foronda, "Informe sobre el estado," 306–7; Olarte, "Informe dado," 321–22.

16. Cacho, "Manifiesto compendioso," 64.

17. Foronda, "Informe sobre el estado," 306.

18. Cacho, "Conquistas espirituales," 1904, 34; Cacho, "Manifiesto compendioso," 64; Foronda, "Informe sobre el estado," 306.

19. Cacho, "Manifiesto compendioso," 64; Foronda, "Informe sobre el estado," 306.

20. Cacho, "Conquistas espirituales," 1904, 34; Cacho, "Manifiesto compendioso," 64; Foronda, "Informe sobre el estado," 306–7.

21. Cacho, "Conquistas espirituales," 1904, 34.

22. Cacho, 33; Cacho, "Manifiesto compendioso," 64.

23. Foronda, "Informe sobre el estado," 304.

24. Francisco Antolín, "Compendio cronologico sobre el camino para Cagayan por la provincia y mision de Ituy" (1790), AUST, APSR, Cagayan, tomo 30, n. 1, 62v; Ferrando and Fonseca, *Historia de los PP.*, 3:726.

25. Antolín, "Compendio cronologico," AUST, APSR, Cagayan, tomo 30, n. 1, 65r.

26. Herzog, *Frontiers of Possession*, 98–99.

27. Seed, *Ceremonies of Possession*, 56–63.

28. Smuts and Gorse, "Introduction," 19; Herzog, *Frontiers of Possession*, 104; Andrade, "Political Spectacle."

29. Biedermann, Gerritsen, and Riello, "Introduction," 1–8.

30. Osorio, *Inventing Lima*, 61.

31. Seed, *Ceremonies of Possession*, 54–55.

32. Herzog, *Frontiers of Possession*, 102.

33. Voigt, *Spectacular Wealth*, 7–11, 13–15.

34. Junker, *Raiding, Trading, and Feasting*, 298–303.

35. Clulow, "Gifts for the Shogun," 213–15.

36. Biedermann, Gerritsen, and Riello, "Introduction," 7.

37. Antolín, "Compendio cronologico," AUST, APSR, Cagayan, tomo 30, n. 1, 62v.

38. Dizon, "Social and Spiritual Kinship," 377–79.

39. Andaya, "Historicising 'Modernity,'" 401–3.

40. Andaya, 401–2; Riello, "With Great Pomp and Magnificence," 257.

41. Andaya, "Historicising 'Modernity'"; Riello, "With Great Pomp," 239, 263; Junker, *Raiding, Trading, and Feasting*, 240–46.

42. Carrillo, *Breve relacion*, 1–2.

43. Carrillo, 3–5.

44. Carrillo, 6.

45. Carrillo, 8–9.

46. Carrillo, 9.

47. Carrillo, 10–11.

48. Carrillo, 10.

49. Carrillo, 10–11.

50. Carrillo, 11.

51. Villoria Prieto, "Los agustinos," 13.

52. Geertz, "Centers, Kings, and Charisma"; Geertz, *Negara*; Roque, *Headhunting and Colonialism*, 40–69.

53. Weber, *Bárbaros*, 243.

54. Ruiz, *King Travels*, 72, 76–84, 146–92; Osorio, *Inventing Lima*, 61–63, 72–74; Cañeque, *King's Living Image*, 123–25.

55. Ruiz, *King Travels*, 13, 23, 157, 182; Osorio, *Inventing Lima*, 58, 63, 71–72; Cañeque, *King's Living Image*, 122, 124–25.

56. Ruiz, *King Travels*, 13, 182; Cañeque, *King's Living Image*, 125.

57. Antolín, "Compendio cronologico," AUST, APSR, Cagayan, tomo 30, n. 1, 229v.

58. Rosaldo, *Ilongot Headhunting*, 38–48, 54–61; Tsing, *Friction*, 186–202.

59. Tsing, *Friction*, 176–77, 186.

60. Rosaldo, *Knowledge and Passion*, 84.

61. Ileto, "Religion and Anti-Colonial Movements," 208, 211–13; Ileto, "Rizal," 308–9, 333; Andaya and Andaya, *History*, 9.

62. Carrillo, *Breve relacion*, 25.

63. Carrillo, 28.

64. "Carta de Fray Jose de San Pascual" (Aleveg, May 12, 1755), AFIO 89/87, 2v.

65. "Carta de Pedro Manuel de Arandia sobre bautismo de ilongotes en Manila" (Manila, July 24, 1757), AGI, Filipinas, 160, n. 16, 1r–1v.

66. "Carta de Pedro Manuel de Arandia," AGI, Filipinas, 160, n. 16, 1v–2r.

67. "Carta de Pedro Manuel de Arandia," AGI, Filipinas, 160, n. 16, 2r–3r.

68. "Carta de Pedro Manuel de Arandia," AGI, Filipinas, 160, n. 16, 3r–3v.

69. "Carta de Fray Jose de San Pascual," AFIO 89/87, 2v.

70. Quirk and Vigneswaran, "Mobility Makes States."

71. Smuts and Gorse, "Introduction," 16; Cañeque, *King's Living Image*, 19–26, 120–32.

72. Geertz, "Centers, Kings, and Charisma," 125–34; Perdue, *China Marches West*, 409–29; Chang, *Court on Horseback*, 75–86; Taylor, "Early Kingdoms," 166.

73. Guevara-Gil and Salomon, "'Personal Visit,'" 8–9.

74. Geertz, "Centers, Kings, and Charisma," 125.

75. Mundy, *Mapping of New Spain*, 8–9; cited in Smuts and Gorse, "Introduction," 19.

76. Cited in Guevara-Gil and Salomon, "'Personal Visit,'" 9; Mundy, *Mapping of New Spain*, 9.

77. Brendecke, *Empirical Empire*, 17–26; Smuts and Gorse, "Introduction," 19; Guevara-Gil and Salomon, "'Personal Visit,'" 9–10.

78. Ruiz, *King Travels*, 10–30.

79. Osorio, *Inventing Lima*, 83–85.

80. Osorio, 96–98.

81. Osorio, 89–96; Díaz-Trechuelo López-Spínola, "Filipinas en el siglo," 285–86; Curcio-Nagy, "Commemorating the Conquest," 187.

82. Osorio, *Inventing Lima*, 96–97, 101; Flores and Marcocci, "Killing Images," 474.

83. Cañeque, *King's Living Image*, 19–29, 119–27.

84. Antolín, "Compendio cronologico," AUST, APSR, Cagayan, tomo 30, n. 1, 62v; Santa Rosa, "Carta-relación," 102.

85. Cañeque, *King's Living Image*, 26–29, 119–32; Osorio, *Inventing Lima*, 81–102.

86. Clulow, "Gifts for the Shogun," 201–4; Andrade, "Chinese under European Rule," 2; Blussé, "Batavia, 1619–1740," 162.

87. Cañeque, *King's Living Image*, 25, 128, 144–45, 148.

88. Osorio, *Inventing Lima*, 57–79; Hidalgo Nuchera, "La entrada"; Cañeque, *King's Living Image*, 120–27.

89. Hidalgo Nuchera, "La entrada," 616–24, 626, 637.

90. Cañeque, *King's Living Image*, 35–36.

91. Brendecke, *Empirical Empire*, 111–50; Grafe, *Distant Tyranny*, ix–11.

92. Osorio, *Inventing Lima*, 70; Herzog, *Ritos de control*, 11–12, 53; Céspedes del Castillo, "La visita."

93. Radding, "Environment, Territory," 71, 76.

94. Céspedes del Castillo, "La visita," 1004–5; Radding, "Environment, Territory," 76; Weber, *Spanish Frontier*, 220.

95. Weber, *Spanish Frontier in North America*, 204–15; Hidalgo, "Visitas a la tierra," 207–9.

96. Hidalgo, "Visitas a la tierra," 208–9.

97. Libro 2, título 31 in *Recopilación*, 1:276v–80r.

98. Hidalgo, "Visitas a la tierra," 210–11; Dueñas Olmo, "Contribución al estudio," 51–52, 87.

99. "Carta de la Audiencia de Manila sobre continuación de las visitas generales" (Manila, June 14, 1702), AGI, Filipinas, 164, n. 1.

100. Zanolli, "'Visitas de la tierra,'" 155–60; Herzog, *Ritos de control*, 4; Dueñas Olmo, "Contribución al estudio," 52.

101. Dueñas Olmo, "Contribución al estudio," 54.

102. Dueñas Olmo, 39–40.

103. "Carta de Fausto Cruzat sobre visita a provincias" (Manila, May 12, 1696), AGI, Filipinas, 16, r. 1, n. 1; Dueñas Olmo, "Contribución al estudio," 80–81, 406.

104. "Carta de la Audiencia de Manila," AGI, Filipinas, 164, n. 1; "Duplicado de carta de la Audiencia de Manila remitiendo autos de la visita de José Ignacio de Arzadun" (Manila, July 18, 1743), AGI, Filipinas, 556, n. 1.

105. "Carta de la Audiencia de Manila," AGI, Filipinas, 164, n. 1; Dueñas Olmo, "Las ordenanzas"; "Ordenanzas de Arzadun" (1734), AUST, APSR, Cagayan, tomo 13, n. 13.

106. Pan, *Documentos para la historia*.

107. "Piden los de Camarag se vuelva su pueblo a su antiguo lugar" (June 15, 1792), AUST, APSR, Cagayan, tomo 24, n. 10, 141v.

108. Malumbres, *Historia de Cagayán*, 65.

109. Herzog, *Ritos de control*, 6–9.

110. Dueñas Olmo, "Contribución al estudio," 40–41, 128, 130–31; "Carta de Fausto Cruzat sobre reducciones de indios" (Manila, May 12, 1700), AGI, Filipinas, 122, n. 28, 1.

111. "Orden sobre reducción de indios infieles y apóstatas" (Madrid, November 14, 1696), AGI, Filipinas, 331, l. 9.

112. "Carta de Torralba sobre visita de Pangasinan" (Manila, June 21, 1704), AGI, Filipinas, 165, n. 9.

113. "Carta de Torralba," AGI, Filipinas, 165, n. 9, 8–9, 15–18.

114. "Carta de Torralba," AGI, Filipinas, 165, n. 9, 19.

115. Dueñas Olmo, "Contribución al estudio," 196; "Carta de la Audiencia de Manila," AGI, Filipinas, 164, n. 1, 2v.

116. Mora Mérida, "La visita eclesiástica como institución en Indias," 60; Manchado López, *Conflictos Iglesia-Estado*, 20–21.

117. Zanolli, "'Visitas de la tierra,'" 143; Salinas, "Reclamos y multas," 199.

118. Juan Ormaza, "Breve relacion de algunas cosas" (Buhay, February 25, 1743), AUST, APSR, Cagayan, tomo 29, n. 33, 528v, 530v.

119. Phelan, *Hispanization of the Philippines*, 32–38; Manchado López, *Conflictos Iglesia-Estado*, 21, 24–25; Díaz-Trechuelo López-Spínola, *Filipinas*, 220; "Carta de Diego Camacho sobre confirmaciones" (Manila, June 16, 1699), AGI, Filipinas, 75, n. 41.

120. "Carta de Diego Camacho," AGI, Filipinas, 75, n. 41, 2, 12.

121. "Carta de Diego Camacho," AGI, Filipinas, 75, n. 41, 2–3, 12–13.

122. "Carta de Diego Camacho," AGI, Filipinas, 75, n. 41, 1; Foronda, "Informe sobre el estado," 308.

123. "Carta de Fausto Cruzat sobre conquista de infieles" (Manila, June 12, 1691), AGI, Filipinas, 14, r. 3, n. 35, 1r.

124. Phelan, *Hispanization of the Philippines*, 41–71; Rafael, *Contracting Colonialism*, 84–109.

125. Concepción, "Informe del Provincial," 126.

126. Bautista Martínez, "Informe del P. Provincial," 127–29.

127. Bautista Martínez, 129.

128. Junker, *Raiding, Trading, and Feasting*, 221–46; Andaya, *To Live as Brothers*, 75–78; Andaya and Andaya, *History*, 27–30, 45–48.

129. Lockhart, *Nahuas after the Conquest*, 14–58; Mumford, *Vertical Empire*, 27–39.

130. Villoria Prieto, *Un berciano en Filipinas*; González Cuellas, *Presencia berciana en Filipinas*, 35–118; Villoria Prieto, "Fray Antolín de Alzaga"; Villoria Prieto, "La labor del agustino vasco."

131. Cacho, "Manifiesto compendioso," 62; Dizon, "La misión del Caraballo," 40.

132. Cacho, "Conquistas espirituales," 1904, 31.

133. Cacho, 31.

134. Villoria Prieto, "Fray Antolín de Alzaga," 119.

135. "Registro desde 1690 hasta 1722" (1722), APAF 35-A, 51v.

136. Cacho, "Conquistas espirituales," 1904, 32–33; Cacho, "Compendioso manifiesto," 362.

137. Alzaga, "Carta," 304.

138. Cacho, "Conquistas espirituales," 1904, 32–33; Cacho, "Compendioso manifiesto," 363.

139. Cacho, "Conquistas espirituales," 1904, 33; Cacho, "Compendioso manifiesto," 363.

140. "Misiones de Pampanga: Padrón de todos los cristianos nuevos" (1707), APAF 97/1, 70; Antolín, "Compendio cronologico," AUST, APSR, Cagayan, tomo 30, n. 1, 59r, 72r; "Carta del Padre Fray Francisco Maza" (Bagtar, January 28, 1703), AGI, Filipinas, 296, n. 36, 2; Villoria Prieto, "Los agustinos," 13.

141. "Carta de Fray Jose de San Pascual," AFIO 89/87, 2v.

142. "Misiones de Pampanga," APAF 97/1, 70; Antolín, "Compendio cronologico," AUST, APSR, Cagayan, tomo 30, n. 1, 72r.

143. José Tomás Marín, "Documentos interesantes," *Libertas*, February 23, 1905.

144. Antolín, "Compendio cronologico," AUST, APSR, Cagayan, tomo 30, n. 1, 66r.

145. Antolín, "Compendio cronologico," AUST, APSR, Cagayan, tomo 30, n. 1, 64v.

146. Antolín, "Compendio cronologico," AUST, APSR, Cagayan, tomo 30, n. 1, 59r, 63r.

147. Antolín, "Compendio cronologico," AUST, APSR, Cagayan, tomo 30, n. 1, 64v.

148. Antolín, "Compendio cronologico," AUST, APSR, Cagayan, tomo 30, n. 1, 64v.

149. Antolín, "Compendio cronologico," AUST, APSR, Cagayan, tomo 30, n. 1, 64v; "Carta del Padre Fray Francisco Maza," AGI, Filipinas, 296, n. 36, 2.

150. Antolín, "Compendio cronologico," AUST, APSR, Cagayan, tomo 30, n. 1, 64v–65r; "Carta del Padre Fray Francisco Maza," AGI, Filipinas, 296, n. 36, 2.

151. Antolín, "Compendio cronologico," AUST, APSR, Cagayan, tomo 30, n. 1, 65r–65v; "Carta del Padre Fray Francisco Maza," AGI, Filipinas, 296, n. 36, 3.

152. Antolín, "Compendio cronologico," AUST, APSR, Cagayan, tomo 30, n. 1, 65v–66r; "Carta del Padre Fray Francisco Maza," AGI, Filipinas, 296, n. 36, 3–4.

153. Antolín, "Compendio cronologico," AUST, APSR, Cagayan, tomo 30, n. 1, 66r; "Carta del Padre Fray Francisco Maza," AGI, Filipinas, 296, n. 36, 3.

154. Antolín, "Compendio cronologico," AUST, APSR, Cagayan, tomo 30, n. 1, 66r–66v; "Carta del Padre Fray Francisco Maza," AGI, Filipinas, 296, n. 36, 4.

155. Antolín, "Compendio cronologico," AUST, APSR, Cagayan, tomo 30, n. 1, 67r; "Carta del Padre Fray Francisco Maza," AGI, Filipinas, 296, n. 36, 4–5.

156. Antolín, "Compendio cronologico," AUST, APSR, Cagayan, tomo 30, n. 1, 67r–67v; "Carta del Padre Fray Francisco Maza," AGI, Filipinas, 296, n. 36, 5.

157. Antolín, "Compendio cronologico," AUST, APSR, Cagayan, tomo 30, n. 1, 67r; "Carta del Padre Fray Francisco Maza," AGI, Filipinas, 296, n. 36, 5.

158. Conklin, Lupaih, and Pinther, *Ethnographic Atlas of Ifugao*, 97.

159. "Misiones de Pampanga," APAF 97/1, 190–201; Cacho, "Compendioso manifiesto," 373–83.

160. Cacho, "Conquistas espirituales," 1997, 343.

161. Cacho, "Compendioso manifiesto," 373.

162. Cacho, 373–74.

163. Cacho, 374–76.

164. Cacho, 376–77.

165. Cacho, 377.

166. Antolín, "Compendio cronologico," AUST, APSR, Cagayan, tomo 30, n. 1, 68r; "Carta del Padre Fray Francisco Maza," AGI, Filipinas, 296, n. 36, 6.

167. Malumbres, *Historia de Nueva-Vizcaya*, 18; Antolín, "Compendio cronologico," AUST, APSR, Cagayan, tomo 30, n. 1, 63r.

168. Antolín, "Compendio cronologico," AUST, APSR, Cagayan, tomo 30, n. 1, 68r–68v; "Carta del Padre Fray Francisco Maza," AGI, Filipinas, 296, n. 36, 5–6.

169. Fernandez, "Pigu's Account"; Beltrán Pigu, "Pigu's Narrative."

170. Cacho, "Compendioso manifiesto," 384.

171. Antolín, "Compendio cronologico," AUST, APSR, Cagayan, tomo 30, n. 1, 92r.

172. Antolín, "Compendio cronologico," AUST, APSR, Cagayan, tomo 30, n. 1, 72v.

173. Antolín, "Compendio cronologico," AUST, APSR, Cagayan, tomo 30, n. 1, 72v.

174. Antolín, "Compendio cronologico," AUST, APSR, Cagayan, tomo 30, n. 1, 72v–73r.

175. "Carta del Hermano Fray Domingo Maza al Padre Vicario Provincial Fray Joseph Vila" (Burubur, February 12, 1703), AGI, Filipinas, 296, n. 36, 8; Villoria Prieto, "Los agustinos," 17.

176. Fernandez, "Pigu's Account," 132–33.

177. Villoria Prieto, "Los agustinos," 27.

178. "Carta del Hermano Fray Domingo Maza al Padre Fray Francisco Marquez" (Burubur, February 12, 1703), AGI, Filipinas, 296, n. 36.

179. Dizon, "Social and Spiritual Kinship," 372–79.

180. Santa Rosa, "Carta-relación," 94.

181. Carsten, "Introduction."

182. "Carta de Fray Jose de San Pascual al Provincial Padre Alejandro Ferrer" (Aleveg, September 2, 1755), AFIO 89/88, 3v; Andaya, *To Live as Brothers*, 23–29.

183. Jose de San Pascual, "Breve relacion de las nuevas misiones de los Montes de Tabueyon" (Aleveg, August 30, 1754), AFIO 89/80, 20.

184. San Pascual, "Breve relacion," AFIO 89/80, 20–21.

185. San Pascual, "Breve relacion," AFIO 89/80, 21.

186. Antolín, "Compendio cronologico," AUST, APSR, Cagayan, tomo 30, n. 1, 63r.

187. Janowski, "Feeding the Right Food," 13.

188. Janowski, 11–13, 20.

189. Carsten, "Substance of Kinship."

190. "Carta de Fray Jose de San Pascual," AFIO 89/87, 1v–2r.

Chapter Two

1. "Traslado del memorial de fray Francisco Jiménez" (San Juan del Monte, June 12, 1703), AGI, Filipinas, 296, n. 36, 1–2.

2. "Traslado del memorial," AGI, Filipinas, 296, n. 36, 2.

3. "Traslado del memorial," AGI, Filipinas, 296, n. 36, 3–4.

4. Langfur, "Moved by Terror," 284; Herzog, *Frontiers of Possession*, 11.

5. Langfur, "Moved by Terror"; Langfur, *Forbidden Lands*, 227–61; Ferguson and White-head, "Preface," xxv.

6. Cresswell, "Friction," 108–12; Revill, "Histories," 507–8; Sheller and Urry, "New Mobilities Paradigm," 210.

7. Ferguson and Whitehead, "Preface," xxii–xxvii; Clendinnen, "Fierce and Unnatural Cruelty"; Rodriguez, "Juan de Salcedo."

8. Reid, *Southeast Asia*, 1:121–29; Angeles, "Battle of Mactan," 12–16; Charney, *Southeast Asian Warfare*, 17–18; Charney, "Warfare," 3.

9. George, *Showing Signs of Violence*, 16, 64–67.

10. Angeles, "Battle of Mactan"; Rodriguez, "Juan de Salcedo."

11. Langfur, "Moved by Terror"; Langfur, *Forbidden Lands*, 227–61.

12. Thomas, *Entangled Objects*, 100–110.

13. "Registro desde 1716 hasta 1719" (1719), APAF 36, 69r; Pérez, "Decreto del Rey," 335; Villoria Prieto, "Los agustinos," 27.

14. "Orden sobre reducción de indios infieles y apóstatas" (Madrid, November 14, 1696), AGI, Filipinas, 331, l. 9, 201v–2r.

15. "Carta de Fausto Cruzat sobre conquista de infieles" (Manila, June 12, 1691), AGI, 14, r. 3, n. 35, 1v.

16. "Carta de Fausto Cruzat sobre conquista," AGI, Filipinas, 14, r. 3, n. 35, 1v–5v.

17. "Carta de Fausto Cruzat sobre conquista," AGI, Filipinas, 14, r. 3, n. 35, 2v.

18. "Carta de Fausto Cruzat sobre conquista," AGI, Filipinas, 14, r. 3, n. 35, 4v.

19. "Carta de Fausto Cruzat sobre conquista," AGI, Filipinas, 14, r. 3, n. 35, 4v, 8r–9r, 13r–15r.

20. "Carta de Fausto Cruzat sobre conquista," AGI, Filipinas, 14, r. 3, n. 35, 15v–17v.

21. "Carta de Fausto Cruzat sobre conquista," AGI, Filipinas, 14, r. 3, n. 35, 8r.

22. "Carta de Fausto Cruzat sobre conquista," AGI, Filipinas, 14, r. 3, n. 35, 2r; Junker, *Raiding, Trading, and Feasting*, 83, 240–42.

23. "Carta de Fausto Cruzat sobre conquista," AGI, Filipinas, 14, r. 3, n. 35, 24v–25v.

24. "Carta de Fausto Cruzat sobre conquista," AGI, Filipinas, 14, r. 3, n. 35, 24v–25r.

25. "Carta de Fausto Cruzat sobre conquista," AGI, Filipinas, 14, r. 3, n. 35, 25v.

26. Weber, *Bárbaros*, 161, 164.

27. Kagan, "Projecting Order"; Kagan and Marías, *Urban Images*, 26–28, 36–39.

28. "Carta de Fausto Cruzat sobre reducciones de indios" (Manila, May 12, 1700), AGI, Filipinas, 122, n. 28, 2.

29. "Carta de Fausto Cruzat sobre reducciones," AGI, Filipinas, 122, n. 28, 2–3.

30. Barrio Muñoz, *Vientos de reforma ilustrada*, 109; Barrio Muñoz, "Negritos," 80, 83, 94, 99; Antolín, "Notices," 238.

31. Santa Rosa, "Carta-relación," 97; "Carta de Valdés Tamón sobre ataques de indios infieles" (Manila, July 6, 1733), AGI, Filipinas, 144, n. 9, 128v, 142v.

32. Mozo, *Noticia historico natural*, 32; "Breve relacion de las nuevas misiones de los Montes de Tabueyon" (Aleveg, August 30, 1754), AFIO 89/80, 2v; "Carta de Valdés Tamón," AGI, Filipinas, 144, n. 9, 43r; Villoria Prieto, "Breve relación," 36.

33. "Registro desde 1716 hasta 1719," APAF 36, 56v.

34. "Carta de Valdés Tamón," AGI, Filipinas, 144, n. 9, 43r, 203r–203v.

35. "Breve relacion de las nuevas misiones," AFIO 89/80, 9r–9v.

36. "Breve relacion de las nuevas misiones," AFIO 89/80, 9v.

37. Cacho, "Conquistas espirituales," 1997, 332.

38. "Carta de Valdés Tamón," AGI, Filipinas, 144, n. 9, 12r, 70v; "Petición del dominico Alonso Sandín sobre nuevas conversiones en Filipinas" (August 27, 1696), AGI, Filipinas, 83, n. 52, 32; Mozo, *Noticia historico natural,* 32; Pérez, "Los Aetas e Ilongotes," 316.

39. Santa Rosa, "Carta-relación," 100.

40. Dizon, "Sumpong," 20, 23–26.

41. Santa Rosa, "Carta-relación," 96.

42. Santa Rosa, 93, 96.

43. Santa Rosa, 98–104; Rafael, *Contracting Colonialism,* 167–209; Phelan, *Hispanization of the Philippines,* 59–60, 81–84; Rosaldo, "Grief"; Rosaldo, *Knowledge and Passion,* 31–60, 136–76.

44. Needham, "Skulls and Causality," 75–78; Rosaldo, "Skulls and Causality."

45. "Carta de Valdés Tamón," AGI, Filipinas, 144, n. 9, 48r.

46. Herosa, "Breve insinuación," 244.

47. Herosa, 244.

48. Rosaldo, "Skulls and Causality"; Rosaldo, *Knowledge and Passion,* 137–76.

49. Santa Rosa, "Carta-relación," 93, 96.

50. "Carta de Valdés Tamón," AGI, Filipinas, 144, n. 9, 13v, 19v, 42v, 47v, 199v.

51. "Carta de Valdés Tamón," AGI, Filipinas, 144, n. 9, 11r, 18r, 19v.

52. "Carta de Valdés Tamón," AGI, Filipinas, 144, n. 9.

53. "Petición del dominico Alonso Sandín," AGI, Filipinas, 83, n. 52, 109.

54. "Petición del dominico Alonso Sandín," AGI, Filipinas, 83, n. 52, 109–10.

55. "Carta de Valdés Tamón," AGI, Filipinas, 144, n. 9, 52v, 54v–55r, 57v, 69r.

56. "Carta de Valdés Tamón," AGI, Filipinas, 144, n. 9, 128r–128v.

57. George, *Showing Signs of Violence,* 10–13.

58. Metcalf, "Images of Headhunting," 262–63.

59. "Breve relacion de las nuevas misiones," AFIO 89/80, 8v–9r; "Registro desde 1716 hasta 1719," APAF 36, 56v.

60. "Carta de Valdés Tamón," AGI, Filipinas, 144, n. 9, 49r.

61. Bolton, "Mission."

62. Weber, *Bárbaros,* 143, 166–72; Weber, *Spanish Frontier,* 212, 215.

63. Luengo, "La fortificación," 740–45; Barrio Muñoz, *Vientos de reforma ilustrada,* 403–9; Díaz-Trechuelo López-Spínola, *Filipinas,* 212–13; Díaz-Trechuelo López-Spínola, "Filipinas en el siglo," 276–78.

64. Luengo, "La fortificación," 744, 753; Díaz-Trechuelo López-Spínola, "Filipinas en el siglo," 278.

65. "Carta de Valdés Tamón," AGI, Filipinas, 144, n. 9, 191v, 193v, 197v–98r.

66. "Carta de Valdés Tamón," AGI, Filipinas, 144, n. 9, 52r–52v, 97r, 181v.

67. "Carta de Valdés Tamón," AGI, Filipinas, 144, n. 9, 78v–79r.

68. "Carta de Valdés Tamón," AGI, Filipinas, 144, n. 9, 79v–80r.

69. "Carta de Valdés Tamón," AGI, Filipinas, 144, n. 9, 81r.

70. "Carta de Valdés Tamón," AGI, Filipinas, 144, n. 9, 199r–199v.

71. "Carta de Valdés Tamón," AGI, Filipinas, 144, n. 9, 199v–200v.

72. "Carta de Valdés Tamón," AGI, Filipinas, 144, n. 9, 90r, 95r, 97r, 193v–94r, 197r.

73. "Carta de Fausto Cruzat sobre conquista," AGI, Filipinas, 14, r. 3, n. 35, 4r–4v.

74. "Petición del dominico Alonso Sandín," AGI, Filipinas, 83, n. 52.

75. Pan, *Documentos para la historia*, 32.

76. Pérez, "Orden."

77. Weber, "Bourbons and Bárbaros," 82–84; Weber, *Bárbaros*, 8, 141–42, 246.

78. Scott, *Art*, 40–50, 182–207.

79. "Carta de Torrecampo sobre misión de agustinos" (Manila, June 30, 1725), AGI, Filipinas, 140, n. 29, 84v.

80. Mozo, *Noticia historico natural*, 117–18.

81. José Tomás Marín, "Documentos interesantes," *Libertas*, February 15, 1905; Vicente Salazar, "Relacion de los sucesos y progresos de la tropa" (1750), AUST, APSR, Cagayan, tomo 29, n. 19, 153r, 154r.

82. Francisco Antolín, "Compendio cronologico sobre el camino para Cagayan por la provincia y mision de Ituy" (1790), AUST, APSR, Cagayan, tomo 30, n. 1, 171r.

83. Vicente de Salazar, "Relacion de la conquista de Pituy" (Buhay, July 15, 1748), AUST, APSR, Cagayan, tomo 29, n. 23, 201r; Antolín, "Compendio cronologico," AUST, APSR, Cagayan, tomo 30, n. 1, 171r.

84. Cacho, "Informe sobre la divisoria"; Villoria Prieto, *Un berciano en Filipinas*, 159.

85. Carrillo, *Breve relacion*, 18.

86. "Breve relacion de las nuevas misiones," AFIO 89/80, 4v.

87. Salazar, "Relacion de los sucesos y progresos," AUST, APSR, Cagayan, tomo 29, n. 19, 153v.

88. Salazar, "Relacion de los sucesos y progresos," AUST, APSR, Cagayan, tomo 29, n. 19, 153v.

89. José Honorato Lozano, "Álbum: Vistas de las yslas Filipinas y trages de sus abitantes" (1847), BNE, DIB/15/84/49, 138.

90. Lozano, "Álbum," BNE, DIB/15/84/49, 138.

91. "Instruccion que dio el Mariscal de Campo para la expedicion de abrir el paso" (Manila, April 19, 1719), AUST, APSR, Cagayan, tomo 29, n. 5, 57r.

92. "Instruccion que dio el Mariscal de Campo," AUST, APSR, Cagayan, tomo 29, n. 5, 57v.

93. "Carta de Valdés Tamón," AGI, Filipinas, 144, n. 9, 99v.

94. "Carta de Valdés Tamón," AGI, Filipinas, 144, n. 9, 99r.

95. "Carta de Felipe Pardo denunciando la inutilidad de los presidios de Cagayan" (Manila, June 10, 1686), AGI, Filipinas, 75, n. 18, 15.

96. Thomas, *Entangled Objects*, 87.

97. Manuel de Jesus Maria Joseph de Olivencia, "Relación de los progresos de la misión de San Antonio de Padua de los montes Emotlen" (Santa Ana de Sapa, June 28, 1755), AGI, Filipinas, 301, n. 24, 7–8.

98. "Carta de Valdés Tamón," AGI, Filipinas, 144, n. 9, 180v–81r.

99. "Carta de Valdés Tamón," AGI, Filipinas, 144, n. 9, 232v–33r.

100. Junker, *Raiding, Trading, and Feasting*, 221–46.

101. "Petición del dominico Alonso Sandín," AGI, Filipinas, 83, n. 52, 36.

102. "Petición del dominico Alonso Sandín," AGI, Filipinas, 83, n. 52, 36.

103. "Carta de Valdés Tamón," AGI, Filipinas, 144, n. 9, 202r.

104. "Carta de Valdés Tamón," AGI, Filipinas, 144, n. 9, 53v–54r.

105. "Carta de Valdés Tamón," AGI, Filipinas, 144, n. 9, 54v–55r.

106. Weber, *Bárbaros*, 221–50.

107. "Carta de Valdés Tamón," AGI, Filipinas, 144, n. 9, 55v.

108. "Carta de Valdés Tamón," AGI, Filipinas, 144, n. 9, 57v.

109. "Carta de Valdés Tamón," AGI, Filipinas, 144, n. 9, 57v.

110. "Carta de Valdés Tamón," AGI, Filipinas, 144, n. 9, 184r–184v, 194r, 196v.

111. "Carta de Valdés Tamón," AGI, Filipinas, 144, n. 9, 98v–99r, 193v–94r.

112. "Carta de Valdés Tamón," AGI, Filipinas, 144, n. 9, 193v.

113. Raj, "Go-Betweens."

114. "Carta de Valdés Tamón," AGI, Filipinas, 144, n. 9, 243r–47r; "Respuesta sobre delitos de indios infieles y negros" (El Pardo, January 23, 1735), AGI, Filipinas, 333, l. 13.

115. Mawson, "Convicts or Conquistadores?"

116. "Informe anonimo sobre las misiones de los Ilongotes" (1783), AFIO 89/70, 13–14.

117. "Petición del dominico Alonso Sandín," AGI, Filipinas, 83, n. 52, 32, 38–39.

118. "Petición del dominico Alonso Sandín," AGI, Filipinas, 83, n. 52, 38.

119. Lee, "Military Revolution," 63.

120. "Descripciones con planos y figuras de la capital de Manila, puerto de Cavite, fuerzas de los presidios y otras fortificaciones" (1753), AGI, MP-Libros Manuscritos, 81, 79–82.

121. "Petición del dominico Alonso Sandín," AGI, Filipinas, 83, n. 52, 109.

122. "Carta de Felipe Pardo," AGI, Filipinas, 75, n. 18, 19–20.

123. "Carta de Felipe Pardo," AGI, Filipinas, 75, n. 18, 20.

124. "Carta de Felipe Pardo," AGI, Filipinas, 75, n. 18, 20.

125. "Petición del dominico Alonso Sandín," AGI, Filipinas, 83, n. 52, 110.

126. Mawson, "Convicts or Conquistadores?," 111; Mawson, "Philippine Indios," 391.

127. Cáceres Menéndez and Patch, "'Gente de Mal Vivir'"; García de los Arcos, *Forzados y reclutas*; Mawson, "Convicts or Conquistadores?"

128. García de los Arcos, *Forzados y reclutas*, 12–13, 228.

129. Antolín, "Compendio cronologico," AUST, APSR, Cagayan, tomo 30, n. 1, 61r.

130. "Carta de Francisco de la Cuesta sobre misiones de Casiguran y Baler" (Manila, June 18, 1720), AGI, Filipinas, 132, n. 32, 8–9.

131. "Petición del dominico Alonso Sandín," AGI, Filipinas, 83, n. 52, 36.

132. "Petición del dominico Alonso Sandín," AGI, Filipinas, 83, n. 52, 36.

133. "Petición del dominico Alonso Sandín," AGI, Filipinas, 83, n. 52, 36.

134. Huetz de Lemps, *L'archipel des épices*, 26–34, 49; Robles, *Philippines*, 98–136.

135. Weber, *Bárbaros*, 169–72; White, *Middle Ground*, 94–141; "Petición del dominico Alonso Sandín," AGI, Filipinas, 83, n. 52, 38, 111; "Carta de Felipe Pardo," AGI, Filipinas, 75, n. 18, 15.

136. "Carta de Felipe Pardo," AGI, Filipinas, 75, n. 18, 18.

137. "Petición del dominico Alonso Sandín," AGI, Filipinas, 83, n. 52, 38.

138. "Petición del dominico Alonso Sandín," AGI, Filipinas, 83, n. 52, 39.

139. "Duplicados de cartas del presidente y oidores de Audiencia" (1743), AGI, Filipinas, 557, 18v–19v.

140. "Petición del dominico Alonso Sandín," AGI, Filipinas, 83, n. 52, 108–9.

141. "Duplicados de cartas del presidente y oidores de Audiencia" (Manila, July 18, 1743), AGI, Filipinas, 559, n. 1, 7r–7v.

142. "Petición del dominico Alonso Sandín," AGI, Filipinas, 83, n. 52, 111.

143. "Carta de Felipe Pardo," AGI, Filipinas, 75, n. 18, 19.

144. "Petición del dominico Alonso Sandín," AGI, Filipinas, 83, n. 52, 111.

145. "Petición del dominico Alonso Sandín," AGI, Filipinas, 83, n. 52, 111.

146. Mawson, "Convicts or Conquistadores?," 96–105.

147. Mawson, 100–102.

148. Cáceres Menéndez and Patch, "'Gente de Mal Vivir,'" 367–69.

149. García de los Arcos, *Forzados y reclutas*, 217–24.

150. "Petición del dominico Alonso Sandín," AGI, Filipinas, 83, n. 52, 110.

151. García de los Arcos, *Forzados y reclutas*, 233.

152. "Carta de Felipe Pardo," AGI, Filipinas, 75, n. 18, 19.

153. "Petición del dominico Alonso Sandín," AGI, Filipinas, 83, n. 52, 111; "Carta de Felipe Pardo," AGI, Filipinas, 75, n. 18, 19.

154. "Carta de la Audiencia de Manila sobre continuación de las visitas generales" (Manila, June 14, 1702), AGI, Filipinas, 164, n. 1, 76v–77v.

155. "Descripciones con planos y figuras," AGI, MP-Libros Manuscritos, 81, 50v–53v, 79–83.

156. Antolín, "Notices," 235, 237; Malumbres, *Historia de Nueva-Vizcaya*, 55.

157. "Carta de Felipe Pardo," AGI, Filipinas, 75, n. 18, 7–8.

158. "Carta de Felipe Pardo," AGI, Filipinas, 75, n. 18, 7; "Petición del dominico Alonso Sandín," AGI, Filipinas, 83, n. 52, 110.

159. "Petición del dominico Alonso Sandín," AGI, Filipinas, 83, n. 52, 110.

160. Charney and Wellen, "Introduction," 10–11; Reid, *Southeast Asia*, 1:121–24; Angeles, "Battle of Mactan," 19–23, 41.

161. Charney, *Southeast Asian Warfare*, 1–6, 18–21.

162. George, *Showing Signs of Violence*, 70–71; Hoskins, "Heritage of Headhunting," 223–25.

163. Charney and Wellen, "Introduction," 9, 13–15, 18–19.

164. Cited in Malumbres, *Historia de la Isabela*, 32.

165. Alzaga, "Cartas, informes y otros documentos," 333.

166. Cacho, "Compendioso manifiesto," 391.

167. Dizon, "Social and Spiritual Kinship," 368–84; Lopez, "Kinship, Islam, and Raiding," 76–88; Pulsipher, "Gaining the Diplomatic Edge," 29–31.

168. Cacho, "Compendioso manifiesto," 393.

169. "Traslado del memorial," AGI, Filipinas, 296, n. 36, 3.

170. "Traslado del memorial," AGI, Filipinas, 296, n. 36, 3.

171. Santa Rosa, "Carta-relación," 93; Mozo, *Noticia historico natural*, 32.

172. Mozo, *Noticia historico natural*, 34–35.

173. Mozo, 35.

174. Olivencia, "Relación de los progresos," AGI, Filipinas, 301, n. 24, 15; Mozo, *Noticia historico natural*, 32–33.

175. Mozo, *Noticia historico natural*, 33.

176. Santa Rosa, "Carta-relación," 101–2.

177. "Relacion del descubrimiento y entrada de los religiosos de N.P.S. Francisco en los pueblos o rancherias de los montes altos de Baler" (Orihuela, 1756), AFIO 89/71, 11; Dizon, "Sumpong," 21.

178. Rosenwein, *Emotional Communities*, 7–10; Metcalf, "Images of Headhunting," 270–74; Ferguson and Whitehead, "Preface to the Second Printing," xx–xxii; Ferguson and Whitehead, "Violent Edge of Empire," 28; Rosaldo, *Knowledge and Passion*, 32–34; Rosaldo, "Grief."

179. "Carta de Valdés Tamón," AGI, Filipinas, 144, n. 9, 100v–101v.

180. Ferguson and Whitehead, "Preface," xxiii–xxv.

181. Roque, *Headhunting and Colonialism*, 17–100; Hoskins, "On Losing."

182. Diaz, *Parrocho de indios instruido*, 44r–44v.

183. Diaz, 44v.

184. Diaz, 44r–44v.

185. "Carta de Valdés Tamón," AGI, Filipinas, 144, n. 9, 98r–98v; Barrio Muñoz, "Negritos," 60–61.

186. Salazar, "Relacion de la conquista de Pituy," AUST, APSR, Cagayan, tomo 29, n. 23, 199r.

187. Restall, *Seven Myths*, 142–44; Diamond, *Guns, Germs, and Steel*, 74–77.

188. Malumbres, *Historia de la Isabela*, 21.

189. "Petición del dominico Salvador Contreras sobre misiones dominicas" (March 17, 1739), AGI, Filipinas, 298, n. 21, 12r–12v.

190. Pérez, "Carta del P. Jose González."

191. "Descripciones con planos y figuras," AGI, MP-Libros Manuscritos, 81, 47r–53v.

192. Vivar, "Relación," 146; Malumbres, *Historia de la Isabela*, 60.

193. Malumbres, *Historia de Nueva-Vizcaya*, 25.

194. Antolín, "Notices," 234–35; Ferrando and Fonseca, *Historia de los PP.*, 3:404–5; Malumbres, *Historia de Nueva-Vizcaya*, 24–25; Scott, *Discovery of the Igorots*, 84–85.

195. Collantes, *Historia*, 493–96; Ferrando and Fonseca, *Historia de los PP.*, 3:405–10.

196. Collantes, *Historia*, 493–94.

197. Cited in Malumbres, *Historia de Nueva-Vizcaya*, 89; Antolín, "Notices," 235.

198. Collantes, *Historia*, 494–95.

199. Antolín, "Compendio cronologico," AUST, APSR, Cagayan, tomo 30, n. 1, 73r; Beltrán Pigu, "Pigu's Narrative," 140; Scott, *Discovery of the Igorots*, 79.

200. Mariano Pérez de los Cobos, "Manifiesto canónico-político-moral en que se hace ver lo vil y precioso del presente estado de las tres missiones de Puncan, Caranglan y Pantabangan" (September 14, 1785), AFIO 292/12, 176–77.

201. "Petición del dominico Alonso Sandín," AGI, Filipinas, 83, n. 52, 110; Salazar, "Relacion de la conquista de Pituy," AUST, APSR, Cagayan, tomo 29, n. 23, 199r.

202. Salazar, "Relacion de los sucesos y progresos," AUST, APSR, Cagayan, tomo 29, n. 19, 153r, 154v; Antolín, "Notices," 235.

203. Salazar, "Relacion de los sucesos y progresos," AUST, APSR, Cagayan, tomo 29, n. 19, 153r.

204. Salazar, "Relacion de los sucesos y progresos," AUST, APSR, Cagayan, tomo 29, n. 19, 154v.

205. Salazar, "Relacion de los sucesos y progresos," AUST, APSR, Cagayan, tomo 29, n. 19, 153r.

206. Ferrando and Fonseca, *Historia de los PP.*, 3:405; Malumbres, *Historia de Nueva-Vizcaya*, 24.

207. Langfur, "Moved by Terror"; Langfur, *Forbidden Lands*, 227–61.

208. Macdonald, "Folk Catholicism," 88–90; Aguilar, *Clash of Spirits*, 38–44.

209. Carrillo, *Breve relacion*, 24.

210. Antolín, "Compendio cronologico," AUST, APSR, Cagayan, tomo 30, n. 1, 101r, 102r.

211. Juan Ormaza, "Breve relacion de algunas cosas que han sucedido en esta mission de Ytuy y la muerte del viejo Apnuan" (Buhay, February 25, 1743), AUST, APSR, Cagayan, tomo 29, n. 33, 529v–30r.

212. Ormaza, "Breve relacion de algunas cosas," AUST, APSR, Cagayan, tomo 29, n. 33, 529v.

213. Salazar, "Relacion de la conquista de Pituy," AUST, APSR, Cagayan, tomo 29, n. 23, 199v.

214. Salazar, "Relacion de la conquista de Pituy," AUST, APSR, Cagayan, tomo 29, n. 23, 199v.

215. "Petición del dominico Alonso Sandín," AGI, Filipinas, 83, n. 52, 36, 104, 120.

216. "Petición del dominico Alonso Sandín," AGI, Filipinas, 83, n. 52, 36.

217. "Petición del dominico Alonso Sandín," AGI, Filipinas, 83, n. 52, 16.

218. Barrio Muñoz, "Negritos," 82–84, 87–90.

219. "Expediente sobre misiones de Filipinas y China" (Manila, July 13, 1747), AGI, Filipinas, 152, n. 19, 32r.

220. Olivencia, "Relación de los progresos," AGI, Filipinas, 301, n. 24, 11.

221. Olivencia, "Relación de los progresos," AGI, Filipinas, 301, n. 24, 11.

222. Ormaza, "Breve relacion de algunas cosas," AUST, APSR, Cagayan, tomo 29, n. 33, 533v–35r.

223. Ormaza, "Breve relacion de algunas cosas," AUST, APSR, Cagayan, tomo 29, n. 33, 533v–34r.

224. "Consulta que dicho M.R.P. Provincial hizo al Superior Gobierno" (Ituy, January 26, 1704), AUST, APSR, Cagayan, tomo 29, n. 2, 28r–28v.

225. "Consulta que dicho M.R.P. Provincial hizo," AUST, APSR, Cagayan, tomo 29, n. 2, 24v, 27r.

226. "Consulta que dicho M.R.P. Provincial hizo," AUST, APSR, Cagayan, tomo 29, n. 2, 25r–25v; Antolín, "Compendio cronologico," AUST, APSR, Cagayan, tomo 30, n. 1, 70v.

227. Antolín, "Compendio cronologico," AUST, APSR, Cagayan, tomo 30, n. 1, 71r–71v; Villoria Prieto, "Los agustinos," 22–24.

228. Antolín, "Compendio cronologico," AUST, APSR, Cagayan, tomo 30, n. 1, 71r.

229. Antolín, "Compendio cronologico," AUST, APSR, Cagayan, tomo 30, n. 1, 71r–71v.

230. Angeles, "Battle of Mactan," 23; Charney, *Southeast Asian Warfare*, 10.

231. "Consulta que dicho M.R.P. Provincial hizo," AUST, APSR, Cagayan, tomo 29, n. 2, 28v.

232. Cresswell, "Friction," 108–9.

Chapter Three

1. Altić, "Jesuit Contribution"; Quirino, *Philippine Cartography*, 72–91; Villoria Prieto, "La producción cartográfica"; Sofia Tomacruz, "Ever Heard of the 1734 Murillo Velarde Map and Why It Should Be Renamed?," *Rappler*, September 20, 2019; Pardo de Tavera, *El mapa de Filipinas*.

2. Carpio, *South China Sea Dispute*, 99, 121, 164; Padrón, "Las Indias olvidadas," 1.

3. Villoria Prieto, "La producción cartográfica," 139.

4. Antolín, "Notices," 191.

5. Murillo Velarde, *Geographia Historica*, 8:61.

6. Pardo de Tavera, *El mapa de Filipinas*, 4.

7. Francisco Antolín, "Compendio cronologico sobre el camino para Cagayan por la provincia y mision de Ituy" (1790), AUST, APSR, Cagayan, tomo 30, n. 1.

8. Pérez-González, "Royal Roads"; Grafe, *Distant Tyranny*, 102–15; Mundy, *Mapping of New Spain*, 8–9; Sellers-García, *Distance and Documents*, 34–38.

9. Sellers-García, *Distance and Documents*, 38–48.

10. Mundy, "Questionnaire," 227–29.

11. Mundy, 228–29.

12. Scott, *Art*, 43–48; Cresswell, "Friction," 109–10.

13. Sellers-García, *Distance and Documents*, 51.

14. Akerman, "Introduction," 8–10; Pooley, *Mobility, Migration and Transport*, 32–36.

15. Braudel, *Mediterranean*, 1:276–77.

16. Edwards, "Tyranny of Proximity"; Guldi, *Roads to Power*, 1–24; Scholz, "Protection"; Scholz, "La strada proibita."

17. Odyniec, "Negotiating."

18. Seijas, "Royal Road."

19. Scott, *Art*; Pooley, *Mobility, Migration and Transport*, 115.

20. Delano-Smith, "Milieus of Mobility," 27.

21. Pooley, *Mobility, Migration and Transport*, 105–8, 115.

22. Delano-Smith, "Milieus of Mobility," 30.

23. Grandjean, *American Passage*, 5, 45–75, 138–68.

24. Sellers-García, *Distance and Documents*, 41–42, 53.

25. Langfur, *Forbidden Lands*, 47–50, 202–3.

26. Seijas, "Royal Road," 295; Pérez-González, "Royal Roads," 194; Conti, "Connections and Circulation," 267–73.

27. Delano-Smith, "Milieus of Mobility," 29–33.

28. Grandjean, *American Passage*, 131–32.

29. Revill, "Histories," 506–8.

30. García de los Arcos, "¿Avanzada o periferia?," 48–50.

31. Braudel, *Mediterranean*, 1:281–84; Braudel, *Civilization and Capitalism*, 1:415–16, 422.

32. Braudel, *Civilization and Capitalism*, 1:429.

33. Scott, *Art*, 43–47; Braudel, *Mediterranean*, 1:29–32, 284–90.

34. Aduarte, *Historia de la provincia*, 636.

35. Carrillo, "Breve y verdadera relación," 124.

36. Antolín, "Compendio cronologico," AUST, APSR, Cagayan, tomo 30, n. 1, 229r.

37. Antolín, "Compendio cronologico," AUST, APSR, Cagayan, tomo 30, n. 1, 229r.

38. Braudel, *Civilization and Capitalism*, 1:418.

39. "Duplicados de cartas del presidente y oidores de Audiencia" (Manila, July 18, 1743), AGI, Filipinas, 559, n. 1, 6v–7r; "Duplicados de cartas del presidente y oidores de Audiencia" (1743), AGI, Filipinas, 557, 18v–19v, 23r; "Duplicado de carta de la Audiencia de Manila remitiendo autos de la visita de José Ignacio de Arzadun" (Manila, July 18, 1743), AGI, Filipinas, 556, n. 1, 170v, 499r–501v.

40. "Carta de Domingo de Zabalburu sobre derrota de galeones" (Manila, May 26, 1702), AGI, Filipinas, 125, n. 27, 14r–14v.

41. "Carta de Domingo de Zabalburu," AGI, Filipinas, 125, n. 27, 1–6; Schurz, *Manila Galleon*, 248–49.

42. "Carta de Domingo de Zabalburu," AGI, Filipinas, 125, n. 27, 52r, 54r–54v.

43. Villoria Prieto, "Los viajes a Filipinas," 64–65.

44. "Carta de Domingo de Zabalburu," AGI, Filipinas, 125, n. 27, 41r.

45. de Jesus, *Tobacco Monopoly*, 142.

46. Cited in Malumbres, *Historia de la Isabela*, 32.

47. "Carta del P. Santiago de Jesus Maria al Provincial dandole cuenta del estado de la mision" (Casiguran, April 26, 1721), AFIO 89/63, 1v; Santa Rosa, "Carta-relación," 88.

48. "Carta del Padre Juan de Ocaña al Provincial Padre Alejandro Ferrer" (Baler, July 4, 1754), AFIO 89/81, 2r.

49. Andaya and Andaya, *History*, 3.

50. Pérez, "Los Aetas e Ilongotes," 309.

51. "Carta del Padre Juan de Ocaña," AFIO 89/81, 2r–2v; Santa Rosa, "Carta-relación," 88, 104.

52. Aduarte, *Historia de la provincia*, 331; "Carta de Domingo de Zabalburu," AGI, Filipinas, 125, n. 27, 6r.

53. Jose de San Pascual, "Breve relacion de las nuevas misiones de los Montes de Tabueyon" (Aleveg, August 30, 1754), AFIO 89/80, 4v; "Carta de Torrecampo sobre misión de agustinos" (Manila, June 30, 1725), AGI, Filipinas, 140, n. 29, 62r, 66r.

54. "Carta del Padre Juan de Ocaña," AFIO 89/81, 2v.

55. Carrillo, "Breve y verdadera relación," 124.

56. San Pascual, "Breve relacion," AFIO 89/80, 4v.

57. Diaz, *Parrocho de indios instruido*, 112v.

58. Antolín, "Notices," 229.

59. Antolín, "Compendio cronologico," AUST, APSR, Cagayan, tomo 30, n. 1, 50v, 112r.

60. "Dos copias simples de los authos que se comenzaron a formar en Manila el año de 1722 sobre añadir tres misioneros mas" (Manila, July 29, 1727), APAF 374/2-a, 12r; "Carta de Torrecampo," AGI, Filipinas, 140, n. 29, 68v, 83v.

61. "Dos copias," APAF 374/2-a, 14v; "Carta de Torrecampo," AGI, Filipinas, 140, n. 29, 80r–80v.

62. "Carta de Fray Jose de San Pascual al Provincial Padre Alejandro Ferrer" (Aleveg, September 2, 1755), AFIO 89/88, 1r; Alzaga, "Carta," 305; Carrillo, "Breve y verdadera relación," 123; Vivar, "Relación," 159.

63. Vivar, "Relación," 141.

64. Malumbres, *Historia de la Isabela*, 52–53; Malumbres, *Historia de Nueva-Vizcaya*, 24.

65. Scott, *Art*, 61.

66. Foronda, "Informe sobre el estado," 317.

67. "Duplicado de carta de la Audiencia de Manila," AGI, Filipinas, 556, n. 1, 578v–79r.

68. Antolín, "Notices," 192.

69. San Pascual, "Breve relacion," AFIO 89/80, 3r.

70. Fermoselle, *Relación del descubrimiento*, 7.

71. Fermoselle, 6; José Tomás Marín, "Documentos interesantes," *Libertas*, March 10, 1905; "Carta de Fray Juan de Ocaña al Provincial Padre Alejandro Ferrer" (Baler, December 15, 1755), AFIO 89/84, 1r.

72. Manuel de Jesus Maria Joseph de Olivencia, "Relación de los progresos de la misión de San Antonio de Padua de los montes Emotlen" (Santa Ana de Sapa, June 28, 1755), AGI, Filipinas, 301, n. 24, 2.

73. "Duplicado de carta de la Audiencia de Manila," AGI, Filipinas, 556, n. 1.

74. "Traslado de los autos de la pesquisa secreta de la de la provincia de Cagayan" (Manila, July 18, 1743), AGI, Filipinas, 556, n. 23, 193r.

75. "Traslado de los autos," AGI, Filipinas, 556, n. 23, 192v.

76. "Traslado de los autos," AGI, Filipinas, 556, n. 23, 208v–9r, 292r–292v, 305r–6r, 394v–95r.

77. "Duplicado de carta de la Audiencia de Manila," AGI, Filipinas, 556, n. 1, 425r–32r.

78. "Duplicado de carta de la Audiencia de Manila," AGI, Filipinas, 556, n. 1, 427v, 428v.

79. Libro 1, título 15, ley 14 y 22; libro 6, título 10, ley 17; and libro 6, título 12, ley 6; "Duplicado de carta de la Audiencia de Manila," AGI, Filipinas, 556, n. 1, 609r–609v; *Recopilación*, 1:78v, 79v; *Recopilación*, 2:237r, 242r.

80. "Duplicado de carta de la Audiencia de Manila," AGI, Filipinas, 556, n. 1, 431r–32r.

81. "Duplicado de carta de la Audiencia de Manila," AGI, Filipinas, 556, n. 1, 554v–55r.

82. "Duplicado de carta de la Audiencia de Manila," AGI, Filipinas, 556, n. 1, 555r–555v.

83. "Duplicado de carta de la Audiencia de Manila," AGI, Filipinas, 556, n. 1, 618v–19r.

84. "Duplicado de carta de la Audiencia de Manila," AGI, Filipinas, 556, n. 1, 619r.

85. "Duplicado de carta de la Audiencia de Manila," AGI, Filipinas, 556, n. 1, 619v.

86. "Duplicado de carta de la Audiencia de Manila," AGI, Filipinas, 556, n. 1, 619v.

87. "Duplicado de carta de la Audiencia de Manila," AGI, Filipinas, 556, n. 1, 654r–56r.

88. Pérez-González, "Royal Roads," 199, 207; Seijas, "Inns, Mules," 59, 61, 63–64, 68; Conti, "Connections and Circulation," 269–73; Braudel, *Mediterranean*, 1:284–85; Braudel, *Civilization and Capitalism*, 1:429–30.

89. Antolín, "Notices," 219.

90. Sellers-García, *Distance and Documents*, 40–41, 51.

91. Marín, "Documentos interesantes," March 10, 1905.

92. Antolín, "Notices," 232.

93. Olivencia, "Relación de los progresos," AGI, Filipinas, 301, n. 24, 5.

94. "Duplicado de carta de la Audiencia de Manila," AGI, Filipinas, 556, n. 1, 655v.

95. Grandjean, *American Passage*, 45–75, 110–37; Sellers-García, *Distance and Documents*, 16–21; Braudel, *Mediterranean*, 1:363–68.

96. "Carta del P. Santiago de Jesus Maria," AFIO 89/63, 1r.

97. Braudel, *Civilization and Capitalism*, 1:430.

98. "Carta del P. Santiago de Jesus Maria," AFIO 89/63, 1r.

99. Marín, "Documentos interesantes," March 10, 1905.

100. "Carta de Fray Juan de Ocaña," AFIO 89/84, 1r.

101. "Carta de Fray Juan de Ocaña," AFIO 89/84, 1v.

102. "Carta de Fray Juan de Ocaña," AFIO 89/84, 1v.

103. "Carta del P. Pedro de la Cruz Alcocer al Provincial dandole cuenta del estado de las misiones" (Casiguran, March 28, 1721), AFIO 89/65, 1r.

104. "Carta de Fray Jose de San Pascual," AFIO 89/88, 1r.

105. Antolín, "Compendio cronologico," AUST, APSR, Cagayan, tomo 30, n. 1, 111r, 124r, 125v, 202v, 204v; Carrillo, "Breve y verdadera relación," 124; "Informe al gobernador sobre reduccion de los indios a poblado" (1732), AFIO 7/24, 4v; "Piden los de Camarag se vuelva su pueblo a su antiguo lugar" (June 15, 1792), AUST, APSR, Cagayan, tomo 24, n. 10, 143r; "Carta de Valdés Tamón sobre ataques de indios infieles" (Manila, July 6, 1733), AGI, Filipinas, 144, n. 9, 12r, 15r, 41v, 43v, 200v–201r; "Expediente formado a peticion del P. Provincial para que las escoltas concedidas para construir iglesias y conventos" (Nueva Segovia, 1755), AUST, APSR, Cagayan, tomo 29, n. 27, 397v.

106. Pérez-González, "Royal Roads," 200.

107. Pérez-González, 196–97, 215–18.

108. Braudel, *Mediterranean*, 1:371–72.

109. Zamora, *Las corporaciones religiosas*, 277; González Cuellas, *Presencia berciana en Filipinas*, 84–85.

110. José Tomás Marín, "Documentos interesantes," *Libertas*, March 9, 1905.

111. "Duplicado de carta de la Audiencia de Manila," AGI, Filipinas, 556, n. 1, 125v–27r; Dueñas Olmo, "Contribución al estudio," 190.

112. "Carta de la Audiencia de Manila sobre nombramiento de visitador a Arzadun" (Manila, July 15, 1739), AGI, Filipinas, 180, n. 11, 28v–29r.

113. "Petición del dominico Salvador Contreras sobre misiones dominicas" (March 17, 1739), AGI, Filipinas, 298, n. 21, 13r–13v; Pedro Jiménez, "Descripcion de Paniqui" (1690), AUST, APSR, Cagayan, tomo 29, n. 32.

114. "Otra de dicho M.R.P. en que informa del estado de las misiones de Cagayan" (August 4, 1740), AUST, APSR, Cagayan, tomo 29, n. 12, 123r–123v.

115. "Carta de Fausto Cruzat sobre conquista de infieles" (Manila, June 12, 1691), AGI, Filipinas, 14, r. 3, n. 35, 28v.

116. "Carta de Gaspar de la Torre sobre misiones dominicas" (Manila, July 14, 1742), AGI, Filipinas, 150, n. 40, 5–6.

117. "Carta de Gaspar de la Torre," AGI, Filipinas, 150, n. 40, 6–7.

118. "Informe del P. Manuel del Rio sobre las misiones de Cagayan" (Manila, August 4, 1740), AUST, APSR, Cagayan, tomo 29, n. 25, 385v.

119. Antolín, "Compendio cronologico," AUST, APSR, Cagayan, tomo 30, n. 1, 168v.

120. Antolín, "Notices," 233.

121. Antolín, 233.

122. Dueñas Olmo, "Contribución al estudio," 185, 409.

123. "Carta de la Audiencia de Manila sobre continuación de las visitas generales" (Manila, June 14, 1702), AGI, Filipinas, 164, n. 1, 1r.

124. "Petición del dominico Salvador Contreras," AGI, Filipinas, 298, n. 21, 12r.

125. "Carta de Fausto Cruzat sobre conquista de infieles," AGI, Filipinas, 14, r. 3, n. 35, 28r–29r.

126. "Carta de Fausto Cruzat sobre conquista de infieles," AGI, Filipinas, 14, r. 3, n. 35, 28v.

127. "Carta de Fausto Cruzat sobre conquista de infieles," AGI, Filipinas, 14, r. 3, n. 35, 6v.

128. "Carta de Fausto Cruzat sobre conquista de infieles," AGI, Filipinas, 14, r. 3, n. 35, 27v.

129. "Carta de Francisco de la Cuesta sobre sublevaciones de naturales" (Manila, July 13, 1720), AGI, Filipinas, 132, n. 43, 1; Antolín, "Compendio cronologico," AUST, APSR, Cagayan, tomo 30, n. 1, 222v.

130. Collantes, *Historia de la provincia,* 340–48; Ferrando and Fonseca, *Historia de los PP.,* 4:196–204; Malumbres, *Historia de Cagayán,* 55–57; Salgado, *Cagayan Valley,* 1:125–27.

131. Díaz-Trechuelo López-Spínola, *Filipinas,* 211; Díaz-Trechuelo López-Spínola, "Filipinas en el siglo," 275.

132. "Carta de Francisco de la Cuesta sobre sublevaciones," AGI, Filipinas, 132, n. 43, 13, 5–6.

133. Collantes, *Historia de la provincia,* 345.

134. "Carta de Francisco de la Cuesta sobre sublevaciones," AGI, Filipinas, 132, n. 43, 3.

135. "Carta de Francisco de la Cuesta sobre sublevaciones," AGI, Filipinas, 132, n. 43, 3–4.

136. "Carta de Francisco de la Cuesta sobre sublevaciones," AGI, Filipinas, 132, n. 43, 4.

137. "Carta de Francisco de la Cuesta sobre sublevaciones," AGI, Filipinas, 132, n. 43, 6.

138. "Instruccion que dio el Mariscal de Campo para la expedicion de abrir el paso desde la provincia de Nueva Segovia hasta la Pampanga" (Manila, April 19, 1719), AUST, APSR, Cagayan, tomo 29, n. 5, 55r–59r; "Carta de Francisco de la Cuesta sobre sublevaciones," AGI, Filipinas, 132, n. 43, 6–10; "Carta de Torrecampo sobre estado de las misiones" (Manila, June 30, 1725), AGI, Filipinas, 141, n. 6, 46v; Antolín, "Compendio cronologico," AUST, APSR, Cagayan, tomo 30, n. 1, 223r.

139. "Instruccion que dio el Mariscal de Campo," AUST, APSR, Cagayan, tomo 29, n. 5, 55r, 56r.

140. "Instruccion que dio el Mariscal de Campo," AUST, APSR, Cagayan, tomo 29, n. 5, 55r–55v, 57v.

141. "Carta de Francisco de la Cuesta sobre sublevaciones," AGI, Filipinas, 132, n. 43, 9; Antolín, "Compendio cronologico," AUST, APSR, Cagayan, tomo 30, n. 1, 223r.

142. "Carta de Torrecampo sobre estado de las misiones," AGI, Filipinas, 141, n. 6, 5r; Villoria Prieto, *Un berciano en Filipinas,* 96–97.

143. Díaz-Trechuelo López-Spínola, *Filipinas,* 212.

144. Villoria Prieto, *Un berciano en Filipinas,* 93, 97.

145. Cacho, "Compendioso manifiesto," 382.

146. "Carta de Torrecampo sobre estado de las misiones," AGI, Filipinas, 141, n. 6, 46v–48v.

147. Villoria Prieto, *Un berciano en Filipinas,* 99.

148. Cacho, "Compendioso manifiesto," 382–83.

149. "Carta de Torrecampo sobre estado de las misiones," AGI, Filipinas, 141, n. 6, 40r–40v.

150. "Carta de Francisco de la Cuesta sobre sublevaciones," AGI, Filipinas, 132, n. 43, 10.

151. "Petición del dominico Salvador Contreras," AGI, Filipinas, 298, n. 21, 3r, 4r; "Carta de Gaspar de la Torre," AGI, Filipinas, 150, n. 40, 6; Malumbres, *Historia de Nueva-Vizcaya,* 42–43, 45; Langfur, *Forbidden Lands,* 175–79.

152. "Petición del dominico Salvador Contreras," AGI, Filipinas, 298, n. 21, 3r.

153. Antolín, "Compendio cronologico," AUST, APSR, Cagayan, tomo 30, n. 1, 121v.

154. Antolín, "Compendio cronologico," AUST, APSR, Cagayan, tomo 30, n. 1, 121v–22r.

155. Antolín, "Compendio cronologico," AUST, APSR, Cagayan, tomo 30, n. 1, 122r.

156. Antolín, "Compendio cronologico," AUST, APSR, Cagayan, tomo 30, n. 1, 79r–92v, 98r–98v; Malumbres, *Historia de la Isabela,* 24–43; Fernandez and Juan, "Social and Economic Development," 108–20; Scott, *Discovery of the Igorots,* 80–82; Villoria Prieto, *Un berciano*

en Filipinas, 196–201; Villoria Prieto, "Un Totanero en Filipinas," 96–97; Salgado, *Cagayan Valley*, 1:504–18.

157. Antolín, "Compendio cronologico," AUST, APSR, Cagayan, tomo 30, n. 1, 121r.

158. Cacho, "Conquistas espirituales," 1997, 343.

159. Cacho, 343.

160. Antolín, "Compendio cronologico," AUST, APSR, Cagayan, tomo 30, n. 1, 93r–93v, 121v.

161. Antolín, "Compendio cronologico," AUST, APSR, Cagayan, tomo 30, n. 1, 93r–93v; Cacho, "Compendioso manifiesto," 398.

162. Junker, *Raiding, Trading, and Feasting*, 85–113, 345–49; Abinales and Amoroso, *State and Society*, 32–33; Scott, *Art*, 50–61.

163. Antolín, "Compendio cronologico," AUST, APSR, Cagayan, tomo 30, n. 1, 93v.

164. Dizon, "Social and Spiritual Kinship."

165. Cacho, "Conquistas espirituales," 1997, 343, 346–48.

166. Antolín, "Compendio cronologico," AUST, APSR, Cagayan, tomo 30, n. 1, 121v.

167. Cacho, "Compendioso manifiesto," 397.

168. Cacho, "Conquistas espirituales," 1997, 346, 348.

169. "Carta de Diego Camacho sobre confirmaciones que ha hecho y visitas de los provinciales" (Manila, June 16, 1699), AGI, Filipinas, 75, n. 41, 3, 22; Cacho, "Compendioso manifiesto," 397.

170. "Carta de Valdés Tamón sobre progreso de las misiones" (Manila, July 8, 1737), AGI, Filipinas, 148, n. 18, 22v.

171. Santa Rosa, "Carta-relación," 104, 106.

172. Santa Rosa, 97.

173. Olivencia, "Relación de los progresos," AGI, Filipinas, 301, n. 24, 5.

174. Olivencia, "Relación de los progresos," AGI, Filipinas, 301, n. 24, 5.

175. Aduarte, *Historia de la provincia*, 638.

176. Cacho, "Conquistas espirituales," 1997, 346.

177. Cacho, 350.

178. Cacho, "Compendioso manifiesto," 386.

179. Cacho, "Conquistas espirituales," 1997, 350–51.

180. Cacho, 351.

181. Phelan, *Hispanization of the Philippines*, 55–56; Río, *Relación de los successos*, 14; Correa de Castro, *Breve relacion*, 16.

182. Cacho, "Conquistas espirituales," 1997, 351.

183. Cacho, 350.

184. Antolín, "Compendio cronologico," AUST, APSR, Cagayan, tomo 30, n. 1, 93v.

185. Antolín, "Compendio cronologico," AUST, APSR, Cagayan, tomo 30, n. 1, 121v.

186. Antolín, "Compendio cronologico," AUST, APSR, Cagayan, tomo 30, n. 1, 93v.

187. Antolín, "Compendio cronologico," AUST, APSR, Cagayan, tomo 30, n. 1, 122r.

188. Cacho, "Conquistas espirituales," 1997, 350.

189. "Petición del dominico Salvador Contreras," AGI, Filipinas, 298, n. 21, 8r–8v; Río, *Relación de los successos*, 4–5; Antolín, "Compendio cronologico," AUST, APSR, Cagayan, tomo 30, n. 1, 79r, 95r–95v.

190. "Petición del dominico Salvador Contreras," AGI, Filipinas, 298, n. 21, 8v–9r.

191. Río, *Relación de los successos,* 6–7; Correa de Castro, *Breve relacion,* 7–8; Antolín, "Compendio cronologico," AUST, APSR, Cagayan, tomo 30, n. 1, 79v–80r.

192. Río, *Relación de los successos,* 7–8; Correa de Castro, *Breve relacion,* 8–10; Antolín, "Compendio cronologico," AUST, APSR, Cagayan, tomo 30, n. 1, 80r.

193. Río, *Relación de los successos,* 8; Correa de Castro, *Breve relacion,* 9–10; Antolín, "Compendio cronologico," AUST, APSR, Cagayan, tomo 30, n. 1, 80r.

194. "Petición del dominico Salvador Contreras," AGI, Filipinas, 298, n. 21, 6r–6v.

195. Río, *Relación de los successos,* 11–13; Correa de Castro, *Breve relacion,* 13–15; Antolín, "Compendio cronologico," AUST, APSR, Cagayan, tomo 30, n. 1, 80r.

196. Río, *Relación de los successos,* 12–13; Correa de Castro, *Breve relacion,* 14–15.

197. Río, *Relación de los successos,* 13–14; Correa de Castro, *Breve relacion,* 15–16; Antolín, "Compendio cronologico," AUST, APSR, Cagayan, tomo 30, n. 1, 80r.

198. Río, *Relación de los successos,* 7, 28; Correa de Castro, *Breve relacion,* 9, 30.

199. Antolín, "Compendio cronologico," AUST, APSR, Cagayan, tomo 30, n. 1, 80r.

200. Ustariz, *Relación de los sucessos,* 2.

201. Río, *Relación de los successos,* 15, 17; Correa de Castro, *Breve relacion,* 17, 19; Antolín, "Compendio cronologico," AUST, APSR, Cagayan, tomo 30, n. 1, 80v.

202. Antolín, "Compendio cronologico," AUST, APSR, Cagayan, tomo 30, n. 1, 81v.

203. Antolín, "Compendio cronologico," AUST, APSR, Cagayan, tomo 30, n. 1, 82r.

204. Río, *Relación de los successos,* 16–17; Correa de Castro, *Breve relacion,* 18.

205. Río, *Relación de los successos,* 19; Correa de Castro, *Breve relacion,* 21.

206. Dizon, "Sumpong," 29–32.

207. Río, *Relación de los successos,* 17; Correa de Castro, *Breve relacion,* 18–19.

208. Antolín, "Compendio cronologico," AUST, APSR, Cagayan, tomo 30, n. 1, 81r–81v.

209. "Carta de Joseph Gonzalez" (Buhay, October 24, 1738), AUST, APSR, Cagayan, tomo 29, n. 24; Antolín, "Compendio cronologico," AUST, APSR, Cagayan, tomo 30, n. 1, 81r.

210. Antolín, "Compendio cronologico," AUST, APSR, Cagayan, tomo 30, n. 1, 80v, 82v, 91v–92r; Río, *Relación de los successos,* 19–20; Correa de Castro, *Breve relacion,* 20–22; Alvarez del Manzano, *Compendio,* 375–76; Malumbres, *Historia de Cagayán,* 61, 354; Malumbres, *Historia de la Isabela,* 8, 39–40; Fernandez and Juan, "Social and Economic Development," 114–16; Scott, *Discovery of the Igorots,* 80; Salgado, *Cagayan Valley,* 1:513–15.

211. "Viajes del P. Fr. Jose Tomas Marin en el radio de las misiones de los mandayas, y a Dingras" (1740), AUST, APSR, Cagayan, tomo 13, n. 7; Scott, *Discovery of the Igorots,* 91–99.

212. "Carta de Joseph Gonzalez," AUST, APSR, Cagayan, tomo 29, n. 24, 179v–80r; Antolín, "Compendio cronologico," AUST, APSR, Cagayan, tomo 30, n. 1, 81v.

213. "Carta de Joseph Gonzalez," AUST, APSR, Cagayan, tomo 29, n. 24, 179v; Antolín, "Compendio cronologico," AUST, APSR, Cagayan, tomo 30, n. 1, 81v.

214. Antolín, "Compendio cronologico," AUST, APSR, Cagayan, tomo 30, n. 1, 91v–92v, 98r, 225v–26r; Fernandez and Juan, "Social and Economic Development," 114–16.

215. Antolín, "Compendio cronologico," AUST, APSR, Cagayan, tomo 30, n. 1, 118v.

216. Antolín, "Compendio cronologico," AUST, APSR, Cagayan, tomo 30, n. 1, 226r; San Pascual, "Breve relacion," AFIO 89/80, 3r–3v.

217. Antolín, "Compendio cronologico," AUST, APSR, Cagayan, tomo 30, n. 1, 91v, 226r.

218. Río, *Relación de los successos*, 20.

219. Antolín, "Compendio cronologico," AUST, APSR, Cagayan, tomo 30, n. 1, 91v, 226r; Río, *Relación de los successos*, 20–21; Correa de Castro, *Breve relacion*, 21–22.

220. Antolín, "Compendio cronologico," AUST, APSR, Cagayan, tomo 30, n. 1, 91v.

221. Río, *Relación de los successos*, 20–21; Correa de Castro, *Breve relacion*, 22; Antolín, "Compendio cronologico," AUST, APSR, Cagayan, tomo 30, n. 1, 91v, 226r.

222. Río, *Relación de los successos*, 28–29; Correa de Castro, *Breve relacion*, 32–33.

223. Antolín, "Compendio cronologico," AUST, APSR, Cagayan, tomo 30, n. 1, 91v, 226v.

224. Correa de Castro, *Breve relacion*, 24; Río, *Relación de los successos*, 22.

225. Antolín, "Compendio cronologico," AUST, APSR, Cagayan, tomo 30, n. 1, 98r–98v, 227r; Antolín, "Notices," 212–13; Fernandez and Juan, "Social and Economic Development," 118–19.

226. "Carta de Gaspar de la Torre sobre misiones de Ituy y Paniqui" (Manila, June 18, 1741), AGI, Filipinas, 150, n. 11, 5v–7v.

227. Antolín, "Notices," 234–35; Scott, *Discovery of the Igorots*, 84–85.

228. Marcus, "Ethnography"; Junker, *Raiding, Trading, and Feasting*, 315–25.

229. "Sobre los progresos y augmento de las nuebas missiones de Ituy y Paniqui" (Manila, August 20, 1741), AUST, APSR, Cagayan, tomo 29, n. 33, 541r.

230. Cacho, "Conquistas espirituales," 1997, 358.

231. Antolín, "Compendio cronologico," AUST, APSR, Cagayan, tomo 30, n. 1, 99v.

232. Scott, *Discovery of the Igorots*, 93–99.

233. Río, *Relación de los successos*, 21–22; Correa de Castro, *Breve relacion*, 23–24.

234. Antolín, "Compendio cronologico," AUST, APSR, Cagayan, tomo 30, n. 1, 98r.

235. Villoria Prieto, *Un berciano en Filipinas*, 224, 230.

236. Antolín, "Compendio cronologico," AUST, APSR, Cagayan, tomo 30, n. 1, 98r.

237. Pérez, "Decreto del Rey," 340–41.

238. "Sin título" (1741), APSR, Pangasinan, tomo 1, n. 20, 333v, 336r; Villoria Prieto, *Un berciano en Filipinas*, 155–56.

239. "Sin título," APSR, Pangasinan, tomo 1, n. 20, 331r–331v.

240. "Consulta de dicho M.R.P. Provincial al Superior Gobierno" (Santo Domingo, April 10, 1739), AUST, APSR, Cagayan, tomo 29, n. 7, 66v.

241. "Consulta de dicho M.R.P. Provincial," AUST, APSR, Cagayan, tomo 29, n. 7, 67r.

242. "Carta de Juan Ormaza" (Buhay, September 12, 1741), AUST, APSR, Cagayan, tomo 29, n. 24, 249v.

243. "Carta de Juan Ormaza" (Buhay, February 2, 1744), AUST, APSR, Cagayan, tomo 29, n. 24, 213r.

244. Quirk and Vigneswaran, "Mobility Makes States," 7–8, 19–20.

245. "Lista de los títulos, y mercedes que piden los principales de los montes que se presentaron ante el Señor Gobernador" (n.d.), AUST, APSR, Cagayan, tomo 29, 526r.

246. "Carta de Juan Ormaza," AUST, APSR, Cagayan, tomo 29, n. 24, 249v.

247. Cited in Villoria Prieto, *Un berciano en Filipinas*, 238.

248. "Carta de Juan Ormaza" (Buhay, October 18, 1740), AUST, APSR, Cagayan, tomo 29, n. 24, 210r.

249. "Carta de Juan Ormaza," AUST, APSR, Cagayan, tomo 29, n. 24, 210r.

250. "Carta de Juan Ormaza," AUST, APSR, Cagayan, tomo 29, n. 24, 210r.

251. Pérez-González, "Royal Roads," 197, 215–16.

252. Seijas, "Royal Road," 296, 299–300.

253. "Carta de Gaspar de la Torre sobre misiones," AGI, Filipinas, 150, n. 11, 10v; "Sobre los progresos," AUST, APSR, Cagayan, tomo 29, n. 33, 541v.

254. Herosa, "Breve insinuación," 239.

255. Scholz, *Borders*, 12, 87–127.

256. "Carta de Juan Ormaza" (Buhay, April 29, 1743), AUST, APSR, Cagayan, tomo 29, n. 24, 322v.

257. "Carta de Juan Ormaza," AUST, APSR, Cagayan, tomo 29, n. 24, 322v–23r; Antolín, "Compendio cronologico," AUST, APSR, Cagayan, tomo 30, n. 1, 102v.

258. "Carta de Juan Ormaza," AUST, APSR, Cagayan, tomo 29, n. 24, 323r.

259. Ferguson and Whitehead, "Preface," xix–xxii, xxvii.

260. Antolín, "Compendio cronologico," AUST, APSR, Cagayan, tomo 30, n. 1, 98v.

261. Carrillo, "Breve y verdadera relación," 125.

262. Antolín, "Compendio cronologico," AUST, APSR, Cagayan, tomo 30, n. 1, 99v.

263. Antolín, "Compendio cronologico," AUST, APSR, Cagayan, tomo 30, n. 1, 101r.

264. "Carta de Juan Ormaza y Lucas de San Vicente" (Dupax, May 19, 1741), AUST, APSR, Cagayan, tomo 29, n. 24, 222v.

265. Antolín, "Compendio cronologico," AUST, APSR, Cagayan, tomo 30, n. 1, 101r; "Carta de Juan Ormaza y Lucas de San Vicente," AUST, APSR, Cagayan, tomo 29, n. 24, 223v–24r.

266. "Carta de Juan Ormaza y Lucas de San Vicente," AUST, APSR, Cagayan, tomo 29, n. 24, 224r.

267. "Carta de Juan Ormaza y Lucas de San Vicente," AUST, APSR, Cagayan, tomo 29, n. 24, 222v–23r.

268. Antolín, "Compendio cronologico," AUST, APSR, Cagayan, tomo 30, n. 1, 111r.

269. Antolín, "Compendio cronologico," AUST, APSR, Cagayan, tomo 30, n. 1, 102v.

270. "Razon del estado de la casa de Buhay y su mision" (Buhay, March 20, 1743), AUST, APSR, Cagayan, tomo 29, n. 18, 148r.

271. "Carta de Gaspar de la Torre sobre misiones," AGI, Filipinas, 150, n. 11, 5v–7v.

272. "Carta de Gaspar de la Torre sobre misiones," AGI, Filipinas, 150, n. 11, 6v.

273. "Carta de Juan Ormaza y Lucas de San Vicente" (Buhay, December 27, 1740), AUST, APSR, Cagayan, tomo 29, n. 24, 212v.

274. "Carta de Juan Ormaza," AUST, APSR, Cagayan, tomo 29, n. 24, 209v–10r.

275. "Carta de Juan Ormaza," AUST, APSR, Cagayan, tomo 29, n. 24, 210r.

276. "Carta de Gaspar de la Torre sobre misiones," AGI, Filipinas, 150, n. 11, 6v–7r.

277. "Carta de Juan Ormaza," AUST, APSR, Cagayan, tomo 29, n. 24, 210r.

Chapter Four

1. Francisco Antolín, "Compendio cronologico sobre el camino para Cagayan por la provincia y mision de Ituy" (1790), AUST, APSR, Cagayan, tomo 30, n. 1, 183r, 197r.

2. Alvarez del Manzano, *Compendio*, 476; Fernandez, "18th-Century Report," 454–56; Scott, "Notices," 177–80.

3. Antolín, "Compendio cronologico," AUST, APSR, Cagayan, tomo 30, n. 1, 182r–235r.

4. Antolín, "Compendio cronologico," AUST, APSR, Cagayan, tomo 30, n. 1, 183v.

5. Antolín, "Compendio cronologico," AUST, APSR, Cagayan, tomo 30, n. 1, 183v.

6. Antolín, "Compendio cronologico," AUST, APSR, Cagayan, tomo 30, n. 1, 183v.

7. Antolín, "Compendio cronologico," AUST, APSR, Cagayan, tomo 30, n. 1, 185r–185v.

8. Mumford, *Vertical Empire*, 27–28, 30–31, 35.

9. Antolín, "Compendio cronologico," AUST, APSR, Cagayan, tomo 30, n. 1, 228v–29r.

10. Antolín, "Compendio cronologico," AUST, APSR, Cagayan, tomo 30, n. 1, 196r.

11. Antolín, "Compendio cronologico," AUST, APSR, Cagayan, tomo 30, n. 1, 229v.

12. Antolín, "Compendio cronologico," AUST, APSR, Cagayan, tomo 30, n. 1, 228v.

13. Cagle, *Assembling the Tropics*, 6, 9.

14. Antolín, "Compendio cronologico," AUST, APSR, Cagayan, tomo 30, n. 1, 197v.

15. Antolín, "Compendio cronologico," AUST, APSR, Cagayan, tomo 30, n. 1, 196r–196v, 229v.

16. Junker, *Raiding, Trading, and Feasting*, 240–42.

17. Antolín, "Compendio cronologico," AUST, APSR, Cagayan, tomo 30, n. 1, 189v.

18. "Relación del descubrimiento de Tuy por Luis Pérez das Mariñas" (July 7, 1591), AGI, Filipinas, 6, r. 7, n. 86, 1.

19. "Petición del dominico Salvador Contreras sobre misiones dominicas" (March 17, 1739), AGI, Filipinas, 298, n. 21, 2v.

20. "Carta de Fray Jose de San Pascual al Provincial Padre Alejandro Ferrer" (Aleveg, May 12, 1755), AFIO 89/87, 1v.

21. "Carta de Fray Jose de San Pascual," AFIO 89/87, 1v.

22. Grove, *Green Imperialism*, 16–72; Safier, "Tenacious Travels," 150.

23. Cagle, *Assembling the Tropics*, 36–37.

24. Cagle, 37–45.

25. Duárez y Santa Cruz, *Carta ingenua y religiosa*, 6.

26. Aduarte, *Historia de la provincia*, 329, 636.

27. Antolín, "Compendio cronologico," AUST, APSR, Cagayan, tomo 30, n. 1, 195v; Malumbres, *Historia de Nueva-Vizcaya*, 18.

28. "Intento de pacificación de Ituy y retirada por peste" (July 19, 1654), AGI, Filipinas, 285, n. 1, 39r.

29. Foronda, "Informe sobre el estado," 312; Cacho, "Conquistas espirituales," 1997, 337, 364–65.

30. Mozo, *Noticia historico natural*, 30–31; Cacho, "Conquistas espirituales," 1997, 340.

31. Antolín, "Compendio cronologico," AUST, APSR, Cagayan, tomo 30, n. 1, 220r; Foronda, "Informe sobre el estado," 312–13.

32. Antolín, "Compendio cronologico," AUST, APSR, Cagayan, tomo 30, n. 1, 218v–19r.

33. Cagle, *Assembling the Tropics*, 7, 11.

34. Cagle, 293.

35. Antolín, "Compendio cronologico," AUST, APSR, Cagayan, tomo 30, n. 1, 58v, 81r–81v, 188v, 208r.

36. Antolín, "Compendio cronologico," AUST, APSR, Cagayan, tomo 30, n. 1, 81v.

37. Antolín, "Compendio cronologico," AUST, APSR, Cagayan, tomo 30, n. 1, 198v.

38. "Carta de la Audiencia de Manila sobre nombramiento de visitador a Arzadun" (Manila, July 15, 1739), AGI, Filipinas, 180, n. 11, 5r, 29v, 49r; Alvarez, "Misión de San Agustín," 210.

39. "Duplicado de carta de la Audiencia de Manila remitiendo autos de la visita de José Ignacio de Arzadun" (Manila, July 18, 1743), AGI, Filipinas, 556, n. 1, 579r.

40. Antolín, "Compendio cronologico," AUST, APSR, Cagayan, tomo 30, n. 1, 198v.

41. Antolín, "Compendio cronologico," AUST, APSR, Cagayan, tomo 30, n. 1, 220r.

42. Antolín, "Compendio cronologico," AUST, APSR, Cagayan, tomo 30, n. 1, 221v.

43. "Duplicado de carta de la Audiencia de Manila," AGI, Filipinas, 556, n. 1, 556r, 564r, 575v.

44. Sutter, "Tropics"; Safier, "Tenacious Travels," 141–43, 172.

45. Reed, *City of Pines*.

46. Antolín, "Compendio cronologico," AUST, APSR, Cagayan, tomo 30, n. 1, 188r–188v.

47. Antolín, "Compendio cronologico," AUST, APSR, Cagayan, tomo 30, n. 1, 188r–188v.

48. Antolín, "Compendio cronologico," AUST, APSR, Cagayan, tomo 30, n. 1, 53r; Antolín, "Notices," 187.

49. Scott, *History on the Cordillera*, 65–66.

50. Antolín, "Notices," 193–94, 200–201.

51. Antolín, 193.

52. Antolín, 200.

53. Arnold, *Problem of Nature*, 150–52; Sutter, "Tropics," 184; McNeill, *Mosquito Empires*, 15–62, 91–136.

54. McNeill, *Mosquito Empires*, 15–62.

55. Newson, *Conquest and Pestilence*, 10–23.

56. Newson, *Conquest and Pestilence*.

57. Arnold, *Problem of Nature*, 141–68; Sutter, "Tropics"; Driver and Martins, "Views and Visions."

58. Cosgrove, "Tropic and Tropicality," 213.

59. "Duplicado de carta de la Audiencia de Manila," AGI, Filipinas, 556, n. 1, 588v–89r, 610r.

60. Antolín, "Compendio cronologico," AUST, APSR, Cagayan, tomo 30, n. 1, 199r.

61. Foronda, "Informe sobre el estado," 313.

62. Foronda, 311.

63. Foronda, 311.

64. Bautista Martínez, "Informe del P. Provincial," 129; Antolín, "Compendio cronologico," AUST, APSR, Cagayan, tomo 30, n. 1, 200r, 220r, 230v–31r.

65. Antolín, "Compendio cronologico," AUST, APSR, Cagayan, tomo 30, n. 1, 228v.

66. Antolín, "Compendio cronologico," AUST, APSR, Cagayan, tomo 30, n. 1, 207r, 219r.

67. Antolín, "Compendio cronologico," AUST, APSR, Cagayan, tomo 30, n. 1, 200v, 206v.

68. Antolín, "Compendio cronologico," AUST, APSR, Cagayan, tomo 30, n. 1, 207v.

69. Bautista Martínez, "Informe del P. Provincial," 129.

70. De Bevoise, *Agents of Apocalypse*, 142–43; Deb Roy, *Malarial Subjects*, 71–72.

71. "Otra de dicho M.R.P. en que informa del estado de las misiones de Cagayan" (August 4, 1740), AUST, APSR, Cagayan, tomo 29, n. 12, 121v.

72. "Repuesta del M.R.P. Provincial Fr. Manuel del Rio al Superior Gobierno" (1740), AUST, APSR, Cagayan, tomo 29, n. 11, 115v.

73. De Bevoise, *Agents of Apocalypse*, 143; McLennan, "Changing Human Ecology," 62; Newson, *Conquest and Pestilence*, 174–75, 189, 198.

74. Henley, *Fertility, Food and Fever*, 264–68; De Bevoise, *Agents of Apocalypse*, 143–44.

75. Henley, *Fertility, Food and Fever*, 264; De Bevoise, *Agents of Apocalypse*, 144.

76. Newson, *Conquest and Pestilence*, 213.

77. Henley, *Fertility, Food and Fever*, 268–70; De Bevoise, *Agents of Apocalypse*, 148.

78. Henley, *Fertility, Food and Fever*, 270–74; De Bevoise, *Agents of Apocalypse*, 146–48.

79. Henley, *Fertility, Food and Fever*, 271; De Bevoise, *Agents of Apocalypse*, 143.

80. Deb Roy, *Malarial Subjects*, 11–16, 73.

81. McNeill, *Mosquito Empires*, 53–54.

82. Yu et al., "*Anopheles* Community."

83. Van Bortel et al., "Eco-Ethological Heterogeneity"; McNeill, *Mosquito Empires*, 56–57.

84. De Bevoise, *Agents of Apocalypse*, 148.

85. Luis Pérez Dasmariñas, "Carta de G. P. Mariñas sobre jornada de Tuy" (Manila, June 1, 1592), AGI, Filipinas, 6, r. 7, n. 94, 1r.

86. Scott, *Barangay*, 46–47, 201.

87. Scott, 262, 265; "Boxer Codex" (ca. 1590), Indiana University, Lilly Library, 19v; Souza and Turley, *Boxer Codex*, 326.

88. Aguilar, "Rice and Magic," 299–304.

89. Herosa, "Breve insinuación," 237; Antolín, "Notices," 194.

90. "Registro desde 1716 hasta 1719" (1719), APAF 36, 56v, 70v.

91. Crosby, *Germs, Seeds & Animals*, 28–44; Fischer, *Cattle Colonialism*, 14–16, 27–29.

92. *Recopilación*, 2:149, 199.

93. Antolín, "Compendio cronologico," AUST, APSR, Cagayan, tomo 30, n. 1, 114r–114v.

94. Fischer, *Cattle Colonialism*, 12–36.

95. Díaz-Trechuelo López-Spínola, *Filipinas*, 221.

96. Malumbres, *Historia de Cagayán*, 340.

97. Basco y Vargas, *D. Joseph Basco*.

98. Foronda, "Informe sobre el estado," 312.

99. Foronda, 311–12.

100. Foronda, 311–12.

101. "Carta de Torrecampo sobre misión de agustinos" (Manila, June 30, 1725), AGI, Filipinas, 140, n. 29, 66v.

102. Malumbres, *Historia de Cagayán*, 339; Antolín, "Compendio cronologico," AUST, APSR, Cagayan, tomo 30, n. 1, 114v.

103. Antolín, "Compendio cronologico," AUST, APSR, Cagayan, tomo 30, n. 1, 111r.

104. "Traslado de los autos de la pesquisa secreta de la de la provincia de Cagayan hecha por el oidor José Ignacio de Arzadun y Rebolledo" (Manila, July 18, 1743), AGI, Filipinas, 556, n. 23, 400r–400v.

105. "Carta de la Audiencia de Manila sobre continuación de las visitas generales" (Manila, June 14, 1702), AGI, Filipinas, 164, n. 1, 46r; Antolín, "Compendio cronologico," AUST, APSR, Cagayan, tomo 30, n. 1, 53r; Antolín, "Notices," 193; Malumbres, *Historia de Cagayán*, 351.

106. Antolín, "Compendio cronologico," AUST, APSR, Cagayan, tomo 30, n. 1, 52r; Antolín, "Notices," 216, 220–21.

107. Antolín, "Notices," 224, 231–32.

108. Herosa, "Breve insinuación," 244; Vivar, "Relación," 136; Reid, *Southeast Asia*, 1:32–36.

109. Herosa, "Breve insinuación," 244–45.

110. Junker, *Raiding, Trading, and Feasting*, 313–25.

111. Antolín, "Notices," 230.

112. Antolín, "Notices: Part 2," 120–21.

113. Antolín, "Compendio cronologico," AUST, APSR, Cagayan, tomo 30, n. 1, 188v.

114. Scott, *Discovery of the Igorots*, 177.

115. Acabado, "Archaeology of Pericolonialism," 14–17, 21–22.

116. Acabado, "Archaeology of Pericolonialism."

117. Antolín, "Compendio cronologico," AUST, APSR, Cagayan, tomo 30, n. 1, 62v, 93r, 95v, 101v.

118. Antolín, "Compendio cronologico," AUST, APSR, Cagayan, tomo 30, n. 1, 62v.

119. Acabado, "Archaeology of Pericolonialism."

120. Malumbres, *Historia de la Isabela*, 33; Rosaldo, *Ilongot Headhunting*, 86–88.

121. Antolín, "Compendio cronologico," AUST, APSR, Cagayan, tomo 30, n. 1, 80v, 202v.

122. Herosa, "Breve insinuación," 238.

123. Antolín, "Notices," 241.

124. Bankoff and Swart, "Breeds of Empire," 13; Bankoff, "Colonising New Lands," 85.

125. Antolín, "Compendio cronologico," AUST, APSR, Cagayan, tomo 30, n. 1, 114v, 229r; Francisco Antolín, "Informe sobre la conveniencia de formar dos provincias en el Valle de Cagayan en lugar de la actual, y sobre la reduccion de infieles" (1787), AUST, APSR, Cagayan, tomo 28, n. 27, 457r, 460v.

126. "Duplicado de carta de la Audiencia de Manila," AGI, Filipinas, 556, n. 1, 555r–555v; Vivar, "Relación," 159.

127. "Duplicado de carta de la Audiencia de Manila," AGI, Filipinas, 556, n. 1, 555r, 556v; "Traslado de los autos," AGI, Filipinas, 556, n. 23, 192v, 292r, 395r.

128. "Duplicado de carta de la Audiencia de Manila," AGI, Filipinas, 556, n. 1, 427r–30r, 432r.

129. Antolín, "Compendio cronologico," AUST, APSR, Cagayan, tomo 30, n. 1, 229r; Antolín, "Informe sobre la conveniencia," AUST, APSR, Cagayan, tomo 28, n. 27, 449v; "Duplicado de carta de la Audiencia de Manila," AGI, Filipinas, 556, n. 1, 569v, 575r.

130. "Duplicado de carta de la Audiencia de Manila," AGI, Filipinas, 556, n. 1, 569v–70r, 574v, 578v.

131. Malumbres, *Historia de Cagayán*, 321, 351; Malumbres, *Historia de la Isabela*, 30.

132. Bankoff, "Colonising New Lands," 86–87.

133. Dizon, "Cartographic Ethnography," 77–79.

134. Mozo, *Noticia historico natural*, 31.

135. Pérez, *Relaciones agustinianas*, 32, 34.

136. Bankoff and Swart, "Breeds of Empire," 95.

137. Antolín, "Compendio cronologico," AUST, APSR, Cagayan, tomo 30, n. 1, 194r.

138. Antolín, "Compendio cronologico," AUST, APSR, Cagayan, tomo 30, n. 1, 189r.

139. Bankoff, "Colonising New Lands," 86.

140. Díaz-Trechuelo López-Spínola, *Filipinas*, 240, 248–49; Hidalgo Nuchera, "La entrada," 633–34.

141. Antolín, "Compendio cronologico," AUST, APSR, Cagayan, tomo 30, n. 1, 229v.

142. "Duplicado de carta de la Audiencia de Manila," AGI, Filipinas, 556, n. 1, 570v.

143. Antolín, "Compendio cronologico," AUST, APSR, Cagayan, tomo 30, n. 1, 186v.

144. Crosby, *Germs, Seeds & Animals*, 28–44.

145. Cacho, "Manifiesto compendioso," 62.

146. Cited in González Cuellas, *Presencia berciana en Filipinas*, 137.

147. Antolín, "Compendio cronologico," AUST, APSR, Cagayan, tomo 30, n. 1, 183r–183v, 204v.

148. Antolín, "Notices," 237; Newson, *Conquest and Pestilence*, 174–75.

149. Antolín, "Compendio cronologico," AUST, APSR, Cagayan, tomo 30, n. 1, 183v.

150. "Sobre los progresos y augmento de las nuebas missiones de Ituy y Paniqui" (Manila, August 20, 1741), AUST, APSR, Cagayan, tomo 29, n. 33, 541v; Newson, *Conquest and Pestilence*, 225, 239.

151. Antolín, "Compendio cronologico," AUST, APSR, Cagayan, tomo 30, n. 1, 186v; Newson, *Conquest and Pestilence*, 240.

152. Antolín, "Compendio cronologico," AUST, APSR, Cagayan, tomo 30, n. 1, 186r.

153. Newson, *Conquest and Pestilence*, 226.

154. González Cuellas, *Presencia berciana en Filipinas*, 122.

155. Mozo, *Noticia historico natural*, 59.

156. Antolín, "Notices," 194.

157. Malumbres, *Historia de Nueva-Vizcaya*, 22.

158. "Sobre los progresos," AUST, APSR, Cagayan, tomo 29, n. 33, 541v.

159. Antolín, "Notices," 200.

160. Antolín, "Compendio cronologico," AUST, APSR, Cagayan, tomo 30, n. 1, 175v, 177r.

161. Aguilar, *Clash of Spirits*, 38–44; Phelan, *Hispanization of the Philippines*, 55.

162. "Carta de Torrecampo," AGI, Filipinas, 140, n. 29, 87r–87v.

163. "Carta de Juan de la Fuente Yepes sobre suspensión de viaje por epidemia de peste" (Manila, June 20, 1756), AGI, Filipinas, 293, n. 71.

164. Antolín, "Compendio cronologico," AUST, APSR, Cagayan, tomo 30, n. 1, 125v–26r, 186r.

165. Antolín, "Compendio cronologico," AUST, APSR, Cagayan, tomo 30, n. 1, 186r; Newson, *Conquest and Pestilence*, 226–27.

166. Antolín, "Compendio cronologico," AUST, APSR, Cagayan, tomo 30, n. 1, 206r.

167. Antolín, "Notices," 221–28.

168. Antolín, 222.

169. Antolín, 224.

170. Carrillo, "Breve y verdadera relación," 122; Pérez, "Los Aetas e Ilongotes," 316; Malumbres, *Historia de la Isabela*, 71.

171. Mozo, *Noticia historico natural*, 59; Carrillo, "Breve y verdadera relación," 122; Antolín, "Compendio cronologico," AUST, APSR, Cagayan, tomo 30, n. 1, 206r.

172. Antolín, "Compendio cronologico," AUST, APSR, Cagayan, tomo 30, n. 1, 163r–67r, 175r–81r.

173. Antolín, "Compendio cronologico," AUST, APSR, Cagayan, tomo 30, n. 1, 178r.

174. Antolín, "Compendio cronologico," AUST, APSR, Cagayan, tomo 30, n. 1, 167r.

175. Antolín, "Compendio cronologico," AUST, APSR, Cagayan, tomo 30, n. 1, 164v–65r.

176. Newson, *Conquest and Pestilence*, 226.

177. Antolín, "Compendio cronologico," AUST, APSR, Cagayan, tomo 30, n. 1, 167v, 180r.

178. "Carta de Juan Ormaza y Lucas de San Vicente" (Buhay, December 27, 1740), AUST, APSR, Cagayan, tomo 29, n. 24, 212r.

179. Newson, *Conquest and Pestilence*, 227.

180. Antolín, "Compendio cronologico," AUST, APSR, Cagayan, tomo 30, n. 1, 178v.

181. Antolín, "Compendio cronologico," AUST, APSR, Cagayan, tomo 30, n. 1, 180r.

Conclusion

1. Navarro García, "Poblamiento y colonización estratégica."

2. Palomo, "Jesuit Interior Indias," 106–7.

3. Francisco Antolín, "Compendio cronologico sobre el camino para Cagayan por la provincia y mision de Ituy" (1790), AUST, APSR, Cagayan, tomo 30, n. 1, 192r–192v, 204v; "Informe anonimo sobre las misiones de los Ilongotes" (1783), AFIO 89/70, 11.

4. Gómez Navarro, "Aportación," 365–68.

5. Gómez Navarro, 366.

6. Navarro García, "Poblamiento y colonización estratégica."

7. Antolín, "Compendio cronologico," AUST, APSR, Cagayan, tomo 30, n. 1, 191r–191v.

8. Newson, *Conquest and Pestilence*, 226–27.

9. Antolín, "Compendio cronologico," AUST, APSR, Cagayan, tomo 30, n. 1, 188v.

10. "Copia simple de una representaion hecha al superior gobierno por el R. P. Fr. Joseph Tasamonte sobre asumptos relativos a la despoblacion de la Pampanga y otros puntos" (1718), APAF 187/4-e, 1.

11. "Copia simple," APAF 187/4-e, 4, 6.

12. "Copia simple," APAF 187/4-e, 6.

13. "Copia simple," APAF 187/4-e, 1; Antolín, "Compendio cronologico," AUST, APSR, Cagayan, tomo 30, n. 1, 183v, 192r.

14. Scott, *Art*; Scott, *Discovery of the Igorots*; Acabado, "Archaeology of Pericolonialism"; Salgado, *Ilongots*.

15. Tappe, "Introduction."

16. Antolín, "Compendio cronologico," AUST, APSR, Cagayan, tomo 30, n. 1, 189r.

17. Acabado, "Archaeology of Pericolonialism."

18. Antolín, "Compendio cronologico," AUST, APSR, Cagayan, tomo 30, n. 1, 166r.

19. Antolín, "Compendio cronologico," AUST, APSR, Cagayan, tomo 30, n. 1, 202v.

Bibliography

Primary Sources

ARCHIVES

Ávila, Spain
   Archivo de la Provincia del Santísimo Rosario
Bloomington, IN
   Lilly Library, Indiana University
Boston, MA
   Boston Public Library
Madrid, Spain
   Archivo Franciscano Ibero-Oriental
   Biblioteca Nacional de España
Manila, Philippines
   Archives of the University of Santo Tomas
Seville, Spain
   Archivo General de Indias
Valladolid, Spain
   Archivo Padres Agustinos Filipinos
Washington, DC
   Library of Congress

PERIODICALS

Libertas
Rappler

BOOKS AND ARTICLES

Aduarte, Diego. *Historia de la provincia del Santo Rosario de Filipinas, Japon y China de la Orden de Predicadores*. Zaragoza: Domingo Gascon, 1693.

Alvarez, Manuel. "Misión de San Agustín de Banná: Costumbres y propiedades de los infieles." In *Relaciones agustinianas de las razas del norte de Luzon*, edited by Angel Pérez, 209–18. Manila: Bureau of Public Printing, 1904.

Alvarez del Manzano, Bartolome. *Compendio de la reseña biográfica de los religiosos de la provincia del Santísimo Rosario de Filipinas desde su fundación hasta nuestros días*. Manila: Estab. tip. del Real Colegio de Santo Tomás, 1895.

Alzaga, Antolín. "Carta del P. Fr. Antolín Alzaga sobre los Italones y Abacaes." In *Relaciones agustinianas de las razas del norte de Luzon*, edited by Angel Pérez, 304–6. Manila: Bureau of Public Printing, 1904.

———. "Cartas, informes y otros documentos sobre la reducción de infieles." In *Relaciones agustinianas de las razas del norte de Luzon,* edited by Angel Pérez, 293–343. Manila: Bureau of Public Printing, 1904.

Antolín, Francisco. "Notices of the Pagan Igorots in 1789." Translated by William Henry Scott. *Asian Folklore Studies* 29 (1970): 177–249.

———. "Notices of the Pagan Igorots in 1789: Part 2." Translated by William Henry Scott. *Asian Folklore Studies* 30, no. 2 (1971): 27–132.

Basco y Vargas, José. *D. Joseph Basco y Vargas Gobernador y Capitan General de las Islas Filipinas, la decadencia que de dia en dia padece a agricultura á causa de los robos y muertes de carabaos reduciría sin duda las islas al mas deplorable estado por tanto ordeno y mando se observen invariablemente las disposiciones siguientes.* Manila, 1782.

Bautista Martínez, Juan. "Informe del P. Provincial, Fr. Juan Bautista Martínez, al Gobernador General de las islas Filipinas, D. Alonso de Abella y Fuertes, sobre la conversión de los infieles." *Archivo Ibero-Americano: Estudios históricos sobre la orden franciscana en España y sus misiones* 2, no. 7 (1915): 126–30.

Beltrán Pigu, Luis. "Pigu's Narrative." Edited by Pablo Fernandez. *Philippiniana Sacra* 24, no. 70 (1989): 136–53.

Cacho, Alejandro. "Compendioso manifiesto del principio y progreso de la misión de italones que los religiosos de nuestro padre San Agustín de la Provincia del Santísimo Nombre de Jesús de Filipinas mantienen en los montes de la Pampanga, así al oriente de dicha provincia." In *Un berciano en Filipinas: Alejandro Cacho de Villegas,* edited by Carlos Villoria Prieto, 360–99. León: Universidad de León, 1997.

———. "Conquistas espirituales de los Religiosos Agustinos Calzados de la Provincia del Santísimo Nombre de Jesús de Filipinas, hechas en estos cuarenta años, y sólo dentro de una Alcaldía que es la de Provincia de la Pampanga." In *Un berciano en Filipinas: Alejandro Cacho de Villegas,* edited by Carlos Villoria Prieto, 327–59. León: Universidad de León, 1997.

———. "Conquistas espirituales de los Religiosos Agustinos Calzados de la Provincia del Santísimo Nombre de Jesús de Filipinas, hechas en estos cuarento años (1700 a 1740) en la alcaldía de la Pampanga." In *Relaciones agustinianas de las razas del norte de Luzon,* edited by Angel Pérez, 25–57. Manila: Bureau of Public Printing, 1904.

———. "Informe sobre la divisoria." In *Relaciones agustinianas de las razas del norte de Luzon,* edited by Angel Pérez, 30. Manila: Bureau of Public Printing, 1904.

———. "Manifiesto compendioso del principio y progresos de la Misión de Italones que los religiosos de N.P. San Agustín de la Provincia del Santísimo Nombre de Jesús de Filipinas mantienen en los montes de la Pampanga, hacia el oriente de dicha provincia." In *Relaciones agustinianas de las razas del norte de Luzon,* edited by Angel Pérez, 61–97. Manila: Bureau of Public Printing, 1904.

Carrillo, Manuel. *Breve relacion de las missiones de las quatro naciones, llamadas Igorrotes, Tinguianes, Apayaos y Adanes, nuevamente fundadas en las Islas Philipinas, en los Montes de las Provincias de Ilocos, y Pangasinan, por los Religiosos de N.P.S. Agustin de la Provincia del Santissimo Nombre de Jesus.* Madrid: Imprenta del Consejo de Indias, 1756.

———. "Breve y verdadera relación de los progresos de las Misiones de Igorrotes, Tinguianes, Apayaos, y Adanes, que los Religiosos Agustinos Calzados tienen nuevamente fundadas en los montes de Pangasinan, é Ilocos de las Islas Filipinas." In

Relaciones agustinianas de las razas del norte de Luzon, edited by Angel Pérez, 119–25. Manila: Bureau of Public Printing, 1904.

Collantes, Domingo. *Historia de la provincia del Santisimo Rosario de Filipinas, China, y Tunquin Orden de Predicadores: Quarta parte desde el año de 1700 hasta el de 1765.* Manila: Imprenta del Colegio y Universidad de Santo Tomas de Manila, 1783.

Concepción, Fernando de la. "Informe del Provincial P. Fernando de la Concepción, al Rey Carlos II, sobre la conversión de los infieles de Filipinas." *Archivo Ibero-Americano: Estudios históricos sobre la orden franciscana en España y sus misiones* 2, no. 7 (1915): 125–26.

Correa de Castro, Geronimo. *Breve relacion, y felizes progresos de los Religiosos del Sagrado Orden de Predicadores de las Islas Philipinas, en la Conquista espiritual, y reduccion de los Gentiles de la Provincia de Paniqui que, media entre las Provincias de Cagayan y Pangasinan, que tambien administra dicha Religion Dominica.* Manila: Colegio y Universidad del Señor Santo Tomás, 1739.

Diaz, Casimiro. *Parrocho de indios instruido. Idea de un perfecto pastor copiada de los SS.PP. y Concilio: Con la resolución de las principales dudas que en la administración de los sacramentos se ofrecen acerca de los indios.* Manila: Imp. de la Compañia de Jesús, 1745.

Duárez y Santa Cruz, Juan. *Carta ingenua y religiosa de Fr. Juan Duarez y Santa Cruz de la Regular observancia de nuestro Seráfico Padre San Francisco en contextacion á la de otro religioso de su misma Orden, que contiene cinco qüésitos.* Madrid, 1786.

Fermoselle, Manuel de Jesus Maria. *Relación del descubrimiento, y entrada de los Religiosos de N.S.P.S. Francisco de la Apostolica Provincia de S. Gregorio de las Islas Philipinas en los Pueblos, ò Rancherias de los Montes altos de Baler, en la contracosta dichas Islas.* Manila, 1754.

Foronda, Sebastián. "Informe sobre el estado de las misiones de la Pampanga." In *Relaciones agustinianas de las razas del norte de Luzon,* edited by Angel Pérez, 301–20. Manila: Bureau of Public Printing, 1904.

Herosa, Benito. "Breve insinuación de la tierra y carácter de los infieles llamados Igorrotes: Sus usos, modales y costumbres." In *Relaciones agustinianas de las razas del norte de Luzon,* edited by Angel Pérez, 235–45. Manila: Bureau of Public Printing, 1904.

Mozo, Antonio. *Noticia historico natural de los gloriosos triumphos y felices adelantamientos conseguidos en el presente siglo por los religiosos del Orden de N.P.S. Agustin en las missiones que tienen à su cargo en las Islas Philipinas, y en el grande Imperio de la China.* Madrid: Andrès Ortega, 1763.

Murillo Velarde, Pedro. *Geographia Historica.* Vol. 8. Madrid: Oficina de D. Gabriel Ramirez, 1752.

Olarte, Juan de. "Informe dado al superior Gobierno sobre nuestra misión de Italones." In *Relaciones agustinianas de las razas del norte de Luzon,* edited by Angel Pérez, 321–23. Manila: Bureau of Public Printing, 1904.

Pan, Felipe del, ed. *Documentos para la historia de la administración de Filipinas: Las ordenanzas de buen gobierno de Corcuera, Cruzat y Raon.* Manila: La Oceanía Española, 1891.

Pérez, Angel, ed. "Carta del P. Jose González misionero de Buhay." In *Relaciones agustinianas de las razas del norte de Luzon,* 300–301. Manila: Bureau of Public Printing, 1904.

———, ed. "Decreto del Rey aprobando la cesión de las Misiones de Ituy." In *Relaciones agustinianas de las razas del norte de Luzon,* 335–41. Manila: Bureau of Public Printing, 1904.

———, ed. "Orden para que los sangleyes de Pantabangán y Bongabón de las misiones de Italones no vivan en dichos pueblos, por ser contra el éxito de las misiones, 1705." In *Relaciones agustinianas de las razas del norte de Luzon*, 295–96. Manila: Bureau of Public Printing, 1904.

———, ed. *Relaciones agustinianas de las razas del norte de Luzon*. Manila: Bureau of Public Printing, 1904.

Recopilación de leyes de los Reynos de las Indias mandadas imprimir y publicar por la Magestad Católica del Rey Don Carlos II. 3rd ed. Vol. 1. Madrid: Andres Ortega, 1774.

Recopilación de leyes de los Reynos de las Indias mandadas imprimir y publicar por la Magestad Católica del Rey Don Carlos II. 3rd ed. Vol. 2. Madrid: Andres Ortega, 1774.

Río, Manuel del. *Relación de los successos de la Missión de Santa Cruz de Ytuy en la Provincia de Paniqui, media entre las de Pangasinan, y Cagayan en las Philippinas: Año de 1739*. Manila, 1739.

Santa Rosa, Bernardo de. "Carta-relación escrita por el P. Fr. Bernardo de Santa Rosa, en la cual describe las costumbres de los Aetas que habitan en los montes de Casiguran y Baler." Edited by Lorenzo Pérez. *Archivo Ibero-Americano: Revista de estudios históricos* 15, no. 88 (1928): 86–106.

Souza, George Bryan, and Jeffrey Scott Turley, eds. *The Boxer Codex: Transcription and Translation of an Illustrated Late Sixteenth-Century Spanish Manuscript Concerning the Geography, Ethnography and History of the Pacific, South-East Asia and East Asia*. Leiden: Brill, 2016.

Ustariz, Bernardo. *Relación de los sucessos, y progressos de la mission de Santa Cruz de Paniqui y de Ytuy, medias entre las de Pangasinan, Cagayan, y Pampanga: Año de 1745*. Manila, 1745.

Vivar, Pedro de. "Relación del establecimiento y estado de las nuevas misiones en la nación de Igorrotes (1755–1756), y cartas de varios padres misioneros." In *Relaciones agustinianas de las razas del norte de Luzon*, edited by Angel Pérez, 133–62. Manila: Bureau of Public Printing, 1904.

Secondary Sources

Abinales, Patricio N., and Donna J. Amoroso. *State and Society in the Philippines*. Lanham, MD: Rowman & Littlefield, 2005.

Acabado, Stephen. *Antiquity, Archaeological Processes, and Highland Adaptation: The Ifugao Rice Terraces*. Quezon City: Ateneo de Manila University Press, 2015.

———. "The Archaeology of Pericolonialism: Responses of the 'Unconquered' to Spanish Conquest and Colonialism in Ifugao, Philippines." *International Journal of Historical Archaeology* 21 (2017): 1–26.

Acabado, Stephen, and Grace Barretto-Tesoro. "Places, Landscapes, and Identity: Place Making in the Colonial Period Philippines." In *The Global Spanish Empire: Five Hundred Years of Place Making and Pluralism*, edited by Christine Beaule and John G. Douglass, 200–221. Tucson: University of Arizona Press, 2020.

Adelman, Jeremy, and Stephen Aron. "From Borderlands to Borders: Empires, Nation-States, and the Peoples in between in North American History." *American Historical Review* 104, no. 3 (1999): 814–41.

Aguilar, Filomeno V. *Clash of Spirits: The History of Power and Sugar Planter Hegemony on a Visayan Island*. Quezon City: Ateneo de Manila University Press, 1998.

———. "Rice and Magic: A Cultural History from the Precolonial World to the Present." *Philippine Studies: Historical and Ethnographic Viewpoints* 61, no. 3 (2013): 297–330.

Akerman, James R. "Introduction." In *Cartographies of Travel and Navigation*, edited by James R. Akerman, 1–15. Chicago: University of Chicago Press, 2006.

Algazi, Gadi. "Introduction: Doing Things with Gifts." In *Negotiating the Gift: Pre-Modern Figurations of Exchange*, edited by Gadi Algazi, Valentin Groebner, and Bernhard Jussen, 9–27. Göttingen: Vandenhoeck & Ruprecht, 2003.

Altenbernd, Erik, and Alex Trimble Young. "Introduction: The Significance of the Frontier in an Age of Transnational History." *Settler Colonial Studies* 4, no. 2 (2014): 127–50.

Altić, Mirela. "Jesuit Contribution to the Mapping of the Philippine Islands: A Case of the 1734 Pedro Murillo Velarde's Chart." In *Mapping Asia: Cartographic Encounters between East and West*, edited by Martijn Storms, Mario Cams, Imre Josef Demhardt, and Ferjan Ormeling, 73–94. Cham, Switzerland: Springer, 2019.

Andaya, Barbara Watson. "Historicising 'Modernity' in Southeast Asia." *Journal of the Economic and Social History of the Orient* 40, no. 4 (1997): 391–409.

———. *To Live as Brothers: Southeast Sumatra in the Seventeenth and Eighteenth Centuries*. Honolulu: University of Hawaii Press, 1993.

Andaya, Barbara Watson, and Leonard Y. Andaya. *A History of Early Modern Southeast Asia, 1400–1800*. Cambridge: Cambridge University Press, 2014.

Andrade, Tonio. "Chinese under European Rule: The Case of Sino-Dutch Mediator He Bin." *Late Imperial China* 28, no. 1 (2007): 1–32.

———. "Political Spectacle and Colonial Rule: The *Landdag* on Dutch Taiwan, 1629–1648." *Itinerario* 21, no. 3 (1997): 57–93.

Angeles, Jose Amiel. "The Battle of Mactan and the Indigenous Discourse on War." *Philippine Studies* 55, no. 1 (2007): 3–52.

Arnold, David. *The Problem of Nature: Environment, Culture and European Expansion*. Oxford: Blackwell, 1996.

Ballantyne, Tony. "Mobility, Empire, Colonisation." *History Australia* 11, no. 2 (2014): 7–37.

Bankoff, Greg. "Colonising New Lands: Horses in the Philippines." In *Breeds of Empire: The "Invention" of the Horse in Southeast Asia and Southern Africa, 1500–1950*, edited by Greg Bankoff and Sandra Scott Swart, 85–103. Copenhagen: NIAS, 2007.

Bankoff, Greg, and Sandra Scott Swart. "Breeds of Empire and the 'Invention' of the Horse." In *Breeds of Empire: The "Invention" of the Horse in Southeast Asia and Southern Africa, 1500–1950*, edited by Greg Bankoff and Sandra Scott Swart, 1–18. Copenhagen: NIAS, 2007.

Barnard, Timothy P. "'We Are Comfortable Riding the Waves': Landscape and the Formation of a Border State in Eighteenth-Century Island Southeast Asia." In *Borderlands in World History, 1700–1914*, edited by Paul Readman, Cynthia Radding, and Chad Carl Bryant, 83–100. Basingstoke, UK: Palgrave Macmillan, 2014.

Barrio Muñoz, José Ángel del. "Negritos contra españoles y filipinos: Notas sobre un conflicto en las Filipinas del primer tercio del siglo XVIII." *Revista española del Pacífico* 24 (2011): 49–100.

―――. *Vientos de reforma ilustrada en Filipinas: El gobernador Fernando Valdés Tamón (1729–1739)*. Madrid: Consejo Superior de Investigaciones Científicas, 2012.

Benton, Lauren. *A Search for Sovereignty: Law and Geography in European Empires, 1400–1900*. Cambridge: Cambridge University Press, 2010.

Berdah, Jean-Francois. "Pyrenees without Frontiers: The French-Spanish Border in Modern Times, 17th to 20th Centuries." In *Frontiers, Regions and Identities in Europe*, edited by Steven G. Ellis and Raingard Esser, 163–84. Pisa: Pisa University Press, 2009.

Bertrand, Romain. "Where the Devil Stands: A Microhistorical Reading of Empires as Multiple Moral Worlds (Manila–Mexico, 1577–1580)." *Past & Present* 242, Supplement 14 (2019): 83–109.

Biedermann, Zoltán, Anne Gerritsen, and Giorgio Riello. "Introduction: Global Gifts and the Material Culture of Diplomacy in Early Modern Eurasia." In *Global Gifts: The Material Culture of Diplomacy in Early Modern Eurasia*, edited by Zoltán Biedermann, Anne Gerritson, and Giorgio Riello, 198–216. Cambridge: Cambridge University Press, 2018.

Blussé, Leonard. "Batavia, 1619–1740: The Rise and Fall of a Chinese Colonial Town." *Journal of Southeast Asian Studies* 12, no. 1 (1981): 159–78.

Bolton, Herbert E. "The Mission as a Frontier Institution in the Spanish-American Colonies." *American Historical Review* 23, no. 1 (1917): 42–61.

Braudel, Fernand. *Civilization and Capitalism, 15th–18th Century: The Structures of Everyday Life: The Limits of the Possible*. Translated by Siân Reynolds. Vol. 1. London: William Collins Sons, 1981.

―――. *The Mediterranean and the Mediterranean World in the Age of Philip II*. Translated by Siân Reynolds. Vol. 1. New York: Harper & Row, 1972.

Brendecke, Arndt. *The Empirical Empire: Spanish Colonial Rule and the Politics of Knowledge*. Translated by Jeremiah Riemer. Berlin: De Gruyter, 2016.

Cáceres Menéndez, Beatriz, and Robert W. Patch. "'Gente de Mal Vivir': Families and Incorrigible Sons in New Spain, 1721–1729." *Revista de Indias* 66, no. 237 (2006): 363–92.

Cagle, Hugh. *Assembling the Tropics: Science and Medicine in Portugal's Empire, 1450–1700*. Cambridge: Cambridge University Press, 2018.

Cañeque, Alejandro. *The King's Living Image: The Culture and Politics of Viceregal Power in Colonial Mexico*. New York: Routledge, 2004.

Cardim, Pedro, Tamar Herzog, José Javier Ruiz Ibáñez, and Gaetano Sabatini. "Polycentric Monarchies: How Did Early Modern Spain and Portugal Achieve and Maintain a Global Hegemony?" In *Polycentric Monarchies: How Did Early Modern Spain and Portugal Achieve and Maintain a Global Hegemony?*, edited by Pedro Cardim, Tamar Herzog, José Javier Ruiz Ibáñez, and Gaetano Sabatini, 3–8. Eastbourne, UK: Sussex Academic Press, 2012.

Carey, Jane, and Jane Lydon. "Introduction: Indigenous Networks, Historical Trajectories and Contemporary Connections." In *Indigenous Networks: Mobility, Connections and Exchange*, edited by Jane Carey and Jane Lydon, 1–26. New York: Routledge, 2014.

Carpio, Antonio T. *The South China Sea Dispute: Philippine Sovereign Rights and Jurisdiction in the West Philippine Sea*. e-book, 2017. http://murillovelardemap.com/south-china-sea -dispute-philippine-sovereign-rights-jurisdiction-west-philippine-sea/.

Carsten, Janet. "Introduction: Cultures of Relatedness." In *Cultures of Relatedness: New Approaches to the Study of Kinship*, edited by Janet Carsten, 1–36. Cambridge: Cambridge University Press, 2000.

———. "The Substance of Kinship and the Heat of the Hearth: Feeding, Personhood, and Relatedness among Malays in Pulau Langkawi." *American Ethnologist* 22, no. 2 (1995): 223–41.

Carter, Paul. *The Road to Botany Bay: An Exploration of Landscape and History*. Minneapolis: University of Minnesota Press, 2010.

Certeau, Michel de. *The Practice of Everyday Life*. Berkeley: University of California Press, 1988.

Céspedes del Castillo, Guillermo. "La visita como institución indiana." *Anuario de Estudios Americanos* 3 (1946): 984–1025.

Chang, Michael G. *A Court on Horseback: Imperial Touring & the Construction of Qing Rule, 1680–1785*. Cambridge, MA: Harvard University Asia Center, 2007.

Charney, Michael W. *Southeast Asian Warfare, 1300–1900*. Leiden: Brill, 2004.

———. "Warfare in Premodern Southeast Asia." *Oxford Research Encyclopedia of Asian History*, April 26, 2018. https://doi.org/10.1093/acrefore/9780190277727.013.238.

Charney, Michael W., and Kathryn Anderson Wellen. "Introduction." In *Warring Societies of Pre-Colonial Southeast Asia: Local Cultures of Conflict within a Regional Context*, edited by Michael W. Charney and Kathryn Anderson Wellen, 1–19. Copenhagen: NIAS Press, 2018.

Clendinnen, Inga. "'Fierce and Unnatural Cruelty': Cortés and the Conquest of Mexico." *Representations*, no. 33 (1991): 65–100.

Clulow, Adam. "Gifts for the Shogun: The Dutch East India Company, Global Networks and Tokugawa Japan." In *Global Gifts: The Material Culture of Diplomacy in Early Modern Eurasia*, edited by Zoltán Biedermann, Anne Gerritson, and Giorgio Riello, 198–216. Cambridge: Cambridge University Press, 2018.

Conklin, Harold C., Puguwon Lupaih, and Miklos Pinther. *Ethnographic Atlas of Ifugao: A Study of Environment, Culture, and Society in Northern Luzon*. New Haven, CT: Yale University Press, 1980.

Conti, Viviana E. "Connections and Circulation in the Southern Andes from Colony to Republic." In *The Oxford Handbook of Borderlands of the Iberian World*, edited by Danna A. Levin Rojo and Cynthia Radding, 267–93. New York: Oxford University Press, 2019.

Cosgrove, Denis. "Tropic and Tropicality." In *Tropical Visions in an Age of Empire*, edited by Felix Driver and Luciana Martins, 197–216. Chicago: University of Chicago Press, 2005.

Crailsheim, Eberhard. "Las Filipinas, zona fronteriza: Algunas repercusiones de su función conectiva y separativa." In *Intercambios, actores, enfoques: Pasajes de la historia latinoamericana en una perspectiva global*, edited by Aarón Grageda Bustamante, 133–52. Hermosillo, Mexico: Universidad de Sonora, 2014.

Cresswell, Tim. "Friction." In *The Routledge Handbook of Mobilities*, edited by Peter Adey, David Bissell, Kevin Hannam, Peter Merriman, and Mimi Sheller, 107–15. London: Routledge, 2014.

Crewe, Ryan. "Transpacific Mestizo: Religion and Caste in the Worlds of a Moluccan Prisoner of the Mexican Inquisition." *Itinerario* 39, no. 3 (2015): 463–85.

Crosby, Alfred W. *Germs, Seeds & Animals: Studies in Ecological History*. Armonk, NY: M. E. Sharpe, 1994.

Crossley, John N. *The Dasmariñases, Early Governors of the Spanish Philippines*. London: Routledge, 2016.

———. "Dionisio Capulong and the Elite in Early Spanish Manila (c. 1570–1620)." *Journal of the Royal Asiatic Society* 28, no. 4 (2018): 697–715.

Curcio-Nagy, Linda A. "Commemorating the Conquest: Local Politics and Festival Statecraft in Early Colonial Mexico City." In *The Politics of Space: European Courts, ca. 1500–1750*, edited by Marcello Fantoni, Georges Gorse, and R. Malcolm Smuts, 171–89. Rome: Bulzoni, 2009.

Curless, Gareth, Stacey Hynd, Temilola Alanamu, and Katherine Roscoe. "Editors' Introduction: Networks in Imperial History." *Journal of World History* 26, no. 4 (2015): 705–32.

Daniels, Christine, and Michael V. Kennedy, eds. *Negotiated Empires: Centers and Peripheries in the Americas, 1500–1820*. New York: Routledge, 2002.

De Bevoise, Ken. *Agents of Apocalypse: Epidemic Disease in the Colonial Philippines*. Princeton, NJ: Princeton University Press, 1995.

de Jesus, Ed. C. *The Tobacco Monopoly in the Philippines: Bureaucratic Enterprise and Social Change, 1766–1880*. Quezon City: Ateneo de Manila University Press, 1980.

Deb Roy, Rohan. *Malarial Subjects: Empire, Medicine and Nonhumans in British India, 1820–1909*. Cambridge: Cambridge University Press, 2017.

Delano-Smith, Catherine. "Milieus of Mobility: Itineraries, Route Maps, and Road Maps." In *Cartographies of Travel and Navigation*, edited by James R. Akerman, 16–68. Chicago: University of Chicago Press, 2006.

Deloria, Philip J. "What Is the Middle Ground, Anyway?" *William and Mary Quarterly* 63, no. 1 (2006): 15–22.

Diamond, Jared. *Guns, Germs, and Steel: The Fates of Human Societies*. New York: W. W. Norton, 1997.

Díaz-Trechuelo López-Spínola, María Lourdes. "Filipinas en el siglo de la Ilustración." In *Historia general de Filipinas*, edited by Leoncio Cabrero, 249–92. Madrid: Ediciones de Cultura Hispánica, 2000.

———. *Filipinas: La gran desconocida, 1565–1898*. Pamplona: Ediciones Universidad de Navarra, 2001.

Dizon, Mark. "Cartographic Ethnography: Missionary Maps of an Eighteenth-Century Spanish Imperial Frontier." *Imago Mundi* 71, no. 1 (2021): 73–81.

———. "La misión del Caraballo y relaciones sociales en la primera mitad del siglo XVIII." Master's thesis, University of the Basque Country, 2010.

———. "Social and Spiritual Kinship in Early-Eighteenth-Century Missions on the Caraballo Mountains." *Philippine Studies* 59, no. 3 (2011): 367–98.

———. "Sumpong: Spirit Beliefs, Murder, and Religious Change among Eighteenth-Century Aeta and Ilongot in Eastern Central Luzon." *Philippine Studies: Historical and Ethnographic Viewpoints* 63, no. 1 (2015): 3–38.

Driver, Felix, and Luciana Martins. "Views and Visions of the Tropical World." In *Tropical Visions in an Age of Empire*, edited by Felix Driver and Luciana Martins, 3–20. Chicago: University of Chicago Press, 2005.

Dueñas Olmo, Antonio. "Contribución al estudio de las visitas a la tierra de la Audiencia de Filipinas (1690–1747)." Undergraduate thesis, Universidad de Córdoba, 1984.

———. "Las ordenanzas de D. Alonso de Abella Fuertes para las provincias de Cagayan, Ilocos, Pangasinan y Pampanga." Unpublished manuscript, Cordoba, September 1985.

Edwards, Penny. "The Tyranny of Proximity: Power and Mobility in Colonial Cambodia, 1863–1954." *Journal of Southeast Asian Studies* 37, no. 3 (2006): 421–43.

Elliott, J. H. "A Europe of Composite Monarchies." *Past & Present* 137 (1992): 48–71.

Ellis, Steven G., and Raingard Esser. "Introduction: Early Modern Frontiers in Comparative Context." In *Frontiers and the Writing of History, 1500–1850*, edited by Steven G. Ellis and Raingard Esser, 9–20. Hannover-Laatzen, Germany: Wehrhahn, 2006.

Elsner, Jas, and Joan-Pau Rubiés. "Introduction." In *Voyages and Visions: Towards a Cultural History of Travel*, edited by Jas Elsner and Joan-Pau Rubiés, 1–56. London: Reaktion Books, 1999.

Ethington, Philip J. "Placing the Past: 'Groundwork' for a Spatial Theory of History." *Rethinking History* 11, no. 4 (2007): 465–93.

Ferguson, R. Brian, and Neil L. Whitehead. "Preface to the Second Printing." In *War in the Tribal Zone: Expanding States and Indigenous Warfare*, edited by R. Brian Ferguson and Neil L. Whitehead, xi–xxxv. Santa Fe, NM: School of American Research Press, 2000.

———. "The Violent Edge of Empire." In *War in the Tribal Zone: Expanding States and Indigenous Warfare*, edited by R. Brian Ferguson and Neil L. Whitehead, 1–30. Santa Fe, NM: School of American Research Press, 2000.

Fernandez, P., and J. de Juan. "Social and Economic Development of the Province of Nueva Vizcaya, Philippines, 1571–1898." *Acta Manilana*, B, 1, no. 8 (1969): 59–134.

Fernandez, Pablo. "An 18th-Century Report on the Ilongots and Futile Attempts at Their Evangelization." *Philippiniana Sacra* 23, no. 69 (1988): 454–59.

———. "Pigu's Account in the Context of the Evangelization of Nueva Vizcaya (1591–1739)." *Philippiniana Sacra* 24, no. 70 (1989): 122–35.

Ferrando, Juan, and Joaquin Fonseca. *Historia de los PP. Dominicos en las Islas Filipinas y en sus misiones del Japon, China, Tung-kin y Formosa, que comprende los sucesos principales de la historia general de este archipiélago, desde el descubrimiento y conquesta de estas islas por las flotas españolas, hasta el año de 1840*. Vol. 3. Manila: Imprenta y estereotipa de M. Rivadeneyra, 1871.

———. *Historia de los PP. Dominicos en las Islas Filipinas y en sus misiones del Japon, China, Tung-kin y Formosa, que comprende los sucesos principales de la historia general de este archipiélago, desde el descubrimiento y conquesta de estas islas por las flotas españolas, hasta el año de 1840*. Vol. 4. Manila: Imprenta y estereotipa de M. Rivadeneyra, 1871.

Fischer, John Ryan. *Cattle Colonialism: An Environmental History of the Conquest of California and Hawai'i*. Chapel Hill: The University of North Carolina Press, 2015.

Flores, Jorge. *Unwanted Neighbours: The Mughals, the Portuguese, and Their Frontier Zones*. New Delhi: Oxford University Press, 2018.

Flores, Jorge, and Giuseppe Marcocci. "Killing Images: Iconoclasm and the Art of Political Insult in Sixteenth and Seventeenth Century Portuguese India." *Itinerario* 42, no. 3 (2018): 461–89.

Flynn, Dennis O., and Arturo Giráldez. "Born with a 'Silver Spoon': The Origin of World Trade in 1571." *Journal of World History* 6, no. 2 (1995): 201–21.

Fullagar, Kate. "Voyagers from the Havai'i Diaspora: Polynesian Mobility, 1760s–1850s." In *The Routledge Companion to Global Indigenous History*, edited by Ann McGrath and Lynette Russell, 221–40. London: Routledge, 2022.

García de los Arcos, María Fernanda. "¿Avanzada o periferia? Una visión diacrónica de la situación fronteriza de Filipinas." In *Fronteras del mundo hispanico: Filipinas en el contexto de las regiones liminares novohispánicas*, edited by Marta María Manchado López and Miguel Luque Talaván, 47–70. Córdoba, Spain: Universidad de Córdoba, 2011.

———. *Forzados y reclutas: Los criollos novohispanos en Asia, 1756–1808*. Ciudad de México: Potrerillos Editores, 1996.

García-Abásolo, Antonio. "Filipinas: Una frontera más allá de la frontera." In *Fronteras del mundo hispanico: Filipinas en el contexto de las regiones liminares novohispánicas*, edited by Marta María Manchado López and Miguel Luque Talaván, 71–88. Córdoba, Spain: Universidad de Córdoba, 2011.

Gaudin, Guillaume, Antonio Castillo Gómez, Margarita Gómez Gómez, and Roberta Stumpf. "Vencer la distancia: Actores y prácticas del gobierno de los imperios español y portugués." *Nuevo Mundo Mundos Nuevos*, October 2, 2017. http://journals.openedition.org/nuevomundo/71453.

Geertz, Clifford. "Centers, Kings, and Charisma: Reflections on the Symbolics of Power." In *Local Knowledge: Further Essays in Interpretive Anthropology*, 121–46. New York: Basic Books, 1983.

———. *Negara: The Theatre State in Nineteenth-Century Bali*. Princeton, NJ: Princeton University Press, 1980.

George, Kenneth M. *Showing Signs of Violence: The Cultural Politics of a Twentieth-Century Headhunting Ritual*. Berkeley: University of California Press, 1996.

Gómez Navarro, Soledad. "Aportación para una doble efeméride: Carlos III y su obra colonizadora en las prensas; Un estado de la cuestión." *Revista de Historiografía* 27 (2017): 363–81.

González Cuellas, Tomás. *Presencia berciana en Filipinas*. Valladolid, Spain: Ed. Estudio Agustiniano, 1988.

Grafe, Regina. *Distant Tyranny: Markets, Power, and Backwardness in Spain, 1650–1800*. Princeton, NJ: Princeton University Press, 2012.

Grandjean, Katherine. *American Passage: The Communications Frontier in Early New England*. Cambridge, MA: Harvard University Press, 2015.

Grove, Richard. *Green Imperialism: Colonial Expansion, Tropical Island Edens, and the Origins of Environmentalism, 1600–1860*. Cambridge: Cambridge University Press, 1995.

Guevara-Gil, Armando, and Frank Salomon. "A 'Personal Visit': Colonial Political Ritual and the Making of Indians in the Andes." *Colonial Latin American Review* 3, no. 1/2 (1994): 3–36.

Guldi, Jo. "Landscape and Place." In *Research Methods for History*, edited by Simon Gunn and Lucy Faire, 66–80. Edinburgh: Edinburgh University Press, 2012.

———. *Roads to Power: Britain Invents the Infrastructure State*. Cambridge, MA: Harvard University Press, 2012.

Hämäläinen, Pekka. *The Comanche Empire*. New Haven, CT: Yale University Press, 2008.

———. "What's in a Concept? The Kinetic Empire of the Comanches." *History and Theory* 52, no. 1 (2013): 81–90.

Hämäläinen, Pekka, and Samuel Truett. "On Borderlands." *Journal of American History* 98, no. 2 (2011): 338–61.

Henley, David. *Fertility, Food and Fever: Population, Economy and Environment in North and Central Sulawesi, 1600–1930*. Leiden: KITLV Press, 2005.

Herzog, Tamar. *Frontiers of Possession: Spain and Portugal in Europe and the Americas*. Cambridge, MA: Harvard University Press, 2015.

———. *Ritos de control, prácticas de negociación: Pesquisas, visitas y residencias en las relaciones entre Quito y Madrid (1650–1750)*. Madrid: Fundación Ignacio Larramendi, 2011.

Hidalgo Nuchera, Patricio. "La entrada de los gobernadores en Manila: El ceremonial y sus costes." *Revista de Indias* 75, no. 265 (2015): 615–44.

———. "Visitas a la tierra durante los primeros tiempos de la colonización de las Filipinas, 1565–1608." In *Imperios y naciones en el Pacífico*, edited by María Dolores Elizalde, Josep M. Fradera, and Luis Alonso, 1:207–25. Madrid: Consejo Superior de Investigaciones Científicas, 2001.

Hoskins, Janet. "The Heritage of Headhunting: History, Ideology, and Violence on Sumba, 1890–1990." In *Headhunting and the Social Imagination in Southeast Asia*, edited by Janet Hoskins. Stanford, CA: Stanford University Press, 1996.

———. "On Losing and Getting a Head: Warfare, Exchange, and Alliance in a Changing Sumba, 1888–1988." *American Ethnologist* 16, no. 3 (1989): 419–40.

Huetz de Lemps, Xavier. *L'archipel des épices: La corruption de l'administration espagnole aux Philippines (fin XVIIIe–fin XIXe siècle)*. Madrid: Casa de Velázquez, 2006.

Ileto, Reynaldo. "Religion and Anti-Colonial Movements." In *The Cambridge History of Southeast Asia: The Nineteenth and Twentieth Centuries*, edited by Nicholas Tarling, 2:197–248. Cambridge: Cambridge University Press, 1992.

———. "Rizal and the Underside of Philippine History." In *Moral Order and the Question of Change: Essays on Southeast Asian Thought*, edited by David K. Wyatt, Alexander Woodside, and Michael Aung-Thwin, 274–337. New Haven, CT: Yale University Southeast Asia Studies, 1982.

Ingold, Tim. "Culture on the Ground: The World Perceived through the Feet." *Journal of Material Culture* 9, no. 3 (2004): 315–40.

Janowski, Monica. "Feeding the Right Food: The Flow of Life and the Construction of Kinship in Southeast Asia." In *Kinship and Food in South East Asia*, edited by Monica Janowski and Fiona Kerlogue, 1–23. Copenhagen: NIAS, 2007.

Junker, Laura Lee. *Raiding, Trading, and Feasting: The Political Economy of Philippine Chiefdoms*. Quezon City: Ateneo de Manila University Press, 2000.

Kagan, Richard L. "Projecting Order." In *Mapping Latin America: A Cartographic Reader*, edited by Jordana Dym and Karl Offen, 46–50. Chicago: University of Chicago Press, 2011.

Kagan, Richard L., and Fernando Marías. *Urban Images of the Hispanic World, 1493–1793*. New Haven, CT: Yale University Press, 2000.

Keesing, Felix M. *The Ethnohistory of Northern Luzon*. Stanford, CA: Stanford University Press, 1962.

Kennedy, Dane. "Introduction: Reinterpreting Exploration." In *Reinterpreting Exploration: The West in the World*, edited by Dane Kennedy, 1–18. New York: Oxford University Press, 2014.

Langfur, Hal. *The Forbidden Lands: Colonial Identity, Frontier Violence, and the Persistence of Brazil's Eastern Indians, 1750–1830*. Stanford, CA: Stanford University Press, 2006.

———. "Moved by Terror: Frontier Violence as Cultural Exchange in Late-Colonial Brazil." *Ethnohistory* 52, no. 2 (2005): 255–89.

Lee, Wayne E. "The Military Revolution of Native North America: Firearms, Forts, and Polities." In *Empires and Indigenes: Intercultural Alliance, Imperial Expansion, and Warfare in the Early Modern World*, edited by Wayne E. Lee, 49–79. New York: New York University Press, 2011.

Lester, Alan. "Place and Space in British Imperial History Writing." In *The Routledge History of Western Empires*, edited by Robert Aldrich and Kirsten McKenzie, 300–314. London: Routledge, 2014.

Levin Rojo, Danna A., and Cynthia Radding. "Introduction: Borderlands, a Working Definition." In *The Oxford Handbook of Borderlands of the Iberian World*, edited by Danna A. Levin Rojo and Cynthia Radding, 1–19. New York: Oxford University Press, 2019.

Lieberman, Victor. "A Zone of Refuge in Southeast Asia? Reconceptualizing Interior Spaces." *Journal of Global History* 5, no. 2 (2010): 333–46.

Liebersohn, Harry. *The Return of the Gift: European History of a Global Idea*. Cambridge: Cambridge University Press, 2011.

Lockhart, James. *The Nahuas after the Conquest: A Social and Cultural History of the Indians of Central Mexico, Sixteenth through Eighteenth Centuries*. Stanford, CA: Stanford University Press, 1992.

Lopez, Ariel C. "Kinship, Islam, and Raiding in Maguindanao, c. 1760–1780." In *Warring Societies of Pre-Colonial Southeast Asia: Local Cultures of Conflict within a Regional Context*, edited by Michael W. Charney and Kathryn Anderson Wellen, 73–99. Copenhagen: NIAS Press, 2018.

Luengo, Pedro. "La fortificación del archipiélago filipino en el siglo XVIII: La defensa integral ante lo local y lo global." *Revista de Indias* 77, no. 271 (2017): 727–58.

Macdonald, Charles J.-H. "Folk Catholicism and Pre-Spanish Religions in the Philippines." *Philippine Studies* 52, no. 1 (2004): 78–93.

Maier, Charles S. "Transformations of Territoriality, 1600–2000: Space, Place, Territory." In *Transnationale Geschichte: Themen, Tendenzen und Theorien*, edited by Gunilla-Friederike Budde, Sebastian Conrad, and Oliver Janz, 2. Auflage. Göttingen: Vandenhoeck & Ruprecht, 2011.

Malumbres, Julián. *Historia de Cagayán*. Manila: Tip. Linotype de Sto. Tomás, 1918.

———. *Historia de la Isabela*. Manila: Tip. Linotype de Col. de Sto. Tomás, 1918.

———. *Historia de Nueva-Vizcaya y Provincia Montaña*. Manila: Tip. Linotype de Col. de Sto. Tomás, 1919.

Manchado López, Marta M. *Conflictos Iglesia-Estado en el extremo oriente ibérico: Filipinas (1767–1787)*. Murcia, Spain: Universidad de Murcia, 1994.

Marcus, George E. "Ethnography in/of the World System: The Emergence of Multi-Sited Ethnography." *Annual Review of Anthropology* 24 (1995): 95–117.

Markovits, Claude, Jacques Pouchepadass, and Sanjay Subrahmanyam. "Introduction: Circulation and Society under Colonial Rule." In *Society and Circulation: Mobile People and Itinerant Cultures in South Asia, 1750–1950*, edited by Claude Markovits, Jacques Pouchepadass, and Sanjay Subrahmanyam, 1–22. London: Anthem, 2006.

Mauss, Marcel. *The Gift: The Form and Reason for Exchange in Archaic Societies*. Translated by W. D. Halls. London: Routledge, 1990.

Mawson, Stephanie. "Convicts or Conquistadores? Spanish Soldiers in the Seventeenth-Century Pacific." *Past & Present* 232, no. 1 (2016): 87–125.

———. "Philippine Indios in the Service of Empire: Indigenous Soldiers and Contingent Loyalty, 1600–1700." *Ethnohistory* 63, no. 2 (2016): 381–413.

McLennan, Marshall S. "Changing Human Ecology on the Central Luzon Plain: Nueva Ecija, 1705–1939." In *Philippine Social History: Global Trade and Local Transformation*, edited by Alfred W. McCoy and Ed. C. de Jesus, 57–90. Quezon City: Ateneo de Manila University Press, 1982.

McNeill, John Robert. *Mosquito Empires: Ecology and War in the Greater Caribbean, 1620–1914*. New York: Cambridge University Press, 2010.

Metcalf, Peter. "Images of Headhunting." In *Headhunting and the Social Imagination in Southeast Asia*, edited by Janet Hoskins, 249–90. Stanford, CA: Stanford University Press, 1996.

Mora Mérida, José Luis. "La visita eclesiástica como institución en Indias." *Jahrbuch für Geschichte Lateinamerikas = Anuario de Historia de América*, no. 17 (1980): 59–67.

Mumford, Jeremy Ravi. *Vertical Empire: The General Resettlement of Indians in the Colonial Andes*. Durham, NC: Duke University Press, 2012.

Mundy, Barbara E. *The Mapping of New Spain: Indigenous Cartography and the Maps of the Relaciones Geográficas*. Chicago: University of Chicago Press, 1996.

———, ed. "The Questionnaire of the Relaciones Geográficas." In *The Mapping of New Spain: Indigenous Cartography and the Maps of the Relaciones Geográficas*, 227–30. Chicago: University of Chicago Press, 1996.

Navarro García, Luis. "Poblamiento y colonización estratégica en el siglo XVIII indiano." *Temas americanistas* 11 (1994): 40–57.

Needham, Rodney. "Skulls and Causality." *Man* 11, no. 1 (1976): 71–88.

Newson, Linda A. *Conquest and Pestilence in the Early Spanish Philippines*. Honolulu: University of Hawai'i Press, 2009.

Norton, Claire. "Liminal Space in the Early Modern Ottoman-Habsburg Borderlands: Historiography, Ontology, and Politics." In *The Uses of Space in Early Modern History*, edited by Paul Stock, 75–96. New York: Palgrave Macmillan, 2015.

Odyniec, Krzysztof. "Negotiating the Sixteenth-Century Road: Diplomacy and Travel in Early Modern Europe." In *Historians without Borders: New Studies in Multidisciplinary History*, edited by Lawrence Abrams and Kaleb Knoblauch, 219–36. London: Routledge, 2019.

Osorio, Alejandra B. *Inventing Lima: Baroque Modernity in Peru's South Sea Metropolis*. New York: Palgrave Macmillan, 2008.

Padrón, Ricardo. "Las Indias olvidadas: Filipinas y América en la cartografía imperial española." *Terra Brasilis (Nova Série): Revista da Rede Basileira de História da Geografia e Geografia Histórica* 4 (2015): 1–13.

Palomo, Federico. "Jesuit Interior Indias: Confession and Mapping of the Soul." In *The Oxford Handbook of the Jesuits*, edited by Ines G. Županov, 105–27. New York: Oxford University Press, 2019.

Pardo de Tavera, T. H. *El mapa de Filipinas del P. Murillo Velarde*. Manila: Tipo-Litografía de Chofré y Comp., 1894.

Paredes, Oona. *A Mountain of Difference: The Lumad in Early Colonial Mindanao*. Ithaca, NY: Cornell University Southeast Asia Program Publications, 2013.

Perdue, Peter C. *China Marches West: The Qing Conquest of Central Eurasia*. Cambridge, MA: Belknap, 2005.

Pérez, Lorenzo. "Los Aetas e Ilongotes de Filipinas." *Archivo Ibero-Americano: Revista de estudios históricos* 14, no. 84 (1927): 289–346.

Pérez-González, María Luisa. "Royal Roads in the Old and the New World: The 'Camino de Oñate' and Its Importance in the Spanish Settlement of New Mexico." *Colonial Latin American Historical Review* 7, no. 2 (1998): 191–218.

Phelan, John Leddy. *The Hispanization of the Philippines: Spanish Aims and Filipino Responses, 1565–1700*. Madison: University of Wisconsin Press, 1959.

Pooley, Colin G. *Mobility, Migration and Transport: Historical Perspectives*. Cham, Switzerland: Palgrave Macmillan, 2017.

Pouchepadass, Jacques. "Itinerant Kings and Touring Officials: Circulation as a Modality of Power in India, 1700–1947." In *Society and Circulation: Mobile People and Itinerant Cultures in South Asia, 1750–1950*, edited by Claude Markovits, Jacques Pouchepadass, and Sanjay Subrahmanyam, 241–74. London: Anthem, 2006.

Pulsipher, Jenny Hale. "Gaining the Diplomatic Edge: Kinship, Trade, Ritual, and Religion in Amerindian Alliances in Early North America." In *Empires and Indigenes: Intercultural Alliance, Imperial Expansion, and Warfare in the Early Modern World*, edited by Wayne E. Lee, 19–47. New York: New York University Press, 2011.

Quirino, Carlos. *Philippine Cartography, 1320–1899*. Edited by Carlos Madrid. 4th ed. Quezon City: Vibal Foundation, 2018.

Quirk, Joel, and Darshan Vigneswaran. "Mobility Makes States." In *Mobility Makes States: Migration and Power in Africa*, edited by Darshan Vigneswaran and Joel Quirk, 1–34. Philadelphia: University of Pennsylvania Press, 2015.

Radding, Cynthia. "Environment, Territory, and Landscape Changes in Northern Mexico during the Era of Independence." In *Borderlands in World History, 1700–1914*, edited by Paul Readman, Cynthia Radding, and Chad Carl Bryant, 65–82. Basingstoke, UK: Palgrave Macmillan, 2014.

Rafael, Vicente L. *Contracting Colonialism: Translation and Christian Conversion in Tagalog Society under Early Spanish Rule*. Quezon City: Ateneo de Manila University Press, 1988.

Raj, Kapil. "Go-Betweens, Travelers, and Cultural Translators." In *A Companion to the History of Science*, edited by Bernard Lightman, 39–57. Malden, MA: Wiley Blackwell, 2016.

Readman, Paul, Cynthia Radding, and Chad Carl Bryant. "Introduction: Borderlands in a Global Perspective." In *Borderlands in World History, 1700–1914*, edited by Paul Readman, Cynthia Radding, and Chad Carl Bryant, 1–23. Basingstoke, UK: Palgrave Macmillan, 2014.

Reed, Robert R. *City of Pines: The Origins of Baguio as a Colonial Hill Station and Regional Capital*. 2nd ed. Baguio City, Philippines: A-Seven, 1999.

Reid, Anthony. *Southeast Asia in the Age of Commerce, 1450–1680*. Vol. 1. New Haven, CT: Yale University Press, 1988.

Restall, Matthew. *Seven Myths of the Spanish Conquest*. Oxford: Oxford University Press, 2003.

Revill, George. "Histories." In *The Routledge Handbook of Mobilities*, edited by Peter Adey, David Bissell, Kevin Hannam, Peter Merriman, and Mimi Sheller, 506–16. London: Routledge, 2014.

Riello, Giorgio. "'With Great Pomp and Magnificence': Royal Gifts and the Embassies between Siam and France in the Late Seventeenth Century." In *Global Gifts: The Material Culture of Diplomacy in Early Modern Eurasia*, edited by Zoltán Biedermann, Anne Gerritson, and Giorgio Riello, 235–65. Cambridge: Cambridge University Press, 2018.

Robles, Eliodoro G. *The Philippines in the Nineteenth Century*. Quezon City: Malaya Books, 1969.

Roche, Daniel. *Les circulations dans l'Europe moderne: XVIIe–XVIIIe siècle*. Paris: Pluriel, 2011.

Rodriguez, Felice Noelle. "Juan de Salcedo Joins the Native Form of Warfare." *Journal of the Economic and Social History of the Orient* 46, no. 2 (2003): 143–64.

Rodriguez, Inmaculada Alva. "La centuria desconocida: El siglo XVII." In *Historia general de Filipinas*, edited by Leoncio Cabrero, 207–48. Madrid: Ediciones de Cultura Hispánica, 2000.

Roque, Ricardo. *Headhunting and Colonialism: Anthropology and the Circulation of Human Skulls in the Portuguese Empire, 1870–1930*. Basingstoke, UK: Palgrave Macmillan, 2010.

Rosaldo, Michelle Z. *Knowledge and Passion: Ilongot Notions of Self and Social Life*. Cambridge: Cambridge University Press, 1980.

———. "Skulls and Causality." *Man* 12, no. 1 (1977): 168–70.

Rosaldo, Renato. "Grief and a Headhunter's Rage." In *Culture and Truth: The Remaking of Social Analysis*, 1–21. Boston: Beacon, 1989.

———. *Ilongot Headhunting, 1883–1974: A Study in Society and History*. Stanford, CA: Stanford University Press, 1980.

Rosenwein, Barbara H. *Emotional Communities in the Early Middle Ages*. Ithaca, NY: Cornell University Press, 2006.

Rossi, Benedetta. "Kinetocracy: The Government of Mobility at the Desert's Edge." In *Mobility Makes States: Migration and Power in Africa*, edited by Darshan Vigneswaran and Joel Quirk, 149–68. Philadelphia: University of Pennsylvania Press, 2015.

Rubiés, Joan-Pau. "Instructions for Travellers: Teaching the Eye to See." *History & Anthropology* 9, no. 2/3 (1996): 139–90.

Ruiz, Teofilo F. *A King Travels: Festive Traditions in Late Medieval and Early Modern Spain*. Princeton, NJ: Princeton University Press, 2012.

Safier, Neil. "The Tenacious Travels of the Torrid Zone and the Global Dimensions of Geographical Knowledge in the Eighteenth Century." *Journal of Early Modern History* 18 (2014): 141–72.

Salgado, Pedro V. *Cagayan Valley and Eastern Cordillera, 1581–1898*. Vol. 1. Quezon City: Rex Commercial, 2002.

———. *Cagayan Valley and Eastern Cordillera, 1581–1898*. Vol. 2. Quezon City: Rex Commercial, 2002.

———. *The Ilongots, 1591–1994*. Manila: Lucky, 1994.

Salinas, María Laura. "Reclamos y multas en pueblos de indios: La visita de Garabito de León a Corrientes. Río de la Plata, 1649–1653." *Revista Historia y Justicia* 3 (2014): 195–227.

Sánchez Gómez, Luis Ángel. "Estructura de los pueblos de indios en Filipinas durante la etapa española." In *Cuadernos de Historia*, edited by Florentino Rodao. Vol. 1. Manila: Instituto Cervantes de Manila, 1998.

Scholz, Luca. *Borders and Freedom of Movement in the Holy Roman Empire*. Oxford: Oxford University Press, 2020.

———. "La strada proibita: L'uso delle strade nel Sacro Romano Impero in epoca moderna." *Quaderni storici*, no. 2 (2018): 335–51.

———. "Protection and the Channelling of Movement on the Margins of the Holy Roman Empire." In *Protection and Empire: A Global History*, edited by Lauren A. Benton, Adam Clulow, and Bain Attwood, 13–28. New York: Cambridge University Press, 2017.

Schurz, William Lytle. *The Manila Galleon*. New York: E. P. Dutton, 1939.

Scott, James C. *The Art of Not Being Governed: An Anarchist History of Upland Southeast Asia*. New Haven, CT: Yale University Press, 2009.

Scott, William Henry. *Barangay: Sixteenth-Century Philippine Culture and Society*. Quezon City: Ateneo de Manila University Press, 1994.

———. *The Discovery of the Igorots: Spanish Contacts with the Pagans of Northern Luzon*. Revised edition. Quezon City: New Day Publishers, 1987.

———. *History on the Cordillera: Collected Writings on Mountain Province History*. Baguio City, Philippines: Baguio Printing & Publishing, 1975.

———. "Notices of the Pagan Igorots in 1789." *Asian Folklore Studies* 29 (1970): 177–83.

Seed, Patricia. *Ceremonies of Possession in Europe's Conquest of the New World, 1492–1640*. Cambridge: Cambridge University Press, 1995.

Seijas, Tatiana. *Asian Slaves in Colonial Mexico: From Chinos to Indians*. New York: Cambridge University Press, 2014.

———. "Inns, Mules, and Hardtack for the Voyage: The Local Economy of the Manila Galleon in Mexico." *Colonial Latin American Review* 25, no. 1 (2016): 56–76.

———. "The Royal Road of the Interior in New Spain: Indigenous Commerce and Political Action." In *The Oxford Handbook of Borderlands of the Iberian World*, edited by Danna A. Levin Rojo and Cynthia Radding, 295–307. New York: Oxford University Press, 2019.

Sellers-García, Sylvia. *Distance and Documents at the Spanish Empire's Periphery*. Stanford, CA: Stanford University Press, 2014.

Sheller, Mimi, and John Urry. "The New Mobilities Paradigm." *Environment and Planning A* 38 (2006): 207–26.

Sivasundaram, Sujit. *Islanded: Britain, Sri Lanka, and the Bounds of an Indian Ocean Colony*. Chicago: University of Chicago Press, 2013.

Smuts, Malcolm, and George Gorse. "Introduction." In *The Politics of Space: European Courts, ca. 1500–1750*, edited by Marcello Fantoni, Georges Gorse, and R. Malcolm Smuts, 13–35. Rome: Bulzoni, 2009.

Standfield, Rachel. "Mobility, Reciprocal Relationships and Early British Encounters in the North of New Zealand." In *Indigenous Mobilities: Across and Beyond the Antipodes*, edited by Rachel Standfield, 57–77. Canberra: ANU Press, 2018.

———. "Moving Across, Looking Beyond." In *Indigenous Mobilities: Across and Beyond the Antipodes*, edited by Rachel Standfield, 1–33. Canberra: ANU Press, 2018.

Stock, Paul. "History and the Uses of Space." In *The Uses of Space in Early Modern History*, edited by Paul Stock, 1–18. New York: Palgrave Macmillan, 2015.

Stoler, Ann Laura. "Colonial Archives and the Arts of Governance." *Archival Science* 2, no. 1–2 (2002): 87–109.

Stoler, Ann Laura, and Frederick Cooper. "Between Metropole and Colony: Rethinking a Research Agenda." In *Tensions of Empire: Colonial Cultures in a Bourgeois World*, edited by Frederick Cooper and Ann Laura Stoler, 1–56. Berkeley: University of California Press, 1997.

Subrahmanyam, Sanjay. "Connected Histories: Notes towards a Reconfiguration of Early Modern Eurasia." *Modern Asian Studies* 31, no. 3 (1997): 735–62.

———. "Holding the World in Balance: The Connected Histories of the Iberian Overseas Empires, 1500–1640." *The American Historical Review* 112, no. 5 (2007): 1359–85.

Sutter, Paul S. "The Tropics: A Brief History of an Environmental Imaginary." In *The Oxford Handbook of Environmental History*, edited by Andrew C. Isenberg, 178–98. New York: Oxford University Press, 2014.

Tagliacozzo, Eric. "Jagged Landscapes: Conceptualizing Borders and Boundaries in the History of Human Societies." *Journal of Borderlands Studies* 31, no. 1 (2016): 1–21.

Tappe, Oliver. "Introduction: Frictions and Fictions—Intercultural Encounters and Frontier Imaginaries in Upland Southeast Asia." *Asia Pacific Journal of Anthropology* 16, no. 4 (2015): 317–22.

Taylor, Keith W. "The Early Kingdoms." In *The Cambridge History of Southeast Asia: From Early Times to c.1800*, edited by Nicholas Tarling, 1:137–82. Cambridge: Cambridge University Press, 1992.

Thomas, Nicholas. *Entangled Objects: Exchange, Material Culture, and Colonialism in the Pacific*. Cambridge, MA: Harvard University Press, 1991.

Thrush, Coll. *Indigenous London: Native Travelers at the Heart of Empire*. New Haven, CT: Yale University Press, 2016.

———. "Walking the Indigenous City: Colonial Encounters at the Heart of Empire." In *The Routledge Companion to Global Indigenous History*, edited by Ann McGrath and Lynette Russell, 241–55. London: Routledge, 2022.

Tremml-Werner, Birgit, Lisa Hellman, and Guido van Meersbergen. "Introduction. Gift and Tribute in Early Modern Diplomacy: Afro-Eurasian Perspectives." *Diplomatica* 2, no. 2 (2020): 185–200.

Tsing, Anna Lowenhaupt. *Friction: An Ethnography of Global Connection*. Princeton, NJ: Princeton University Press, 2005.

Tuck-Po, Lye. "Before a Step Too Far: Walking with Batek Hunter-Gatherers in the Forests of Pahang, Malaysia." In *Ways of Walking: Ethnography and Practice on Foot*, edited by Tim Ingold and Jo Lee Vergunst, 21–34. Aldershot, UK: Ashgate, 2008.

Van Bortel, Wim, Ho Dinh Trung, Tho Sochantha, Kalouna Keokenchan, Patricia Roelants, Thierry Backeljau, and Marc Coosemans. "Eco-Ethological Heterogeneity of the Members of the *Anopheles minimus* Complex (Diptera: Culicidae) in Southeast Asia and Its Consequences for Vector Control." *Journal of Medical Entomology* 41, no. 3 (2004): 366–74.

van Deusen, Nancy E. *Global Indios: The Indigenous Struggle for Justice in Sixteenth-Century Spain*. Narrating Native Histories. Durham, NC: Duke University Press, 2015.

Villoria Prieto, Carlos. "Breve relación de la misión de los montes de Pantabangán y Caranglán (Filipinas)." *Archivo Agustiniano* 79, no. 197 (1995): 29–48.

———. "Fray Antolín de Alzaga: Un modelo de misionero en Filipinas en el siglo XVIII." *Archivo Agustiniano* 83, no. 201 (1999): 115–35.

———. "La labor del agustino vasco Baltasar de Santa María Isasigana en Filipinas (1665–1717)." *Archivo Agustiniano* 82, no. 200 (1998): 407–26.

———. "La producción cartográfica del jesuita Pedro Murillo Velarde (1696–1753)." In *El Siglo de las Luces: III Centenario del Nacimiento de José de Hermosilla (1715–1776)*, edited by Felipe Lorenzana de la Puente and Francisco J. Mateos Ascacíbar, 147–60. Llerena: Sociedad Extremeña de Historia, 2016.

———. "Los agustinos y la misión de Buhay a principios del siglo XVIII." *Archivo Agustiniano* 81, no. 199 (1997): 3–34.

———. "Los viajes a Filipinas en el siglo XVIII." *Revista de Hespérides*, no. 13 (2011): 62–67.

———. *Un berciano en Filipinas: Alejandro Cacho de Villegas*. León, Spain: Universidad de León, 1997.

———. "Un Totanero en Filipinas: Fr. José González (Totana, 1704–Valladolid, 1762)." *Cuadernos de La Santa* 17 (2015): 91–100.

Vivo, Filippo de. "Walking in Sixteenth-Century Venice: Mobilizing the Early Modern City." *I Tatti Studies in the Italian Renaissance* 19, no. 1 (2016): 115–41.

Voigt, Lisa. *Spectacular Wealth: The Festivals of Colonial South American Mining Towns*. Austin: University of Texas Press, 2016.

Vries, Jan de. "Playing with Scales: The Global and the Micro, the Macro and the Nano." *Past & Present* 242, Supplement 14 (2019): 23–36.

Warf, Barney, and Santa Arias. "Introduction: The Reinsertion of Space into the Social Sciences and Humanities." In *The Spatial Turn: Interdisciplinary Perspectives*, edited by Barney Warf and Santa Arias, 1–10. London: Routledge, 2009.

Weber, David J. *Bárbaros: Spaniards and Their Savages in the Age of Enlightenment*. New Haven, CT: Yale University Press, 2005.

———. "Bourbons and Bárbaros: Center and Periphery in the Reshaping of Spanish Indian Policy." In *Negotiated Empires: Centers and Peripheries in the Americas, 1500–1820*, edited by Christine Daniels and Michael V. Kennedy, 79–103. New York: Routledge, 2002.

———. *The Spanish Frontier in North America*. New Haven, CT: Yale University Press, 1992.

Wenzlhuemer, Roland. *Doing Global History: An Introduction in 6 Concepts*. Translated by Ben Kamis. London: Bloomsbury Academic, 2020.

White, Richard. "Creative Misunderstandings and New Understandings." *William and Mary Quarterly* 63, no. 1 (2006): 9–14.

———. *The Middle Ground: Indians, Empires, and Republics in the Great Lakes Region, 1650–1815*. Twentieth Anniversary edition. New York: Cambridge University Press, 2011.

———. "What Is Spatial History?" Spatial History Lab, February 1, 2010. http://web .stanford.edu/group/spatialhistory/media/images/publication/what%20is%20 spatial%20history%20pub%20020110.pdf.

Wilde, Guillermo. "Political Dimension of Space-Time Categories in the Jesuit Missions of Paraguay (Seventeenth and Eighteenth Centuries)." In *Space and Conversion in Global Perspective*, edited by Giuseppe Marcocci, Wietse de Boer, Aliocha Maldavsky, and Ilaria Pavan, 175–213. Leiden: Brill, 2015.

Withers, Charles W. J., and David N. Livingstone. "Introduction: On Geography and Enlightenment." In *Geography and Enlightenment*, edited by David N. Livingstone and Charles W. J. Withers, 1–28. Chicago: University of Chicago Press, 1999.

Wolters, O. W. *History, Culture, and Region in Southeast Asian Perspectives*. Singapore: Institute of Southeast Asian Studies, 1982.

Yu, Guo, Guiyun Yan, Naixin Zhang, Daibin Zhong, Ying Wang, Zhengbo He, Zhentian Yan, Wenbo Fu, Feilong Yang, and Bin Chen. "The *Anopheles* Community and the Role of *Anopheles minimus* on Malaria Transmission on the China-Myanmar Border." *Parasites & Vectors* 6, no. 264 (2013): 1–8.

Zamora, Eladio. *Las corporaciones religiosas en Filipinas*. Valladolid: Andrés Martín, 1901.

Zanolli, Carlos Eduardo. "'Visitas de la tierra': De su historia europea al terreno en América. Chucuito, Jujuy y Tarija (siglos XVI y XVII)." *Revista Historia y Justicia* 3 (2014): 140–65.

Index

Printed in the USA
CPSIA information can be obtained
at www.ICGtesting.com
LVHW101637190823
755707LV00001B/51

9 781469 676449